GARRETT
AND THE ENGLISH MUSE

LIA NOEMIA RODRIGUES CORREIA RAITT

GARRETT
AND THE
ENGLISH MUSE

TAMESIS BOOKS LIMITED
LONDON

Colección Támesis
SERIE A - MONOGRAFIAS, XCIV

Depósito legal: M. 17021-1983

Printed in Spain by Talleres Gráficos de Selecciones Gráficas
Carretera de Irún, km. 11,500 - Madrid-34

for
TAMESIS BOOKS LIMITED
LONDON

TABLE OF CONTENTS

FOREWORD

In this work modern spelling has been adopted for all titles and quotations, except in the case of titles of periodicals which have not had a later reprint. The reader is referred to *Obras de Almeida Garrett,* 2 Vols (Porto, 1966), which was used throughout, except in the case of *Viagens na minha terra,* for which I have adopted the edition by Augusto da Costa Dias (Lisboa, 1963).

ABBREVIATIONS

B. Nac.	Biblioteca Nacional de Lisboa.
Esp.	Espólio literário de Garrett.
O. A. G.	*Obras de Almeida Garrett,* 2 Vols (Porto, 1966).
P. R. O.	Public Record Office.
Sala F. L.	Sala Ferreira Lima, in Faculdade de Letras, Coimbra.

PREFACE

Garrett is, by general acknowledgement, one of the greatest Portuguese authors of the early nineteenth century, if not the greatest, and much has been written about him. Critical opinion has not been slow to recognise that both his personal achievement in his writings and the major part he played in the revivification of Portuguese literature owe a great deal to his reading of foreign literature and his contacts with foreign countries, and a number of valuable studies have been devoted, in whole or in part, to the examination of the effects such things had on him. Ofélia Paiva Monteiro, in her monumental study A formação de Almeida Garrett, *has paid close attention to what Garrett derived from his knowledge of non-Portuguese authors in his early years; Otto Antscherl, in* J. B. de Almeida Garrett und seine Beziehungen zur Romantik, *has attempted to set Garrett in the wider context of European romanticism; Fidelino de Figueiredo, in* Shakespeare e Garrett, *has drawn a detailed parallel between the two authors. The only attempts to produce a synthesis of Garrett's various debts to England are to be found in two articles by Carlos Estorninho, 'Garrett and England: English Reminiscences in the Life and Work of Almeida Garrett' and 'Garrett e a Inglaterra'. Interesting and intelligent though these are, their limited size leaves much to be said, both in general terms and in matters of detailed research. Apart from that, no one has tried to investigate in depth what effect Garrett's admiration for English writers and his periods of exile in England may have had on him as a man of letters; indeed, more attention has been given to his connections with French literature. Yet it has always been clear that England and English literature were extremely important to Garrett, both in his private life and in his literary career. It is the object of the present study to fill at least some of that gap.*

The work deals essentially with Garrett as a creative writer, and no attempt has been made to assess the extent to which Garrett as a politician and political theorist may have been indebted to English sources. That would be another vast subject in itself, deserving of detailed treatment on its own and quite impossible to include within the necessarily restricted dimensions of this work, though it is to be hoped that some day someone may cover it. It would in fact be a totally different topic from that of Garrett as a man of letters, since his development as a politician is by no means coterminous with his development as a creative writer, despite the inevitable interaction between the two. It thus seems legitimate to consider Garrett here solely in his role as an imaginative artist; the subject forms a coherent whole on its own, and the picture which emerges would not be materially altered, save in its dimensions, if discussion of Garrett's political life were added to it.

Though it would obviously not be possible or desirable to include here anything like a complete biography of Garrett, the first chapter of the work is devoted to an examination of the part played by England and English literature in the general context of Garrett's life; without this preliminary study, it would be impossible to understand or define the significance of his relationship with individual English authors. The subsequent chapters go on to study the impact made on Garrett by those English writers whose work he knew most intimately, Addison, Byron, Scott, Sterne and Shakespeare. This sequence has largely been determined by the order in which each of them first emerged as a distinct force in Garrett's evolution, save that Shakespeare has been discussed last, since it is impossible to identify with precision any period at which he assumed special prominence for Garrett. A conclusion seeks to sum up the overall importance of England and English literature to Garrett as a writer.

I owe a special debt of gratitude to the two supervisors of the thesis on which this work is based, Professor Peter Russell and Dr. Luís de Sousa Rebelo. Professor Russell's help in defining the subject, guiding my first steps, and demonstrating the methods which could be used, was quite invaluable; since he ceased to be my supervisor, I have never turned in vain to him for advice and support. Dr. Sousa Rebelo, who took over my supervision from Professor Russell, has been more than an exemplary guide, he has been a friend. His patience was as inexhaustible as his erudition, and without him the thesis would certainly never have been completed. I am also deeply indebted to the Instituto Nacional de Investigação Científica, which in the year 1977-8 awarded me a research grant to enable me to concentrate on the thesis, and to the Instituto de Alta Cultura for paying my College fees in 1974-5, as well as for giving me a grant to do research in Cambridge, Newcastle and London. My particular gratitude also goes to Professor Maria de Lourdes Belchior, who supported my applications for grants with great kindness. Among those whose valuable assistance was freely given me, I must mention Professor Graham Hough, Professor Ofélia Paiva Monteiro, Dr. Phyllis Horsley, Professor Pierre Castex, Professor Prado Coelho, Dr. Robert Howes, Dr. H. Livermore and Dr. George West, as well as the Librarians of Coimbra and Cambridge, Dr. Maria Luísa Lemos and Mr. John Oates. My thanks also go to Mr. Seldon, of the Library of the Spanish and Portuguese Department, as well as to the Librarians of the Taylor Institution and of the English Faculty in Oxford, of the Newcastle Literary and Philosophical Society, of the Newcastle University Library and of the Northumberland Record Office, for facilitating my research. I am particularly grateful to the Calouste Gulbenkian Foundation, Lisbon, for generously agreeing to assist the publication of this volume. I cannot name all those who kindly helped me with their advice or by making life easier and happier. Among them, however, I must single out my father, who was a continuous source of strength, and my husband, who supported me with infinite patience and wisdom.

LIA NÓEMIA RODRIGUES CORREIA RAITT.

Oxford.

INTRODUCTION

Cultural exchanges of some significance between England and Portugal only take place in the eighteenth century. After the Spanish Domination Portugal, which had a long tradition of cultural links with Spain and France, sought new contacts beyond the confines of the Peninsula. Among the countries with whom Portugal tried to establish closer links France was the first to reciprocate in a meaningful manner; she had replaced Spain as a cultural leader in Europe and when she included Portugal in her new fields of literary exploration Restoration England soon followed her. As a result, a modest stream of literature on Portuguese themes emerges in England at the end of the seventeenth century. Contributions came in the form of impressions from curious travellers, which threw light on Portugal as a country; they also came from those who, like Fielding, sought her as a health resort; and literary praise is found in a passage of Thomson's *Summer* (1727). However, it was not until the earthquake of 1755 that one can speak of a real entrance of Portugal into the world of English letters.[1] From 1756 daily columns in the *Gentleman's Magazine* were devoted to first-hand accounts of the disaster, which continued to be discussed until the end of the century in scientific and popular journals. The activities and writings of Dr. Johnson and of his literary circle contributed to the growing interest in Portuguese letters, which are also indebted to them for assisting Mickle in his translation of *Os Lusíadas* in 1776: Boswell, Goldsmith, John Hoole, and Johnson himself, in turn, helped Mickle.[2] Though the poem was known before in Fanshawe's translation (1655), also made directly from the original, Mickle's version —which was to be vastly enjoyed by the Romantics— played a prominent role in the appreciation of Camões as an epic poet in England. Knowledge of Portugal grew thanks to some earnest exploration of her art and literature by visitors like Murphy, Dillon, and Beckford in particular. Yet such literary and academic productions were directed solely at a restricted elite, and little was known by the English at large until the works of Strangford and Southey gave new impetus to the cultural exchanges between the two countries. Strangford's main academic contribution consisted in revealing the lyric works of Camões, hitherto known almost exclusively as the author of *Os Lusíadas*. His *Poems from the Portuguese of Luis de Camoens* (1803)

---

[1] Felix Walter, *La Littérature portugaise en Angleterre à l'époque romantique* (Paris, 1927), p. 32.
[2] F. Walter, p. 40.

1

awakened widespread enthusiasm and started a vogue for translations. One of the writers of the time that was most moved by the figure and the poetry of the Portuguese bard was W. L. Bowles, who wrote a *Last Song of Camoens,* dedicated to Strangford, and an epic poem, *The Spirit of Discovery; or the Conquest of Ocean* (1804), inspired by *The Lusiads* and by the Portuguese discoveries, with a long address to Camões. Despite the later satire in *English Bards and Scotch Reviewers* Byron himself had been impressed by Strangford's work and led to write *Stanzas to a Lady with the poems of Camoens* in 1805. Like Camões, Inês de Castro had been one of the main sources of inspiration since the seventeenth century, and Benjamin Thompson in 1800 and John Adamson in 1808 added to the works based on her life, translating from the originals of Domingos Reis Quita and Nicolau Luís, as Strangford had done with the sonnets and *redondilhas* of Camões. The somewhat narrow compass of English interest in Portuguese letters was considerably widened by Southey's writings, both critical and creative. They comprise an adaptation of *Amadis de Gaula* and of *Palmeirim de Inglaterra* and a brilliant defence of their Portuguese authorship by Lobeira and by Francisco Morais, poetic works on Portuguese themes and a regular contribution to some of the main periodicals of reviews of works written or inspired by Portuguese. Through literary and historical writings Southey asserted himself as the outstanding authority on things Portuguese.

The joint venture of the British and Portuguese armies against Napoleon's troops gave rise to a proliferation of works of diverse nature —literary, military, geographical or merely anecdotal. The war inspired Wordsworth's defence of Portuguese interests in *Convention of Cintra* (1809), and passages of Scott's *The Vision of Don Roderick* (1811) refer to the resistance of Lusitania against the invaders. To this period, too, belongs Byron's criticism of the Portuguese in *Childe Harold* (1812). With few exceptions, the other publications reflect the prejudices prevailing among the British army. Yet, despite their misleading information, they made the average Englishman more aware of Portugal, and peace in 1815 was followed by a period of prosperity for Portuguese studies: alongside accounts from explorers of the country more discerning than the British soldier, scholarly work was done by keen lusophiles. To the names of Southey, Strangford, Halliday, and Adamson others were added later, like Sir Charles Stuart, Kinsey, and Quillinan. Together with such figures as Lord Holland and Hookham Frere, with the bibliophiles Gooden and Heber, and with the Portuguese correspondents of the Portuguese periodicals in England, they fostered knowledge of Portuguese language and literature.

Whereas in England Portuguese culture had permeated only slowly, Portugal followed France in her admiration for the English Enlightenment. By the end of the eighteenth century English philosophy and science, represented mainly but by no means exclusively by Locke, Bacon and Newton, had penetrated cultural life through the writings of the *estrangeira-dos,* through the activities of the Academies —founded on the model of the Royal Society and the French Académie Royale des Sciences—, through the reformed teaching of the University of Coimbra, as well as through

French translations. It was through translations also, often Le Tourneur's, that English writers like Young, Milton, and Richardson were first read by the Portuguese public. Newspapers, like *Mnemósine Lusitana, Jornal Enciclopédico,* and *Jornal de Coimbra,* took it upon themselves to acquaint their readers with English poetry, offering them translations often accompanied by the original; Pope and the pre-romantics figured most frequently in their pages. As Cidade writes, 'Sente-se que era novo luxo saber inglês!' [3] There was no scarcity of translations from the English original, not only of poetry but also of the novel. Defoe, Richardson, and Swift appear to be the first to be translated —*Robinson Crusoe* in 1786, *Pamela Andrews* in 1790, *Gulliver* in 1793— in a wide stream of translations of English novels recorded by Gonçalves Rodrigues.[4] At the turn of the century there was a slow filtering through of English authors dating from the Enlightenment to romanticism, and Beckford's letters register his surprise at the extent of the knowledge that his friends among the Portuguese aristocracy and intellectuals showed of the literature of his country.

In this general picture of receptivity to English thought and literature there emerge the names of Filinto Elísio (1734 to 1819), of the Marquesa de Alorna (1750 to 1831) and of José Anastácio da Cunha (1744 to 1787) —pre-romantics who varied greatly in the impact they had on their contemporaries, as well as in the extent they experienced the new sensibility and in the way they shared its new interests.

José Anastácio da Cunha, whose compositions were first published only forty years after his death, does not stand out as a formative figure in the introduction of English literature and even today he is not a widely-read author. He appears rather as someone who wrote, mainly for himself, verses that were deeply imbued with an Englishness of feeling that he acquired through his avid reading and translating of English writers —Shakespeare, Pope, Milton, Otway— stimulated by his English fellow-officers at Valença do Minho. Among them was Brigadier Ferrier, who, under the pseudonym of Arthur William Costigan, wrote *Sketches of Society and Manners in Portugal* (1787) and who, in a letter published in a London periodical, reprinted by Dr. Vicente Pedro Nolasco in *Investigador Portuguez em Inglaterra,* recalls José Anastácio's passionate recitations of Shakespeare.[5] The remarkable intelligence of the Portuguese poet and his thorough knowledge of Newton helped him to an academic career at Coimbra, under Pombal, which was cut short by the Inquisition. Tried and sentenced for his deism and his bold explorations of sensibility and passion, he gave up working as a poet and as a translator, and died in obscurity some years later. With Manuel de Figueiredo (1725 to 1801) and with Targini, Baron of S. Lourenço,[6] who wrote briefly but perceptively of Shakespeare's

---

[3] Hernani Cidade, *A obra poética do Dr. José Anastácio da Cunha, com um Estudo sobre o anglo-germanismo nos proto-românticos portugueses* (Coimbra, 1930), p. LVI.

[4] *A novelística estrangeira em versão portuguesa no período pré-romântico* (Coimbra, 1951).

[5] Fidelino de Figueiredo, *Shakespeare e Garrett,* Conselho Estadual de Cultura, Comissão de Literatura (São Paulo, 1970), p. 13.

[6] H. Cidade, p. LXIII.

plays, José Anastácio da Cunha is a precursor of the appreciation of the great Elizabethan in Portugal.

Filinto Elísio, who himself had to flee the country in order to escape the Inquisition, had a wider influence on his younger contemporaries than José Anastácio ever achieved, particularly on the Marquesa de Alorna and even on Garrett's own generation. A classicist through and through, he contributed nonetheless to the introduction of the Romantic spirit, both with his translations of the new writers, namely Thomson and Gray, and with his poetry, which reflected the current interest in forms of folk art (Garrett was to sign *D. Branca,* his first long Romantic poem in the genre, with the initials F. E. as a tribute to the old man's inspiring role).

Pope, Goldsmith, Thomson, Gray, Young, Macpherson and others were translated or imitated by the Marquesa de Alorna, who was also an admirer of Byron. Her own poetry, like that of José Anastácio da Cunha, was profoundly affected by her reading of English authors, but also like José Anastácio da Cunha's, her compositions were published only posthumously, in 1844. Thus, during her life-time, the most effective way in which she contributed to introducing the latest literary currents into Portugal was through her *salon littéraire.* Taught by Filinto in the classic tradition which she never discarded entirely, she nevertheless boldly explored new fields and it was thanks to her activities that the centre of cultural interest was transferred from France to England and Germany, thus winning for her from Herculano the title of the 'Portuguese Mme de Staël'. At a time when English romanticism was beginning to be a matter of individual concern on the part of emigrants like Garrett, the Marquesa de Alorna fostered a general atmosphere of receptiveness to it, sowing the seeds for the creation of a Portuguese romanticism with strong Anglo-Germanic sources of inspiration. To José Augusto França, her salon represents the first cycle in the development of romanticism in Portugal, followed by the liberal emigration to Plymouth and then by the years of liberal government, in both of which Garrett took part.

This then is briefly the context in which one must consider Garrett as the intermediary between the two countries.

I

ENGLAND IN GARRETT'S LIFE

João Baptista da Silva Leitão was born the son of a customs official on 4 February 1799; the fact that he later added the name Garrett, from an Irish grandmother, as well as Almeida from his mother, seems to indicate the extent to which he had moved away from his origins and the attraction which he felt to the English-speaking world.

His family, though conservative in its views, was more progressive than many middle-class Portuguese at the time, but it was not until they moved to the Azores when the French invaded Portugal in 1809 that his education became particularly open to foreign influences. This came about through two uncles, Bishop Frei Alexandre da Sagrada Família and Dr. João Carlos Leitão, both of whom were cultured and, particularly in the case of the Bishop, distinguished men of letters. D. Frei Alexandre, of whom Garrett said that he was 'verdadeiro mestre, educador e segundo pai',[1] combined the love of the classics of ancient Greece and Rome with the cult of sensitivity and expressiveness that prevailed in the second half of the eighteenth century, and he introduced Garrett not only to the main writers of France, Spain and Italy from the sixteenth to the eighteenth centuries, but also to Pope, Thomson and the English theatre —Garrett tells us that the Bishop placed some English and Spanish playwrights even above his beloved Greek classics.[2] As for Dr. João Carlos Leitão, it was probably he who acquainted Garrett with pre-romantic writers such as Bocage and José Anastácio da Cunha, who aroused in the young man such admiration that in Oporto, in 1820, he set himself the task of collecting José Anastácio's unpublished poems and imitated Bocage so successfully in his early verse that Adrien Balbi writes that he was called 'O novo Du Bocage'.[3]

It may well have been an English girl who was responsible for Garrett's decision, on returning from the Azores, to read law at Coimbra rather than entering the Church. His first poems —nine anacreontic odes addressed to

[1] Note to Ode xviii, Book II, MS 53 of *Esp.*, in Ofélia Milheiro Caldas Paiva Monteiro, *A formação de Almeida Garrett, Experiência e criação*, 2 Vols (Coimbra, 1971), Vol. I, p. 43, note 67; see also *Tratado da educação*, O. A. G., Vol. 1, p. 686.
[2] Preface to *Mérope*, O.A.G., Vol. 2, p. 1786.
[3] *Essai statistique sur le royaume de Portugal*, 2 Vols (Paris, 1822), Vol. II, p. clxxiv, quoted by O. P. Monteiro, Vol. I, p. 161, note 142.

'Lília' and probably the ones addressed to 'Isbela'— are believed to have been inspired by a person whom he calls 'Hewson' in his diary: this was no doubt Isabel Hewson, probably the daughter of an English consul posted in the Azores.[4] Other early poems bear the imprint of a different kind of English inspiration, that which came from English writers, who were among the many converging influences to which the young man's open-mindedness, eclecticism and wide reading made him susceptible. The ode 'A primavera', for instance, with its epigraph from Thomson, 'Come, gentle Spring, ethereal mildness, come!', shows that he had the first of The Seasons in mind in composing his own much briefer work.

At the university, Garrett found a ferment of political agitation, normal academic life being disrupted through the presence of the French invaders, followed by that of the English liberators. He was himself drawn to the liberal students who were fired by the ideas of the French philosophes and modern French adversaries of absolutism such as Mme de Staël and Benjamin Constant. After a first year of conscientious study he joined the militant action of the Regeneração movement, and rapidly became a prominent figure, with his tragedies Xerxes, Lucrécia and Mérope, in which he attacked despotism and tyranny, while at the same time showing himself aware, in the latter, of possible new developments in drama in the wake of Alfieri and Ducis.[5] When the Revolution took place on August 24th, Garrett saluted it enthusiastically with two poems, one of which, Hynno patriótico, was sung as a hymn in the Teatro de S. João in Oporto on the 27th at the ceremony held to celebrate the victory of the insurgents. In 1820, his last year in the Faculty, Garrett had become the recognised leader of the liberal students; one of the works of the period is As férias — a um amigo, which is an attack on British rule and the old regime.[6] In June 1821 he was sent by the Minister José da Silva Carvalho, a member of the Regency and head of the Masonic Order in Portugal, to the Azores to convert the islanders to the new constitutional creed, which he did successfully, also bringing about the downfall of the despotic and incompetent governor Garção Stockler.

Garrett wrote a great deal at this time, much of it in support of liberal, constitutional ideas but also fostering his preoccupation with the foundation of a Portuguese national theatre. Notable in the latter campaign was the production of the tragedy Catão in a theatre in Bairro Alto in September 1821. As we shall see later, Catão reflects not only the views of freedom which Garrett derived largely from the French political writers of the Enlightenment, but also his interest in English literature, since outwardly the work is mainly based on Addison's Cato. Garrett's political hostility to British intervention in Portugal, evident in the jaundiced view of England expressed in O Toucador,[7] the journal of feminine instruction which he

---

4 Teófilo Braga, Garrett e o romantismo (Porto, 1903), p. 154.
5 Preface to Mérope, O.A.G., Vol. 2, p. 1787.
6 According to O. P. Monteiro, Vol. I, pp. 180-1, this poem gives some indication of Garrett's peripheral involvement in the conspiracy of 1820.
7 O Toucador, periodico sem política. Dedicado às senhoras portuguesas (Lisboa, Anno II, 1822).

produced with Paulo Midosi in 1822, did not preclude admiration for English authors, though Shakespeare was still too strong meat for his taste, as is revealed by the Prologue to *Mérope*.

He married Luisa Midosi in 1822 and obtained a post in the Ministry 'Secretaria do Reino'. But his prospects of personal happiness and literary success were suddenly cut short by the *Vilafrancada* in 1823, which forced him to flee to England, where he arrived on 8 June 1823. Entrusted with letters from liberal leaders in exile to be taken to Lisbon, Garrett set off again on 26 July from Gravesend, and as he writes in his *Diário da minha viagem a Inglaterra*, he was thrown into prison as he disembarked in Lisbon. According to his biographer, Gomes de Amorim, his arrest, if it ever took place, did not last longer than a few hours,[8] but it left a deep mark on the poet's spirit, recorded in the poem *O cárcere*, with an epigraph from Byron, and in a note included in a collection of odes he prepared in Birmingham, on 8 November of the same year. On his return to England, Garrett hailed the British flag with warm gratitude, and his expectations of safety and freedom in his country of exile were not disappointed.

On arrival, Garrett and his wife enjoyed the hospitality of a wealthy businessman, Thomas Hadley, from Edgbaston, to whom he had been recommended on his first journey. With Thomas Hadley and his cultivated and charming family Garrett and Luisa spent six months which were, he writes in *Camões*, most peaceful and heart-warming. In passages of this work and of the *Diário* he pays homage to the perfect friendship of the Hadleys [9] and in *Viagens* he recalls his reading during that period, which signalled a much closer contact with things English than he had ever had before, and was to begin a radical change in his attitudes, notably to English literature, but also to British political institutions. Though Garrett had already evinced some interest in English writers, and had learned English sufficiently well to read them in the original, his taste had largely been formed on French models, and his nationalistic opposition to British interference in Portuguese affairs had inhibited his acceptance of ways of thought and writings from the other side of the Channel. *O Castelo de Dudley* and Carlos's letter in *Viagens* evoke Garrett's experiences during his stay with the Hadleys, who introduced him to the life and manners of the English upper middle-class and to medieval architecture, and guided him in the subtleties of their language and literature:

> Os mais difíceis e delicados ápices de sua tão caprichosa e tão expressiva língua, as belezas mais sentidas de seus autores queridos, o espírito e tom difícil de sua sociedade tão desdenhosa e fastienta, mas tão completa e tão calculada para sublimar a vida e a desmaterializar —isso tudo, e um indefinível sentimento do *gentil,* que só com natural tacto se adquire, é verdade, mas que se não alcança com ele só— isso tudo o aprendi ali (...) [10]

---

[8] *Memórias biographicas,* 3 Vols (Lisbon, 1881-4), Vol. I, pp. 304-6.
[9] Canto I, ii and note S to Canto I; see also G. de Amorim, Vol. I, p. 313.
[10] *Viagens na minha terra,* henceforth abbreviated to *Viagens,* Introduction and Notes by Augusto da Costa Dias (Lisboa, 1963), Chapt. XLIV, pp. 312-13.

2

It was a period of intense study and creative activity, the importance of which cannot be sufficiently stressed: the period of exploration of English romanticism, which led directly to the planning of *Magriço* and to the first steps in the collection of folk ballads for a future compilation in Scott's manner, and which had its first tangible results in the composition of *Camões* and *D. Branca* shortly afterwards in France.

In fact, the need to make a living forced Garrett to abandon the home of the Hadleys in January and, after moving to Birmingham and to London, to leave England in February 1824 and seek work in France. It was during his stay in Ingouville, near Le Havre, that he gave expression in those two poems to the inspiration first received in Warwickshire. When the publication of the Constitutional Charter by D. João VI in 1826 finally enabled him to return to Portugal, Garrett was reinstated in his post in the Ministry and gave up all literary creation in order to devote himself to the task of enlightening the public about the principles of a constitutional regime.[11] Thus he not only wrote *Carta de guia para eleitores* in September of that year, but also founded the daily paper *O Portuguez* with former companions of the English exile, like Paulo and Luis Francisco Midosi, as well as the weekly *O Chronista,* which he edited almost single-handed. Both dealt with politics and the arts. *O Portuguez* was written in a modern form which reflected the new horizons opened to Garrett and his co-editors by the years spent abroad.[12] Gomes de Amorim writes that political articles of their daily were reproduced in the *Morning Chronicle.*[13] This fact is confirmed by research done in this and in other contemporary English periodicals: issues of 2 March, 10 May, 6, 25 and 30 August 1827 of the *Morning Chronicle* include articles from *O Portuguez;* besides, both the *Morning Chronicle* and the *Foreign Quarterly Review* extolled it for its discernment and balance:

> evidently conducted with great talent and judgement. The Debates in the Two Houses are reported in a masterly manner (...)
>
> M. C. 31 Jan. 1826

> we must not omit the journal called *O Portuguez,* written with great moderation on the constitutional side, and displaying more activity and knowledge than could have been expected under the reign of a strict censorship, and amid a people where little encouragement is given to political speculation (...)
>
> F. Q. R. Vol. 2, Art. VI, 7, 1828.[14]

The impartial political stance of *O Portuguez* made it the target of both liberals and absolutists, and with the restoration of absolutism under D. Miguel, it was closed down, and its editors arrested and tried. *O Chronista,* more outspoken in its political criticism but less influential than the daily paper, came to an end at about the same time, of the editors' own volition.[15] During the period of detention preceding his acquittal

---

11 O. P. Monteiro, Vol. II, p. 46.
12 O. P. Monteiro, Vol. II, p. 49, note 116.
13 G. de Amorim, Vol. I, p. 409.
14 Neither article is included in Felix Walter's Bibliography.
15 O. P. Monteiro, Vol. II, p. 49.

Garrett worked on *Adosinda,* which, as he writes in the Preface, was conceived in exile. Though Garrett does not specify which particular exile, the original inspiration for this poem must be related to his reading in Warwickshire.

As indexes to entry certificates of aliens were not introduced until 1826, Garrett's *Diário* is all one has to go by in the way of sources for the dates of his first two landings in England. Research done in the Public Record Office for the period after 1826, however, has made it possible to ascertain with greater accuracy the dates of his different arrivals, though there is still total lack of information about later entries. But for this third journey, which was part of the great liberal emigration of 1827-8, there is evidence that he entered Falmouth on 19 June 1828, with certificate No 50.[16]

In the years that followed, Garrett, though dismissed from the 'Secretaria do Reino' by D. Miguel's government in 1828, and struggling with financial difficulties, was spared the hardships and sufferings of those other liberals whose fate it was to be allotted to Plymouth.[17] First in Birmingham, where he lived until the spring of 1829, and then in London —it is not certain whether he was appointed attaché or secretary to the Portuguese Embassy—,[18] Garrett was also able to remain comparatively uninvolved in the bitter intrigues that divided the emigrés, and to pursue an intense literary and political activity. His publications followed one another in quick succession: *Adosinda* and *Bernal-Francês* in 1828, *Lírica de João Mínimo,* the poem *Victória da Terceira* and *Tratado da educação* in 1829, and a second edition of *Catão, Carta a Mucio Scevola, Elogio Fúnebre de Carlos Infante de Lacerda* and his remarkably clear-sighted *Portugal na balança da Europa,* part of which had already appeared in the pages of the London periodical *O Popular,* to which Garrett had been a contributor, in 1826. Besides all this, in order to revive the downcast spirit of the emigrés, Garrett also founded two newspapers in London: *O Chaveco Liberal* in 1829, and *O Precursor* in 1831 at Palmela's request and almost exclusively at his own expense.

At that time the most distinguished members of the Portuguese colony moved in the circles of British aristocracy, of which Holland House was outstanding for its hospitality and international atmosphere; thanks to Palmela and to his own post at the Embassy, Garrett gained admission to such spheres, and there has been a certain amount of speculation about his social and cultural life in London, on the strength of evidence found in Garrett's own writings, like *O Inglês* and passages from *Viagens,* and in Amorim's *Memórias biographicas.*[19] According to the Preface to the first edition of *Adosinda* and to Amorim, Garrett had consulted the excellent Portuguese libraries of the well-known bibliophiles Gooden and Richard Heber. It was possibly through them that Garrett met their friend, the

---

16 P. R. O. Ashridge, *Entry Books,* Vol. 25, 1826-8.
17 Vitorino Nemésio, *Exilados (1828-1832). História Sentimental e política do liberalismo na emigração* (Lisbon, n. d.).
18 G. de Amorim, Vol. I, p. 481.
19 Vol. I, p. 473, and ff.

lusophile John Adamson, a leading figure on Tyneside, founder of a number of literary and learned societies, a man of multiple interests like numismatics and conchology, which he pursued with a certain distinction, and who was, above all, a lover of Portuguese literature, which he promoted with unflagging enthusiasm through his writings and in the Literary and Philosophical Society of Newcastle, of which he was secretary.

Research done in various archives in Newcastle-on-Tyne,[20] in an attempt to find links between Garrett and Walter Scott, with whom Adamson's Antiquarian Society of Newcastle maintained regular correspondence mainly over the collecting of ballads, was fruitless. Yet Adamson's Dedication to Garrett in Part II of his *Lusitania Illustrata* (1846), confirms Garrett's interest in Percy and Scott during this period of their acquaintance:

> You will remember when, many years ago, we conversed and corresponded on the subject of the poetical Traditions of your Country; when you, prompted by the example of my Countrymen, Percy and others, who had collected our older Ballads, and by the poetical works of Sir Walter Scott, determined to rescue from oblivion the Minstrelsy of Portugal. You were then an exile in England (...)

Other lines of research about Garrett's connections at that time have proved to be equally disappointing: a poem in French addressed to Mary Shelley (MS 57 of *Esp.*, f. 21 r-v) of which O. Paiva Monteiro quotes nine lines,[21] and which is transcribed in full as an appendix to this study, raised the hypothesis that Garrett might have met Shelley's widow in Lord Holland's salon. Yet no evidence for this has been found in published form or among the Shelley Papers in the Bodleian Library, in Oxford, which include her journal for that period.

Nor does there seem to exist any published record of Garrett's visits to Holland House, though they probably did take place. If Palmela, the Count of Funchal and one or two members of the Embassy were sufficiently distinguished to be mentioned now and again in the *Holland House Diaries*,[22] Garrett possibly rated no higher than any other Portuguese or Spanish refugee to whom the liberal-minded Lord opened his doors.

Despite the fact that this was an invaluable period for Garrett's training in English political and social life, it was not free from illness, financial crises, and worry and frustration over the turn taken by the liberal cause — feelings which are voiced in *Carta a Mucio Scevola*. It does not seem to have been a continuous stay either: according to Amorim, Garrett left for France and Belgium in October 1829, in a vain attempt to join the troops that were being recruited to go to Terceira, but there is no evidence in the P. R. O. for an entry in that month or in the period immediately after. It was only in 1831 that Garrett was finally able to set off for the Azores

---

[20] The Literary and Philosophical Society in Newcastle, the University Library, the Northumberland Record Office and Gateshead Central Library.

[21] Vol. II, p. 139.

[22] *The Holland House Diaries 1831-1840, The Diary of Henry Richard Vassal Fox, Third Lord Holland, with Extracts from the Diary of Dr. John Allen*, edited by Abraham D. Kriedgel (London, 1977).

from Belle-Isle, on borrowed money and on the meagre sum obtained by selling his clothes. Thus ends Garrett's third period of exile in England —rich in literary, political and human experiences, even if they only led to general disenchantment.

After helping Mousinho da Silveira in drawing up his vast social, political and administrative reforms, and joining the liberal occupation of Oporto, Garrett was sent back to England for a fourth time.

In November 1832 Palmela and Mousinho were sent to London by D. Pedro, the ostensible purpose of their official mission being the request for help for the liberals, who were then in a situation of impasse in the besieged town of Oporto, and their respective secretaries were José Balbino de Barbosa e Araújo and Garrett. Perhaps because they were on an official mission, the names of these four men were not recorded in the Entry Books of the Home Office, though there is enough evidence, both Portuguese and English, to confirm their visit. The mission was dissolved on 17 January 1833, but whereas its other three members were taken care of (Palmela was elevated to a dukedom, Mousinho and José Barbosa given funds for repatriation), Garrett, inexplicably, was left stranded in England; his government refused him financial aid then, and years later denied him official recognition of his participation in the mission.[23] Garrett, again on borrowed money, left for Paris, where he was joined by his wife. It was only when England fully recognized the young queen D. Maria that all Portuguese emigrants were allowed to return home. Garrett made his way via England: Entry Book 27 (1832-4), Home Office Section, Ashridge, shows that J. B. L. Garrett entered Southampton on 11 September 1833, with certificate 197, in a hitherto undiscovered visit. He finally set foot in his country in October, at the end of the bitterest of all exiles,[24] destitute, jobless, ill and forgotten, as Gomes de Amorim tells us: 'como se fosse o derradeiro e o mais ínfimo dos liberais portugueses'.[25]

Garrett's career after these years of exile was varied and active in the extreme. Consul-General in Belgium from 1834 to 1836, member of Parliament almost continuously, sometimes in opposition, sometimes in office, eventually Minister of Foreign Affairs and Peer of the Realm, author of projects for reform in education, law and administration, member of committees for the restoration of relations with the Holy See, for the Overseas Provinces, for treaties of commerce with France and the U. S. A., editor and contributor to numerous periodicals, he nevertheless continued to devote much of his remarkable energy and talents to artistic activities, such as the foundation of the National Theatre, of the Conservatoire of Dramatic Art and the Board of Supervision of Theatres, and to the promotion of cultural relations with England.

His own works were known and appreciated among the English lusophiles, and Edward Quillinan, in a review of Um auto de Gil Vicente, in The Quarterly Review, LXXIX (1846-7) alludes in particular to his achievement as the founder of the national theatre and to his encouragement, sometimes

[23] G. de Amorim, Vol. I, pp. 585-7.
[24] O. P. Monteiro, Vol. II, p. 71.
[25] G. de Amorim, Vol. I, p. 592.

overgenerous, to young writers. But Garrett's appearance in the English world of letters may be said to date back to 1829, when William Morgan Kinsey included the *Brief Review of the Literary History of Portugal* —a slightly altered version of MS 82 of *Esp.*, 'Esquisse d'une histoire littéraire du Portugal'— in the second edition of his *Portugal Illustrated* (1829). A long anonymous article in the *Foreign Quarterly Review* (1832) deals with Garrett's *História da língua e literatura portuguesa* preceding *Parnaso Lusitano* (Paris, 1826), and with *Adosinda*. It is a well-informed and detailed review, in which a distinction is made between Garrett's original work for *Parnaso* and its distortion by the compiler P. J. Fonseca; it shows knowledge and appreciation of Garrett's efforts in rescuing the *chacra* from oblivion and of his work as a whole, and translates excerpts from *Adosinda*, which it praises highly. As for John Adamson, his esteem for Garrett is apparent not only in the correspondence between the two men, but in his translation of most of the *Romances reconstruídos*, in *Lusitania Illustrata*, Part II, dedicated to Garrett, and in *Ballads from the Portuguese* (1846). In Notes to *Romances reconstruídos* Garrett includes a quotation in Portuguese on *Adosinda* and *Bernal-Francês*, as part of a letter from Southey to Adamson, written in 1828:

> que estes eram dois monumentos de mais remota antiguidade talvez do que nenhumas daquelas canções irlandesas que ele até ali tivera na conta de serem os vestígios mais antigos de toda a poesia popular das nações do Oeste da Europa [26].

If Garrett's merits were recognized by the English lusophiles, he, for his part, did not neglect to foster the knowledge of English literature in Portugal, or to procure a fitting reward for those who promoted the cause of Portuguese studies in England.

He invited James Sheridan Knowles, by then a well-known playwright who travelled all over Great Britain and made a tour in the United States as a dramatic lecturer, and who had stopped in Lisbon on his way to or from Madeira in 1845, to give a series of lectures on Shakespeare and on English writers from Milton to the present day. Though no record of the Lisbon lectures is to be found in the biographies of Sheridan Knowles, it is possible to reconstitute the gist of their contents on the Shakespearean drama through his notes — collected by his son, Richard Brinsley Knowles,[27] through the programme in the contemporary press, quoted by Fidelino de Figueiredo in *Shakespeare e Garrett*,[28] as well as through Garrett's *Mr. Sheridan Knowles*. A letter from Sheridan Knowles in 1852 recollects his acquaintance with Garrett on the occasion of those lectures in terms of high regard and admiration.

Southey was awarded the Insignia of the Tower and Sword, and the

---

[26] Notes on 'Bernal-Francês', in *Romances reconstruídos*, O. A. G., Vol. I, p. 1811.

[27] *Lectures on Dramatic Literature by James Sheridan Knowles*, revised and edited by F. Harvey in 1873 and 1875.

[28] *Shakespeare e Garrett*, Conselho Estadual de Cultura, Comissão de Literatura (São Paulo, 1970), pp. 50-1.

same decoration was conferred on Adamson, together with that of the Order of Christ, in 1839; such official recognition of their distinguished services to Portuguese letters was in large measure due to Garrett.

Versatile and open-minded, Garrett was deeply sensitive to the best manifestations of English literature, English language, English institutions and the way of life of the English people. His discriminating and generous acceptance of the spirit and manners of English civilization enriched his personality with new dimensions, while, at the same time, defining more sharply his own national traits. Portuguese through and through, Garrett never became Anglicized, but received with warm gratitude the new vigour and life England gave him.

II

ADDISON

The tragedy *Catão* is the first of Garrett's works of some significance to show clear traces of English literary influence. Composed for immediate performance in Coimbra in 1821, and first published in the following year, it belongs to the process of aesthetic evolution that Garrett was going through at the time, from classicism to a neoclassicism imbued with more pathos; it also reveals the civic preoccupations that he shared with the other members of the *movimento da Regeneração,* which inclined them to subscribe to the idea of committed literature supporting social and political enlightenment, and the relevance of the work of art to its time. The tragedy, like the ode, seems to have been one of the forms that Garrett favoured in that period as best suited to his own purpose to move, persuade and arouse an audience, and the themes of a considerable proportion of his compositions in the early years until 1823 reveal his political and didactic motivation: the denunciation of tyranny, the praise of illustrious figures, and the eulogy of liberty and of high moral qualities such as justice and courage. It is not surprising that a man of Garrett's political beliefs should have felt drawn to Addison's *Cato,* in so far as it was eminently apposite to the situation in Portugal, when the *vintistas,* now that the revolution was completed, wanted to promote the defence of freedom within a spirit of moderation and respect for law. Garrett may have been aware of the fact that there was a certain parallel between the Portuguese contemporary scene and the circumstances that had led to the writing of *Cato* in 1713. The heated debates on the problem of succession caused by Queen Anne's failing health had prompted Addison to rekindle the sense of national identity in place of party politics, by setting before his countrymen the example of Cato's moral loftiness and, above all, his love of liberty and of his country. The political approval that was largely responsible for the initial success of *Cato* may have encouraged Garrett in his choice of model: Addison's play had shown in England that the themes of Roman nobility could arouse a contemporary response, such as he himself aimed at with his own experiment. This was also of particular interest to someone like Garrett who believed in the need for a national theatre, not one that necessarily dealt with figures or episodes of national history, but one that struck a chord in the audience by appealing to situations that were directly relevant to their own concerns. The fame of Addison's play, which had repeated revivals and gave rise to a whole series of editions, dedications, burlesques and

14

critical writings, was not restricted to eighteenth-century England. *Cato* enjoyed vast popularity on the continent, where it was not only the object of translations and much critical comment, but also had inspired new plays, or simply imitations and adaptations. Its semi-classical form gave it particular impact in France, where the first translation by Abel Boyer in 1715 was followed by seven more by 1815; it was praised in the *Encyclopédie,* by Voltaire in his *Lettres philosophiques,* and elsewhere. In spite of the general success achieved by *Cato,* its only direct repercussion in Portugal, apart from the musical adaptation in Lisbon in 1740 of one of the works it inspired in Italy —Metastasio's *Catone in Utica*— [1] seems to have been Manuel de Figueiredo's translation, about 1775-6. The staging of *Catão* in 1821, more than one hundred years after the original was written, was thus a cultural event of some significance. It met with immediate acclaim, described in these glowing terms by Garrett's biographer: «(...) a mais completa ovação que talvez conseguisse nenhum dos nossos Poetas».[2] Garrett had correctly assessed the impact that a theme like *Catão*'s would have on a politically aware audience such as his, and the vigorous manner of his writing, not often found among his contemporaries, was yet another factor in the extraordinary success of his play.

When Garrett read *Cato* he subscribed in tragedy to the ideal of Voltaire —who was one of his formative authors— and that of Ducis. Hence in his reading of Addison's play, first in a French adaptation, then in Figueiredo's translation, and lastly in the original,[3] he judged it largely by Voltaire's standards.[4] And when he wrote *Catão* in 1821 he did so according to the principles of 'mixed genre', which he saw as a harmonious compromise of the classical and the Romantic genres, and whose highest exponents were, in his eyes, Voltaire and Ducis.[5] Nevertheless, the resemblance of Garrett's play to Addison's was obvious to his contemporaries. In *Carta a um amigo,* inserted in the first edition, in 1822, and in the Preface to the second, dated London 1830, Garrett tries to refute the accusations of plagiarism in an off-hand manner, by openly avowing the passages that he did imitate and by professing misgivings on the literary merit of *Cato,* echoing some of the adverse criticism that had been made since John Dennis and quoting

---

[1] Andrée Crabbé Rocha, *O teatro de Garrett,* 2nd ed. (Coimbra, 1954), p. 98.

[2] G. de Amorim, Vol. 1, p. 224.

[3] *Carta a um amigo,* O. A. G., Vol. 2, p. 1622.

[4] In *Lucrécia,* O. A. G., Vol. 1, p. 16, Garrett refers to Voltaire as 'mestre da cena moderna'. In O. P. Monteiro, Vol. 1, p. 253.

[5] According to Antscherl, p. 23, the notion of 'mixed genre' was suggested to Garrett by Voltaire's *Dissertation sur la tragédie ancienne et moderne* preceding his *Sémiramis.* Garrett's views on this literary genre are voiced in *A quem ler* and in *Carta a um amigo,* in the first edition of *Catão:* «Mas o que não me lembro de ler é que este género romântico, combinando-se com o clássico, dando-se e recebendo mútuos socorros, formassem um género novo, cujos caracteres são bem salientes e cuja beleza incontestável», and «O *misto,* que principalmente se deve a Voltaire e a Ducis, participa das belezas dum e doutro, sem cair nos defeitos do *romântico,* aformoseia visivelmente o *clássico. Zaira, Tancredo, Alzira, Otelo* e o *Rei Lear* (de Ducis) provarão, melhor que todas as teorias, esta verdade.» O. A. G., Vol. 2, p. 1610 and p. 1624.

Schlegel. Yet he is clearly on the defensive; he makes an incomplete admission of the extent to which his play is influenced by *Cato* and suggests that any similarities between them arise from the reading of Plutarch or from common reactions to the same situations, thus making it a case of tradition and polygenesis rather than direct imitation.[6] Tradition and polygenesis are to some extent present in *Catão*, it is true. The fact, however, that the statement is belied by the evidence of the text justifies the conclusion that this, like his reference to Metastasio in *Carta a um amigo* is, as A. Crabbé Rocha suggests and as we shall see, another red herring,[7] and it shows Garrett in that form of creative activity designated by Bloom as *daemonization,* in which the author attempts to 'generalize away his precursor's uniqueness' and in which he himself 'is made more of a daemon and his precursor more of a man'.[8]

A close look will be taken at the two plays, in order to study Garrett's process of assimilation of *Cato,* and, unless otherwise stated, the London edition of *Catão*, usually regarded as the definitive, will be the one adopted. Reference will also be made to the first edition, particularly for an assessment of *Catão's* varying degree of verbal closeness to its precursor. As for the variants of the third and fourth editions, they are minimal and of no relevance to this work and will therefore be ignored.

The conclusion of the comparison of the English and the Portuguese texts is that Garrett keeps its moral, political and patriotic themes; he also keeps the structure of the plot, particularly in Acts I, II and V, as well as characters and relationships, and verbal reminiscences and translations.

Like *Cato,* Garrett's play is a didactic, moralising work, teaching by the illustration of exemplary behaviour. The message they share is that true patriotism must be regulated by the dictates of reason and by the interest of the *res publica:* obedience to the law and civic responsibility must prevail over individualistic reactions and feelings. The true patriot, though fearless of death, does not seek glory for self-aggrandisement or foolhardy self-sacrifice: the enlightened love of liberty and of one's country may demand, alongside deeds of overt bravery, other more self-effacing courses of action — like the temporary retreat from the scene of war that the protagonist recommends to Marco Bruto in Act V, ix, parallel to Cato's words to Portius in Act IV, i, or to his supporters, for whom he provides ships that may lead them to safety — or like suicide, which deprived the conqueror of his triumph. The moral arguments for the suicide are similar in the two plays — disenchantment and general weariness play their part, heightened by the disclosure of treason and the death of the protagonist's son — but the main justification is the emphatically repeated message that death is preferable to dishonour and slavery. Plato's doctrine of another, better existence, where the soul is free from oppression and decay, lends added weight to the moral justification of suicide in both cases. Garrett

---

[6] Dámaso Alonso, 'Tradition or polygenesis', *Annual Bulletin,* MHRA, 32 (1960), pp. 17-34.

[7] A. Crabbé Rocha, pp. 97-8.

[8] Harold Bloom, *The Anxiety of Influence, A Theory of Poetry* (New York, 1973), pp. 15 and 106.

also follows Addison in reassuring the audience that, in spite of the protagonist's personal tragedy, or rather because of it, tyranny will meet its merited punishment.

In addition to such thematic similarities it is possible to indicate affinities in the structure of the plot of the two plays: with the exception of passages resulting from divergences in characters and subplots, which will be discussed later, it can be said that to a great extent events and ideas unfold in close parallel in Acts I, II and V.

Thus in Act I of both works action takes place at dawn on the fateful day when a meeting of the Senate called by Cato will decide the future of Utica, besieged by Caesar.[9] The main characters, except for Cato himself, are introduced and their speeches convey what are basically the same ideas, in very much the same sequence, the difference consisting in a minor reshuffling by Garrett in the identity of those who utter them. In both plays the characters refer to the fearful nature of the decisive day, to the corruption of the Roman Senate, to the helpless situation of Cato and his supporters in a degenerate world, to the insignificant numbers of Cato's own Senate, survivors of Pharsalia, and to the impetuous temperament of one of Cato's sons (Marcus and Marco Bruto, in the English and in the Portuguese play, respectively). In both plays this is followed by the disclosure of Sempronius's treason, of his dissembling in the form of incitement to resistance, and of the worries that his duplicity causes him. Act I of both works also contains the eulogy of Cato as a public figure and as a family man, Sempronius's criticism of the imitation of Cato by his sons, to whom the word 'sententious' is applied in both plays, and expressions of filial love and concern for Cato from Pórcio in *Catão*, Act I, v, and from Juba and Marcia in *Cato*, Act I, iv.

Close parallels in content and sequence can also be found in Act II, which deals in both plays with the meeting of the Senate and with the peace message sent by Caesar. Common traits are Cato's opening speech to the assembly; his admonishing words about the intemperate patriotic zeal displayed by Garrett's Marco Bruto and by Addison's Sempronius, who are parallel figures to the extent that they represent unreasoned, fiery behaviour, sincere or feigned; the counsel given by those two other parallel figures, the moderating senators Mânlio and Lucius, which earns them the accusation of treason from Marco Bruto and from Sempronius, respectively; Cato's speech on liberty rather than death; the announcement by one of Cato's sons of the arrival of Caesar's emissary; Cato's reply to Caesar's proffered peace, which includes in both plays a reference to the tyrant's unrepresentative and corrupt Roman Senate; the turning down of Caesar's terms of peace by Mânlio and Lucius. With the exception of Semprónio's offer of a dictatorship to Cato and of the passages connected with the love intrigue and with the Syphax subplot, excluded by Garrett, the structure of Act II in both works is essentially the same.

It is only in Acts III and IV that Garrett strikes out a line for himself

---

[9] In order to avoid repetition of the names Cato/Catão, etc., the characters will be referred to by their English names only, whenever the action or the speeches are common in the two plays.

and makes what would be regarded in Bloom's terminology as a correction of *Cato,* through such means as new nuances of the political content and structural divergences, thus ensuring a degree of autonomy to his play. This is felt more forcefully in Act III, where the only point of contact with Addison —Sempronius's treason and his attempts to implicate Juba— is treated by Garrett in an independent manner; the same may be said of his approach in Act IV to such parallels as the exposure of Sempronius and the death of one of the protagonist's sons. Yet, in spite of Garrett's original conception of Act IV as a whole, it is possible to distinguish the influence of Addison in the lines on obedience to law as a basis for liberty, which may be related to Cato's speech in Act III; one can also establish a link in Act IV of the two plays, in *Cato,* IV, i, and in *Catão,* IV, iii, in the protagonist's attitude of growing discouragement and disillusion at the idea of Juba's treason.

In Act V Garrett returns openly to his English model, though not in such close parallel as in the first two Acts. From *Cato* he keeps the initial scene, in which the protagonist, sitting by a drawn sword, reads a book and then embarks on a soliloquy on the subject of life and death and on the existence of an eternal life, in the light of Plato's doctrine; the dialogue on the theme of suicide between Cato and Portius, which in *Catão* takes place in expanded form between the protagonist and Mânlio; the tidings of Caesar's imminent arrival, brought by Juba and Lucius, and which Garrett reserves for Juba alone; the offer of help from Pompey's son, which, conveyed by Juba in Addison's play, is announced by Mânlio in Garrett's; the protagonist's repeated expressions of advice and concern for the future and safety of those around him —the ships in the port, the refuge in the Sabine fields, his daughter's marriage—; and, finally, the act of suicide, which evokes similar reactions from Lucius «Now is Rome fallen indeed! » and from his counterpart Mânlio «Expiraste, ó Roma! ».

During this brief comparison of the structure of the two plays the existence of affinities between the characters, mentioned earlier on, will have become apparent. Garrett does, in fact, keep from *Cato,* in exact correspondence or with only minor alterations, characters and relationships for which there is no evidence in Plutarch, whom he quotes as a common source.[10] Thus he imitates Addison in modifying Plutarch's account in *Life of Cato Minor,* according to which the stoic leader had only one son in his company —Portius, the eldest— during the siege of Utica, by representing him surrounded by a number of children. To Addison's real sons Portius and Marcus and to the adopted Juba Garrett presents an obvious parallel in one real son, Pórcio, and two adopted, Marco Bruto and Juba. The role of the Numidian prince, cast as Cato's foster son and loyal supporter against Caesar's besieging troops, has not the historical foundation that the imprecision of Garrett's Note I to Act I may lead the reader to believe; for, according to Plutarch's *Life of Cato Minor* and *Life of Caesar,* it was in fact Juba's father, King Juba, who acted as an ally to Cato during the siege, and not the prince, whose life Garrett relates in his Note. King Juba

---

[10] *Catão,* Preface to the 2nd and 3rd ed., O. A. G., Vol. 2, pp. 1614 and 1618.

was defeated by Caesar's advancing troops and ran away to a mountain, where he awaited Cato's decision. Prince Juba must therefore be regarded as an imitation from *Cato*. In Plutarch there is no evidence either for Décio or for Semprónio, who are further imitations from *Cato*. The same applies to Mânlio, inspired by the figure of Lucius, who, in spite of his historical existence, performs in Addison's play a role that is not warranted by Plutarch's account.

These characters correspond largely in temperament and behaviour to their English models. The three young men in *Catão* are united to the protagonist by the same feelings of filial reverence, loyalty and affection as in Addison's play, and they serve similar purposes of intensification of pathos, either through their own deaths or through their sorrow for the death of their father. Their temperaments, too, are cast in similar moulds: Pórcio's disposition mirrors Portius's combination of bravery with reason, Marcus and Marco Bruto are shown as equally impetuous and strong-headed in their boldness, and the two Jubas are depicted alike as intrepid soldiers, utterly devoted to the protagonist, deeply conscious of being mere barbarians and filled with admiration for Rome and her civilization. The character of Semprónio, too, is closely modelled on that of Addison's creation, with only such differences in behaviour as must result from divergences in plot. It should also be noted that Garrett attributes to Marco Bruto some of the lines which, in his model, were spoken by Sempronius, as part of his process of reshuffling; such are, for instance, the intervention in the Senate, voting for war, in Act II, i, of both plays, which causes them to be rebuked by Cato for their impetuous zeal, and the desire to take the law in their own hands, which, again, is reproved by the civic-minded leader (*Cato*, Act III, i, and *Catão*, Act IV, i). But on the whole, and apart from Sempronius's qualified interest in Marcia, the motivation is exactly the same for the two characters: resentment, jealousy and hatred of Cato, mingled with ambition for the honours that may accrue to the followers of a triumphant Caesar. Their duplicity induces in both similar feelings of disquiet and guilt, and is disguised as loud vocal support for Cato —too loud for discerning ears— and as incitement to war. Like Semprónio, Décio has an identical role to that of his English original, as the bearer of Caesar's offer of peace in exchange for Cato's friendship. The argument in the discussion of terms between him and the besieged leader runs roughly along the same lines in the two plays, with Decius evoking the victor's generosity and personal admiration for Cato's virtue, and speaking of the shedding of tears that would follow, should his proposal be unheeded —the difference being that, while in *Cato* the tears are Roman, in the Portuguese play Décio speaks of Utican tears...

No less important than the affinities already pointed out are the verbal similarities between the two plays, in the form of imitations, translations of varying degrees of fidelity, paraphrases or simple reminiscences, some of which are admitted in *Carta a um amigo*. The second edition of *Catão* shows a further approximation to its precursor, while acquiring greater autonomy through deviations in a different direction. This may sound like a paradox, but the turning away from his model to correct it is still an aspect of Garrett's being open to the influence of Addison's play, in so far as it presupposes his continuing awareness of it. A comparison of texts of *Cato* and of the two first versions of *Catão* show the following main points of verbal assimilation:

a) Lines 77-81 in Marco Bruto's speech beginning 'Olha, vês tu a aurora?' (Act I, i), acknowledged by Garrett as an imitation of the first four lines of the passage by Portius 'The dawn is overcast, the morning lowers (...)' (Act I, i), are followed by a compressed adaptation of the last seven lines. This is not mentioned by Garrett, and the variant of the 1830 edition shows an even greater approximation to *Cato*.

b) The end of Semprónio's monologue (lines 303-10, Act I, iv), is clearly an imitation of Sempronius's in 'I must dissemble / And speak a language foreign to my heart' and in the last five lines of his final words (Act I, ii). Here, again, the 1830 variant is closer to *Cato*.

c) Pórcio's lines in Act I, v, which start 'Meu Semprónio, abracemonos ainda (...)', are a close parallel to Sempronius's in Act I, ii, 'Good morrow, Portius: let us once embrace (...)'. Garrett admits the correspondence between the two texts; their resemblance is again greater in the second edition of *Catão*.

d) Pórcio's lines in Act I, v, on the meeting of the Senate, 'Aí vão correndo à humilde cúria (...)' are, on Garrett's admission, parallel to the first three lines of Portius's speech in Act I, ii, beginning 'My father has this morning called together (...)'.

e) Juba's reply in praise of Catão, from the lines 'Todo o esplendor da fastuosa Roma, / Toda a sua pompa (...)' (Act I, v) is an imitation, also acknowledged by Garrett, of Sempronius's speech 'Not all the pomp and majesty of Rome (...)' (Act I, ii) which becomes closer to *Cato* in the 1830 variant.

f) In another imitation, only partially acknowledged by Garrett, Catão's opening address to the Senate (Act II, i) incorporates an adaptation of the parallel speech by Cato (Act II, i), as can be seen from the following excerpts:

> Fathers, we once again are met in council;
> Caesar's approach has summoned us together,
> And Rome attends her fate from our resolves.
> How shall we treat this bold aspiring man?
> Success still follows him, and backs his crimes.

> Padres de Roma, augustos senadores
> Da pátria moribunda único apoio,
> Quanto ainda folgo de vos ver unidos, (...)
> Esta pátria, esta Roma o seu destino
> De vós espera agora: a vós incumbe
> Decidir de seu fado. —César chega: (...)
> Que nos convém fazer? Como devemos

20

Tratar esse homem temerário, ardido,
Ambicioso, insaciável? —A fortuna
Tem coroado seus crimes com vitórias.

g) Marco Bruto's long intervention in the Senate, Act II, i, 'Eu voto a guerra (...)' is an amplification of Sempronius's lines from 'My voice is still for war (...)' to 'Of his thronged legions, and charge home upon him', and then from 'The corps of half her Senate (...)' to 'Great Pompey's shade complains that we are slow', in Act II, i. Garrett acknowledges the resemblance between the texts.

h) Catão's admonishment of Marco Bruto 'Bruto, esse furor não é romano (...)' in Act II, ii, corresponds, as admitted in *Carta,* to Cato's rebuff of Sempronius's excessive fieryness 'Let not a torrent of impetuous zeal (...)' in Act II, i.

i) Catão's speech on his terms for peace (Act II, iii) is parallel to two of Cato's (Act II, i), on Garrett's own admission. The first, in reply to Decius's request '(...) And name your terms', begins 'Bid him disband his legions (...)', and is clearly imitated as 'As condições são estas: Desarme as legiões (...)'. The second, 'Nay, more, though Cato's voice was ne'er employed / To clear the guilty (...)' is incorporated in the London variant in a form that is even closer to Addison, as 'Jamais no foro, / No Senado se ergueu meu brado austero / Para defender crimes (...)'.

Besides these affinities, common to the first two editions of *Catão,* there are others which were introduced only in the much revised and expanded second edition. Such are, for instance, Sempronius's fear and guilt as a plotter (*Cato,* Act I, iii, and *Catão* Act III, vi), and the announcement of his treason, followed by a reaction of surprised indignation and general condemnation (*Cato,* IV, i, and *Catão,* IV, iii), which are major significant elements in the fuller development of this character in the second edition, as analyzed by O. P. Monteiro.[11] Most important of all is the introduction of Catão's soliloquy in Act V, ii, which has also been discussed by the same critic as an essential alteration in the Stoic's psychological make-up, to whose motivations for suicide is now added the Platonic belief in a life beyond. Catão's monologue, with its reference to Plato —a meditation on the dread of nothingness, the longing for immortality, the uncertainty of man's life with its trials and hopes, the intimations of a happier existence that Heaven puts into his soul— is clearly inspired by the first half of Cato's soliloquy in Act V, i, when he is about to commit suicide. Another variant in Act V, ix of the second edition —the Stoic's indignation at the fact that his sword had been taken away from him— becoming closer to Addison's parallel episode in Act V, i, with strong verbal affinities, corroborates the fact that the English playwright, and not Lamartine, as tentatively suggested by O. P. Monteiro,[12] is the source of this climactic passage in *Catão.*

Apart from these passages there are further verbal reminiscences scat-

---

11 O. P. Monteiro, Vol. II, pp. 286-7.
12 O. P. Monteiro, Vol. II, p. 285, note 183.

21

tered throughout the play, which reveal that Garrett had read *Cato* very closely indeed, as in the Stoic's lines over the corpse of his son. Compare:

> Thanks to the gods, my boy has done his duty.
>
> ....
>
> (...) Here lay him down, my friends
> Full in my sight, that I may view at leisure
> The bloody corpse, and count these glorious wounds.
> —How beautiful is death when earned by virtue!
>
> *Cato,* Act IV, i
>
> Deram-te abençoada morte os deuses.
>
> ....
>
> Ânimo! vinde, aproximai-vos dele;
> Contemos as feridas gloriosas
> Deste cadáver. Nunca tão formoso
> Me pareceste, meu querido Pórcio...
>
> *Catão,* Act IV, v

Counterbalancing the similarities and imitations that he acknowledged and which are far from complete, Garrett tries to establish the originality of his work by emphasizing differences in plot, characters and content. Thus he eliminates from the stage Addison's love scenes and all feminine figures, thereby achieving greater cohesion of action. In adopting this course and in writing disapprovingly of the love interest in *Cato* Garrett does no more than reflect the adverse criticism that had been voiced from the outset [13] and which had become generalised by 1820. It is even highly probable that he, who mentions Voltaire's admiration for the play in *Carta a um amigo,* should have read the disparaging lines in *Zaïre* on the insipidness of the feminine characters, and on Addison's having ruined a masterpiece through the love subplot to please his audience, in *De la tragédie anglaise.* Yet it is not Voltaire's, but rather Schlegel's more detailed criticism in the *Cours de littérature dramatique* that Garrett quotes to justify his views on *Cato* in general. His own words on the subject of the love scenes are inspired by Schlegel, both in *Carta* and in the Preface to the second edition, but he pushes the point further with questionable fairness:

> Seis namoros! (...) no *Catão* de Addison são verdadeiramente —verbos de encher; tanto têm eles com a acção capital, como os nossos antigos *graciosos* das óperas do Judeu com Medeia e Jasão. Demais a mais têm a habilidade de ocupar quasi sempre a cena, e deixar raras vezes aparecer sobre ela o principal actor e acção. A traição de Semprónio Sífax é motivada por namoro, as mortes de Semprónio e Marco por namoro, toda a *intriga* ou nexo do drama por namoro; Catão entretém-se também com todos estes namoros (...) [14]

[13] Lady Mary Montagu, even before the play was performed, declared that the love interest was not relevant to the main action; Pope's information that it had been added as an afterthought seems to be corroborated by the fact that an edition of *Cato... without the love scenes* was made in London in 1764, apparently without any damage to the success of the work. See Peter Smithers, *The Life of Joseph Addison,* 2nd ed. (Oxford, 1968), p. 271.

[14] *Carta a um amigo.*

Garrett deviates from Addison by also eliminating the Syphax subplot, in which the love intrigue is combined with and subordinated to the political theme, and by replacing it with the complications of Marco Bruto's parentage. This provides the play with added action on the stage and off it: it prolongs the presence of Décio and introduces the reported action of César's *amours* with Servília, Catão's sister. Besides, it has the double effect of contributing to an increase in tension through the hints, in the speeches of Marco Bruto and Juba, of an eventual parricide — and simultaneously reassuring the audience, in the tradition of the Enlightenment, that the tyrant will ultimately be overthrown. Yet the problems of Marco Bruto's bonds with César lend a melodramatic note to the play, and the same applies to the delivery of the letter, remarked on by A. Crabbé Rocha.[15] Besides, such complications are liable to incur a similar criticism to that which Garrett made of the love interest: that it diverts attention from the main action. This divergence in subplots partly accounts for the independent structures of Acts III and IV of the two plays. It is true that they lead eventually to the same situations that confirm Cato in his decision to commit suicide in Act V —the exposure and punishment of Sempronius, Cato's disenchantment at the news of treason and sorrow for the loss of his son, Caesar's imminent arrival— but their convergence at the climax of the tragedy is achieved through different means. Thus in Addison's Act III the action deals with the love intrigue, the treason of Sempronius in association with the leaders of the mutiny, and his plotting with Syphax to seize Marcia by force; in Act IV the main points are the onstage killing of Sempronius by Juba, and the stoic reaction of Cato at the sight of his dead son. In Garrett, on the other hand, the main peripeteia of Act III are connected with Marco Bruto's parentage and with the trap Semprónio sets for the unsuspecting Juba; this is followed in Act IV by an encounter between Mânlio and the rebel soldiers, the arrest and banishment of Semprónio, and, finally, Catão's emotional reaction to the death on stage of his son Pórcio.

As far as dramaturgy is concerned, there is greater flexibility in the observance of the neoclassical rules in *Catão* than in its English model, to the advantage of the Portuguese play. Schlegel points out in Lesson XV of his *Cours* that Addison's strict adherence to them in *Cato* has an inhibiting effect and that certain privileges and freedoms authorized by Shakespeare's example are forgone without any corresponding gain. In fact Addison's concern with unity of place causes him to set the action in the same scene throughout the play, with the result that *Cato* depends almost exclusively on the power of discourse and is deprived of the dramatic effects which might have been achieved by resorting to the technique of scene construction that was a legacy of the Elizabethans and of the Restoration theatre. Garrett avoids the pitfall of monotony by interpreting the classical rule of the unity of place with a certain degree of latitude. Thus he sets the action in Utica, but moves it from a square in Act I to the dilapidated interior of a barbarian building in Acts II and III, to the city

---

[15]   A. Crabbé Rocha, p. 113.

3

gates in Act IV, and finally, in Act V, to a gallery with a view over the sea with ships on one side and part of the city walls on the other.

In contrast with Addison's laconic stage indications, those of Garrett denote his concern with spectacle, to which he may partly have resorted as a means to counteract the paucity of action in the play. One may, for instance, compare Addison's stage directions for Act II, i, 'The Senate (sitting)', with Garrett's detailed instructions on the form of entry and seating arrangements of the senators, followed by the entrance of the lictors and Catão after them. Another parallel scene where Garrett achieves a greater sense of spectacle is that of Catão killing himself with his sword in full view of the audience rather than behind the curtain as Cato does. On the whole, in spite of such scenes in Addison's play as the encounter of Cato and his guards with Sempronius and the leaders of the mutiny (Act III, i), or Sempronius's fight with Juba, each with his retinue of soldiers (Act IV, i), there is much more spectacle in *Catão*, where the characters are often followed by a body of lictors, guards and soldiers, where the confusion of the struggle between Mânlio and a group of rebels is added to by the arrival of Marco Bruto and his cohort of soldiers, closely followed by Catão, who comes preceded by lictors and Roman soldiers bearing torches (Act IV, i, ii, iii), and where the crowd, spreading over the stairway, actually participates in the action (Act V, v).

One important respect in which Garrett differs from Addison is in the role he assigns to the people. In accordance with strict neoclassical practice, Addison had included in his *Cato* only characters of high rank and station. Garrett, on the other hand, had, as a liberal revolutionary, a much keener awareness of the impact political events had on the common people, and indeed of the part played by the people in wars and upheavals. So in *Catão* he includes the important scene in Act V, v, in which the populace of Utica vainly beg Catão to leave with them. The political significance of the play is considerably widened by this device, which removes the drama from the restricted milieu of princes and senators, and recognises that the whole population, from the highest to the lowest classes, is involved in the affairs of state.

Garrett deviates further from Addison by adding new elements to the common substance of their political message, so that *Catão* becomes more directly relevant to the Portuguese scene, particularly after the alterations introduced in the London edition of 1830. Though he denies that there is a change of political outlook between the first and the second editions,[16] the variants introduced in the latter reveal a disenchantment with revolution and with man in all ranks of society, which has no parallel in *Cato* and which seems to spring from the same feelings against the liberal leadership that dictate his *Carta a Mucio Scevola*, of the same year; they may also be related to his disappointment with the *movimento regenerador* and with the open discords prevailing among liberal exiles.[17] Thus certain lines of

16 Preface to the third edition.
17 He writes in Act IV, iv: '(...) Que lucrámos na mudança / Perigosa? (...) A mesma corrupção, —mais desfaçada, / Mais clara só, mais despejada. —E é esta, / É esta a liberdade que nos destes!'.

Mânlio's speech in Act II, i, appear to be an allusion to Palmela and his associates, when he refers to the invidious position of those who, having the responsibility of government in a period of civil strife, become easy targets for all manner of accusations; the same may be said of Mânlio's remarks on the pride of such leaders, who presume to be able to guide a divided nation to safety.

The importance that Garrett attaches to the people in the first edition —and which, as said above, has no counterpart in Addison— is increased in the second, where one finds in Juba's speech in Act III, vii, a reference to the *Povo-Rei* in terms that may be regarded as republican. Yet at the same time, in a passage in Act IV, iii —already present in the first edition—, Catão reflects realistically on the fundamental inconstancy of the people:

> (...) —O que é o povo?
> O que são homens! —Ontem expulsastes
> A Coriolano, poque ousou negar-vos
> Os baldios comuns: hoje, fugindo,
> Abandonais à fúria dos patrícios
> Graco que vo-las dava!

Likewise, in the denunciation of demagogy by Marco Bruto (Act III, i), one may sense a recognition of the fact that the people —'incauta prole'— can easily be swayed by unscrupulous manipulators. The significance of the social role of the people is heightened in *Catão* by the repeated message that tyranny thrives on the decay of virtue in institutions and in the heart of the citizens: 'Roma é serva / No coração, tem alma escrava há muito (...)' says Catão in Act V, vii. And the death of the tyrant —whom Catão compares to a hydra of a hundred faces—, does not necessarily entail the end of tyranny:

> Desafogar a pátria de um tirano,
> É transitório alívio: empiora a miúdo
> Co esse remédio o mal; tens cem tiranos
> Em vez de um: nem talentos nem virtudes
> Ocuparão, no Estado, o grau supremo
> Entre vis demagogos repartido
> Por facções, por subornos, peitas, crimes.
>
> Act IV, iii

Garrett's message to his contemporaries is thus one of evolution rather than revolution, and reflects his adherence to the ideas of Montesquieu and Filangeri. The second edition develops the idea of the original *Catão*, that the way to healing lies in the purging of the institutions that regulate society and in the obedience to law and justice. To this moralizing and moderating message Garrett adds a note of encouragement, by reminding his countrymen of the love of freedom among their ancestors, the Lusitanians.

In spite of such differences in plot, dramaturgy and political content, the parallels between the two plays were too evident for Garrett to escape the charge of imitation that prompts *Carta a um amigo* —in which he tries to prove the fundamental independence of his work while acknowledging his debt to Addison—, and justifications in the Prefaces to the editions of 1830 and 1839. It would be perhaps unreasonable to expect a full and sincere avowal of the extent of his borrowings. Besides, as Garrett reminds us in 1830, he was only twenty-one then, and the play, completed in twenty-odd days, was already under rehearsal as it was being written. This may incline the present day reader to be more lenient when judging Garrett's acknowledgement, which was specious and half-hearted. Thus, after a criticism of *Cato* which is, to a certain degree, a biased version of Schlegel's, he makes the following remarks on the differences between the two plays:

> O muito que me afastei de Addison, da simples comparação destes reparos o podes colher. A personagem de Bruto, que é a segunda na minha tragédia, não aparece na dele; eu não tenho damas nem namoricos; a exposição, o nexo, a catástrofe da minha peça são outras absolutamente.

The same desire to disclaim similarities with *Cato* reappears in the Preface to the second edition, where he writes: 'fábula, interesse, mecanismo dramático, tudo é diferente nas duas tragédias'. The comparison carried out above indicated that, on the contrary, *Catão* is deeply indebted to Addison's play in essential points, such as the sharing of the main themes of death rather than slavery, and patriotism above personal interest, subject to reason and to state laws and institutions; affinities in the structure of the plot, where, but for the replacement of the love interest and of the Syphax subplot by Marco Bruto's, ideas and events unfold in close parallel in content and sequence, particularly in Acts I, II and V; parallels and affinities between the characters and their relationships, even in the case of Marco Bruto, who shares some of the traits of Marcus and of the speeches of Sempronius; parallel development of the events leading to the climax, and parallel motivation for suicide.

Garrett is particularly severe in his criticisms of what he describes as the lack of climactic build-up in *Cato:* he writes in *Carta* that the suicide is caused by the general loss of liberty but that there is no immediate, direct motivation, and that, therefore, the denouement is unnecessarily suspended throughout the whole play. Nevertheless it has just been shown that the reasons for suicide in *Catão* are parallel to those in *Cato:* growing disenchantment disclosed in the dialogue with the moderating senators Lucius/Mânlio, brought about by the news of treason and of the death of the protagonist's son; the main motivation is, however, the refusal to fall alive into the tyrant's hands, so that suicide takes place when Caesar's arrival is imminent. Cato's lines about the immediate cause, in Act IV, i, are sufficiently clear:

> Is there aught else, my friends, I can do for you?
> The conqueror draws near. Once more, farewell!
> If e'er we meet hereafter, we shall meet
> In happier climates, and on a safer shore,
> Where Caesar never shall approach us more.

26

That Garrett, who attributes the same motives to Catão's suicide, should fail to recognize them in *Cato,* is hardly believable. One feels tempted to doubt his sincerity, particularly as further down on the same page he criticizes the monologue in Act V, i, as being undramatic and inappropriate to the situation — a monologue that he imitates and sets in an identical scene in his own Act V, ii, and which he does not include in his list of lines indebted to Addison. Their real extent in the first edition is not admitted in *Carta,* and the second edition variants of some of those passages, which, as shown above, bring them even closer to Addison, are not once referred to in the Prefaces to the second and third editions. There, on the contrary, Garrett tries to make out the case that the source of similarities lies in their common reading of Plutarch — in statements belied by the above analysis of his characters. The reasons why Garrett should thus try to bring in new and easily disproved arguments to deny his considerable debt to Addison as late as 1830 and 1839, when immaturity is no excuse, may be said to fall within the case of daemonization, as suggested above. Garrett was in fact caught in the tensions arising from the divergence between the Enlightenment and the Romantic notions of poetical influence. His late disavowals of Addison's presence in *Cato* may be seen as a manifestation of his share in the prevailing unease about 'filial relationship' in poetry.[18] They may also be seen as stemming from a desire to be consistent, in his prime, with his earlier stance as a youth, when he defended himself from the accusation of plagiarism. Whatever his motivations, one should not look at Garrett as an isolated case but rather place him in the wide context of literary creation, where no one is free from intra-poetic influence. As Bloom puts it,

> Weaker talents idealize; figures of capable imagination appropriate for themselves. But nothing is got for nothing, and self-appropriation involves the immense anxieties of indebtedness, for what strong maker desires the realization that he has failed to create himself?[19]

What matters ultimately is the assessment of *Catão* in relation to its precursor, what Bloom calls 'clinamen' — the moving away from the model in order to improve it. For *Catão* is in fact a correction and a prolongation of *Cato,* and develops away from it to an entity of its own, despite the bold and brazen appropriations that have been uncovered, and this is achieved in the second edition through divergences in characters and structure, through the ideas of immediate political relevance to the Portuguese situation, through its concept of the sociological and theatrical role of the people, through its more modern and flexible dramaturgy. In spite of the strictures of some critics on its arcadian verse *Catão* is alive and still has the power to appeal to a present day audience in a way that perhaps *Cato* has not; and although the replacement of Addison's two subplots by Marco Bruto's is still a diversion, Garrett's play has a greater cohesion and gathers momentum in an unimpeded way that is not achieved

[18] H. Bloom, pp. 26-7.
[19] H. Bloom, p. 1.

in *Cato*. It may not mark the beginning of contemporary drama, as is claimed in the Preface to the fourth edition, but nonetheless it stands out in the general perspective of the dramatic production of its author and of his Portuguese contemporaries. It is the last and most accomplished of Garrett's writings for the theatre in the early period before exile, when, after having sought classical themes directly in Brumoy's *Le Théâtre des Grecs*, he looks for them in the interpretation of writers like Voltaire, Alfieri and Addison. At this stage French influences loom large in Garrett in comparison with English: they are present even in his choice of Addison as a model, in so far as *Cato* was a successful adaptation of the French concept of classical tragedy, and in his decision to write in a genre inspired by Voltaire and Ducis. It is only during the years of emigration that follow soon after *Catão* that Garrett's reading of English literature appears to be free from French aesthetic judgements. Just as the restraint and the universal appeal of *Cato* are a product of the Augustan age, so does *Catão* reflect the spirit of its time in such features as greater subjectivity in character portrayal and freer expression of emotion —which at times reaches passionate or pathetic accents—, as well as in its specific political message. By emphasizing in his successive Prefaces now one now another aspect of the political content of *Catão*, Garrett is able to maintain its relevance to the Portuguese scene for about two decades: from a cautionary message to revolutionaries in the first edition, it becomes a defence of the excellence of constitutional or monarchic freedom in the second, and finally, in the third, it is presented as the most national of his creations.[20] The same capacity to adjust *Catão* to the political situation of the moment enabled Garrett to stage successful revivals, like the performances in Count Moreley's theatre, organized by Paulo Midosi to raise the morale of the Portuguese exiles confined to the 'Depósito' in Plymouth,[21] and mentioned by Garrett in the Preface to the second edition:

> Também exilada na geral proscrição de 1828, veio aparecer em Plymouth, onde, se houvermos de crer os jornais ingleses desse tempo, tão perfeitamente desempenhada foi por vários oficiais e outros distintos emigrados portugueses, —que até dos 'spectadores britanos' se não poderá o autor queixar (...)[22]

Indeed it met with such applause that it was performed three times, and reprinted in London in 1830.

In *Viagens na minha terra* (1843) Garrett generously makes up for the ungracious lack of recognition of his debt as a fledgeling writer to the author of *Cato*. There warm tribute is paid to Addison for achieving distinction in many diverse capacities — as a statesman and as a philosopher, as a poet and as a writer of elegance, humour and talent.[23] These lines in praise of Addison's multiplicity of gifts are also an ironical dig at the narrow-mindedness of the contemporary Portuguese, who could not conceive

20 A. Crabbé Rocha, p. 115.
21 V. Nemésio, p. 57.
22 O. A. G., Vol. 2, p. 1615.
23 *Viagens*, Chapt. IV, p. 29.

that talent in the arts was compatible with seriousness and stature in politics; and they contain an element of self-congratulation, in view of the evident parallels between Garrett's own versatility and that of Addison the Magdalen scholar, the Whig Secretary of State and the editor of *The Spectator,* as evinced in the self-portrait in the Preface of *Viagens,* ascribed to the Editors. Garrett's tribute culminates in the lines:

> E eu trago aqui na algibeira o meu Addison —um dos poucos livros que não largo nunca— (...) e Addison (...) é muito maior filósofo do que Démades (...)
> O erudito e amável leitor (...) compre um *Spectator* que é um livro sem que se não pode estar e veja passim.[24]

Such an admiration for the successful daily paper is no surprise when one remembers Garrett's linguistic and literary interests and his deep concern with middle class culture, and a number of essays immediately occur as most likely to have attracted the attention of the Portuguese writer, — those on the Ballad, on Milton, on Language, on Authors and Writing, on Taste and the Pleasures of Imagination. There is indeed specific evidence of intratextual influence in the chapter in question —Chapter IV—, in which Garrett opposes Demades and gives Addison full support for rating modesty above all other virtues. Garrett's treatment of the theme —the charm of modesty and its primordial value, the excess of modesty as a lack of social grace, and its indispensable nature, without which beauty becomes contemptible— echoes similar opinions in essays of *The Spectator:* Steele's No. 154, Addison's No. 213, 435 and 458, and, in particular, Budgell's No. 395, with which the text in *Viagens* presents affinities in content, vocabulary and imagery. Besides, there is the fact that the manner of the chapter as a whole —humorous, learned and yet simply communicative— is reminiscent of that of the Spectatorial papers. Addison's style, based on that of the cultured gentlemen of the eighteenth century, is one in which the distinction between conversation and writing tends to be diluted, and must be regarded as another —far from negligible— contribution to the varied style of *Viagens* and to one of its most pronounced features —the spoken manner.

It seems almost inevitable that the admirer of *The Spectator* should devote some space to the coffee-house — and one does indeed find the well-known passage on 'o café do Cartaxo'[25] where Garrett, like another Addison, goads the owner of the place to give his views on local news and politics. Just as Addison had written in «Sensations in a coffee-house» (Essay No. 403) that it was his habit to visit such establishments in order to become acquainted with the opinions of his 'Ingenious Countrymen', so does Garrett present the 'café' as a main source of study of the middle-class:

> O café é uma das feições mais características de uma terra. O viajante experimentado e fino chega a qualquer parte, entra no café, observa-o, examina-o,

---

[24] *Viagens,* Chapt. IV, p. 29.
[25] *Viagens,* Chapt. VII.

estuda-o, e tem conhecido o país em que está, o seu governo, as suas leis, os seus costumes, a sua religião.[26]

Though there is no evidence of any direct connection between *The Tatler* and *The Spectator* and the periodicals for women in which Garrett collaborated —*O Toucador, periódico sem política. Dedicado às senhoras portuguesas* (1822), the projected *Lyceu das damas* (MS 127 of Esp., 1822-3), which eventually found partial realisation in *O Chronista* (1827) and *O Correio das damas* (1836)— Addison and Steele must be named at least as inspirations, even if at some distance, in their pioneering role in promoting feminine education and instruction, as well as reformation of manners, through the periodical essay.

Addison, then, can be said to have been a constant in Garrett's life, from the beginning to the peak of his literary career. Through his early education in the spirit of the Enlightenment already permeated by sensitivity, Garrett was receptive to the poetry of *Cato*. His own versatility found a model to emulate in the English scholar who so successfully branched out from the sheltered world of classical studies to the more public activities of playwriting, statesmanship and journalism, combining throughout a purist's love of words and language with the pressing desire for effective communication. And Garrett, through the continued study of the language and literature, classical and modern, of his own and of other countries; through the growing critical powers which enabled him to assess for himself —as a rule most judiciously, and independently from current trends— the specific qualities of the authors that he studied; and who, through the knowledge thus acquired fashioned his own original work in a way that opened new linguistic and literary horizons in Portugal, certainly fits Addison's definition of a 'Man of a Fine Taste'.

---

[26] *Viagens*, Chapt. VII, p. 50.

BYRON

Leva-to além das passadas eras
Do bardo misterioso o eterno canto,
A harpa sublime agora pendurada
Nos louros do Pamiso —onde um suspiro
De morte lhe quebrou a extrema corda
Que Eleutéria divina lhe afinara—,
Do cantor que no alento derradeiro
Ouviram as cidades contendoras
Pelo berço de Homero, em canção última
De moribundo Cisne, o brado ingente
Alçar da glória aos filhos acordados
De Leónidas que dorme...

Camões, C. V. xiii, l. 20-31

Thus does Garrett pay tribute to Byron the poet and the champion of Greek freedom, in a passage interpolated in a description of the beauties of Sintra, which he wrote with lines of *Childe Harold* echoing in his mind. These reminiscences of the English poem, and Garrett's admiration for Byron, who had only recently died in Missolonghi, are given more explicit expression in an explanatory note (Note D to Canto V, first edition):

Lorde Byron, que em seu extraordinário e inimitável poema, o *Child* (sic) *Harold,* fala de Sintra com o entusiasmo que as belezas da Natureza excitam em génios como o dele. Este grande poeta, o maior do século presente, acabava de expirar na Grécia, onde o levara a nobreza de seus sentimentos, quando isto se escrevia; e à sua morte aludem os seguintes versos, que são imitados de uns do seu amigo e biógrafo, o suavíssimo Anacreonte do Norte, Tomás Moore:

Onde um suspiro
De morte, etc.

Despite the fact that a record of Garrett's library [1] mentions only one copy of Byron's *Complete Works* of a comparatively late date —Paris, 1837— there is every reason to believe that he became acquainted with them at a much earlier stage. In fact, quotations from *Childe Harold,* the *Prisoner of Chillon, Lara,* and *The Corsair,* used as epigraphs in poems

---

[1] MS Mov. 5-7-1, Sala F. L.

of *Lírica de João Mínimo* and *Flores sem fruto,* or as the motto of the London-published *Chaveco Liberal;* references to Byron in prefaces, in notes, in appendices and in the texts themselves, apart from those contained in that important source for Garrettian studies, his correspondence; unpublished material in *Espólio* [2] — all these provide external evidence of the

[2] *a)* Epigraph from *Childe Harold,* C. I., xiii, l. 2 and l. 7, in 'O mar' (*Fl. s. f.,* O. A. G., Vol. II, p. 17-24, dated 182...).

> He seized his harp which he at times could string...
> While flew the vessel on her snowy wing
>
> *Child* [sic] *Harold*

As a result of internal analysis O. P. Monteiro suggests in *A formação de Almeida Garrett,* Vol. II, pp. 96-7 and n. 29, that stanzas VII, VIII and IX of this poem were not part of the initial composition, which, according to Garrett, is dated 1821, but were rather added, together with the epigraph, in 1827, when it was first published in *O Chronista,* Vol. I, n. IV, 1827, pp. 78-85, and later included in the collection of *Fl. s. f.* She draws attention to Garrett's allusion to Hobbes, showing him at variance with the English philosopher. Though it is possible to see the influence of Chateaubriand in the sea imagery of these stanzas, it is also arguable that Byron might be in Garrett's mind, in such ideas as the formation of the universe from a chaotic mass, the cycles of existence, man as a link between the cycles and as a thinking animal, his mixture of greatness and misery, his preoccupation with deciphering the secrets of the universe, preoccupations that will be dealt with later in this chapter. This hypothesis is strengthened by the epigraph and by the treatment of the sea, which, if it can be related to Chateaubriand, is also reminiscent of the ocean stanzas at the end of *Childe Harold,* C. IV.

b) Epigraph from 'Sonnet on Chillon', preceding 'The Prisoner of Chillon' in 'O cárcere', dated August, 1823 (*Lírica,* O. A. G., Vol. II, p. 1633).

> Brightest in dungeons, liberty, thou art
> For there thy *tabernacle* is the heart

It is in fact a misquotation of Byron's line, which reads 'thy habitation'. The end of Garrett's poem is a paraphrase of the idea of the two quatrains of the sonnet that Byron wrote in memory of the patriot Bonnivard: the glory of martyrdom for those who suffer imprisonment for the cause of liberty. There is also an analogy with Byron's preoccupation with the insignificance of man, in the image of the atom tossed about.

c) Lines from *Lara* as an epigraph for 'O emprazado' (*Fl. s. f.,* 1841, O. A. G., Vol. II, pp. 104-7). The poem appears on MS. 122 of *Espólio,* pp. 91-4, with the first four stanzas, and the date 'Lisboa, 16. Fev. 1827' on p. 91, and the note 'Acabado —Lisboa Março 22— 1844' on p. 94. Stanzas V and VI appear in the same MS, p. 97, dated 1844. The poem is also part of MS 51, with the date 1841, i. e., the same as the date in *Fl. s. f.* (in O. P. Monteiro, Vol. II, pp. 136-7, n. 130). The lines chosen for the epigraph are 450-4 of C. II, xviii:

> They seemed, unto the last
> To... forget the present in the past
> To share between themselves some separate fate,
> Whose darkness none beside should penetrate.

The complete lines of Byron's poem are: 'They seem'd even then —that twain— unto the last / To half-forget the present in the past'. There is an analogy in the oblique way the two stories are told —an obliqueness that can be said to be carried to excess in the Portuguese poem—, as well as in elements of the plot: a challenge for a mysterious reason that is never clarified and which ultimately leads to the fact that Garrett took an interest in Byron that can be traced back to his first emigration, and which was to last throughout the period of his mature writings.

The text of 'Esquisse d'une histoire littéraire du Portugal', which, under the title *Brief review of the literary history of Portugal*, appeared as an appendix to the second edition of Kinsey's *Portugal Illustrated*, 1829,[3] has a passage, characteristically lacking in understatement, in which Garrett informs the reader of his good knowledge of the language and literature of France and England, and discloses his preferences in English literature, describing himself as a man 'qui connaît notre Shakespeare et notre Byron comme il connaît son Camoens'. The association of the English poets with the name of the Portuguese bard shows in what high regard they were held by Garrett.

Reflexions on the poetry of Mr. de la Martine [sic] in MS 122, of *Espólio*,[4] reiterate Garrett's esteem for Byron:

> De Lamartine, entusiasta admirador de Lord Byron, e seu imitador, esforça-se por contrastar o mal ortodoxo inglês com as suas cristianíssimas composições —Poeta, e grande ingenho [sic] é sem dúvida este Martine, mas não o porei eu de par com Byron.[5]

About twenty years later, a humorous passage in *Viagens* reasserts Garrett's view of the leading position occupied by Byron in contemporary literature — the ironic tone revealing his awareness of partisan excesses prevailing among the Romantics:

> Realmente o século estava muito atrasado: Milton não se tinha ainda sentado no lugar de Homero, Shakespeare no de Eurípedes, e lord Byron acima de todos (...)[6].

The amount of external evidence of Garrett's admiration for Byron, of which the above are a few examples, leads us to search for further signs of the presence of the English Romantic in his work, through a close reading of texts by both men, and we shall start doing so with the poem that marks the beginning of romanticism in Portugal — *Camões*.

---

death of challenger and challenged; the third person in the triangle, the woman, is also a victim of the tragedy she finds herself involved in. It should be noted that, in using the lines from *Lara* as an epigraph, Garrett does not apply them to a lovers' relationship, as Byron does, but rather to the secret between the contending brothers.

    d) Lines from *The Corsair*, C. I. in *Camões*, C. I. ii, and in *Chaveco Liberal*:

> O'er the glad waters of the dark blue sea
> Our thoughts as boundless, and our souls as free.

    e) Garrett wrote a summary of *The Siege of Corinth* and transcribed some passages of it in MS 122 of *Espólio* (in O. P. Monteiro, Vol. II, p. 136, note 129).

[3] O. P. Monteiro, Vol. II, pp. 135 and 143: MS 82, p. 2.
[4] O. P. Monteiro, Vol. II, p. 143, and note 148.
[5] The MS is undated; O. P. Monteiro believes it was written between 1823 and 1828.
[6] *Viagens*, p. 42.

Byron's presence in *Camões* goes beyond the eulogies in verse and in prose that were quoted at the beginning of this chapter. Garrett himself, in a letter to a friend and in the preface to the first edition of *Camões,* throws some light on a connection with Byron in the conception of his poem. Writing to Duarte Lessa from France on 27 July 1824, to ask him to find subscribers for *Camões,* which he was about to finish, Garrett says:

> Dei-lhe um tom e um ar de romance para interessar os menos curiosos de letras, e geralmente falando o estilo vai moldado ao de Byron e Scott (ainda não usado nem conhecido em Portugal) mas não servilmente e com *macacaria,* porque *sobretudo* quis fazer uma obra nacional.

In these lines, while maintaining that his main purpose was to create a work with national character, and that he had consciously avoided any servile aping of Byron and Scott, Garrett states that he was introducing a new style into Portuguese letters, and that his work was fashioned after these two English Romantics. The idea of Byron as a literary source was more forcefully put forward in the Preface to the first edition, through irony, in the form of apparent denial: Garrett overtly disclaims any pretensions to join the French in imitating his style — a task only fit for the truly great, says Garrett modestly, with an irony that is reinforced by the hyperbolic terms in which he defines the talents required to be a successful imitator.

Following the Romantic cult of originality, Garrett made a double experiment in *Camões,* weaving one poem within the other,[7] and combining what the new school saw as Romantic in the sixteenth century with what was characteristic of their own nineteenth-century romanticism:[8]

> (...) mas o género romântico injustamente envolvido na proscrição do seis-centismo, esse desprezado e perseguido, ninguém curou dele, julgaram-no sem o entender, condenaram-no sem o ouvir.
> No meu poemazinho de Camões aventurei alguns toques, alguns longes de estilo e pensamentos, enunciei, para assim dizer, a possibilidade da restauração deste género, que tanto tem disputado na Europa literária com aqueloutro, e que hoje coroado dos louros de Scott, de Byron e de Lamartine vai de par com ele, e não direi vencedor, mas também não vencido.

Despite his protestations of independence of school, be it classical or Romantic,[9] Garrett thought of Camões as a genius singled out by misfortune, born under a star or fate —*fado, sina* are the words he uses—, predestined to immortalize the name of the Portuguese: in short, a romantic figure to which he added some of the traits commonly associated with that composite abstraction known as the 'Byronic hero'.

We use the expression as it has been established by convention but a short clarification is called for. What often passed as a 'Byronic hero' is no more than an amalgamation of Lara, Manfred and Cain, with traits borrowed

---

7 Letter to Duarte Lessa (27 July 1824), O. A. G., Vol. I, p. 1382.
8 *Ao Sr. Duarte Lessa,* O. A. G., Vol. I, p. 1750.
9 Preface to the first edition of *Camões.*

from Childe Harold and from his immediate posterity, says Escarpit.[10] But to try to reduce the gallery of Byron's characters to that common denominator accepted as the 'Byronic hero' is to ignore their variety in age, temperament and appearance, as well as the context they are set in and which is one of the means of defining them. Juan and Marino Faliero, for example, belong to opposite generations; as for character, Sardanapalus is voluptuous, Lara is ascetic, Selim, in the *Bride of Abydos,* is above reproach, and Juan, a sympathetic youngster whose breaches of accepted behaviour stem from thoughtlessness and great capacity of feeling, rather than viciousness, is just 'a little spoil'd', 'a little blasé'.[11] So not all his characters are hero-villains, or titan-rebels, or exult in crime, or are necessarily sinful and repentant, even though some undoubtedly are. When talking about Byronic traits in Garrett's characters we shall indicate which of Byron's creations we have in mind, when they do not simply correspond to the standard view of the 'Byronic hero'.

In Camões, a man sinned against rather than sinning, there are some features of that composite portrait: he is a Man of Feeling, melancholy and solitary, inclined to meditative contemplation; he is surrounded by an aura of mystery, derived from the intrinsic superiority which divides him from the dull crowd that cannot understand him: he is proud and courageous, and bears that characteristically Byronic trait of being ostracized by an unjust, corrupt society, which, by setting his peers against him, turn him into a rebel against the Establishment, i. e., a political figure.

More significant of the Byronic presence than the portrait of the hero, however, is the way the author stands vis-à-vis his creation. Garrett's attitude towards Camões bears a strong resemblance to Byron's towards Harold. In both poems the authors present themselves as distinct from their heroes, though the distinction is blurred at times by what they have in common, in terms of suffering, psychological traits, particulars of life. The author uses his creation as a method of self-expression, and his feelings, experiences or meditations are imperceptibly prolonged and merged with the hero's. This happens in the first three Cantos of *Childe Harold,* and it is also the case of Canto I of *Camões,* when Garrett's reflections on exile and return to his country are prolonged into the narration itself, in a stanza depicting Camões's own feelings and arrival in Lisbon. Or again, at the beginning of Canto VII, the reader, after following Garrett in his evocation of England and her melancholy medieval poetry, is taken to the more pleasing prospects of Portugal and Sintra, and suddenly finds that Sintra has become both a place in Garrett's memory and the scene for Sebastian's court, in a process of juxtaposition and change from the level of the narrator's biography to that of the narrative. By this technique of ambiguous shifting between the level of the narrator and that of the fictional hero, Byron offers an important new possibility to the Portuguese poet, in his quest for novel forms of expression. This technique, pursued and perfected in later writings like *Magriço* and *Viagens,* is one of the

---

[10] Robert Escarpit, *Lord Byron. Un tempérament littéraire,* 2 Vols (Paris, 1955), Vol. II, p. 147.
[11] *Don Juan,* C. X, 23; XII, 41, 48; XIV, 41.

most innovatory aspects of Garrett's work and seems to have escaped the attention of the critics, in so far as its English sources and its use in *Camões* and *Magriço* are concerned. I shall return to this point later on when dealing with *Viagens* and with Sterne.

Equally interesting, from the point of view of a connection with Byron, is the use that Garrett makes of *saudade*. The choice of that most Portuguese feeling as the muse invoked by Garrett reflects his determination to create a national work. Besides being a part of the Portuguese ethos, it is also an element of the myth of Camões, as José Augusto França points out.[12] *Saudade* both defines and determines the elegiac nature of this very Portuguese poem. Yet, at the same time, it is through the use of the self-same *saudade* that Garrett establishes a fundamental link between his poem and *Childe Harold*.

Just as the central theme of mortality runs through *Childe Harold*, *saudade* runs through *Camões* and gives it unity through the sustained feeling of transience and decay that is experienced in the fate of the lost empire of the sixteenth century, to which the personal fate of the epic bard is closely associated, to the point of becoming its Myth; and *saudade* links the fictional voices of the past with the voice of the author, the exile poet of the tottering Portugal of the eighteen-twenties, who regards himself as a modern parallel of his Renaissance hero.

Garrett defines *saudade* in Canto I, Note A, first edition of *Camões:*

> ... o verdadeiro sentido de saudade é —os sentimentos ou pensamentos da soledade ou solidão ou soidão; o desejo melancólico do que se acha na solidão, ausente, isolado de objectos porque (sic) suspira, amigos, amante, pais, filhos, etc.

A *saudade* that corresponds to this definition is found in the longings of the exiles Camões and Garrett for their distant country, for their mistress, for the grotto in Macao, for Sintra, for Albion; but mixed with such longings is the feeling of mortality and decay that becomes increasingly more powerful and dense when Natercia's death and its annihilating impact on the warrior-poet are followed, in an atmosphere of moral corruption, by the rout at Alkazer-Kibir —death of King and Country— coinciding with and symbolized by the death of Camões.

Within the bonds of this transient world, the way to achieve immortality, i.e., liberation from the nothingness of Death, is through the work of art, namely through *Os Lusíadas,* which will maintain alive the feats of mortal heroes, and through the poem of Garrett, who vindicates the memory of the bard, forgotten by an ungrateful country.[13] This very interweaving of the matter of fiction with biographical truth is characteristically Byronic.

In the context of the poem as set out above the meaning of *saudade* should be widened, to encompass not only the definition proposed by Garrett, of 'a feeling of loneliness and longing for a person or an object that one wants to be with again', but, more significantly, 'a longing for

---

[12] *O Romantismo em Portugal,* 6 Vols (Lisbon, 1974), Vol. I, p. 102.
[13] *Camões,* C. III, xxi; C. IV, vii; C. X, xxiii.

things irrevocably lost'; because in this poem there is no hope for a future and the stress is on the ephemeral nature of human life and achievement. Garrett thus appears to be using the word in a wider meaning than his definition suggests, and with a shift of emphasis.

It is this colouring of the word *saudade* that produces an affinity with *Childe Harold* and indeed with *Don Juan* as well, with their common stress on the theme of mortality. But *Childe Harold* is more relevant to the study of *Camões,* and Garrett's explicit references to it in his notes [14] seem to guide the reader to this poem, with its main theme of lament for love lost and lost empire, for the decay of life and human creations, from which art alone can be the rescuer.[15] In *Childe Harold* the forms of art presented as a means of escape from the triumph of time are sculpture, architecture and literature. Garrett, too, turns to architecture, to ruined monuments, but he clearly gives literature a primary role, with his oft-repeated reminder of the poet's power and mission.

Another similarity between the two poems is that the concern with the lost glory of the empire in Europe, and in Portugal, is connected with the preoccupation with the revival of national dignity and independence — Byron hoping for freedom for Italy and Greece, Garrett for the liberation of his country from tyranny.

Ruins of castles, of religious monuments, and of altars are used by Garrett in ways that seem to have been borrowed from *Childe Harold.* They are a starting point for reflections on mortality and they also provide a link between past and present, for time and voice shifting. In this way they contribute to the creation of an atmosphere of ambiguity, like the passages in which the sorrows of the narrator and of the hero are so closely interwoven that the distinction between them is blurred.

Again as in *Childe Harold,* ruined monuments are used in *Camões* as one way of humanizing a landscape, others being the presence of the hermit-poet Bernardim like that of the religious hermit Honorius, the allusions to classic and contemporary literature, the historical associations and personal recollections, all of which move away from the description of nature for its own sake, and widen the scope and variety of the poem through the introduction of new topics.

The process of description seems to develop in a parallel way in the two poems, from picturesque scenes depicted with an eye to realistic detail to landscapes that suggest that they are remembered, retained in the memory, and therefore more vague than if they had been the result of a recent experience. But in the description of scenery the affinities are even closer, in the choice of places and in the way they are presented. So, for instance, Byron's stanzas on Lisbon and the Tagus have a counterpart in Garrett's descriptions of the same places, only more fully developed, with the suggestion of a paraphrase of both *Childe Harold* and *The Corsair.* In Note C to Canto I of the first edition Garrett mentions the connection

[14] *Camões,* C. I, Note K; C. V, Note D.
[15] M. K. Joseph, *Byron the Poet* (London, 1966), p. 27.

between lines of the second stanza and the opening verses of *The Corsair:*

> O'er the glad waters of the dark blue sea,
> Our thoughts as umbounded [sic] as our souls are free.[16]

Another allusion to Byron is made by Garrett in his notes to *Camões,* where he refers the reader to *Childe Harold:*

> 'Piloto!' gritam: e a um sinal de bordo... p. 41.
>
> É de ver no riquíssimo poema de Byron, o *Child* [sic] *Harold,* a descrição da entrada de Lisboa, etc. O leitor português encontrará aí coisa que não é muito para lisonjear o amor-próprio nacional: mas tenha paciência, que ainda assim não é muito grande a injustiça do nobre lorde.
>
> Note K, C. I, first edition.

Though there is no further mention of Byron, I believe that not only this passage from *Childe Harold* but also lines from *The Corsair* (Canto I, iii, iv, v) were at work in Garrett's mind, consciously or not, when he describes the joyful arrival of the ship, sailing swiftly over the waves, the lowering of the boat, the expectations and fears of the seamen, and the idea of the happy reunion ahead (Canto I, iv, v, vii, ix, xvii). Though the scene is viewed from two different angles —Byron focuses on the feelings of the relatives of the seamen, while in *Camões* the emphasis is on the thoughts and hopes of the seamen themselves— the reading of one poem brings the other one to mind, in its theme and in its imagery.

Sintra is sought by both pilgrims, and even the detail of Monserrate, originally planted by D. João de Castro and acquired by Beckford in the eighteenth century, is brought into the picture. The place is described in both poems with similar images of breakers hitting the foot of the promontory, fugitive visions of golden fruits amidst luxuriant green, and similar expressions of exalted praise.[17] Compare

> Lo! Cintra's glorious Eden intervenes
> In variegated maze of mount and glen [18]
>
> Oh, Christ, It is a goodly sight to see
> What Heaven hath done for this delicious land [19]

with

> Oh Sintra! oh! saudosíssimo retiro [20]
>
> Sintra, amena estância,
> Trono de vicejante Primavera [21]

---

[16] O. P. Monteiro, Vol. II, p. 88, draws attention to this note and discusses Garrett's paraphrase of Byron's lines. In footnote 5 she points out Garrett's alteration of the second verse, and refers to the adoption of these opening lines of *The Corsair* in the epigraph of *Chaveco Liberal.*

[17] J. A. França, Preface to *Camões,* Colecção Horizontes Clássicos, 1 (Lisboa, 1973), p. 17.

[18] *Childe Harold,* C. I, xviii.

[19] *Childe Harold,* C. I, xi.

[20] *Camões,* C. V, xi.

[21] *Camões,* C. V, xiii.

There is no doubt that Byron was very much present in Garrett's mind when he wrote the Sintra stanzas. There is an explicit reference in a footnote to the line 'Do bardo misterioso o eterno canto' in Canto V, xiii, which reads: 'Byron's *Child* [sic] *Harold's Pilgrim* [sic]'. In doing this Garrett is following Byron's own practice in the *Childe,* where his descriptions are often qualified or completed by literary reminiscences, as Escarpit points out.[22]

Another instance of the impact of *Childe Harold* on Garrett is apparent in the first Canto of *Camões,* where his stanzas on exile and on an imaginary journey home led by *saudade* seem to echo, in reverse, Harold's departure from the ancient hall into exile in the wide world. His utter loneliness and consequent despair

> My greatest grief is that I leave
> Nothing to claim a tear

are matched in intensity and in wretchedness by the feelings of the

> infeliz proscrito
> Dos entes o misérrimo na Terra.

The *saudade* felt by the narrator in *Camões* for the absent friend, the absent mistress, the distant home, plays on the same chord of human attachments that brings sighs to page and seaman in Harold's 'Good-night' song. And both Pilgrim and *proscrito* face the journey into the seas in the same spirit of vigorous resolution:

> With thee, my bark, I'll swiftly go
> Athwart the foaming brine
> Nor care what land thou bear'st me to,
> So not again to mine

cries Harold recklessly.[23] And Garrett, anxious to leave an exile where he was pining away, in Ingouville, exclaims eagerly like Harold and like the pirates of *The Corsair:*

> Largo! aos mares
> Livres corramos sobre as ondas livres [24]

A return home from exile and a departure from home in ostracism inspire feelings as divergent as the opposite directions of the two journeys. Yet the elements in common are there —the theme of exile with its corollaries, coupled with a solution sought across the rough seas— strengthened by affinities in imagery, and a reading of this passage of *Camões* startles us with the impression of familiar echoes, which can be traced back to the *Childe.*

In *Camões* Garrett wanted to create a modern work, in the manner of a romance, after Byron and Scott, as he said in his letter of 27 July 1824

---

22 Escarpit, Vol. II, p. 65.
23 *Childe Harold,* C. I, 10.
24 *Camões,* C. I, ii.

to Duarte Lessa, quoted above. Though the canons of invocation and dedication are still observed, though the *verso branco* so dear to the Arcadians may be too unyielding for the full expression of Romantic ideas and feelings, though Garrett, in these and other respects, was not able to free himself from the encumbrances of his classical past, *Camões* is a major step forward, a necessary transition between his early works and his period of maturity, as O. Paiva Monteiro points out.[25] It diverges from the classical poem in the way it develops, and has, in fact, the character of a romance that Garrett aimed at. The interest of *Camões* depends less on the sequence of incidents and on the variety of scenes than on the inner conflicts of the hero, and these are in large part defined by his relationship with man and nature around him, and by the author's digressions.

The statements made by Garrett in the writings quoted above point to Byron as a source for *Camões,* as well as for *D. Branca,* which was being written simultaneously during his exile in Ingouville, as an antidote for the deep nostalgia that enveloped the composition on the Portuguese poet.[26]

Apart from Byron and Scott Garrett also named Ariosto and Wieland as literary background for *D. Branca,* in Note C to Canto I, and in his 'Esquisse d'une histoire littéraire du Portugal'.[27] But both Ariosto and Wieland, as well as Casti and Pulci amongst others, were Byron's models for the comic epic; Shakespeare, Fielding, Sterne and Scott are among the immediate literary sources of *Don Juan.* To try to extricate the maze of influences at work in Byron's own epic poem and separate in detail what Garrett might have learned at first hand from what he found incorporated in Byron is a well-nigh impossible task. We shall have to establish affinities as we find them between *D. Branca* and the works of Byron; Garrett's debt to Scott, Sterne and Shakespeare will be discussed later.

So having in mind the native and foreign tradition behind Byron's *Don Juan,* I shall simply say that *D. Branca* presents, in common with it, the form of an open narrative poem, with the irregular length of the Cantos, the loose digressive manner, the medley style in which a wealth of topics and a variety of tones are held together and given a framework by an inner unity, rather than by plot.

Such unity was provided in *Camões* by the feeling of *saudade,* which was akin to the central theme of *Childe Harold,* as has been pointed out. In *D. Branca* Garrett makes a conscious experiment in the medley style as it had been perfected in *Don Juan.* He himself refers to the heterogeneous nature of the poem and hence to its affinities with *Don Juan* when he writes in 'Esquisse d'une histoire littéraire du Portugal':

> C'est du sérieux, c'est du sentimental, c'est du burlesque, c'est du philosophique — encore du merveilleux: puis des fées, des enchantements, des moines, des

[25] O. P. Monteiro, Vol. II, p. 247.
[26] O. P. Monteiro, Vol. II, p. 24.
[27] O. P. Monteiro, Vol. II, p. 241, note 74.

princes — sans être licencieux ni impie comme le *D. Juan* de Byron, c'est aussi extravagant...[28]

It is his deliberate attempt at a Romantic unity in a diversity of tones that gives *D. Branca* a place of particular interest in the study of Garrett's literary evolution, and, indeed, of Portuguese romanticism. It was not until ten years later, in 1835, that Herculano was to try to establish the theory behind this principle, which Garrett started to put into practice, first in *Camões,* and then explored more fully in *D. Branca,* without ever coming to the point of formulating it in abstract terms.[29]

The actual carrying out of Garrett's plan to bring together the different elements in the poem was not always successful. The failure is particularly apparent in the passages of transition from lyrical to burlesque: Garrett had not yet learnt Byron's precept that the burlesque should not be vulgar. Yet a main idea emerges, colouring the great themes of the poem, love and war. This main idea that gives unity to *D. Branca* is the transience of man's life and passions, and man's paradoxical nature. It is expressed implicitly in the plot, and explicitly in commentaries and in imagery such as this: 'insecto de um só dia', 'o mais raro fenómeno da Terra, / Incompreensível, único', 'vidro obscuro e quebradiço, / Em ti só concentraste o prisma inteiro / Das belezas do mundo repartidas!' In Garrett's eÿes, man is unique in his combination of elements of spiritual grandeur and misery, which appear in Byron's own imagery as 'mercurial clay' and 'fiery dust'. The vulnerability of man's condition is intensified by his lowly place on earth, itself an insignificant part of the cosmos:

> tu misérrimo dos entes
> Que se arrastam no espaço circunscrito
> De um dos mínimos globos do Universo...[30]

In this there are clear parallels with Byron's own preoccupations, as evinced in the following quotations:

> It was the comparative insignificance of ourselves and our world, when placed in competition with the mighty whole, of which it is an atom, that first led me to imagine that our pretensions to eternity might be overrated.[31]

> In the midst of myriads of the living and the dead worlds —stars— systems —infinity— why should I be anxious about an atom?[32]

Recent discoveries in geology had given a new complexion to the already familiar idea of the vastness of the Universe, and of the minimal place that Earth occupied in it.[33] For Byron —and possibly for Garrett as well—

---

[28] MS 82 Esp., p. 70. See O. P. Monteiro, Vol. II, p. 137, n. 132; p. 166; p. 185, note 89.
[29] O. P. Monteiro, Vol. II, pp. 168-9.
[30] *D. Branca,* C. II, ii.
[31] *Letters and Journals,* II, 222, in M. K. Joseph, p. 120.
[32] *Letters and Journals,* III, 408, in M. K. Joseph, p. 120.
[33] M. K. Joseph, p. 119.

such an idea was derived from Fontenelle's *Entretien sur la pluralité des mondes,* from Pope, from Young, and from Voltaire's *Micromégas.*[34] But what was disturbing and depressing was the new idea of man's insignificance on earth and in time, prompted by the recent findings of geological science, which invited a revision of man's relationship with and concept of God. Garrett, whether he had come to such worries through his readings of Byron, or in some other way, voices them in *D. Branca,* and thus establishes an affinity with *Cain* and *Don Juan.*

What gave inner unity to *D. Branca* was already present in *Don Juan:* the idea of the paradoxical nature of man, merging with the ideas of transience and decay, and the idea of the corruption of nature. It is against this common background that the major themes of both poems are set —themes which, in keeping with the tradition of epic, hence of epic satire, are love and war. And, of the two, in *D. Branca* as in *Don Juan,* love —and woman— is given the greater prominence.

By resorting to commentary and digression Garrett focuses on a number of attitudes towards woman that are found in *Don Juan,* which relies more, on that score, on the episodes themselves.[35] Both poets commiserate with the lot of woman in man's hands: to Byron's 'Poor thing of usage! Coerced, compelled, / Victim when wrong and martyr oft when right',[36] Garrett presents a counterpart: '(...) Mas tiranos / Não somos nós, injustos, opressores?'[37] Garrett's commentaries on man's oppressive treatment of woman, not only in Muslim seraglios but within that most venerable institution —the convent— recall harem scenes in such works as *The Giaour, Conrad* or *Don Juan,* as well as Byron's attacks on the marriage of convenience in the latter poem. Both poets see woman as the bearer of Beauty, as maker and unmaker,[38] and not only as 'seduced' but as 'active seducer': in their different forms of humour they allude to the provocation and to the plots of women, in lines such as 'Com moças: moças são coisas do diabo, / Se é que o diabo não são elas mesmas'[39] and 'The single ladies wishing to be double, / The married ones to save virgins trouble'.[40] In *Don Juan* not only the hero, but also the narrator-commentator, and through him, all mankind, feel a strong attraction for woman, and the poem exudes a strong feeling of sexuality, as M. K. Joseph says.[41] This has its parallels in Garrett's commentaries on the need that man has for woman at all ages in life[42] and in the heightened sense of voluptuousness experienced by the characters; it is also conveyed in the direct or oblique description of the charms of the Fairy Queen and of the two princesses, in the suggestive quotation from the Song of Songs, in the incidents themselves and in the commentaries.

---

34 M. K. Joseph, p. 119.
35 M. K. Joseph, p. 242.
36 *Don Juan,* C. XIV, 23.
37 *D. Branca,* C. II, iii.
38 *Don Juan,* XIV, 23 and *D. Branca,* II, iii; see M. K. Joseph, pp. 242-8.
39 *D. Branca,* C. VI, xiii.
40 *Don Juan,* C. XII, 58.
41 M. K. Joseph, p. 242.
42 *D. Branca,* C. II, iii.

Love, in its multiple forms, is at the centre of each episode of *Don Juan*, except for the one concerning the Siege of Ismail. And Garrett, through his characters, illustrates a number of the kinds of love that are seen in action in Byron's poem.

Thus Branca —and her case is generalized to include all women who take a vow without vocation— corresponds to Julia in that they both exemplify love as self-deceit, in the form of idealism, 'platonic love', 'love divine', to use Byron's terminology. Both girls deceive themselves about the purity of their feelings and about their virtue, sharing the belief that the duties of their state will enable them to master the repressed desires of their nature. Garrett's moralizing on the dangers that await Branca for her misguided obedience to her father and to her confessor in Canto II, ii echoes what Byron says in his concise ironical manner: 'The precipice she stood on was immense, / So was her creed in her own innocence.' [43]

The case of Oriana and Mem do Vale, presented ambiguously as the possibility of the existence of 'pure love' after all, brings to mind Juan and Leila, themselves linked in an ambiguous undefined relationship, the love of a protector for an innocent protégée.

The love of Branca and Aben-Afan illustrates Byron's concept of love as a source of supreme happiness, and its vulnerability in man's conflicting nature of spirit and clay. Alina's palace is not merely a magnificent abode to harbour and heighten the couple's enjoyment of love: it is more than just a setting, for its exquisite splendour helps to define the precious quality of their feelings. But even such total mutual love is frail, and Ben-Afan's, mixed with sensuality and lust, wears itself out through its own intensity. Love, which is the creative power on earth, is subject to the corruption of human nature and thus becomes the symbol for the transience of all things. This is basically the moral message of *D. Branca,* as of *Don Juan,* and the inner source for their unity. The sorrow that must spring from love, from love's change and decay, is evoked in plaintive incantatory stanzas at the beginning and end of Canto X, which narrates the destruction of Branca's happiness, the dissolution of the palace and Aben-Afan's death:

> —Gozo da vida, amor, tão breve passas!
> Males que deixas são tão duradoiros!
> ....
> Flor da existência desfolhou-se n'hástia;
> Ramos que amarelecem vão caindo;
> Vegeta o tronco ainda: —mas é vida
> Esse viver que se alimenta em lágrimas? [44]

It is perhaps not impossible to connect some of the theme and imagery of *D. Branca,* as dealt with above, with a passage from *The Giaour,* lines 384-411:

> And all its hidden secrets sleep,
> Known but to Genii of the deep,

---

[43] *Don Juan,* C. I, 106.
[44] *D. Branca,* C. X, i and C. X, xxxviii.

Which, trembling in their coral caves,
They dare not whisper to the waves.
....
As rising on its purple wing
The insect queen of eastern spring,
O'er emerald meadows of Kashmeer
Invites the young pursuer near,
And leads him on from flower to flower
A weary chase and wasted hour,
Then leaves him as it soars on high,
With panting heart and tearful eye:
So Beauty lures the full-grown child,
With hue as bright, and wing as wild;
A chase of idle hopes and fears,
Begun in folly, closed in tears.
If won, to equal ills betray'd,
Woe waits the insect and the maid;
A life of pain, the loss of peace,
From infant's play, and man's caprice:
The lovely toy so fiercely sought
Hath lost its charm by being caught,
For every touch that woo'd its stay
Hath brush'd its brightest hues away,
Till charm, and hue, and beauty gone,
'Tis left to fly or fall alone.
With wounded wing, or bleeding breast,
Ah! where shall either victim rest?

The secret place alluded to in the first four lines might be linked with Alina's palace, only known to the world of magic. The image of the insect queen, which later merges into the image of Beauty, suggests the figure of the Fairy Queen, and the exoticism of her charms and of her magnificent palace is conjured up by the association of such visual images as 'purple wing', 'eastern spring' and 'emerald meadows of Kashmeer'. There are parallel features in the two chases, in the explicit reference to the disturbed state of mind of the pursuer/wanderer when he finds himself alone, and in the qualified happiness offered to both, with its warning of unavoidable final sorrow for the lovers, in the verses which I have italicized. Coupled with 'the maid', and linked with the pain caused by the weariness of love, the image of the insect dissociates itself from the Queen to merge with that of the 'full-grown child', the double meaning of which reappears in the verse 'From infant's play, and man's caprice'. Here one might find the inspiration for Garrett's metaphor for man, 'insecto de um só dia'. The last section of Byron's passage could be read as the end of the tale of Aben-Afan and Branca, told in metaphorical terms.

A few minor details found in *The Giaour* and in *D. Branca* alike reinforce the conjecture that Garrett might have drawn from this Turkish Tale, consciously or not. Such are the dark steep cliff behind which disappears the black warrior on a black steed, the grappling of two foes in the last stage of their duel, the element of Gothic terror involving monks, and an episode of vampires that will be examined later. Too flimsy to be accorded any importance on their own, their combination, however, invites one to speculate on *The Giaour* as a stimulus to the Portuguese poem.

I have been dealing with love and love's decay as one of the central themes of both poems. War, the other major theme, is also coloured in the two epics by the same feeling of *vanitas vanitatum*. In both, war is dealt with less extensively than love, and both Byron and Garrett seem to hold the view that war, only defensible in the case of national independence, is a destructive power to be condemned, in spite of the recognized charisma of heroes. War is acceptable only on condition that it is a 'just' war,[45] and, while condemning it in general, the two poets do not refrain from expressing praise for the bravery and courage it demands. Byron's condemnation of war and his pity for its victims is forcefully expressed, particularly in the stanzas on the Siege of Ismail, with their powerful battle scenes and with the irony he directs at a complacent insensitive world, and with what was in Byron's view a false concept of honour and glory:

> Amidst some groaning thousands dying near —
> All common fellows, who might writhe and wince
> And shriek for water into a deaf ear — [46]

Of all great heroes in history, two alone are spared by Byron, and even revered:

> Not so Leonidas and Washington,
> Whose every battlefield is holy ground,
> Which breathes of nations saved, not worlds undone.[47]

In *D. Branca* the horrors of the battlefield are nowhere near the realism and scope of *Don Juan* in the limited world of 'romance', where, to a great extent, war is dealt with in linear development rather than in large pictures; it is closer to the fighting in the Turkish Tales, like *The Giaour*, for example. But in his sympathy for both sides Garrett shows his acceptance of what is ultimately a war of independence and a fight for national territory for Christians and Moors alike: for while the former were reconquering what had been their own, the latter were defending what they had come to regard as home, after centuries of settlement. So, on the one hand Garrett exalts the Christians in the true manner of a romance of chivalry; on the other hand his hero is a Moor, as brave and valorous as the Mestre de Santiago himself, and in his indictment of the belligerent Portuguese there are echoes of the author's sympathy for the persecuted.[48] The nationalist feelings of the narrator and his nostalgic evocations of the glorious past are balanced by the aura that surrounds Aben-Afan, on the level of the narrative, an aura which is heightened as he takes on the value of a

---

[45] M. K. Joseph, p. 280.
[46] *Don Juan*, C. VIII, 11.
[47] *Don Juan*, C. VIII, 5.
[48] In the fragment *Affonso de Albuquerque* Garrett also enlists the sympathy of the reader for the cause of the enemy. See O. P. Monteiro, Vol. I, p. 406.

symbol. In his impartiality Garrett strikes a parallel attitude to Byron's, who as M. K. Joseph points out, was to die for Greek independence and yet chose to take the siege of the Turkish city of Ismail as the pretext for his major condemnation of war in *Don Juan*.[49]

In *D. Branca* as in *Don Juan* the themes of war and love merge into each other. Aben-Afan dies when he follows an inner urge for glory and the excitement of war, after bringing ruin to Branca through his desertion. It was said above that he was given a symbolic value: his leaving, with the unbearable sorrow it entailed, symbolizes the victory of the destructive power of war over the more vulnerable force of love; his death stands for the idea that, behind such a destructive power as war, brought about by society, lies the intrinsic corruption of human nature.

Garrett's pity for mankind, his irony against the inanity of war itself, is reflected in the accents of lament in which the death of Aben-Afan is told, and in the following lines from the siege of Silves:

> Pregam no campo frades indulgências,
> Na cidade os ímanes novas promessas
> Fazem de huris e paraísos: folga
> Entretanto a Morte, e para a ceifa crua
> Com pérfido sorriso a fouce afia.[50]

Byron's perception of war as both heroism and folly makes *Don Juan* stand out among war-books for its maturity. Garrett, possibly as a result of his own experiences, holds the same view, which will be taken up again in *Viagens*.

Turning now to the characters in *D. Branca*, we find in Aben-Afan, as in Camões and as in Carlos, another Byronic hero. In him there are overtones of the harp-playing, pantheistic Harold and of the gallery of the loving-warring Conrads, Giaours or Laras, with the treason to his own people that we see in Lara and in Alp, the hero of the *Siege of Corinth*. He is above all a Byronic hero in the combination of spark and clay that has been analysed in connection with the major themes. And he and his country —the Algarve— are used by Garrett as elements of Eastern exoticism, which owed so much of its popularity to Byron's writings.[51] In both poets the technique of portrayal of the hero is achieved through dramatization and dialogue, after an initial description; and M. K. Joseph's remarks on Byron's use of the eye and regard as means of expression [52] show affinities with Garrett's own method, extensively analyzed by Lawton.[53]

The digressive form in *Don Juan* and in *D. Branca* was used to

[49] M. K. Joseph, p. 281.

[50] *D. Branca*, C. VIII, i.

[51] Garrett's interest in Arabic civilization is already shown in *Lyceu das damas* and was stimulated by his experiences in exile. He translates Arabic poems from the Latin version by William Jones, *Poeseos Asiaticae Commentatorium libri sex* (1744) in *Lyc.*, pp. 216-19. In *D. Branca*, C. III, Note G, he alludes to Sir W. Jones's *Essays on Eastern Poetry and on the Imitative Arts* (1777). See O. P. Monteiro, Vol. I, p. 355, note 13.

[52] M. K. Joseph, p. 265.

[53] R. A. Lawton, *Almeida Garrett, l'intime contrainte* (Paris, 1966), Ch. II.

introduce what is one of the main topics in both poems: literature, in the form of the poem itself, and literature in general. Garrett develops this device more fully in *Viagens,* but it is already sufficiently exploited in the epic poem to be worth mentioning as a point of affinity with *Don Juan.*

Byron's digressions on and allusions to literature achieve a multiple effect: they enlarge the scope of the poem with the introduction of new material, they make for variety through the change of tone and the shift of perspective from the narrator's to the commentator's voice, and create a distancing effect, akin to Brecht's *Verfremdung.*[54] His extensive digressions on literature past and present show his literary tastes and form a most interesting part of *Don Juan.* Byron also writes on his reasons for writing and about the poem itself: on what he proposes to create in *Don Juan,* on its moralising and instructive purpose, on its development and on its characters, on his chaste independent Muse and on the way it was misunderstood by his former admirers:

> Even I, albeit I'm sure I did not know it
> Nor sought of foolscaps to be king,
> Was reckoned a considerable time
> The grand Napoleon of the realms of rhyme.
>
> But Juan was my Moscow...[55]

In many stanzas, but without real success, Garrett tries to imitate the ease, the light, ironical manner of most of Byron's digressions: above all, he tries to achieve effects similar to those listed above. Like Byron, he writes on the poem and on his literary views and independent stance. Thus, for instance, he discourses on his Muse, which is chaste, like Byron's:

> Eu pudibundo,
> Austero, vate, salmear só quero
> Em coro de donzelas inocentes [56]

Or he talks about a new character he is going to introduce, Mestre Gil Vaz, in terms of a figure in a painting or of a actor in a play,[57] or digresses extensively on the recollected tales of childhood that provide subject matter for *D. Branca,* and will appear in later works like *Romanceiro* and *Adozinda;* he gives his views on the inadequacy of foreign mythology in Portuguese literature, and on the place that should be given to the native tradition of 'bruxas' and 'moiras encantadas'.[58] The principles of harmony and truth, and consonance between matter and form provide him with yet further topics of digression.[59] 1824, the time when Garrett was in Ingouville writing *Camões* and *D. Branca,* was a critical year for French romanticism,[60]

---

54 M. K. Joseph, p. 323.
55 *Don Juan,* C. XI, 55-6.
56 *D. Branca,* C. VII, ii.
57 *D. Branca,* C. II, x.
58 *D. Branca,* C. III, iii, iv, v.
59 *D. Branca,* C. III, v.
60 Edmond Estève, *Byron et le romantisme français* (Paris, 1907), p. 128.

and this is echoed in Garrett's work, when he reasserts humorously his independent position in the classic-romantic conflict:

> Disputa *sine* fine travariam
> Sobre ele as duas bélicas falanges
> Que ora na arena literária pugnam,
> E aos grasnantes jornais dão tema eterno
> Para encher as políticas lacunas.
> Já se vê que de *clássicos românticos,*
> Guelfos de letras, gibelinos de arte,
> Falar entendo: paz seja com eles...[61]

This is not a literary pose. It is the expression of an independence of mind on which Garrett's attitudes rest, both as a writer and a politician, and which made him reject patronage in art, as well as adherence to a system in the abstract, for its own sake, if it did not serve the reality of the moment. Garrett suffered throughout his life for this independence of mind, which happened to be a natural affinity with a fundamental element of Byron's personality. In *Don Juan* Byron, too, professes his independence and shows his willingness to pay the price for placing himself in the opposition.[62] The scandal caused by the publication of the first three Cantos of *Don Juan* in 1819 had largely subsided by the time Garrett was writing in Ingouville, Byron's death for Greek freedom playing no small role in winning back the esteem of his English and French audiences. But there had been a heated controversy around Byron and a small proof that Garrett was well acquainted with current literary opinions is shown in the lines 'Simples é meu canto, meu contar singelo, / Dar-me-ão as mamãs a ler às filhas',[63] followed by a footnote in French — 'La mère en permettra la lecture à sa fille'. They suggest that Garrett had read Defaucompret's *Une année à Londres en 1819,* in which the author voiced the consternation and shock felt about the first two Cantos of *Don Juan* by the majority of writers and critics of the *Restauration:*

> la mère, dit un autre, ne se contentera pas d'interdire à sa fille la lecture de ce poème, elle se la défendra à elle-même, pour peu qu'elle ait de respect pour les moeurs et pour la religion.[64]

Another small instance in *D. Branca* of Garrett's awareness of the literary scene of the day in its connections with Byron lies in Note A to Canto V, from which it becomes apparent that he knew about the controversy around Polidori's *The Vampire,* falsely attributed to the English poet.[65] This note leads us back to Byron's presence in Garrett's work, namely to the lines of Gothic terror in Canto V, depicting a vampire supping on his own relatives:

---

[61] *D. Branca,* C. III, xii.
[62] *Don Juan,* C. XV, 22; C. IX, 26; C. XII, 54-55.
[63] *D. Branca,* C. VII, ii.
[64] Estève, p. 69 ff.
[65] Mario Praz, *The Romantic Agony* (London, 1970), p. 78.

> (...) — descompassadas vozes
> De mortos ressurgidos n'hora aziaga,
> E em banquete de horror sobre um sepulcro
> Embriagando-se em sangue de parentes,
> De amigos... talvez filhos, que no berço
> Deixaram quando a morte os tomou súbito [66]

It is arguable that they echo the following extract from *The Giaour:*

> But first, on earth as Vampire sent,
> Thy corse shall from its tomb be rent:
> Then ghastly haunt thy native place,
> And suck the blood of all thy race;
> There from thy daughter, sister, wife,
> At midnight drain the stream of life;
> Yet loathe the banquet which perforce
> Must feed thy livid living corse:
> Thy victims ere they yet expire
> Shall know the demon for their sire,
> As cursing thee, thou cursing them,
> Thy flowers are wither'd on the stem.[67]

At the beginning of the present discussion of *D. Branca* mention was made of its medley style and of its connections with Byron. To complete the reference to the use of contrasts in this poem, one should add, to the already discussed contrasts of subject and consequent contrasts of tone, the contrast of form provided by a different metre. This is found in Alina's song and in the chorus of the monks, arousing the sleeping congregation to fulfill the devotion of the *tremenda.* In these passages Garrett introduces a lyrical and a burlesque mood in a different metre, thus adding to the variety created by other devices, one of the most interesting of them consisting in the sections of dialogue that show the inner dynamics of Aben-Afan and Branca. With different degrees of success, parallel methods had already been exploited in *The Bride of Abydos,* and in *Childe Harold's Pilgrimage,* for instance, or in *Don Juan,* and this is yet another of Garrett's debts to Byron, who, as Kroeber says, was the first poet of his time to realize that such contrasts in subject and in form were required in a sustained narrative adventure.[68]

Don Juan continued to be a model for Garrett, in a work which, if one is to believe the anonymous biography published in *Universo Pitoresco,* Vol. III, 1843, occupied him on and off for about nine years, from the early days of Warwickshire to his stay in the Azores as a member of the liberal expedition. Also according to the *Autobiografia,* the manuscript of the poem, *Magriço ou os doze de Inglaterra,* was lost together with other writings in the wreck of a ship, the *Amélia,* off Oporto in 1832.[69] From

---

[66] *D. Branca,* C. V, iii.
[67] *The Giaour,* l. 755-66.
[68] Karl Kroeber, *Romantic Narrative Art* (London, 1966), p. 141.
[69] *Autobiografia,* in *Obras completas de Almeida Garrett,* grande edição popular, de Teófilo Braga (Lisboa, 1904), Vol. I, p. XLI.

his correspondence with José Gomes Monteiro one gathers that by 17 January 1831 twenty-two of the twenty-seven cantos he envisaged had been written; by 15 February of the same year, *Magriço* had been completed except for about a canto and a half, and the first page was being printed.[70] Garrett's efforts to reconstruct the lost poem from memory resulted in the fragments of the first six cantos that were posthumously published under the direction of Teófilo Braga.[71] Referring to *Magriço* in the *Autobiografia* Garrett writes:

> (...) era um poema de um género caprichoso entre o *Orlando* de Ariosto e o *D. João* de lord Byron; e o seu título e acção principal era o *Magriço e os doze de Inglaterra;* mas, excêntrico e indeterminado na sua esfera, abraçava todas as coisas antigas e modernas, e ora filosofava austeramente sobre os desvarios do mundo, ora se ria com eles; umas vezes remontava às mais sublimes regiões da poesia do coração ou do espírito; outras descia a seus mais humildes vales a colher uma flor singela, a apanhar talvez às bordas do ribeiro a pedrinha, que só era curiosa ou extravagante. Este poema (...) em que tinha consignado as impressões de suas variadas viagens, e que era, finalmente, uma rica e imensa colecção de variadíssimos estilos poéticos (...)[72]

Orlando Furioso and *Don Juan* are thus the avowed models for *Magriço*. From this passage it can also be inferred that the influence of the English poet is to be found in the digressive, medley style that Garrett had already experimented with, first tentatively in *Camões* and then more fully in *D. Branca. Don Juan* can also be recognized as a model in other aspects referred to in Garrett's passage: in the moralizing purpose of correcting the folly of the world through laughter and satire; in the consciously undefined scope of the work; in the merging of past and present; and in the recording of the author's travels.

Two direct allusions to Byron occur in the extant fragments of *Magriço*, which throw light on Garrett's reading of the English poet, and provide yet another example of the consonance of their ideas:

> De eras feudais relíquia mui devota,
> Mui fidalga, e até muito legítima.
> Legítima é a frase consagrada
> Neste século de ouro, em que vivemos,
> De ouro... em que lhe pese
> A milord Byron e a seus guapos versos
> Do carmen secular, pois oiro é tudo
> Quanto hoje se faz, desfaz e impera em tudo.

Canto IV[73]

In this passage Garrett relates his disenchantment with the materialism of the time to the denunciation of the all-corrupting power of gold in one of

---

[70] *Cartas a Gomes Monteiro*, O. A. G., Vol. I, pp. 1396-7.
[71] *Obras posthumas*, Vol. II, in *Obras completas de Almeida Garrett*, ed. Teófilo Braga (Lisboa, 1914).
[72] *Autobiografia*, p. XLI.
[73] One line in this passage is incomplete.

Byron's best satires, *The Age of Bronze, or Carmen Seculare et Annus Haud Mirabilis,* stanzas xiv, xv and xvi.[74] Further close examination of Byron's poem shows that there is more in it than has been seen so far. In Canto VI, in a literary digression which is, in itself, a Byronic influence, as was shown apropos of *Camões* and *D. Branca,* Garrett expresses an aspiration for literary freedom and reform under the banner of the English poet:

> Alça, ó bardo sublime, eterno Byron,
> Os pendões da poética reforma.
> Do francês ouropel caíu o brunido
> Aos magros esqueletos de seus versos.
> O carunchoso trono desfaçamos
> Da legitimidade enquanto geme
> ....
> ... Livre ao menos
> Às etéreas mansões remonte o génio.[75]

The principle of legitimacy was a 'bête noire' for Garrett, for the threat it posed to national independence. To introduce it in these two allusions to Byron, who himself repeatedly attacked the consortium of nations that upheld it —'the impious alliance which insults the world with the name of Holy!'[76]— denotes a sharing of ideals that seems to have escaped the attention of the critics.

Both Byron and Garrett were ardent opponents of absolutism and, as with Pope and the Augustans, in their eyes poetry was naturally associated with politics. In the case of Garrett, he connected a rigid concept of classicism inside Portugal with this form of government, as one of its manifestations.[77] This explains why the idea of legitimacy is introduced into his plea for literary reform under Byron's aegis. The allusion to legitimacy in the first quotation, within the context of a criticism of materialism, suggests that Byron assumed in Garrett's view the role of a paladin of spiritual values, which included liberalism. For Byron, as is shown in his treatment of Southey and Milton, there is a correlation between moral and political integrity, as well as poetical achievement,[78] and this applies equally to Garrett. As for the manner in which the idea of legitimacy is introduced in these two passages, which may at first sight appear somewhat incongruous, it has a precedent in *Don Juan,* Canto I, 211, where the Holy Alliance is playfully related to a matter of literary bribery.

The fragments of *Magriço* cast interesting light on Garrett's crisis of disenchantment, from the early days when he sang of 'natureza augusta' to the years of 'experiência fatal', and its use of irony makes it a revealing

---

[74] The connection between these works is pointed out by Antscherl, p. 89.

[75] Two lines in this passage are incomplete.

[76] *Don Juan,* Preface to C. VI-VII; see also *The Age of Bronze,* st. viii.

[77] R. A. Lawton, 'O conceito garrettiano do romantismo', in *Estética do romantismo em Portugal.* Primeiro Colóquio, 1970, Centro de Estudos do Século XIX do Grémio Literário (Lisboa, 1974), pp. 95-104.

[78] George M. Ridenour, *The Style of 'Don Juan',* reprint of Yale Studies in English, Vol. 144 (Archon Books, 1969), p. 11.

example of Byronic influence. Garrett's disillusion, interpreted in the light of the *Magriço* fragments, does not take the form of passive acceptance of defeat. It looks as if, having realised the hopelessness of fighting directly for a better world, Garrett learns with Byron how to use irony to express his refusal to accommodate himself to his experience of reality, and, at the same time, to satisfy his inner urge to go on struggling for the ideal that fills his mind. He was too committed a pedagogue and a reformer to retreat into silence. So he follows the path of the English romantic: he writes *Magriço*, a forerunner of *Viagens*, as Byron writes *Don Juan*, using irony as a means to denounce and moralize.

The *Weltanschauung* expressed in *Magriço* is a development of the pessimism already present in *Camões* and *D. Branca* and its affinities with Byron's own vision have been pointed out in the analysis of those poems. The early pessimism assumes predominantly the shape of a melancholy awareness of the transience of life, and of the limitations and ambiguities derived from the complex nature of man. In *Magriço* Garrett discards melancholy; he declares his intention to laugh cynically with Diogenes, in words that may possibly be an echo of the use of the same topos in *The Age of Bronze*.[79] Thus he strikes basically the same pose as Byron when he says in *Don Juan:* 'and if I laugh at any mortal thing, / 'Tis that I may not weep'.[80] These lines explain the reason for the irony of *Don Juan* and apply equally well to *Magriço*. It is possible, in fact, to establish a close resemblance in the evolution of the two poets, by comparing Canto I of *Magriço* with Cantos IV and VII of *Don Juan*. In the course of the confessional introduction Garrett says:

> Por lá cantei de amor purezas e mimos,
> Doçuras de amizade, enlevos d'alma.
> (...) Experiência fatal, tu me roubaste
> A tão doce ilusão, em que eu vivia!
> (...) Tal como ele é vi o homem! Aos meus olhos
> De vergonha e de dó vieram lágrimas.
> Chorei —tão louco fui!— Só gargalhadas
> As loucuras do mundo nos merecem.
> E assim foi que, atentando mais de perto,
> Vi tanta asneira, vi tanta sandice,
> Que desatei a rir, por fim, de tudo.
> (...) Quero rir com Diógenes, com ele
> No cínico tonel entrincheirar-me
> Contra as sandices deste parvo mundo.

A parallel progression from romantic delusion to disappointment and scepticism, and a similar recourse to laughter in an insane world are to be found in passages such as

---

[79] *The Age of Bronze*, st. x, l. 478-81: 'Be slaves who will, the cynic shall be free; / His tub hath tougher walls than Synope!'
[80] *Don Juan*, C. IV, 4.

> The sad truth which hovers o'er my desk
> Turns what was once romantic to burlesque.[81]
>
> When we know what all are, we must bewail us.
> But ne'ertheless I hope it is no crime
> To laugh at all things, for I wish to know
> What after all are all things —but a show? [82]
>
> And in this scene of all-confessed inanity,
> By saint, by sage, by preacher, and by poet,
> Must I restrain me through the fear of strife
> From holding up the nothingness of life? [83]

Garrett introduces more than one level in *Magriço:* the level of the narrative, and that of the narrator, who is partly a fictitious *persona.* In this he adopts a technique similar to that of *Don Juan:* Byron as a fictitious narrator appears at the end of Canto I as an old friend of the family, a figure who is soon replaced by Byron as he chooses to reveal himself, so that he can be regarded throughout as a kind of fiction,[84] without identification of the author with the narrator. As for Garrett, he describes how he comes to write his poem: the priest who had ordered the purging of the library of Don Quixote is in purgatory, and, having to produce a work of chivalry to satisfy the old knight, now elevated to the status of a saint, he chooses Garrett to do it. Garrett depicts himself as a dozing figure by the fire, but he also interpolates an autobiographical allusion to the days in Warwickshire, when he first thought of writing the poem:

> Sorriu-se o cura, e continuou: «Olhando
> Pois, como eu 'stava, a herética Britânia,
> Vi-te a ti modorrando ao pé do fogo.
> E que eras trovador te li na cara.
> Trovador, ocioso, e pelo geito
> De tuas romanescas celebreiras (...) [85]

Thus Garrett, like Byron, uses a process of simultaneous self-dramatization and self-detachment from the narrative, and, through the Byronic technique of continuous shifting from story to interpolated commentary, he achieves a distancing effect between the reader and the reality he presents him with — a practice already applied in *Camões* and *D. Branca.*

The world of chivalry is ironically transformed in *Don Juan,* and Byron's awareness of the fact that the idealism and the absurdity of romance were obsolete in his time [86] is apparent, for instance, when he writes: ' "Fierce loves and faithless wars" —I am not sure / If this be the right reading— 'tis no matter' (*Don Juan,* C. VII, 8), thus parodying by inversion the lost line of the opening stanza of the *Fairie Queene,* 'Fierce

---

81 *Don Juan,* C. IV, 3.
82 *Don Juan,* C. VII, 2.
83 *Don Juan,* C. VII, 6.
84 M. K. Joseph, p. 199.
85 *Magriço,* C. I, p. 123.
86 M. K. Joseph, p. 179.

warres and faithful loues shall moralize my song'.[87] The jocular terms employed by Garrett in the self-portrait quoted above, in the presentation of the theme of *Magriço* in Canto II, or in the irreverent description of São Dom Quixote show an attitude similar to Byron's.

What is of real interest to both writers is the contemporary world, which is brought in through digressions. 'I choose a modern subject as more meet', says Byron.[88] As for Garrett, he says in the *Autobiografia* that his poem 'abraçava todas as coisas antigas e modernas'.[89] And his letter to Gomes Monteiro, dated 17 January 1831, shows that behind the story of *Magriço* Garrett proposed to allude to the political events that must at least partly have been at the root of his crisis:

> (...) Mas que há-de ser se o Magriço esteve todo este tempo metido em Tomar com uns *Pedreiros-livres* ou coisa que o valha (...); e os companheiros pespegados no Porto, onde têm feito coisas nunca vistas. Faz lá ideia o diacho dos rapazes o que revolveram a nossa boa terra! (...) Mas enfim estou já mais descansado, que os embarquei a toda a pressa (...) para esta nobre ilha (que a leve o demo!) e estão a desembarcar por instantes em Plimude. Até se me não engano, já vi nos jornais, que havia sinal naquele porto de *portuguese* [sic] *man of war off* da barra de Plimude (...)[90]

O. Paiva Monteiro puts forward the plausible hypothesis that the ambiguous episode of *Belfastada*, the hardship of the exiles in the Plymouth barracks and other events of the liberal resistance were among the contemporary facts alluded to in *Magriço*.[91]

The *Autobiografia* had revealed that the moralizing intention was one of the aspects of *Don Juan* that Garrett meant to imitate, and this is apparent in the fragments extant — in the digressions and in the satirical treatment of the episode of Lorvão. Garrett's debt to Byron is multiple and O. Paiva Monteiro penetratingly sums up most aspects of its complexity.[92] At this time, however, Garrett had not yet assimilated Byron's work fully. In fact, the comedy and humour in *Don Juan* suggest a complex reaction to the world which is not attained in *Magriço*, where the only tone is one of sarcasm, often tainted with gross vulgarity. And vulgarity, as was observed earlier in relation to *D. Branca*, was condemned by Byron. It is only in *Viagens* that Garrett draws closer to the irony of *Don Juan*, where Byron comes to terms with the world and with its wrongness, in an act of acquiescence, as Ridenour puts it.

The conclusion drawn from this analysis of *Magriço* is that its main interest to this study lies in the evidence it gives of Garrett's continued Byronian apprenticeship, and of his affinities with Byron in the way he envisaged the world and reacted to it in a period of deepening crisis. By the time Garrett writes *Viagens* the disenchanting world in which he seems

[87] M. K. Joseph, p. 241.
[88] *Don Juan*, C. IV, 6.
[89] *Autobiografia*, p. XLI.
[90] O. A. G., Vol. I, p. 1395.
[91] O. P. Monteiro, Vol. II, p. 291.
[92] O. P. Monteiro, Vol. II, pp. 134-7 and 298.

to flounder in *Magriço* is viewed with a degree of amused and ironical detachment that brings to mind Byron's 'addresses from the throne'.[93]

In the interplay of form and content, the consequences of the replacement of the stability and values of the neo-arcadian world of Garrett's youth by a heightened sense of mobility and of paradox in man's behaviour were not restricted to the subject-matter of his creations. They were also reflected in the reassessment of form, on which he expounds his views in an article in *O Chronista*, in 1827:[94] the novel and the drama, which were hardly practised in Portugal at the time but were already part of the native tradition of the countries of his exile, England and France, were the authentic creations of contemporary literature, because, unlike their classical counterparts, the epic and the tragedy, says Garrett, they did not paint an imaginary world of ideal beauty but dealt rather with the complexities of life as it was.

Of Garrett's experiments in novel writing, the fragments entitled *Memórias de João Coradinho*[95] show certain affinities with *Don Juan* from the point of view of its scepticism, irony and exploration of man's paradoxical nature, as well as in the denunciation of social evils, but it would be hard to take the parallel very far. As for *Viagens,* although its digressive medley form escapes classification —'este despropositado e inqualificável livro das minhas VIAGENS' is how Garrett refers to it[96]— it encompasses in its scope a romantic story which, although it has almost the dimensions of a novel, is an intrinsic part of its structure, rather than a mere interpolation.[97] The Byronic influence in this story as well as in several other features of *Viagens* as a whole give the English poet a place of particular prominence among the range of writers who inspired Garrett in this work.

One of the multiple forms of Byron's presence in *Viagens* concerns it as a travel book, which is one of the several levels on which it may be read. Garrett's interest in the genre can be inferred from the lines in *Autobiografia*, where he says that *Magriço* is a record of his various travels, or from reviews in *O Chronista*. Of particular interest is the article *Literatura inglesa — Viagens. Lady Morgan, e sua Itália*,[98] which sheds light on the importance he attributed to the projection of the author's personality and concept of life in a travel book. Answering a rhetorical question on what reader could be found for the description of an already familiar country, he writes:

> Respondo que todo o homem de bom senso e gosto, se as reflexões do viajante, o seu modo novo de ver cousas velhas, se a sua instrução e talento semearem uma estrada batida e retrilhada, das viçosas flores do engenho e dos sazonados frutos da razão e da ciência (...).

[93] *Don Juan*, C. III, 96.
[94] *Literatura alemã e francesa — Romances*, in *Chronista*, Vol. I, no. 2, pp. 28-32.
[95] MS of *Esp.*, dated 1825, and only partially published. See O. P. Monteiro, Vol. II, p. 302.
[96] *Viagens*, cap. xxxii, p. 228.
[97] R. A. Lawton, p. 167.
[98] *O Chronista*, Vol. I, n. vii, 1827.

The contempt for the majority of authors of travel books that he expresses in another passage of the same article reappears about twenty years later, when he dissociates himself from them:

> (...) não cuide que são quaisquer rabiscaduras da moda que, com o título de Impressões de Viagem, ou outro que tal, fatigam as imprensas da Europa sem nenhum proveito da ciência e do adiantamento da espécie.[99]

In this excerpt Garrett reflects, consciously or not, the attitude adopted by Byron in the stanza

> I won't describe; description is my forte,
> But every fool describes in these bright days
> His wondrous journey to some foreign court
> And spawns his quarto and demands your praise.
> Death to his publisher, to him 'tis sport,
> While Nature, tortured thousand ways
> Resigns herself with exemplary patience
> To guide-books, rhymes, tours, sketches, illustrations.[100]

What both authors object to in these passages is not travel writing, but to the way it was largely practised, with description for its own sake. By 1843, when the first chapter of *Viagens* appeared in *Revista Universal Lisbonense*,[101] Garrett was consequently adopting an attitude similar to that of writers such as Gautier and Nerval in France, who had likewise rejected the grand descriptive manner of Chateaubriand and his imitators, in favour of a more informal and humorous style. For the French writers of the 1840s and 1850s, the models were Sterne, Hoffmann, and Heine; Garrett may well not have known Hoffmann or Heine, but he certainly had read Sterne, and he saw Byron as belonging to a similar tradition. The fact that only Xavier de Maistre is named in connection with *Viagens* as a travel book does not exclude the two English writers from being considered as possible stimuli. Sterne's presence will be examined later in this study. As for Byron, Garrett is clearly continuing some of the methods learned in *Childe Harold* and *Don Juan,* and it is even possible to discern a certain parallel between the ways in which the two writers developed.

These two of Byron's poems are inseparable, and no true reading of *Don Juan* is complete without *Childe Harold:* they are intimately connected as the beginning and the end of Byron's literary and spiritual evolution. Nonetheless, one feels inclined to relate *Viagens* to *Childe Harold* primarily at the level of the sight-seeing tour, and to *Don Juan* at the level of the metaphysical journey in the heart of man. For *Childe Harold,* like *Viagens,* belongs in a way to the tradition of the travelogue. Its reputation was established mainly through its merits as a romantic poem, but it should be remembered that it was also vastly enjoyed as a travel book and that, as such, it became for half a century a vademecum for British travellers,

---

[99] *Viagens,* cap. I, p. 16.
[100] *Don Juan,* C. V, 52.
[101] *R. U. L.,* Vol. II, p. 593 and ff. *Viagens* was published in this magazine in 1845-6 and appeared in book form in 1846.

and favourite reading for those who had to resign themselves to vicarious travelling. *Childe Harold*'s success lay in the fact that it provided objective, factual information in the form of 'digested' commentaries, through which external reality was related to and modified by the experiences of its author.[102] In view of the lines quoted from the article on Lady Morgan it becomes clear that this personal approach to travel writing would have appealed to Garrett, who perfects in *Viagens* the Byronian way of describing a landscape, as it was developed in the last cantos of *Childe Harold* and which he had first tried in *Camões:* the replacement of picturesque and immediate impressions by scenes evoked and recreated in the poet's mind with the admixture of personal experience and literary allusion, scenes which are used as central points for moralizing and historical meditations. The visit to the triumphal arch of Afonso Henriques in Santarém, in Chapter XXXVI, illustrates this type of description, in which considerations on a monument of the past lead to the theme of the ruin of the nation in the present. The description of the olive grove in Santarém, which Garrett regards as a national monument, is equally related to the theme of past grandeur and present decay, and enriched with an allusion to Tasso:

> (...) O mais belo contudo de seus ornatos e glórias suburbanas, ainda o possui a nobre vila, não lho destruíram de todo; são os seus olivais. Os olivais de Santarém cuja riqueza e formosura proverbial é uma das nossas crenças populares mais gerais e mais queridas! ... os olivais de Santarém lá estão ainda. Reconheceu-os o meu coração e alegrou-se de os ver; saudei neles o símbolo patriarcal de nossa antiga existência. Naqueles troncos velhos e coroados de verdura, figurou-se-me ver, como nas selvas encantadas do Tasso, as venerandas imagens de nossos passados; e no murmúrio das folhas que o vento agitava a espaços, ouvir o triste suspirar de seus lamentos pela vergonhosa degeneração dos netos...
>
> Estragado como os outros, profanado como todos, o olival de Santarém é ainda um monumento.[103]

In a digression on one of the main themes —war— in Chapter VIII, there are also obvious reminiscences of *Childe Harold:* in the Waterloo stanzas in Canto III, xvii-xx and xxix-xxx, Byron broods on the futility of a war that has destroyed Napoleon in vain, for it has brought no freedom from oppression; and while he pays tribute to the gallantry of those who fell on the battlefield, he queries the validity of the sacrifice of their lives. The gist of Garrett's reflexions on the uselessness and sufferings of the Portuguese civil war and of Waterloo —which he, too, like Byron, has visited— suggest that this famous passage did not leave him unmoved:

> Foi depois da batalha de Almoster, uma das mais lidadas e das mais ensanguentadas daquela triste guerra.
> Toda a guerra civil é triste.
> E é difícil dizer para quem mais triste, se para o vencedor se para o vencido.

[102] Escarpit, Vol. II, Chapt. 3, pp. 61-84.
[103] *Viagens,* Chapt. XXVII, pp. 199-200.

(...) verão que, na totalidade de cada facção em que a nação se dividiu, os ganhos, se os houve, não balançam os padecimentos, os sacrifícios do passado, e menos que tudo, a responsabilidade pelo futuro...

(...) estive no campo de Waterloo, sentei-me ao pé do Leão de bronze sobre aquele monte de terra amassado com o sangue de tantos mil, vi —e eram passados vinte anos— vi luzir ainda pela campina os ossos brancos das vítimas que ali se imolaram a não sei quê... Os povos disseram que à liberdade, os reis que à realeza... Nenhuma delas ganhou muito, nem para muito tempo com a tal vitória...

Mas deixemos isso. Estive ali, e senti bater-me o coração com essas recordações, com essas memórias dos grandes feitos e gentilezas que ali se obraram.

Porque será que aqui não sinto senão tristeza (...)

Eu moía comigo só estas amargas reflexões, e toda a beleza da charneca desapareceu diante de mim.[104]

Thus in a roughly parallel development to Byron's, Garrett moves from considerations on war to the thought of heroic deeds —which may be seen as the counterpart of the battle stanzas— to end up in a mood that matches that of the lines dedicated to Howard, with the shadow of death shutting out all perception of the beauty around them.

Meditations of this kind often form the substance of digressions, of which there is an increased use both in *Don Juan* and in *Viagens,* in a remarkably improved manner: the language is largely free from the poetic diction of the earlier stages, and has become more flexible, novel, colloquial. The digressive, conversational manner in *Viagens* must also be related to Sterne, to whom Byron himself is indebted. The literary allusions and digressions on literature, begun in *Childe Harold,* are carried to such an extreme in *Don Juan* that Byron was accused of plagiarizing by the *Monthly Magazine.*[105] This abundance has its parallel in Garrett: the first conscious attempts to include literature as a theme in *Camões* and *D. Branca* are fully developed in *Viagens,* where frequent and extensive ironical passages are devoted to particular kinds of literature, to particular authors and their writing, as well as to the nature and state of progress of the work itself.

Byron is one of the writers who are explicitly alluded to in *Viagens.* Thus, early in the work, when Garrett is crossing the Tagus at the beginning of his journey, he refers to Byron in the following way:

Não me lembra que lord Byron celebrasse nunca o prazer de fumar a bordo. É notável esquecimento no poeta mais embarcadiço, mais marujo que ainda houve, e que até cantou o enjoo, a mais prosaica e nauseante das misérias da vida![106]

In this passage there is a double reference: one to Byron's cigar, hymned

---

[104] *Viagens,* Chapt. VIII, pp. 60-1.
[105] Elizabeth French Boyd, *Byron's Don Juan. A Critical Study* (New York, 1958), p. 115; M. K. Joseph, p. 173.
[106] *Viagens,* p. 11.

in *The Island,* Canto II, 19, and widely in fashion among the Jeunes-France after 1824,[107] and another to Canto II, 19-20, of *Don Juan.*[108]

Byron is also brought into *Viagens* in a half-humorous, half-satirical digression on the fact that Portuguese wines were no longer bought by the English, who preferred French and German products instead. The digression itself is another clear example of the Byronic avoidance of description *per se* referred to above, replaced by historical and literary considerations: after a few lines of physical description of Cartaxo, Garrett devotes over two pages to the recent history of its wine-trade, its rising fortune during the Peninsular wars and its decay after a change of taste on the part of the oldest ally. In lines of mild humour Garrett denounces the dangers that threaten the British, whose national ethos is inseparable from Portuguese wines: 'O que é um inglês sem Porto ou Madeira... sem Carcavelos ou Cartaxo?' And after ascribing to Portuguese wines the creative power of such figures as Shakespeare, Milton and Bacon, Garrett continues

> Com todas as suas dietas, Newton nunca se lembrou de beber Johannisberg; Byron antes beberia *gin,* antes água do Tamisa, ou do Pamiso, do que essas escorreduras das areias de Bordéus.[109]

One hazards the hypothesis that Byron's stanzas on hock and soda water may have inspired this passage on wine.

In his digressions on the literary trends of the time, Garrett, like Byron, places himself once again above the classic-romantic antinomy and condemns ironically the more extremist Romantics of the time, just as he had satirized the exaggerations of rigorous classicists in *Magriço.* This is not a matter of influence, but rather of consonance of thought — yet another of the several instances of affinity between the two men, which may explain Garrett's particular receptivity to Byron's work. A comparison of extracts from *Viagens* and of writings from Byron shows that both, classicists by upbringing, were men of their time, and as such, Romantic in feeling and in their search for new forms; that they were fundamentally in favour of true art, and had no time for romanticism as a superficial phenomenon, a mere school of new conventions. Byron's disregard for the controversy is apparent in the lines:

---

[107] Estève, p. 129.

[108] This is an ironical passage in which the young hero's grief for leaving Spain and Donna Julia, heightened by the reading of her pathetic letter, is abruptly resolved into a fit of seasickness, caused by the sudden lurches of the ship, instead of ending in a lyrical effusion, as might be expected. Garrett himself, in the poem 'Longa viagem por mar', 1821, tried with considerably less success to create humour by resorting to a similar situation: the poet's sentimental expressions of longing for friends and shore were abruptly interrupted by a sudden swell of the sea that sent pen and paper flying away from him. One wonders whether it is a case of coincidence, or whether Garrett had already read *Don Juan,* of which Cantos I and II had been published in 1819. Garrett's failure results from the fact that the dramatic tension in Donna Julia's episode, which originated in its ambiguous reality, is absent from the straightforward situation depicted in 'Longa viagem por mar'.

[109] *Viagens,* p. 55.

I perceive that in Germany, as well as in Italy, there is a great struggle about what they call *Classical* and *Romantic,* terms which were not subjects of classification in England, at least when I left it four or five years ago. Some of the English Scribblers, it is true, abused Pope and Swift, but the reason was that they themselves did not know how to write either prose or verse, but nobody thought them worth making a sect of. Perhaps there may be something of the kind sprung up lately, but I have not heard much about it, and it would be such bad taste that I shall be very sorry to believe it.[110]

To Byron's dissociation from any school Garrett offers a counterpart in the sentence 'Não sou clássico nem romântico',[111] which is paraphrased throughout his work, as, for example, in 'Pois, amigo e benévolo leitor, eu nem em princípios nem em fins tenho escola a que esteja sujeito (...)'.[112]

The lack of craftsmanship of the future Romantics, denounced in the latter part of Byron's quotation, had already been prophesied earlier in a letter to Moore:

> The next generation (from the quantity and facility of imitation) will tumble and break their necks off our Pegasus, who runs away with us; but we keep the *saddle,* because we broke the rascal and can ride. But though easy to mount, he is the devil to guide; and the next fellows must go back to the riding-school and the manège, and learn to ride the great horse.[113]

A similar preoccupation is found in *Viagens:* an attack in Chapter V on those whose work was no more than a copy of characters, situations and words picked at random from French models and thrown together without rhyme or reason is continued in an ironic digression on the Romantics of the time in Chapter XXII, in which Garrett focusses on their deficient literary foundations:

> Se algum deles era capaz de escrever com menos lógica (com menos gramática, sim) e com mais triunfante desprezo das absurdas e escravizantes regras dessa pateta dessa escola clássica que não produziu nunca senão Homero e Virgílio, Sófocles e Horácio, Camões e o Tasso, Corneille e Racine, Pope e Molière, e mais algumas dúzias de outros nomes tão obscuros como estes? [114]

The two poets' aversion to belonging to a school may be interpreted as part of their refusal of 'systems', about which both write explicitly. O. Paiva Monteiro remarks on Garrett's loss of belief in ideals and absolutes, brought about by the political events between the revolution and 1823, and on his increasingly pragmatic attitude.[115] His subsequent experiences

---

110 *Letters and Journals,* V, 104 (from suppressed dedication of *Marino Faliero* to Goethe), in M. K. Joseph, pp. 299-300.

111 *Camões,* Preface to first edition (Paris, 22 February 1825).

112 *Viagens,* Chapter XXXI, p. 227; see Preface to third edition of *Catão,* O. A. G., Vol. 2, p. 1619.

113 *Letters and Journals,* Vol. IV, pp. 196-7 (to Moore, 2 February 1818), in M. K. Joseph, p. 296.

114 *Viagens,* Chapter XXIV, p. 174. A similar attack on those who criticized the rules of old teachings is found in a poem in *Lyc. das d.* (1822-3), first published in *O Chronista,* Vol. I, 1827, p. 180. See O. P. Monteiro, Vol. I, p. 401.

115 O. P. Monteiro, Vol. I, p. 302.

in exile and back in Portugal were such that they confirmed him in his sceptical outlook. And indeed, taking a line similar to Byron's,[116] Garrett vigorously denounced the fallacy of systems in articles in *O Chronista*[117] in 1827, as well as years later in *Tratado da Educação*. But it is in *Viagens* that he gives aesthetic expression to such a denunciation, and there one finds, time and time again, explicit sallies against abstraction divorced from fact:

> Detesto a filosofia, detesto a razão, e sinceramente creio que num mundo tão desconchavado como este, numa sociedade tão falsa, numa vida tão absurda como a que nos fazem as leis, os costumes, as instituições, as conveniências delas, afectar nas palavras a exactidão, a lógica, a rectidão que não há nas coisas, é a maior e mais perniciosa de todas as incoerências.[118]

Just as they both opposed 'system', understood as irrelevance to reality, they also denounced the lack of congruence between words and things, between principle and practice. In one of the digressions in *Viagens* Garrett writes:

> Mas aqui é que me aparece uma incoerência inexplicável. A sociedade é materialista; e a literatura, que é a expressão da sociedade, é toda excessiva-mente e absurdamente e despropositadamente espiritualista! (...) —É a literatura que é uma hipócrita: tem religião nos versos, caridade nos romances, fé nos artigos do jornal— como os que dão esmolas para pôr no Diário, que amparam orfãs na *Gazeta*, e sustentam viuvas nos cartazes e nos teatros.
> E falam no Evangelho! Deve ser por escárneo...[119]

Such a denunciation of hypocrisy in literature has its parallel in Byron, who writes during the controversy with Bowles in 1817: 'This immaculate period, this moral millennium of expurgated editions in books, manners and royal triads of divorce'.[120] But the quotations above show that Garrett's concern with hypocrisy and with lack of consistency between moral ideal and reality was not restricted to the area of literature; it extended to all walks of life and the things he refers to are equally attacked by Byron, whose views on the subject are summarized at another point in the course of the same controversy:

> The truth is, that in these days the grand 'primum mobile' of England is *cant;* cant political, cant poetical, cant religious, cant moral; but always

---

[116] *Don Juan*, C. XIV, 1-3; *Letters and Journals*, 2nd letter on Bowles controversy.

[117] *O Chronista*, Vol. I, No. IX, p. 188, *Da actual Regência de Portugal e de seu princípio constitutivo:* «Nunca eu gostei em nenhum género de coisas destes *sistemas* tiranos, obra e feitura de nossas mãos, que tanta gente forma para seu tormento, e a quem alevanta altares e tronos para sua escravidão. / O homem de sistemas sacrifica a verdade, a razão, a justiça e a própria moral a seus princípios con-vencionais (...) / Desta mania me defenda Deus, porque a temo mais que nenhuma das desgraças da terra.» See also *Teremos guerra ou paz?*, in Vol. I, pp. 104-5.

[118] *Viagens*, Chapt. XXXVIII, p. 277.

[119] *Viagens*, Chapt. III, p. 25.

[120] *Letters and Journals*, V, 575, in M. K. Joseph, p. 274; *Don Juan*, V, 1-2; *Don Juan*, Pref. to C. VI-VII.

cant, multiplied through all the varieties of life. (...) I say *cant,* because it is a thing of words, without the smallest influence upon human actions; the English being no wiser, no better, and much poorer, and more divided amongst themselves, as well as far less moral, than they were before the prevalence of this moral decorum.[121]

The pragmatic choice of constant adjustment to reality and the consequent rejection of 'systems' had similar repercussions in the political career of both writers, preventing them from giving permanent allegiance to any one particular party — a fact misunderstood by many of their contemporaries, so that at some stage in their lives both Byron and Garrett found themselves in situations in which they had to justify their political 'mobility'.[122] Their experiences in politics were alike in some respects —as members of Parliament, and participating in the underground activities of secret societies and in a national movement of liberation— and their subsequent disenchantment, as well as its literary expression, have been part of the present study. In *Viagens* one finds another affinity with Byron in this particular area, in the way Cervantes's epic is connected with the evolution and illustration of their *Weltanschauung*. Ridenour draws attention to the clue Byron gives his readers as to the role of *Don Quixote* in his literary career, in C. XIII, 8-9, where he says that, although he does not love or hate any longer with the same intensity of youth, he still is

> very willing to redress
> Men's wrongs, and rather check than punish crimes
> Had not Cervantes, in that too true tale
> Of Quixote, shown how all such efforts fail.
>
> Of all tales 'tis the saddest — and more sad,
> Because it makes us smile: his hero's right,
> And still pursues the right; — to curb the bad
> His only object, and 'gainst odds to fight
> His guerdon: 'tis his virtue makes him mad!
> But his adventures form a sorry sight; —
> A sorrier still is the great moral taught
> By that real epic unto all who have thought.[123]

In these stanzas Byron's spiritual evolution from the idealism of youth to the days of experience is related to the replacement of the romance (for *Childe Harold* is a 'Romaunt', as the subtitle stresses) by the epic, as a lesson learnt from *Don Quixote,* the 'real epic', that puts an end to illusion. *Don Juan,* as Byron insists elsewhere, is about the real world, and that is the domain of epic. Since Don Quixote is right, it follows that laughter is the only way to approach a reality that has no place for virtue. Hence the already quoted lines about the sad truth which turns what was once romantic to burlesque. If *Don Quixote* can thus be presented as the point of

---

121 *Letters and Journals,* V, p. 542, in M. K. Joseph, p. 284.
122 Preface to the third edition of *Catão,* O. A. G., Vol. 2, p. 1617; *Discussão da lei da Décima,* O. A. G., Vol. I; R. A. Lawton, p. 505.
123 Ridenour, pp. 98-9.

departure to an ironical approach in Byron, in *Viagens* it is related to Garrett's irony as a point of arrival. The loss of 'innocence' and 'romance', and the progressive disillusionment that finds an extreme expression in *Magriço* —where the multiplication of one knight into a dozen is a clear mockery of the values upheld by Don Quixote— had their correlative in the experiments in the epic satire, and in the new prose forms. In *Viagens* Garrett appears as a more detached spectator, who, in recognizing that the march of Progress is alternately effected by the opposites spiritualism and materialism, accepts that, in fact, the march leads nowhere; and he laughs sadly at a world in which no system, however idealistic and bent on good, will possibly work. His irony in *Viagens* corresponds partially to his acceptance, which is also Byron's. Irony, the denunciation of systems and pragmatism emerge thus as essential features of the book. And the failure of systems —be it Quixote's or Sancho's—, which is an intrinsic part of *Viagens* at a symbolic level, provides the link with the tale of 'A menina dos rouxinóis', through its projection on the figures of Frei Diniz and Carlos. They act it out in their lives, on a personal and a political level, and the fallacy of the abstractions they fight for mirrors symmetrically on the level of the reality of the tale the fallacy of the values symbolised by Cervantes's ill-assorted pair.[124]

In the light of the connection established in *Don Juan* and in *Viagens* with Cervantes's epic one could then say that their main subject is ultimately the loss of innocence. This encompasses the interrelated major themes of the paradoxical nature of man, and of transience and decay, that were discussed earlier in the course of the analysis of *D. Branca*. Elizabeth Boyd suggests that *Don Juan* can be viewed in terms of the oppositions Nature versus Civilization, or Truth versus Feigning.[125] These may be considered as facets of the fundamental loss of innocence, and can be applied to *Viagens* with equal aptness. The intellectual content of *Don Juan* has evoked a variety of approaches which, taken individually, can only partially reflect its complexity. This complexity derives, to a certain extent, from the host of themes and from their combination — a device that did not escape Garrett's attention. *Viagens* shares some of the main themes and topics of digression of *Don Juan*, like love, war, religion, travel, literature, politics, education, and personal confessions. This chapter has focused on the affinities in the views and attitudes of both writers in some of these areas. Love, which is at the centre of most cantos of *Don Juan*, is introduced in *Viagens* chiefly through the story of 'A menina dos rouxinóis', where Byron's presence is felt in various ways, like the portrayal of some characters and the relationship of the author with the hero, the role of the narrator as a dramatic persona, thematic associations and imagery. The story of Carlos and Joaninha forms an integral part of *Viagens*, as was stressed above, and even in the way in which it relates to the context of the work as a whole, it displays the influence of Byron.

One of the links is provided by the central figure of the narrator, who,

---

[124] Compare with Helder Macedo, 'As *Viagens na minha terra* e a menina dos rouxinóis' in *Colóquio / Letras*, No. 57, September 1979.
[125] E. Boyd, p. 58.

in *Don Juan* as in *Magriço*, appears as a self-dramatization of the author, moving on a different level from that of the narrative. As a fictitious persona the narrator is more sharply defined than in the English poem, through his presentation as a traveller; his credibility as a fictional character is heightened by the disclosure, in the last chapter, that he was a former comrade of the hero. This revelation and the meeting with Frei Diniz bridge the gap between the level of the narrator and the level of the narrative, including the autobiographical elements contained in Carlos's letter. In this one may discern an affinity with the procedure used in the Norman Abbey cantos, where the level of the narrator moves closer to that of the narrative: they are autobiographical to the extent that they show reminiscences of Byron's ancestral home, Newstead, and of his experience of English society as a youth. The greater individualization of the speaker as a persona and the final convergence of levels suggest that in *Viagens* Garrett takes practices learnt from Byron one stage further.

As for the pose adopted by Garrett for his narrator, it is essentially the same as in *Don Juan*. In the satire of European society that runs through the poem, and particularly in the Dedication and in the gourmet's menu of the banquet in Norman Abbey, in Canto XV, 63-71, the Byronian speaker is a sophisticated man of the world, a cosmopolitan, unlike the Lakers, who are derided because of their provincialism:

> You gentlemen, by dint of long seclusion
>   From better company, have kept your own
> At Keswick, and through still continued fusion
>   Of one another's minds at last have grown
> To deem, as a most logical conclusion,
>   That poetry has wreaths for you alone.
> There is a narrowness in such a notion,
> Which makes me wish you'd change your lakes for ocean.[126]

Likewise, the narrator in *Viagens* boasts of the exquisite pleasures of high life in Paris, in contrast with the limited horizons of the parochial *lisboetas*, whose intellectual needs are satisfied by some old-fashioned melodrama imported from the Porte Saint-Martin theatre:

> E passam a sua vida entre o Chiado, a rua do Ouro, e o teatro de S. Carlos, como hão-de alargar a esfera dos seus conhecimentos, desenvolver o espírito, chegar à altura do século?[127]

The narrator's pose in *Don Juan* is extended to the protagonist who, as Ridenour remarks, is a world-traveller, and equally cosmopolitan.[128] Juan, Byron tells us, has the 'art of living in all climes with ease' (C. XV, 11). Garrett's parallel concern with his own hero is shown in Carlos's travels and contact above that of his Portuguese peers. From this point of view, his travels can be regarded as a counterpart of Juan's, as *Wanderjahre* in

---

[126] *Don Juan*, Dedication, 5.
[127] *Viagens*, Chapter VII, p. 49.
[128] Ridenour, pp. 17-18.

retrospect.[129] Carlos is a projection of Garrett, and one is reminded of the self-portrait in the Preface to the first edition, which reads:

> (...) se não fosse, além de tudo o mais, um verdadeiro homem do mundo, que tem vivido nas cortes com os príncipes, no campo com os homens de guerra, no gabinete com os diplomáticos e homens de Estado, no parlamento, nos tribunais, nas academias, com todas as notabilidades de muitos países —em salões enfim com as mulheres e com os frívolos do mundo, com as elegâncias e com as fatuidades do século.[130]

Garrett's descriptions of himself, either under the cover of fictional publishers in *Viagens,* or in the voice of the narrator, or in his alter ego Carlos —as well as in other works [131]—, betray the preoccupations of the man of talent wanting to assert himself among the members of the old aristocracy. In this one may see yet another affinity with Byron, who, by nature and upbringing, did not feel that he belonged entirely to the Establishment.[132] Their awareness of being outsiders may have given them their independence of mind in literature and in politics, as a positive element to counterbalance the need for approval and admiration that their pose suggests, and which may be related to their emulation of Brummel.

From the viewpoint of the relationship of the author with the protagonist 'A menina dos rouxinóis' can be related to the autobiographical *Childe Harold,* in so far as the main events in Carlos's life are a projection of Garrett's, and his physical and psychological portrait an idealized version. On the other hand the authorial attitude of benevolent ridicule of the hero links *Viagens* to *Don Juan,* where the serious manner is not sustained for long, not even in the case of the pure love of the Haidée cantos. There is a constant change of tone —be it from meditative, romantic or heroic— to the farcical, which may be introduced through a new element in the situation, or through an unexpected comic rhyme, or an ironical commentary. The examples are multiple and illustrate Byron's permanent perception of the duality of human nature and of life itself. One of the prominent objects of Byron's criticism of Juan —and indeed of mankind— is 'mobility', about which he writes as follows in a footnote to Canto XVI, 97, 1.4:

> (...) It may be defined as an excessive susceptibility of immediate impressions — at the same time without *losing* the past; and is, though sometimes apparently useful to the possessor, a most painful and unhappy attribute.

As, in Byron's view, love is of all things the most subject to mobility, all love episodes in Juan's career are ironically treated from this point of view. The same approach is to be found in *Viagens:* Carlos is not taken entirely in earnest, any more than Juan, and it is primarily his mobility in love

---

[129]   E. Boyd, p. 73.
[130]   *Viagens,* Preface to the first edition, p. 3.
[131]   *Discussão da lei da Décima,* O. A. G., Vol. I, p. 1320; *Diário da Câmara dos Deputados,* 25 June 1852, in G. de Amorim, Vol. III, p. 338; R. A. Lawton, p. 302; J. Prado Coelho, 'Garrett e os seus mitos', *Problemática da história literária* (Lisboa, 1961), pp. 152-3.
[132]   M. K. Joseph, p. 302.

that becomes a target for irony, either in the course of the narrative, like the dialogue of the sentinels,[133] or in the narrator's descriptions and commentaries. Thus, when Carlos is meditating on the sacredness of his feelings for Georgina and on his moral obligations to her, the narrator's ironical intervention waves away the tone of 'romance': 'Oh obrigações de amor, obrigações de amor! se vós não sois, se vós já não sois senão obrigações! ...'[134] Carlos's unwitting self-deceit is exposed, and the duality of man's heart brought in as a theme to be developed. Later on, in Chapter XXIII, when Carlos's solemn resolution to remain faithful to Georgina is shaken by recurring thoughts of Joaninha, Garrett derides his conflicting feelings in a passage that is simultaneously self-ironical because of the identification which, one senses, he has at this point with his hero: Carlos's mobility, a source of torment and delight, puts him in the class

> destes sonhadores acordados que andam pelo mundo e a quem a douta faculdade chama *nervosos;* em estilo de romance *sensíveis,* na frase popular *malucos.*[135]

The chapter ends in a similar tone of mockery, with Garrett relating Carlos's highly poetic thoughts on the two objects of his passion to the conventional themes and terminology of the Romantics — they, says Garrett, cannot compete with his protagonist in the refinements of romanticism:

> E que viesse cá algum menestrel de fraque e chapéu redondo, algum trovador renascença de colete à Joinville, lutar com o meu Carlos em pontos de romantismo vago, descabelado, vaporoso, e nebuloso![136]

When Carlos's sentimental life is put on trial by the traveller and his companions, this is done flippantly and sceptically, and once again, in association with the ridicule of exaggerated romanticism:

> —Oh horror, horror, maldição, inferno! Ferros em brasa, demónios pretos, vermelhos, azuis, de todas as cores! Aqui sim que toda a artilharia grossa do romantismo deve cair em massa sobre esse monstro, esse...
> —Esse quê? Pois em se acabando o coração à gente!
> —Eu não creio nisso. Acaba-se lá o coração a ninguém! ...[137]

The linking of the ironical treatment of the protagonist with literary allusions has its parallel in *Don Juan.* Thus, when Byron depicts Juan's wandering in the woods, lost in thoughts of callow adolescent love, he relates it ironically to the romantic poetry of Campbell, to Wordsworth's obscurity and to Coleridge's metaphysics.[138] A similar case of literary reference in connection with Juan's adventures is found in Canto IV, 94-7: his virtuous refusal to be seduced by the Romagnole of the troupe of singers is linked to the scandal caused by the publication of the first two

---

[133] *Viagens,* Chapt. XXI, pp. 158-9.
[134] *Viagens,* Chapt. XXII, p. 163.
[135] *Viagens,* Chapt. XXIII, p. 168.
[136] *Viagens,* Chapt. XXIII, p. 174.
[137] *Viagens,* Chapt. XXXVI, p. 258.
[138] *Don Juan,* C. I, 88-91.

cantos of *Don Juan*, and to Byron's complaint that the writings of Smollett, Prior, Ariosto and Fielding were no purer than his.

From these examples one may conclude that Garrett shared Byron's attitude of good-humoured irony towards his protagonist, and that he also adopted the Byronic device of associating it with literary allusions or digressions. It is also possible to establish that Garrett followed Byron in shifting the irony from the hero to the narrator. This procedure was pointed out in the discussion of the ironical presentation of Carlos in Chapter XXIII, pp. 167-8. It reappears further on in the same chapter, when a description of the hero's mobility develops into an ambiguous reference —ironical but ultimately complimentary— to poets in general, and by implication, to the narrator or, rather, to Garrett himself:

> O desgraçado... — Porque não hei-de dizer a verdade? — o desgraçado era poeta.
> Inda assim! não me esconjurem já o rapaz... Poeta, entendamo-nos; não é que fizesse versos: nessa não caiu ele nunca, mas tinha aquele fino sentimento de arte, aquele sexto sentido do *belo,* do *ideal* que só têm certas organizações privilegiadas de que se fazem os poetas e os artistas.[139]

Byron uses this device in Canto II, 164-6, for instance, when, after describing the charming scene of Haidée teaching Juan her language, he proceeds to recall similar experiences he had in his youth — the irony first focused on Juan is turned on himself in the next three stanzas, beginning

> 'Tis pleasing to be schooled in a strange tongue
> By female lips and eyes, that is, I mean,
> When both the teacher and the taught are young,
> As was the case where I have been.

Byron's influence on Garrett in the area of presentation of the hero and of the relationship between him and the author, or the narrator, goes beyond what has been shown above: the specifically Byronic technique of interweaving personal data into the image of the fictional character, and of establishing a shifting relationship between the hero and the self-portrait, which had such a large impact on continental romanticism,[140] does not escape Garrett's attention. This technique, first attempted in *Camões,* as was shown earlier in this chapter, is fully developed in the story of 'A menina dos rouxinóis'. In a way, Carlos may be termed the perfect illustration of a Byronic hero, for in him the fictional elements that are combined with Garrett's biography, and with his physical and psychological traits,[141] are clearly inspired by Byron's early works. The painful mystery surrounding his family; the sense of social ostracism that leads him to seek a self-imposed exile; the political role he performs as the lover-warrior, in an overlapping of the fictional and the autobiographical; his uniqueness, which places him, 'homem singular', beyond the grasp of those around

---

[139] *Viagens*, Chapt. XXIII, p. 171.
[140] Graham Hough, *The Romantic Poets* (London, 1967), p. 101.
[141] G. de Amorim, Vol. III, p. 83.

him; his generosity and, simultaneously, his inability to forgive an offence, the mobility that makes him oscillate between the poles of sternness and affection — all these elements are obviously reminiscent of Harold and Lara. The duality of his character reflected in his eyes, the awareness of his undoubted and undisputed superiority betrayed in the contemptuous smile are typically Byronian psychological traits, and equally Byronian is the means chosen to convey them. Further parallels can be drawn from Carlos's confessional letter — the reference to an evil star under which he was born, and which prevents him from enjoying the tranquil delights of home and fatherhood to which he was naturally inclined; his refusal to admit guilt, and to seek excuse instead in his condition as a man, and in the fact that his heart had a greater capacity for love than most; and, ultimately, his blaming fate for the suffering he had caused, bring to mind lines from *Childe Harold* and from *Lara:*

(Born beneath some remote inglorious star) [142]

And print on thy soft cheek a parent's kiss, —
This, it would seem, was not reserved for me;
Yet this was in my nature: [143]

With more capacity for love than earth
Bestows on most of mortal mould and birth,
His early dreams of good outstripp'd the truth,
And troubled manhood follow'd baffled youth;

....

But haughty still, and loth himself to blame,
He call'd on Nature's self to share the shame,
And charged all faults upon the fleshly form
She gave to clog the soul, and feast the worm;
Till he at last confounded good and ill,
And half mistook for fate the acts of will: [144]

But Carlos is more than a mere compound of self-portraiture and of early Byronic heroes, as one would hope in a work of Garrett's maturity like *Viagens*. The influence of *Don Juan* in the story of 'A menina dos rouxinóis' has been established in such points as the ironical treatment of the hero, and its shift to self-irony. It is also apparent in the composition of Carlos's psychological make-up: through the admixture of a few traits borrowed from Juan's own character and behaviour, Carlos stands apart from the melancholy heroes with whom he was linked above. The final result is a more realistic and no less Romantic creation. In Garrett's presentation of Carlos, as in Byron's Juan, stress is laid on his original innocence and good intentions: he is 'a thing of impulse' and 'without malice' like Juan (Canto VIII, 24-5) and, like him, made 'a little blasé' by the circumstances (Canto XII, 81). There are still other similarities: both are honourable in their way, and, in spite of appearances, they do not make a prey of women; and both have a chameleon-like capacity to adapt to new environments.[145]

[142] *Childe Harold*, C. II, xl.
[143] *Childe Harold*, C. III, cxvi.
[144] *Lara*, C. I, xviii.

The interest of Carlos's figure for this study is heightened by the fact that it is through him that one may discern affinities with some of the more prominent features of *Don Juan:* it is in him, and in the story of his successive loves, that one finds the link between *Viagens* and the theme of loss of innocence, or Nature versus Civilization or Truth versus Feigning, that are also part of the substance of the English poem; it is in connection with Carlos that Garrett reveals a parallel approach to Byron's Rousseauism and its associations with the Myth of the Fall; and Carlos's life becomes the illustration of the idea, borrowed from Byron's digressions on the loss of youth and love, that politics and miserliness are the activities left to the middle and late years of life — which were equally the object of digressions by Garrett.

A further affinity between the Portuguese and the English works lies in the points of contact that exist between the Haidée Cantos and the story of 'A menina dos rouxinóis'.[146] Tales of quintessential love, they stand apart from the succession of events. The sense of isolation is largely created by their idyllic beauty and by the fact that the love they present is uniquely pure, in contrast with a series of relationships of varying degrees of sincerity. The setting itself contributes to the feeling of remoteness from the world: Haidée finds Juan asleep in a cove of her island, washed ashore after the shipwreck; and Carlos, himself brought back in the violence of war, discovers Joaninha slumbering in the seclusion of a grove in no man's land. Their brief idylls develop in an atmosphere free from the demands and commitments of the outside world, until it returns in the figures of Lambro and Georgina; the ensuing madness and death of Haidée and Joaninha —'They had too little clay' (Canto IV, 9)— are followed by the desolation that falls over the island and the house in the valley. Ridenour relates the presentation of the idyll between the shipwreck and Lambro's violence to the classical motif of beauty in the lap of horror,[147] and this may not be an inappropriate association to establish with the story of Joaninha, which stands out as a point of edenic peace amid the devastation of war.

Other details reinforce the suggestion that there may have been a connection in Garrett's mind between the Haidée Cantos and his own tale. Thus there is a basic similarity in the description of the girls. In Canto II, 202, beginning 'Haidée was Nature's bride (...) / Haidée was Passion's child', her innocence is linked with her passionate nature, made for total commitment; the combination of opposites continues in the fact that she, 'Nature's child', appears in the banquet stanzas as a regal figure, in poise and attire. Joaninha's innocence is repeatedly emphasized, like Haidée's; and, she, too, is naturally endowed with graces that only the most sophisticated civilization can develop. She had, Garrett writes,

[145] M. K. Joseph, p. 262; *Don Juan*, XV, 15-16.
[146] On the Haidée Cantos see Graham Hough, pp. 113-15.
[147] Ridenour, p. 44.

(...) toda a elegância nobre, todo o desembaraço modesto, toda a flexibilidade graciosa que a arte, o uso e a conversação da corte e da mais escolhida companhia vêm a dar a algumas raras e privilegiadas creaturas no mundo.

Mas nesta foi a natureza que fez tudo, ou quase tudo, e a educação nada ou quase nada.[148]

And, being an angel, like Haidée, she, too, was a woman of passion: 'rosto sereno como é sereno o mar em dias de calma, porque dorme o vento... Ali dormiam as paixões'.[149]

The Byronic use of antithetical description in Haidée and throughout *Don Juan*, remarked on by Ridenour,[150] is also adopted by Garrett and abundantly illustrated in the passage introducing Joaninha:[151]

Joaninha não era bela, (...) mas era o tipo de gentileza, o ideal de espirituali-dade (...) Poucas mulheres são muito mais baixas, e ela parecia alta (...)

E não era o garbo teso e aprumado da perpendicular *miss* inglesa (...); não, mas flexível e ondulante como a hástia jovem da árvore que é direita mas dobradiça, forte na vida de toda a seiva com que nasceu, e tenra que a estala qualquer vento forte.

Era branca, mas não desse branco importuno das louras, nem do branco terso, duro, marmóreo das ruivas — sim daquela modesta alvura da cera que se ilumina de um pálido reflexo de rosa de Bengala.[152]

(...) Os olhos eram verdes... não daquele verde descorado e traidor (...), não daquele verde mau e destingido (...), não, eram verdes-verdes (...)[153]

Besides the use of antithesis of portraiture, another parallel between the two stories can be found in the association with birds. It is true that in his introductory description of the house in the valley Garrett explicitly relates the nightingales to Bernardim Ribeiro's and that, as Helder Macedo reminds us,[154] further associations with *Menina e moça* are to be found in Joaninha's name —Joana being an anagram for Aonia— and in the fact that her story, like Aonia's, is told to the narrator by one of his companions. Besides, in Joaninha's green eyes Garrett touches on a theme that is dear to Portuguese lyric poetry throughout the centuries, *Menina e moça* included. But notwithstanding the 'Portugueseness' of Joaninha's story, it is arguable that her nightingales should not be solely restricted to the native tradition and that their introduction may be regarded as a case of converging influen-ces. Just as the songs of the nightingales are given great prominence in Garrett's story, as a leit-motif of Joaninha's presence,[155] and as a prelude

---

[148] *Viagens*, Chapt. X, p. 85.
[149] *Viagens*, Chapt. X, p. 85.
[150] Ridenour, p. 67; see *Don Juan*, C. IV, 43.
[151] In a description of Frei Diniz, for instance, Garrett contrasts the monk's hard and insensitive appearance with his inner weakness and vulnerability '(...) a viva dor de alma que o consumia. O frade estava por fora, o homem por dentro'. *Viagens*, Chapt. XX, p. 149.
[152] *Viagens*, Chapt. X, p. 85.
[153] *Viagens*, Chapt. X, p. 88.
[154] H. Macedo, p. 20.
[155] *Viagens*, pp. 72, 73, 74, 142, 143, 144.

to the sad love story that begins in the grove,[156] the image of birds is used in the description of Haidée and of her love for Juan, as Ridenour points out.[157] Haidée's voice 'was the warble of a bird' (Canto II, 51), every morning she would come to the cave 'to see her bird reposing in his nest' (Canto II, 68), when their love was consummated she 'flew to her young mate like a young dove' (Canto II, 190), the lovers' language is 'like to that of birds' (Canto IV, 14); the natural quality of their relationship is again conveyed through images of birds: 'There was no reason for their loves / More than for those of nightingales or doves' (Canto IV, 19), these being the 'sweetest song-birds' (Canto IV, 28). Birds, suggests Ridenour, 'are a Byronic symbol of natural innocence and beauty (...) in contrast with the earlier animal symbols of natural depravity'.[158] That Garrett was aware of the use of animal imagery in *Don Juan* seems to be confirmed not only by the association of Joaninha —the personification of innocence and grace— with the nightingales, and by her being compared to a dove among the soldiers,[159] but also by the sarcastic lines devoted to the description of the baron of the liberal society:

> Porque o barão é o mais desgracioso e estúpido animal da criação. Sem exceptuar a família asinina que se ilustra com individualidades tão distintas como o Ruço do nosso amigo Sancho, o asno da Pucela de Orléans e outros.
> O barão (*onagrus baronius*, de Linn., *l'âne baron* de Buf.) é uma variedade monstruosa engendrada na burra de Balaão (...)[160]

But the Haidée Cantos and 'A menina dos rouxinóis' have yet other affinities, which may be related to the grand background theme of Nature versus Civilization. In spite of their innate elegance and dignity, both Haidée and Joaninha are essentially presented as Nature's children; and just as in the English Cantos Lady Adeline can be regarded as Haidée's civilized counterpart, it might not be too farfetched to attribute a similar role to Georgina in the Portuguese tale. For, in the same way as in Newstead Juan's travels seem to reach a high point in his progress towards sophistication, and Lady Adeline may be seen as the epitome of the graces of English aristocracy, with whom Juan may eventually fall in love, the stay in Warwickshire is the culmination of Carlos's process of transformation from the natural to the social man, and Georgina its most decisive figure.

This aspect of loss of innocence in *Viagens* —the antinomy of the natural and of the social man— has been viewed by most critics exclusively in the light of Rousseau's theories.[161] It is, however, arguable that Garrett's approach to the problem of evil in man should not be considered as a case

---

156 *Viagens*, Chapt. XX, pp. 147-8.
157 Ridenour, pp. 41-3.
158 Ridenour, p. 43.
159 *Viagens*, Chapt. XIX, p. 143.
160 *Viagens*, Chapt. XIII, pp. 93-4.
161 For a more developed treatment of Rousseau's influence in *Viagens* see J. Prado Coelho, 'Garrett, Rousseau, e o Carlos das *Viagens*', in *A letra e o leitor* (Lisboa, 1969), pp. 108-11. Antscherl, pp. 158-9, refutes the validity of Rousseauism in Garrett.

71

of straight Rousseauism, and that it should not be studied separately from his references to Eden and the Fall. The hypothesis raised here is that in *Viagens* Garrett strikes a parallel attitude to Byron's —a combination of Rousseau's ideas with the Myth of the Fall—, in which Love, as the major principle in life, is related in its multiple forms to Eden and the protagonists of that first of all dramas. In the explanation of the duality of Carlos's character and in the love scenes Garrett's references to Eden and the Fall are clearly reminiscent of Byron's own allusions in most episodes of Juan's career. A few examples from the Haidée Cantos and from *Viagens* illustrate the similarity in their reference to Eden in moments of happiness and in the description of pure love. Thus, in Canto II, 204, speaking of Juan and Haidée after the consummation of their love, Byron says 'Each was an angel, and earth Paradise'; in Canto IV, 10, 'They were alone once more; for them to be / Thus was another Eden'; or in Canto III, 101-3, the poet relates the happiness of 'the lady and her lover' to the religious mood of the Ave Maria stanzas. In *Viagens* Garrett refers to the valley —the setting of Joaninha's love— as a place of beatitude: 'Imagina-se por aqui o Eden que o primeiro homem habitou com a sua inocência e com a virgindade do seu coração'; [162] the first embrace and the first kiss are described metaphorically, in religious terms: 'porque os reflexos do céu na terra são limitados e imperfeitos (...) Senão... invejariam os anjos a vida da terra';[163] and when Carlos and Joaninha, leaving the grove, are roughly awakened from their dreamy state by the realities of war, their situation is related to the expulsion from Paradise and they themselves to Adam and Eve:

> Daquele sonho encantado que os transportara ao Éden querido da sua infância, acordaram sobressaltados... viram-se na terra erma e bruta, viram a espada flamejante da guerra civil que os perseguia, que os desunia, que os expulsava para sempre do paraíso de delícias em que tinham nascido...[164]

Then the paragraph develops as a denunciation of the destruction of what is holy in man by the false principles that stifle and twist society, and thus illustrates the combination of the Myth of the Fall with Rousseau's theory. The same combination appears in the first pages of Chapter XXIV, usually quoted to prove Garrett's Rousseauism. There one finds that Garrett not only uses one of the characteristic Byronian devices —thematic association— but that he also chooses the same themes, those of Canto I, 127-33 of *Don Juan*. In these stanzas, which are a prelude to the narrative of Juan's first love, Byron alludes to the tree of knowledge and to the consequences of the 'ambrosial' sin of experience: the strangeness of that animal, man, with his opposite capacities for creativeness and destruction. 'First and passionate love', Byron says,

stands alone,
Like Adam's recollection of his fall.

---

[162] *Viagens*, Chapt. X, p. 71.
[163] *Viagens*, Chapt. XX, p. 152.
[164] *Viagens*, Chapt. XX, pp. 154-5.

72

The tree of knowledge has been plucked; all's known,
And life yields nothing further to recall
Worthy of this ambrosial sin (...)
Man's a strange animal and makes strange use
Of his own nature and the various arts, (...)
Man's a phenomenon, one knows not what,
And wonderful beyond all wondrous measure.

In similar fashion, Garrett introduces the analysis of Carlos's sentimental hesitations with a passage in which the ideas of Eden and of Rousseau's corrupting society are interwoven, as was seen above, and in which the tree of knowledge and the strangeness of man —in the image of an animal— are also brought in. As a combined result of the Fall and of the restrictions of the 'systems' of society, man, once the paragon of creation, 'Rei nascido de todo o criado', who remembers his original wonderful being, has become 'o animal mais absurdo, o mais disparatado e incongruente que habita a terra',[165] 'ente absurdo e disparatado, doente, fraco, raquítico',[166] forced to eat for survival from the 'árvore da ciência do bem e do mal'. J. Prado Coelho draws attention to Garrett's use of Rousseau's terminology 'flutuar', 'flutuante', to reinforce the idea of his influence.[167] The use of Byronic expressions like 'mobilidade' e 'sistema', and the association of the Myth of the Fall suggest that Garrett's original reading of Rousseau was 'contaminated', so to speak, by Byron's acceptance of the views of the French philosopher as a merely partial explanation of the evil in man.[168]

Another case of affinity in thematic association can be found between *Viagens,* Chapters IX and XI, and *Don Juan* Canto I, 215-16, Canto XI, 76-85, and Canto XII, 1-15. In the Byronic stanzas the themes of time, love, ambition, money and poetry are first introduced partially and then taken up for fuller development. The final idea that emerges from the digressions on these associated themes is that, in man's middle age, 'the most barbarous of all Middle Ages', when the time for romantic love, with its illusions, is past, the ways that remain open to him are ambition —in the form of the marriage of convenience, or of a career in politics, for instance—, and miserliness. Parodying Scott's line 'Love rules the camp, the court, the grove',[169] Byron launches into a satire against the omnipotence of money: 'Without cash, camps were thin, and courts were none. / (...) So cash rules love the ruler...'[170] Money is the dominant power, and behind the

---

[165] *Viagens,* Chapt. XXIV, p. 175.
[166] *Viagens,* Chapt. XXIV, p. 176.
[167] J. Prado Coelho, p. 109.
[168] In Chapt. XXXV, p. 249, there is another instance of a love scene related to the Myth of the Fall, in a way that is reminiscent of *Don Juan,* C. II, 189. Compare: «(...) And all the burning tongues the passions teach / Found in one sigh the best interpreter / Of nature's oracle, first love, that all / Which Eve has left her daughters since her fall» and «E Georgina disse com aquele som de voz irresistível que as filhas de Eva herdaram de sua primeira mãe, e que a ela ou lho tinham antes ensinado os anjos, ou o aprendeu depois da serpente, — um som de voz que é a última e mais decisiva das seduções femininas (...)».
[169] *Lay of the Last Minstrel,* C. III, 2, 5-7.
[170] *Don Juan,* C. XII, 13-14.

politicians of opposite factions, be they royalist or liberal, behind 'Bonaparte's noble daring', reign Rothschild, Baring and Lafitte, 'the true lords of Europe'. The miser, concludes Byron ironically, 'is your only poet'. These themes are dealt with less extensively in *Viagens*, and presented in a different order. Yet the basic idea is essentially the same: a satire on all-powerful money and the view of poetry as the supreme value. Taking as a starting point for his initial digression Manuel de Figueiredo's *Poeta em anos de prosa* —an ambiguous title, which may apply to man's middle age, equated with inability for poetry, or to the materialism of the century— Garrett dwells on the theme that the only 'three great poets' of the time are Bonaparte, Silvio Pellico and Rothschild: they are 'os três agentes, as três entidades, as três divindades da época'. The poetry of miserliness, that of Rothschild's, is the only one that has been translated into Portuguese — in an adulterated version too, adds Garrett as a last gibe at the decay of national values. Then he takes up this thematic association two chapters later, and digresses on the poet's exemption from the bondages of time, which enables him to retain, undestroyed, his ability to love.

Though one cannot establish a parallel for every detail in the treatment of the themes, there is enough evidence to indicate that Byron was a source of inspiration for these passages of *Viagens*. The interest of the links afforded between *Don Juan* and *Viagens* by this particular thematic grouping is heightened by the fact that it is related to the careers of the two heroes. M. K. Joseph sees the earlier cantos as a kind of a thematic introduction to the English ones.[171] Thus the theme of pure, uncorrupted love, first introduced in the person of Haidée, is embodied in the English Cantos in Aurora Raby, both Nature's daughters, 'the difference in them / Was such as lies between a flower and a gem';[172] and the theme of the marriage of convenience is abundantly illustrated in the members of the society that Juan finds himself in, and with whom he becomes involved in one way or another. In the case of *Viagens*, the theme of the digressions discussed above —in its particular aspect of ambition and miserliness being the options left when the time for love is past—, is integrated in the narrative, in Carlos's becoming a politician and a rich baron of liberalism:

> —Que um belo dia caíu no indiferentismo absoluto, que se fêz o que chamam céptico, que lhe morreu o coração para todo o sentimento generoso, e que deu em homem político ou em agiota.[173]

> Creio que me vou fazer homem político (...); e quem sabe? ... talvez darei por fim em agiota, que é a única vida de emoções para quem já não pode ter outras.[174]

Both the first passage —an excerpt from a dialogue between the narrator and the imaginary reader— and the second —a paragraph of Carlos's letter— are reminiscent of the substance of Byron's own reflexions:

171 M. K. Joseph, p. 245.
172 *Don Juan*, C. XV, 58.
173 *Viagens*, Chapt. XXXVI, pp. 257-8.
174 *Viagens*, Chapt. XLVIII, p. 339.

No more —no more— oh never more, my heart,
  Canst thou be my sole world, my universe!
(...) The illusion's gone forever, and thou art
  Insensible, I trust, but none the worse (...)
My days of love are over (...)
  (...) The credulous hope of mutual minds is o'er,
  (...) So for a good old-gentlemanly vice,
I think I must take up with avarice.[175]

Another instance of affinity in thematic association may be established between an often quoted passage of *Viagens* and *Don Juan*. Thus in Canto XV, 17-18, Byron digresses on the fallibility of knowledge, raised to the status of a science, with particular reference to experimentalism, and alludes to the misuse of Christ's teachings through the ages — with a footnote to dispel any doubts as to the identity of the figure he addresses as 'Thou diviner still':

(...) the good will amiably err
  And eke the wise, as has often been shown.
Experience is the chief philosopher,
  But saddest when his science is well known.
And persecuted sages teach the schools
  Their folly in forgetting they are fools.

Was it not so, great Locke, and greater Bacon?
  Great Socrates? and Thou diviner still,
Whose lot it is by men to be mistaken
  And thy pure creed made sanction of all ill?

A treatment of similar themes is found in Chapter XLII of *Viagens*, in the passage beginning 'Mas ainda espero melhor todavia porque o povo povo está são: Os corruptos somos nós os que cuidamos saber e ignoramos tudo'. There Garrett denounces the fallacy of philosophical abstractions, 'as nossas teorias presunçosas', which, he says, are based on narrow and unreliable analysis — 'a acanhada análise que procede curta e mesquinha dos dados materiais insignificantes e imperfeitos'; this is followed by the eulogy of what he calls 'aquele senso íntimo do povo que vem da Razão divina'. That is to say, Garrett rejects in this passage the validity of the analytical approach of the experimental doctrines, and their attack on innate ideas. To this theme of refutation of experience as a science, parallel to the scepticism of the Byronic stanzas, Garrett associates the theme of Christ, whom he evokes in a similar light to Byron's as a punisher of the vendors of the Temple —identified with the liberal barons— for misusing religion as a cover for their greed:

Jesus Cristo, que foi o modelo da paciência, da tolerância, (...) perdoou ao matador, à adúltera, ao blasfemo, ao ímpio. Mas quando viu os barões a agiotar dentro do templo, não se pôde conter, pegou num azorrague e zurziu-os sem dor.[176]

[175] *Don Juan*, C. I, 215-16.
[176] *Viagens*, Chapt. XLII, p. 301.

The affinities in temperament and outlook between the two men and the notable similarities in their fortunes made Garrett particularly able to respond to Byron's individual genius. Both were courageous, passionate and sincere; both struggled with 'words and deeds' for political freedom and democracy, and both fought against the tyranny of thought in its manifold expressions of dogmatism, hypocrisy and philistinism. Garrett's thorough and perceptive reading of Byron saves him from being an imitator, like so many writers of his generation in France, who saw only the outer mannerisms of the poet, and to whom Byronism meant chiefly satanism, exoticism and dandyism. The techniques he learnt from Byron taught him how to formalize his own experiences of Romantic freedom and rebellion, which could not be explored within the restrictions of rigid neo-classicism. The open form in the poem and in the narrative of *Viagens,* the medley, digressive style, the ambiguity created by the shifting from narrator to narrative, and by simultaneous self-dramatization and self-detachment, were tools which Byron had shown him how to use to express the Romantic awareness of being in a world of paradox and mobility, of tragedy and laughter, the world of Quixote and Sancho Panza, that could only be acceptable through irony. Garrett was a most talented and sensitive interpreter of Byron, and their kinship of temperament enabled him not only to recognize the deepest wellsprings of the English poet's creativity but also to discover himself in his true personality as a writer. More than any other English author, Byron changed the course of Garrett's career, so decisively that in his turn Garrett opened up new horizons for Portuguese literature.

IV

SCOTT

'Nenhuma coisa pode ser nacional se não é popular' — these often quoted words from the Preface to the second edition of *Adosinda* in 1843 define one of the prominent characteristics of Garrett's romanticism, and it is an idea which from the days of his first exile is reiterated and put into practice in his writings. In the Introduction to his *Romanceiro* —the product of nearly two decades of devoted work for the restoration and preservation of the popular heritage— such an idea is the theme for a renewed appeal to younger generations to complete his task of Romantic reform based on a return to national sources: once again Garrett urges his fellow-writers to shake off classical and foreign influences of 'Gregos, romãos e outra gente' and to be themselves, reawakening the feeling of national ethos and of native literature through the study of what today would simply be termed 'folklore', and through the revival of medieval poetry, which he describes as a form of romanticism — 'singela, romanesca, apaixonada, de uma espécie lírico-romântica'.[1]

Popular tradition and nationalism, guide-lines of Garrett's literary reform, cannot be studied without close reference to Scott, whose romances and collections of medieval poetry he read during the days in Warwickshire, together with Percy's *Ancient Reliques*,[2] and as a result of which he developed a new understanding of Gothic architecture, recorded in his *Diário* in 1823,[3] within a general receptiveness to medieval art forms.[4] Scott's writings had another valuable effect on Garrett, confirming him in his interest in the tales, superstitions and popular customs on which his maid Brígida had nurtured him in his childhood. A letter to Duarte Lessa written from Le Havre on 19 November 1824 recalls the conversations between the two men on their ambition to emulate English and German antiquarians, and presents such plans as a stimulus for the writing of *D. Branca*. And four years later, in the Preface to the first edition of

---

[1] *Carta a Duarte Lessa* (1828), O. A. G., Vol. I, p. 1748.
[2] T. Braga, p. 323.
[3] T. Braga, p. 324, and Antscherl, p. 30.
[4] Later, Garrett would associate the appreciation of medieval poetry with Gothic sculpture and architecture, in *Ao. Sr. Duarte Lessa* (1828), O. A. G., Vol. I, p. 1748.

Adosinda in London,[5] several passages point specifically to the extent to which Scott inspires Garrett as a medievalist and as a collector — of all contributions made to rouse and spread the taste for medieval poetry in Europe, in the past and in his day, Scott's is the most decisive, writes Garrett; and as for himself, Scott has a major role in his writing on popular themes:

> Lendo depois os poemas de Walter Scott, ou mais exactamente, suas novelas poéticas, as *Baladas* alemãs de Burger [sic], as inglesas de Burns [sic], comecei a pensar que aquelas rudes e antiquíssimas rapsódias nossas continham um fundo de excelente e lindíssima poesia nacional, e que podiam e deviam ser aproveitadas.[6]

The sources of inspiration for his first attempt in the Romantic vein, *Camões*, are Byron and Scott, as pointed out earlier in connection with Byronic influences. A passage then quoted:

> Dei-lhe um tom e um ar de romance para interessar os menos curiosos de letras, e geralmente falando o estilo vai moldado ao de Byron e Scott (ainda não usado nem conhecido em Portugal) mas não servilmente e com *macacaria*, porque sobretudo quis fazer uma obra nacional[7]

suggests that the nationalism in the poem —different from the nationalism of early works, for it lies not only in the theme, but above all, in the expression of its creator's Portuguese ethos— can be ascribed to Scott's influence. The technique of the poem within the poem in *Camões* may have been inspired by Scott's *The Lay of the Last Minstrel.* Scott's influence is also apparent in *D. Branca,* not only in its chivalric pageantry but, more significantly, in the novelty of replacing classical by national mythology. This is a case of a stimulus that leads to originality. Garrett discerns one of the most meaningful aspects of Scott's writings —their wholly national character— which he will enthusiastically praise two years later, in *O Chronista;* and it is arguable that the 'Essay on Fairies and Popular Superstitions', included in the introductory pages of *The Minstrelsy* as part of Scott's study of the inhabitants of the Border, could have drawn Garrett's attention to the place of native mythology in literature; so, sensitive though he is to the poetry of bards and troubadours of medieval Britain, and to the spirit of their mythology, he moves away in disaffection (*Camões,* Canto VII, i-iii and *D. Branca,* Canto III, iii) and cries:

> Vivam as fadas, seus encantos vivam!
> Nossas lindas ficções, nossa engenhosa
> Mitologia nacional e própria
> Tome enfim o lugar que lhe usurparam
> Na Lusitana antiga poesia...[8]

---

5 *Ao. Sr. Duarte Lessa* (1828), O. A. G., Vol. I, pp. 1747-54.
6 O. A. G., Vol. I, p. 1751.
7 Letter to *Duarte Lessa* (27 July 1824), O. A. G., Vol. I, p. 1382.
8 *D. Branca,* C. III, vii.

The next stage in the development of Garrett's literary use of folk material comes in 1828, with the composition of *Adosinda* and *Bernal-Francês*, based on two folk poems, 'Silvana' or 'Silvaninha' and 'Bernal-Francês'. The original texts of those poems were included in the first edition of *Adosinda*, the former as a note to the Introduction and the latter as part of the letter to Duarte Lessa that was published as the Preface to Garrett's poem. 'Silvana' and 'Bernal-Francês' belong to a number of *xácaras* and legends from the oral tradition in Extremadura and Minho, collected from old *'amas-secas* e lavadeiras e saloias' by a lady of Garrett's acquaintance while he was abroad; to this unidentified friend he addresses the Introduction to *Adosinda*. To her material and Brígida's reminiscences, which form the initial nucleus for the *Romanceiro*, a new and valuable addition is obtained by Duarte Lessa, in the form of a collection of poems copied by Cavaleiro de Oliveira from libraries of old Portuguese houses or taken down from exiled Jews in Holland. Just as Scott had done with Herd's and Alexander Tytler's manuscripts and with those of other collectors,[9] completing his own supply and correcting its deficiencies, so Garrett, with the notes by Oliveira that were found in the copy of Barbosa Machado's *Biblioteca*, enlarges his collection and corrects or completes fragments he had despaired of finishing. Garrett's literary version of 'Bernal-Francês' is the first instance of his intention to write poems like Scott's group of *Imitations of the Ancient Ballad*, that is to say, to make a collection of 'romances reconstruídos e ornados com os efeitos singelos porém simétricos da moderna poesia romântica'.[10] The spirit in which he writes *Bernal-Francês* persists throughout the *Romanceiro* and will be discussed later. *Adosinda*, meant to be another 'romance reconstruído', exceeds the originally intended length and takes the form of a more extended poem in cantos, preceded by an Introduction addressing his unidentified helper as 'Elisa', in which meditations on the joys of friendship are interwoven with descriptive passages. Its similarity with *Marmion* —with cantos introduced by one or more stanzas of a musing and descriptive character, addressed to Scott's friends— is apparent. The metre is another important affinity: just as Scott adopts, with the exception of the interpolated songs and bard recitals,[11] the octosyllabic couplet in *Marmion*, Garrett wants to restore the popular octosyllabic verse —abandoned for two centuries, as he says— as an important part of his attempt to recapture the authentic accents of popular expression. The choice of an excerpt from the address to Erskine introducing Canto III of *Marmion* for the epigraph to the Introduction to *Adosinda* is another link between the two poems. Thus, while the repeated references to Scott in the Prefaces to the two editions of *Adosinda*, some of which have been quoted above, point to Scott as a main source of inspiration in Garrett's general efforts

[9] *Sir Walter Scott's Minstrelsy of the Scottish Border*, edited by T. F. Henderson, 4 Vols (London, 1902), Vol. I, pp. 169-70.

[10] *Ao. Sr. Duarte Lessa* (1828), O. A. G., Vol. I, p. 1752.

[11] T. F. Henderson, 'Sir Walter Scott' in *The Cambridge History of English Literature*, edited by Sir A. W. Ward and A. R. Waller, Vol. XII, Part One (Cambridge, 1964), pp. 1-30 (p. 11).

to preserve and restore national poetry and traditions, there is sufficient internal evidence to regard the author of *Marmion* as a direct stimulus to *Adosinda*. The connection between Garrett's poem and Scott is further confirmed by Note A to its second edition, in 1843:

> O autor deste romance (...) empreende esta nova publicação, cujo assunto é tirado da antiquíssima tradição popular e se refere aos remotos tempos e costumes de nossas épocas heróicas e maravilhosas. Espera ele que não desagradará aos amantes de um género que fez a colossal reputação de *Sir Walter Scott*, e restituíu à antiga Escócia —na república das letras— o nome e independência que há tanto perdera na ordem política.[12]

He ends this note with the hope that his own poem will enable Portuguese letters to stand comparison with any in Europe — from which one may infer his desire to be seen as vying with Scott in his nationalist purpose.

In the period 1834-42 the antiquarian interest awakened by the success of *Adosinda* and *Bernal-Francês* brought fresh contributions from all over the country to Garrett's original collection, already enlarged by the notes taken during his stay in the Azores in 1832. They came from friends and correspondents, some of them anonymous; from Castilho; from Pichon, a former French consul in Oporto; from the librarians Rivara, Rodrigues de Abreu and J. Eloy Nunes Cardoso; above all, from Dr. Emídio da Costa, who supplied him with a considerable number of compositions from the Beiras. Herculano, too, assisted Garrett by making it possible for him to consult the original of *Cancioneiro do Colégio dos Nobres,* which he had perused before in the much criticized Paris edition of Sir Charles Stuart, during his stay in France. As Scott had done in the Introduction to *The Minstrelsy*, Garrett acknowledges and specifies the nature of such contributions in the Introduction to his collection. This Introduction suggests the serious-mindedness with which Garrett devoted himself to rescuing from oblivion such fragments of a vanishing tradition as were still extant; it also demonstrates his interest in the origins and nature of folk poetry. From his references to Schlegel, Millot, Guinguené, Sismondi, Mme de Staël, and above all, to Raÿnouard and his *Recueil des Anciens Troubadours,* one may infer that he was well informed about European writings on this subject. He was also aware of the work done on Castilian balladry by figures like Grimm, Rodd, Depping and Müller; no less important in his eyes were the *Ancient Spanish Ballads* by Scott's son-in-law, Lockhart, which gave him indirectly a measure of the merit of his own work as a pioneer in Portuguese letters.[13] Garrett was indeed a pioneer, not only in Portugal, but also in relation to the rest of the Peninsula. This was acknowledged by contemporaries like the Duke of Rivas, who quotes lines from *Adosinda* as an epigraph in his *El Moro Expósito* (1832), and the Marquis of Valmar, Leopoldo Augusto Cueto, who stresses the priority of Garrett over his Iberian counterparts in the restoration and rehabilitation of the folk ballad;

---

[12] *Adosinda*, O. A. G., Vol. 1, p. 1747.
[13] Garrett's *Romanceiro* was preceded by Ignácio Pizarro Morais Sarmento's *Romanceiro português* (1841). See A. Crabbé Rocha, p. 158. Nevertheless, thanks to *Adosinda, Silvana* and *Bernal-Francês,* his role as a precursor remains undisputed.

it is also recognized by later critics like T. Braga, who establishes Garrett's precedence over Agustín Durán, and Georges Le Gentil who, writing on the Duke of Rivas, presents Garrett as the intermediary between English Romanticism and Spain.[14] Finally Lindley Cintra, after quoting Menéndez Pidal on the pioneering role of Garrett, brings out the full significance of the inclusion of the authentic versions of 'Silvana' and 'Bernal-Francês' in the first edition of *Adosinda,* a fact already alluded to in passing by Leite de Vasconcellos: their publication as early as 1828 gives the Portuguese poet absolute precedence in the history of the collection of Iberian folk ballads obtained directly from the oral tradition.[15]

Equipped as he was with his wide acquaintance of studies and collections, Garrett never ceases to be inspired by the spirit and the methods of Scott's writings. This he acknowledges in the Preface to the second edition of *Adosinda* in 1843, the year of publication of the first volume of *Romanceiro:*

> E tomando para modelo as estimadas colecções de Ellis e do bispo Percy, e a das fronteiras da Escócia por *Sir* Walter Scott, comecei a dar novo método e mais amplos limites à minha compilação que ao princípio intitulara *Romanceiro Português.*

By naming Ellis, Percy and Scott as models, Garrett indicates that he follows the current of English ballad writers and collectors whose criteria were mainly literary or aesthetic, as opposed to the more scientific principles represented by Ritson. For Scott, as for Ellis and Percy before him, the truth of the general impression prevails over strict attention to detail and antiquarian accumulation of facts: though his preference for Ellis rather than for Ritson does not exclude regard for the latter's methods, and though he insists on the need for the 'utmost and most accurate precision' in editing manuscripts, his aim is to recapture the spirit that presided over a composition, rather than establish the facts, as would an historian.[16] Such ideas seem to be adopted by Garrett when he describes to Duarte Lessa his method of dealing with the first body of poems, in which 'Silvaninha' and 'Bernal-Francês' were included: his aim is to embellish them —the verbs

---

[14] Ferreira Lima, *Garrett em Espanha,* Academia das Ciências de Lisboa, Separata das Memórias, Classe de Letras, Tomo III (Lisboa, 1939), p. 140.

[15] 'El fué el primero en hacer cierta la tímida y fallida esperanza que el gran Jacobo Grimm concibió sobre los restos actuales de la primitiva epopeya; y los muchos años que se pasaron antes que Garrett hallase continuadores en otras partes de España prueban lo genial de su cuidado exploratorio...' Menéndez Pidal, *Romancero Hispánico (hispano-portugués, americano y safardí), Teoría e historia* (1953), II, p. 271; Leite de Vasconcellos, *Etnografia portuguesa* (Lisboa, 1933), p. 250; both quoted in Luis Filipe Lindley Cintra, 'Notas à margem do *Romanceiro* de Almeida Garrett', *Boletim Internacional da Bibliografia Luso-Brasileira* (Lisboa, 1967), Vol. VIII, No. 1, pp. 105-35.

[16] 'On Ellis's specimens of early English Metrical Romances', in *The Miscellaneous Works of Sir Walter Scott, Bart,* 30 Vols (Edinburgh, 1870), Vol. XVII, pp. 16-54 (pp. 17-18). See also Edith Batho, 'Scott as a mediaevalist' in *Sir Walter Scott Today - Some retrospective essays & studies,* edited by H. J. C. Grierson (London, 1932), pp. 133-56 (p. 137), and Sigurd Bernhard Hustvedt, *Ballad Books and Ballad Men* (Cambridge, Mass., 1930), p. 22.

he uses are 'ajeitar', 'arranjar e vestir'— while preserving as faithfully as possible the style and the characteristic melancholy tone of those pieces.[17] He continues in the same vein in 1843 when he insists that *Romanceiro* is not intended for the shelves of philologists or antiquarians, and that it has no claims to scientific rigour: his interest lies in the spirit and moral truth of his work, and intuition —'sente-se'— may often provide a clear answer where documents are lacking.[18] And, not unlike Scott when he writes that medieval romances teach us what our ancestors were, whereas the historian will teach what they did, Garrett puts forward the view that the true Portuguese ethos is to be found through the study of 'o povo e as suas tradições e as suas virtudes e as suas crenças e os seus erros'.[19] This listing of the distinct points of study recalls the Introduction to *The Minstrelsy,* where popular traditions, superstitions, legends and the character of the people are discussed in connection with the poetry of the Border. Poetic sensibility in Scott and Garrett surely accounts for their preferring aesthetic criteria to the exclusively objective and scientific or quasi-scientific approach of Ritson. But there was also another reason for printing the poems in a polished form, rather than in their original roughness: as Scott repeatedly points out,[20] Percy's alterations were determined by the basic need for securing public interest in the old ballads, and he himself, despite the advantages gained by the Bishop's achievement, proclaims in the Introduction to *The Minstrelsy* his intention to please the general reader in order to save the native poetry of the Borders from oblivion. In Garrett's case, since he was a veritable pioneer who broke entirely new ground with *Adosinda* and *Bernal-Francês,* his motives for wanting to win an audience are self-evident, and thus the Introduction to *Romanceiro* shows him, like Percy and Scott before him, intent on pleasing readers from a cross-section of society. His purpose is to write a popular and useful book to preserve and restore national poetry and to make it known to the people whom he hopes that his pages will please:

> agradem à mocidade, que as mulheres se não enfadem absolutamente de as ler, e os rapazes lhes não tomem tédio, como a um livro profissional.[21]

The conditions of the period made it necessary for these writers, from Percy to Garrett, to draw attention to their work by presenting it in an

---

[17] In the letter to Duarte Lessa, written in 1828 but modified in 1843 to be used as the Preface to *Adosinda.* Note the parallel between 'ajeitar' and 'accommodate' in Scott's description of Percy's methods: he 'accommodated the ballads with such emendations as might recommend them to the modern taste' ('Introductory Remarks on Popular Poetry', in *The Minstrelsy of the Scottish Border,* Vol. I, p. 37). Further down, in the same letter to Duarte Lessa, Garrett writes: 'O ornato (...) é outro, mas acomodado' (O. A. G., Vol. 1, p. 1753).

[18] *Romanceiro,* O. A. G., Vol. 2, p. 680.

[19] *Romanceiro,* O. A. G., Vol. 2, p. 682.

[20] 'Introductory Remarks on Popular Poetry' in *The Minstrelsy of the Scottish Border,* in 'On Ellis's Specimens of early English Metrical Romances', and 'Evans's Old Ballads' in *The Miscellaneous Works of Sir Walter Scott,* Vol. XVII; see also E. Batho, p. 136.

[21] *Romanceiro,* O. A. G., Vol. 2, p. 680.

attractive way to the general reader, who had not reached the stage where un 'untouched and uncorrupted' text —to use Scott's own words— might be demanded. To similar aims corresponded basically similar methods, but each new collector brought fresh improvements on his predecessor's work. Thus Scott, who wanted to imitate Percy in plan and style, 'observing only more strict fidelity' where his originals were concerned,[22] takes care, unlike his model, to obtain several copies of any individual composition, and shows other signs of scholarship, such as his erudite and profuse prefatory notes. And Garrett, in turn, achieves greater rigour than Scott in apparently keeping away from interpolations, in presenting variants for individual lines, passages or even a whole poem, and in printing parallel compositions from foreign collections. But by and large Garrett follows Scott's method of giving one standard text made up by selection and emendation, without revealing the real extent of his alterations. Scott's criterion for selection is to preserve 'the best or most poetical reading of the passage'[23] and one gathers that Garrett does the same — from his wish to 'ajeitar', from his lines on the more pleasing form of primitive poetry as revived by the Romantics in the letter-preface to *Adosinda,* or from a passage of its Introduction:

> Eu a canção magoada
> Em verso menos rude,
> Mais moldado verti, dei novo corte
> Ao vestido antiquíssimo, à simpleza (...)[24]

Garrett's emendations, according to Leite de Vasconcelos, are essentially restricted to such points as faulty rhythm,[25] which were equally modified by Scott. Unlike Scott, he does not seem to have made emendations in matters of debased diction, but he follows his model in explaining the meaning of obsolete terms.

The references to Scott in the prefatory notes to the individual compositions in *Romanceiro* and *Romances reconstruídos* show that Garrett was not only inspired by him in the more general matter of method but that he also tries to relate his compilations to the author of *The Minstrelsy* in points of detail. Thus, in the note to the *xácara* 'Bela Infanta', after comparing it to one of the ballads in *Reliques of Ancient English Poetry,* London 1823, Book I, p. 261, he quotes a passage from *The Minstrelsy* on the merits of Percy's collection.[26] Then in the comments on the romance 'Conde Yanno', which he believes has been expanded in the Castilian version, he expresses his doubts about the truth of Scott's hypothesis in *The Minstrelsy* that often the compositions handed down by tradition are in fact shortened versions of much longer originals, which the minstrels reduced to two or

---

[22] Cf. Andrew Lang, *Sir Walter Scott and the Border Minstrelsy* (London, 1910), p. 10.

[23] *The Minstrelsy,* Vol. I, p. 167.

[24] *Adosinda,* O. A. G., Vol. 1, p. 1759.

[25] J. Leite de Vasconcelos, *Esboço histórico dos estudos feitos acerca das tradições populares portuguesas,* in F. de Figueiredo, *Pyrene* (Lisboa, 1935), p. 127.

[26] Other references to *Reliques* are made in notes to 'Reginaldo' and 'O Cego'.

three lays, in order to be able to sing them. Discussing the interest in scabrous themes like that of 'Silvaninha' —an incestuous love of a knight for his daughter and her cruel death at his command— Garrett resorts to a passage from *The Minstrelsy* to explain how the rough spirit of our semi-barbarian ancestors needed such violent stimuli to be moved. He is apparently inspired by Scott's reflexions in lines like

> The more rude and wild the state of society, the more general and violent is the impulse received from poetry and music. (...) The music and the poetry of each country must keep pace with their usual tone of mind, as well as with the state of society. The morality of their compositions is determined by the same circumstances.[27]

Further, in order to prove that 'Dom Claros de Além-Mar' belongs to a wide tradition of European romances, Garrett puts a passage in parallel with verses from 'Prince Robert', in *The Minstrelsy* edition of Paris 1838; and in the note to 'A Nau Catrineta' he compares the vivid descriptions of some of the nautical romances with the best pages of *Reddrover* [sic] and Scott's *The Pirate*. In *Romances reconstruídos* Scott is mentioned again, in connection with 'Rosalinda', the theme of which is the transformation of two lovers into the intertwining branches of a tree and a rose-bush. From the several foreign versions of this romance it is to 'Prince Robert' that Garrett turns again, quoting two quatrains, as the closest to the Portuguese, to illustrate the European tradition of the theme. Scott himself, in a note to his ballad, writes that the meeting of the 'birk and the brier' is common to many such compositions and probably originated in an old metrical romance; he substantiates his point with a quotation from *Sir Tristram,* which Garrett reproduces.[28]

Just as Scott had been a decisive figure in the revival of world interest in the romance of balladry, Garrett's *Romanceiro,* within a more restricted field of influence, opened up to specialists a store of ancient native poetry, hitherto unknown, which could stand comparison with that of other countries. His achievement as a true precursor of scientific studies on Portuguese traditions is bound up with the inspiration received from Scott, and the *Romanceiro,* one of Garrett's main literary legacies, has an impact on his original work in its medieval, popular and nationalist features, not unlike the connection between Scott's poetic works and his novels. Hence, even though at one remove, Scott's influence on Garrett's writings for the stage cannot be ignored, from *Um auto de Gil Vicente* (1841), by way of *O alfageme de Santarém* (1841) with its interpolated ballad passages,[29] to *Frei Luís de Sousa* (1843). It is however in Garrett's novel writing that Scott can be regarded as a major, direct source of inspiration, as strong and long lasting as in his verse. In fact, though Garrett's complete novels —'A menina dos rouxinóis' in *Viagens* (in so far as it can be called a novel) and

---

[27] *The Minstrelsy,* Vol. I, pp. 156-7.
[28] *The Minstrelsy,* Vol. III, p. 338; O. A. G., Vol. I, p. 1862.
[29] The passages are adaptations of excerpts from 'Conde de Alemanha', 'Conde Alarcos' and 'Bela Infanta'. Cf. A. do Prado Coelho, *O «Romanceiro» de Garrett,* Clássicos Portugueses (Lisboa, 1943), p. 16.

O arco de Sant' Ana— were only published in his maturity, several manuscripts in *Espólio,* analysed by O. Paiva Monteiro, indicate that his interest in the genre goes back to 1825.[30] The subtitles *Romance histórico* and *História de 1813* to MSS 72 and 73, respectively, suggest that Garrett's attempts at novel-writing included works with an historical background, if not historical novels properly so called. Of these manuscripts only one, MS 79 —which, having no title or date, was catalogued by Ferreira Lima as *Torre do Lavre*— has been explicitly related by O. Paiva Monteiro to Scott, and it consists of a brief sketch of the first seven chapters of an historical novel set in the reign of D. João I.[31] The lack of date makes it impossible to know whether this first project of a novel under Scott's inspiration is previous to *Arco* or contemporary with it, as is the case of MS 73, of 1827-33-44. But if one cannot establish the date of Garrett's first attempt to write a novel on the model created by Scott, his interest in it can be traced back to 1827 with two articles published in *O Chronista.* Though Scott's vogue in France had reached a peak in the years 1820-7,[32] little seems to have been known about him in Portugal at the time and, even in some of that little, French culture played the role of intermediary.[33] The wish to redress the cultural balance of his country in which, to quote Garrett's own words, the French were the most harmful influence, seems to lie behind his series of articles in *O Chronista.* Introducing Scott as a novelist was part of Garrett's aim of bringing contemporary English literature to the attention of his countrymen. His ultimate purpose, as he said in the preamble to those articles, was to widen their horizons, so that, learning from the best writings of all cultivated nations, they might produce an original and national literature.[34] With such a programme in view, it is hardly surprising that one of Garrett's first articles on English literature should have been devoted to Scott, whom he describes as a man whose deep knowledge of ancient and modern literatures had enabled him to avoid the common pitfalls of imitation and who, resorting to a lively imagination, to the direct study of nature and to his intimate acquaintance with the history and the monuments of his country, had opened up new fields and become 'o escriptor mais nacional de que nunca houve memoria'. These are lines from the first article, *Litteratura inglesa — Sir Walter Scott,*[35] in which

---

[30] O. P. Monteiro, Vol. II, pp. 324-7 and p. 335, and 'Viajando com Garrett pelo Vale de Santarém', in V Colóquio Internacional dos Estudos Luso-Brasileiros (Coimbra, 1966).

[31] O. P. Monteiro, Vol. II, p. 326.

[32] Philippe van Tieghem, *Les Influences étrangères sur la littérature française* (Paris, 1961), p. 198.

[33] Before 1827 Scott's presence appears to be restricted to the performance in 1822, in Teatro do Salitre, Lisbon, of *A Morte dos Templários ou as Fogueiras da Inquisição,* translated from Raynouard's adaptation of Scott, *Les Templiers* (1805), and, in 1825, of the 'drama série' *A Dama do Lago,* in São Carlos, Lisbon, with music by Rossini, which was published in book form in the same year, without any reference to *The Lady of the Lake* or its author. Cf. Maria Laura Bettencourt Pires, *Walter Scott e o romantismo português,* Universidade Nova de Lisboa, Faculdade de Ciências Humanas e Sociais (Lisboa, 1979), pp. 104 and 108.

[34] *O Chronista,* Vol. I, Part II.

[35] *O Chronista,* Vol. II, Part II, pp. 87-9.

Garrett presents the author of *Waverley* and *Ivanhoe* as a model for emulation, who, even in minor works like *Woodstock,* always remains original and admirable. In contrast with Byron and Moore, who, according to Garrett, belong to all countries, Scott is praised as a deeply national writer, whose plots, heroes, style and sources of interest spring entirely from his native tradition. In analyzing the factors that contribute to Scott's supremacy in the historical novel, Garrett, like so many other contemporary critics, draws attention to such traits as the instructiveness of his books, not only from an antiquarian and an historical point of view, but also from their abundant quotations, ranging from the most sublime poetry to the simplest popular sayings — which, so Garrett believes, are the repository of the wisdom of all nations. Garrett also follows his fellow-reviewers in associating Scott with Shakespeare, whom he presents, along with the other Elizabethan dramatists, as the novelist's models in his daring irregularities, vigorous phrasing and comic power.

More interesting than such fairly commonplace and somewhat summary remarks, justified though they may be in an introductory article, are Garrett's considerations on the nature of Scott's historical novels and on his delineation of historical characters. Thus Garrett remarks on the admirable way in which Scott depicts political passions, by ascribing a role to ordinary people, on the way historical figures come alive through a faithful rendering of their manner of speech and the description of their attire, and on how the private affairs of fictional heroes are associated with important events. It is through such means, writes Garrett, that Scott recalls past ages and personalises the opinions and beliefs of a class or of a party. In the discussion of historical figures Garrett notes that not only are they not central to the action, but also that the novelist takes care not to bring them on to the scene immediately, and introduces them rather as if by chance. Garrett also stresses the fact that their inner portrait is made, not by the authorial voice, but by those who surround them and that, when they are brought in, only a brief appearance is required to complete the depiction of their public or private character. Garrett relates this method of characterization to the technique of the theatre, rather than that of history, and establishes a distinction between the absolute truth of the historian and the relative truth of the novelist and the dramatist, who may select from history those elements that are most likely to ensure a sustained interest in the work. In these lines on absolute and relative truth Garrett appears to uphold the views put forward by Scott in the Dedicatory Epistle to *Ivanhoe* (1817) and in the Prefatory Letter to *Peveril of the Peak* (1822), comparing the novelist's freedom with that of the painter, who will select from nature the features that suit his taste or pleasure, and defending the novelist's right to move away from the literal rendering of history and to choose the elements he needs, including minor anachronisms, to present a 'lively fictitious picture'.

After thus discussing Scott's methods as a novelist, Garrett proceeds to acknowledge his merits as an historian:

> mas seja qual for o conceito que se faça de W. Scott considerado como historiador, sempre lhe ficará como romancista a bela glória de haver

alargado o quadro do romance e sublimado umas vezes até à dignidade da história, outras até à utilidade da história.

Such lines show that Garrett, at this point, takes Scott's side in the discussions which had started a decade earlier on the accuracy and historical value of his novels.

In *Yu-Kiau-Li, ou As Duas Primas* —a review of a French translation by Abel Rémusat of a Chinese novel published in Paris in 1826— Garrett continues his study of Scott by presenting the recent opinions voiced in France, to which he appears to subscribe. Scott's star, Garrett informs his readers, is waning in France: the blind enthusiasm with which his novels had been hailed was being replaced by an attitude of reappraisal, critical of such points as repetition of motifs and inaccuracy both in matters of fact and in the portraiture of real figures. Before long, writes Garrett, the time will come when Scott will have his due acknowledgement for the real talent of his descriptions, and for his eminently felicitous use of dramatic forms, but when history lovers will seek history outside his novels and those of his imitators. Garrett then goes on to denounce the decadence of the historical novel, brought about by the flood of inferior works —'péssimos romances'— produced by Scott's followers in France as in England.

There is an apparent inconsistency between Garrett's assessment of Scott as an historian in the first article, and the prediction in the second, written only a few months later.[36] It is possible that the reason for it lies in the nature of the articles themselves — in the first, the aim of which is to present Scott as an object of emulation, Garrett's comments are naturally restricted to praise, whereas the more general discussion of the novel as a genre in the second allows him to bring out into the open certain criticisms which he may have preferred to omit before. His assessment of Scott is neither original nor exhaustive. Yet, by the light of modern criticism, it is mostly sound and even perceptive in the importance he attributed to Scott's characterization and in his analysis of it.

The pioneering role of these two articles by Garrett in the study of Scott's influence in Portugal ought to be emphasized, for his efforts anticipated the country's reaction by nearly a decade. In fact, in spite of their habitual receptiveness to literary events in France, the Portuguese did not catch up with the French enthusiasm for Scott until 1837. That year saw the first reviews that seem to have appeared on Scott since those in *O Chronista*. They consisted of no more than a mainly biographical article entitled 'Sir Walter Scott' in *O Archivo popular*, Vol. 1, p. 349, and of notices in *Entre-Acto*, Vol. 1, pp. 2 and 11 —a periodical which Garrett edited—, of the performances in São Carlos of operas inspired by Scott: *Os puritanos*[37] (reviewed by Garrett himself) and *Lucia de Lammermoor*, with music by Bellini and Donizetti, respectively.[38] At about the same time

---

[36] *O Chronista*, Vol. I, Part II, pp. 158-60.
[37] From the French translation, *Les Puritains*, of Scott's *Old Mortality*.
[38] Maria Laura Bettencourt Pires, pp. 150 and 149.

there appeared a steady flow of Portuguese and French translations —these mostly by Defaucompret—, which seems to have begun with *O talisman, conto oriental dos contos das cruzadas,* Lisbon 1835, and *A desposada de Lammermoor,* Lisbon 1836:[39] and Herculano's series of short historical sketches modelled on Scott, published in *Panorama* in 1837 under the title *Quadros da história de Portugal,* gave a decisive impetus to the popularization of the Scottish novelist, with the number of imitations that soon followed. By 1845, when the first volume of *O arco de Sant' Ana — Crónica do Porto* was published,[40] Scott had at last become a household name, known through translations and stage adaptations, and, most important of all, through the numerous novels that he inspired, from Herculano's *Monge de Cister* onwards.[41] Herculano's role as the person who introduced historical fiction in Scott's manner was not disputed, and he himself makes the claim, in the Preface to *Lendas e narrativas,* that his *Quadros da história* were the initial stimulus to the innumerable works in the genre, including *O arco.* Indeed, a contemporary review of Garrett's novel gives the impression that the general appreciation of Scott was coloured by Herculano's works, and that the names of the two writers were bound up together:

> (...) Não é romance grave e sério qual por exemplo o *Eurico*... O autor não quis compor um livro dedicado todo a pintar os costumes da época (...) se tal fora a sua intenção não duvidaríamos afirmar que se iludiu e que nos deu apenas um esboço imperfeito e mesquinho. O que provaríamos com os romances de Walter Scott, modelo indisputável no género.[42]

Garrett's Preface to the second edition of *O arco* in 1851 gives an idea of the nature of the criticisms directed at his work, and shows that he refuses to be ranked with the countless imitators of Scott. In his ironical allusion to the 'severas normas do romance histórico professo e confesso', in his denial of any intention to depict historical *tableaux* and to display antiquarian erudition, Garrett takes an independent stance — which, in itself, shows his disapproval of the narrowness of the way in which his contemporaries conceived the historical novel in the wake of Scott. Another element that points to Garrett's reluctance to be regarded as just another among the many imitators of Scott and to his wish to establish precedence over Herculano in the introduction of the historical novel —even before the publication of *Quadros da história* in 1837—, is found in the Preface to the first edition of the first volume of *O arco, Ao leitor benévolo,* dated December 1844: the novel was begun and was half written in 1832, states Garrett, and he had to interrupt it because its theme —the punishment of a bad bishop by royalty— had become inopportune and even ungenerous in the light of the politics of the day (Garrett is referring to the moderating policy of the *Carta,* which tried to reconcile all factions). However, a study

---

[39] A. Gonçalves Rodrigues, pp. 68 and 28.
[40] Henceforth abbreviated to *O arco.* The second volume appeared in 1850.
[41] *O Monge de Cister* first appeared in serial publication in *Panorama,* 1841.
[42] V. de Az. (Visconde de Azevedo), *Revista Universal Lisbonense,* Vol. III, 2.ª série, p. 317, quoted by Maria Laura Bettencourt Pires, p. 86 and p. 97, note 169.

of MS 64 in Espólio, corresponding to the first volume of *O arco,* by O. Paiva Monteiro suggests that, in reality, the work was less advanced in 1832 than Garrett pretended. As for the reason for the prolonged interruption, the same critic notes that Garrett, having become in the latter part of the 1830s a member of the Ecclesiastical Committee in charge of restoring relations with the Holy See, was not in a position to take up a theme likely to be interpreted as anti-clerical.[43]

O arco occupies an isolated place in the scene of the historical novel of the day; and if contemporary reviewers criticized it for deviating from the norm, its author goes even farther and, as shown above, disclaims in a fit of overreaction any pretension for it to be an historical novel at all. One of the fundamental objections to *O arco* as an historical novel is directed at its explicit political intention, avowed by Garrett on different occasions —in *Ao leitor benévolo,* in the *Advertência* of 1849 and in Chapter XIX. Garrett announces that, with *O arco,* he wishes to redress the excesses derived from the religious revival that Scott and other romantic writers had inspired, through a work in the manner of those very same writers;[44] more specifically, he wishes to teach, through an episode of the past, that kings and the people had joined forces against the abuse of power by ecclesiastical and aristocratic feudalism; and, after admitting that though the subject belongs to the fourteenth century, it is written under the impressions of the nineteenth, he makes no attempt to deny the didactic purpose of his novel, of 'rir castigando'. Such premises do differ from the method by which history is presented in Scott's novels, but do not prevent Garrett from following Scott in essential points, as we shall see. Garrett is not so entirely successful in his methods to relate the past to the present, in so far as he resorts to frequent references to contemporary facts and events, which seldom occur in his model. Such references in Garrett are mainly in the realm of politics, and are often ironically humorous. Thus in Chapter XXXII — of which the title itself, 'Bile de Indemnidade', is an instance of the author's practice of describing the past in terms of the present, the meeting of the people of Oporto with the town councillors is depicted as a burlesque of a nineteenth-century parliamentary session, with such remarks as:

> Hilaridade geral. E faltam os *apoiados* nas notas taquigráficas, porque não as usavam ainda então: estávamos, bem vêem, muito atrasados.[45]

Even in the description of the hero's clothing in Chapter XXV, p. 322, Garrett succumbs to characterization in blatantly contemporary terms.[46] Such

[43] O. P. Monteiro, Vol. II, pp. 329-30.
[44] In Preface to *Mérope* (1841), Garrett writes: 'Romantismo, cá o houve sempre; essa moléstia (...) nunca saíu da nossa Península. Mas a vacina, como a prepararam Goethe e Scott, essa é que não havia: e creio que fui eu que a introduzi.' O. A. G., Vol. 2, p. 1785.
[45] *O arco,* Chapt. XXXXII, O. A. G., Vol. 1, p. 359.
[46] For Garrett's freedom in the use of time cf. O. P. Monteiro, 'Algumas reflexões sobre a novelística de Garrett', in *Colóquio Letras,* Nr. 30 (Março 1976), pp. 13-29.

comments, intended to establish a past-present relationship, place too often an excessive strain on the reader's goodwill, if the illusion of fictional veracity is not to be destroyed. Yet this is not the only manner in which past and present are connected in *O arco*. Garrett also relates the past to the present in the same way as Scott does, that is, by bringing to life a past which, in itself and without the aid of explicit commentaries, is felt to be the necessary pre-history of the present, to use Lukács's terms: [47] his choice of a social crisis in the fourteenth century, in which the burghers eventually triumph over the feudal aristocracy, with the monarch's aid, is felt by the reader precisely as the pre-history of Portuguese liberalism. The relation between the two crises is emphasized by the fact that in 1832, when Garrett wrote the beginning of *O arco*, the town of Oporto was besieged by the troops of the apostolic party, as Braga remarks. [48] It is true that in *O arco* the plot consists, in its narrow historical sense, of no more than the rebellion of the citizens of Oporto against their Bishop, as Fidelino de Figueiredo notes with disapproval. [49] Yet, by the recurrent nature of the alliance between people and monarch against feudal lords in medieval Portugal, the rebellion is part of a much wider movement towards the abolition of class distinction and therefore towards progress, which lends to Garrett's work the historical breadth and character that one associates with Scott's novels.

The crisis is not presented in theoretical terms, but in its interaction with the lives of the characters, and in this respect Garrett shows how well he understood the feeling of what Lukács calls historical necessity and which is one of Scott's achievements. In the way in which the burghers are affected in their private lives and spurred into action by the heavy tributes exacted from them and by the unscrupulous violation of their homes, in the unromantically depicted self-interest that presides over the alliance of the king with the people, in the glimpses into the institutions of chivalry and of the medieval church afforded by the actions of the Bishop, Paio Guterres and Frei João Arrifana, Garrett reenacts historical reality and puts into practice the form of dramatic construction praised in his articles in *O Chronista*. In the process he adopts his model's stance of a narrator who does not take sides, and such impartiality is all the more striking as one contrasts it with the avowed satirical purpose of *O arco:* one is reminded once more that Garrett's prefaces and *advertências,* like those of other writers, may be somewhat misleading in relation to what he actually does in the work itself. The narrative in *O arco* implicitly holds up the past as an effective lesson to the present, and one cannot help regretting that Garrett should have marred his novel by the addition of his too explicit commentaries.

In following the example of *Waverley* by adopting a dramatic form, Garrett gives vent to his natural propensity for the theatre and carries

---

[47] Georg Lukács, *The Historical Novel,* transl. from the German by Hannah and Stanley Mitchell (Harmondsworth, 1962), p. 67.
[48] T. Braga, p. 528.
[49] Fidelino de Figueiredo, *História da literatura romântica (1825-1870),* 2.ª edição revista, Biblioteca de Estudos Históricos Nacionais, IV (Lisboa, 1932), pp. 74-5.

Scott's practice a stage further, by condensing the action into a period of twenty-four hours, as Lawton remarks.[50] The result of this condensation is that Garrett has fewer pretexts on which to hang antiquarian interest, external local colour or descriptions of landscapes —points to which we shall come back later— and that he does not indulge in Scott's leisurely discursiveness. But what the novel may have lost by the absence of such elements it has gained in speed of narrative and in its power to hold the reader's attention — qualities in which Scott's novels excel at certain moments. The description of the structure of *O arco* as a succession of scenes in which the characters become familiar to the reader through their behaviour, rather than by authorial analysis, and in consequence of which the dialogue has great significance, brings to mind passages by Scott on his own writing. One such passage is the dialogue between Dick Tinto and the Author at the beginning of *The Bride of Lammermoor:*

> (...) and how is it possible for an author to introduce his *personae dramatis* to his readers in a more interesting and effectual manner than by dialogue in which each is represented as supporting his own appropriate character? [51]

Garrett must have been acquainted with this passage, considering the popularity of this particular novel in Portugal and the fact that he owned a set of the *Waverley Novels* of 1829.[52] One should not exclude the hypothesis that Garrett, whose interest in English literature has been sufficiently proved, and who had in his personal library four volumes of the *Foreign Quarterly,*[53] might have read Scott's unsigned article on *Tales of My Landlord* in the *Quarterly Review,* xvi, p. 431, in 1817.[54] There Scott refers to his practice of 'keeping both the actors and the action continually before the reader' and comparing it to the way in which, in a play, all the information the audience has is what is shown on the stage. The gist of Garrett's words on his own technique is similar to that of Scott's passages:

> Mas não cansemos o pincel a retratar nem este nem os outros importantes caracteres da nossa história: deixemo-los *daguerreotiparem-se* aos olhos mesmos do leitor, e à luz dos seus próprios ditos e gestos, segundo lhos vamos contando.[55]

What is certainly true is that Garrett had read Scott's novels and that, like them, *O arco* has a dramatic construction, with dialogue having supreme importance: Garrett's heroes, like Scott's, are revealed by what they do and say, and, in the case of Briolanja Gomes and Gil Eanes, peculiarities

---

[50] R. A. Lawton, p. 164.
[51] W. Scott, *The Bride of Lammermoor,* in *The Waverley Novels,* Dryburgh Edition (London, 1892), p. 9.
[52] In MS Mov. 5-7-1, Sala F. L.
[53] Ibidem.
[54] Cf. 'Walter Scott: an unsigned review, «Quarterly Review»', in *Scott. The Critical Heritage,* edited by John O. Hayden, The Critical Heritage Series (London, 1970), pp. 113-44 (p. 114).
[55] *O arco,* Chapt. V, O. A. G., Vol. 1, pp. 242-3.

of speech are used simultaneously for characterization and for comic effect, in a way that brings to mind a creation like Bradwardine in *Waverley*.

The language spoken by the characters in *O arco* is contemporary with Garrett's, and in this and other anachronisms —deliberate, according to the Preface to the second edition—, Garrett shows his adherence to principles stated by Scott in the Dedicatory Epistle to *Ivanhoe*, which were briefly alluded to above in relation to the lines on absolute and relative truth in *O Chronista:*

> It is true that I neither can nor do pretend to the observation of complete accuracy, even in matters of outward costume, much less in the more important points of language and manners. But the same motive which prevents my writing the dialogue of the piece in Anglo-Saxon or in Norman French, (...) prevents my attempting to confine myself within the limits of the period in which my story is laid. It is necessary for exciting interest of any kind that the subject assumed should be, as it were, translated into the manners, as well as the language, of the age we live in...

In the dramatic construction and in the dialogue of *O arco* Garrett shows an understanding of the function of such elements in Scott's novels which is extended to other points, like the use of traditional or impromptu verse interpolated in the text. Thus Vasco breaks into song —*coplas* and *trovas*— in the course of his conversation with Gertrudes and, later, with Pero Cão (Chapt. III, pp. 236-6 and VI, p. 247), as so often happens in Scott: — for instance, when Henry Seyton, as a reply to Roland Graeme, sings the fragment of an old ballad (*The Abbot*, Chapt. XXVII, p. 293) or when Fergus answers Bradwardine with a traditional Scottish stanza (*Waverley*, Chapt. XLIII, p. 312); like Waverley (*Waverley*, Chapt. XXXIII, p. 262 and LIV, p. 370), Vasco, talking to himself, concludes his thought in verse, recalling a popular quatrain (Chapt. III, p. 237); during the heated armistice talks a *caldeireiro* unwittingly contributes to easing the tension by singing a mocking stanza (Chapt. XXXIV, p. 327), like the smith's wife who taunts her husband with a canticle against his honour and thus diverts the anger of the mob surrounding Waverley (*Waverley*, Chapt. XXX, p. 246); finally, in the description of the marching rebellious populace (Chapt. XXV, p. 321), which is itself reminiscent of the episode of riotous revellers breaking in upon the election of the Abbot of St. Mary's (*The Abbot*, Chapt. XIV-XV) in its horrific burlesque and din, a chant is sung against the Bishop, which may be related, through its content and through its role in the scene, to the ballad that Scott's mob sings against Popery.

Garrett appears also as an attentive and perceptive reader of Scott in the portrayal of his main characters. It is true that his minor figures, like Briolanja Gomes, the town councillors and even the brothers Vaz are only sketchily drawn; they are flat characters, and lack the vitality of the immense gallery of their Scottian counterparts, from Evan Dhu to Caleb or to Wamba. It is true also that feminine characters like Aninhas and Gertrudes are not sufficiently developed either, but this is a fault they share with a number of Scott's own heroines: and one may discern in

Gertrudes's lively and determined behaviour a reflexion of Diana Vernon's habitual manner in *Rob Roy*. In his handling of the three male figures, however, Garrett puts effectively into practice, as Hugo did not, his understanding of Scott's creations, of which he had given an idea in *O Chronista*. Thus Vasco shows the characteristics of a Scottian hero both in his portrayal and in his function in the novel. He belongs to the family of such figures as Waverley and Bertram in *Guy Mannering*, of whom Scott wrote in the self-depreciatory lines of his review of *Tales of My Landlord* in the *Quarterly Review*, that they are a

> (...) very amiable and very insipid sort of young men. (...) His chief characters are never actors, but always acted upon by the spur of circumstances, and have their fates uniformly determined by the agency of the subordinate persons.[56]

Like the heroes named above, or like Francis Osbaldistone in *Rob Roy*, Vasco is a reluctant hero who discovers himself in the course of an action imposed on him: it is prompted by Gertrudes and by his mother that he espouses the common cause of the abducted Aninhas, the despoiled burghers and the victimized Jewess, and, from a light-hearted and apparently irresponsible student turns into the undisputed leader of the commune, capable of establishing his authority over the people and of facing the king himself. In the manner of Scott's heroes, Vasco is torn by divided loyalties and occupies a central place between the opposing forces in the struggle: he is a middle figure, who by his reputedly high but unknown parentage (another Scottian feature) and by the Bishop's protection belongs to the upper stratum, but whose love for Gertrudes makes him join the ranks of the insurgent burghers. And, true to the role of a central figure, he acts as a link between the opposing parties —the burghers and the Bishop—, and, in the end, like Waverley, reconciles, through his marriage, the old world with the progressive new one. Again like Waverley, that prototype of the passive hero, who, as A. Welsh remarks,[57] is not 'neutral' but 'stands committed to the prudence and superiority of civil society', Vasco struggles to stay within the bonds of law even when he appears to want to breach it — a point that is particularly evident in the way he leads the populace and legalizes the revolution in the meeting with the town councillors. In the stance attributed to Vasco one may see a convergence of the pattern of behaviour of Scott's passive hero with Garrett's own inclination for legality over violence, discussed earlier in connection with *Catão*.

Scott's presence in *O arco de Sant' Ana* has so far been studied in relation to the Scottish novels, but one must also turn to *Ivanhoe* as a source, among other things, for the figure of the Bishop. Critics have compared this character with Claude Frollo for his lust and abuse of power, basing themselves on a passage of a letter from Garrett to Gomes Monteiro, dated 12 June 1833:

---

[56] Art. cit. in *Scott — The Critical Heritage*, p. 115.
[57] Alexander Welsh, 'Scott's Heroes', in *Walter Scott*, edited by D. D. Devlin, Modern Judgements (London, 1968), pp. 63-70 (pp. 69-70).

Comecei ali um romance em prosa a que dei o título de *Arco de Sant'Anna* —e cujas cenas principais se passam na cidade velha (...) Se leu *Notre Dame de Paris,* de Victor Hugo, é um tanto nesse género o meu romance; se a não leu recomendo-lhe que o faça.

The influence of Hugo's novel in the central role of the Arch and in some aspects of the witch Ester-Guiomar is undeniable. It is however arguable that the Bishop has more traits in common with Brian de Bois-Guilbert. Both are depicted essentially as men of arms, who hold their respective posts in the secular Church and in the Order of the Templars for the privileges they bring to them and not out of any sense of vocation: their characters are a combination of military valour with greed and unbridled lust, without any religious scruples whatsoever. And yet in the course of the action they reveal in their inner conflicts a redeeming basic humanity and capacity for love, and their authors give them a sympathetic treatment by preserving their dignity in their downfall. Another important point they share is the ruin they bring to a Jewish family, and that that sin is part of the chain of events that leads to their undoing. Apart from such largely external affinities, there is also the similarity of the function of the two figures in their respective novels: though Scott and Garrett are both capable of recapturing the spirit of medieval romance, their handling of these representatives of medieval chivalry may be described as anti-romantic, and their defeat is symbolic of the transition from the adventurous world of feudal privilege to the prosaic but more homogeneous age of bourgeois society.[58] The anti-chivalric view is furthered by the light in which the Jewish element is presented in the two novels: like Isaac of York and his daughter,[59] Zacuto and Ester play the role of Good Samaritans and their charity is enhanced by their victimization at the hands of Christian knights and priests. Also like Scott,[60] Garrett uses the Jews as a pretext to contrast the Christian and the Hebrew traditions, highlighting their mutual prejudices; in this respect the function of the Zacuto family is parallel to that of Isaac's and Rebecca's.

Ester-Guiomar as the Bruxa de Gaia is regarded by Fidelino de Figueiredo as the product of Shakespearian influence.[61] Like other romantic witches, she may ultimately be traced back to the Elizabethan playwright, but her relationship with Scott, already pointed out by Antscherl, is more direct.[62] In fact, when she is shown as a hellish figure, singing and hopping about in her tavern (Chapt. XVIII, pp. 287-8), she is reminiscent of the prophetic witchlike women in *The Bride of Lammermoor* (Chapt. XXII, pp. 221-3); more significant, however, are her affinities with Meg Merrilies, not only in matters of detail (Chapt. XX, pp. 295, 297, 298 in *O arco* and Chapt. VIII, p. 49 and LV, p. 403 in *Guy Mannering*), but in her role

---

[58] Joseph E. Duncan, 'The Anti-Romantic in *Ivanhoe*', in *Walter Scott,* edited by D. D. Devlin, Modern Judgements (London, 1968), pp. 142-7 (pp. 147 and 146).
[59] Ibidem.
[60] Ibidem.
[61] Fidelino de Figueiredo, *Shakespeare e Garrett,* Conselho Estadual de Cultura (São Paulo, 1970), p. 37.
[62] Antscherl, p. 179.

in the novel, in so far as she is the main figure contributing to the exposure of crime and leading the hero to the discovery of his true identity, after having protected him from childhood, as a mysterious, beneficent presence.

In the presentation of D. Pedro and in the delineation of his character Garrett puts into practice the perceptive views put forward in *O Chronista* on Scott's recreation of historical personages. In *O arco* the ground is from the outset carefully prepared for the actual appearance of the king, through allusions and commentaries which show him as an individual and as a social entity. Thus in the initial conversation between Aninhas and Gertrudes the king is depicted psychologically and in conjunction with the outline of the situation, as the people's last hope for the redressing of their grievances. Their common aspiration is summed up in Gertrudes's words:

> (...) que nos valha com a sua justiça, e venha açoitar este malvado Bispo, e enforcar os seus cónegos, os seus frades e portageiros.[63]

Pedro's traits as a man and a monarch, in his more prominent positive and negative aspects, emerge from such a method of indirect portraiture, carried on gradually throughout the novel: his courage, for instance, is casually revealed in a dialogue between the brothers Vaz;[64] from the conversation between Guiomar and her son the reader learns about his doings and motivations;[65] Guiomar's suggestion that the king acts for personal gain, under the guise of liberating the people, is confirmed by a remark in the narrator's voice[66] and reinforced by Paio Guterres's warning in the cathedral of the dangers attending the people in an alliance with the king. When he finally appears in the climactic scene of Vasco's arrest in the cathedral, he acts in conformity with the portrait that was almost completely given beforehand, and his intervention is felt not only as opportune, but as indispensable and decisive, as is the appearance of Richard or Robin Hood. The final touches added to his character complete the traditional image of a monarch who is crafty and severe, but also humane and convivial. The figure of D. Pedro illustrates the solidarity with the people that one finds between certain of Scott's leaders and those they lead:[67] his ultimate interests are the same as those of the Bishop's vassals, in the movement against feudal power and towards a victorious middle-class as a basis for monarchy; and in his admixture of selfish gain and patriarchal justice he corresponds to the bourgeois mentality of those he rules, dominated by the idea of profit and by strong community ties.

Despite his words of praise in *O Chronista* for such features as descriptions, historical detail and local colour in Scott's novels, Garrett only resorts to them in moderation, incurring thereby the criticism of his contemporaries and of later writers, like Fidelino de Figueiredo[68] and

---

[63] *O arco,* Chapt. II, O. A. G., Vol. 1, p. 234.
[64] *O arco,* Chapt. XXXIV, O. A. G., Vol. 1, p. 373.
[65] *O arco,* Chapt. XXI, O. A. G., Vol. 1, p. 301.
[66] *O arco,* Chapt. XIX, O. A. G., Vol. 1, p. 294.
[67] Lukács, p. 41.
[68] F. de Figueiredo, pp. 72-3.

Antscherl,[69] which seems to be dictated by a superficial understanding of Scott. Among such Scottian devices in *O arco* one finds a show of historical erudition in notes appended to the novel; popular verse and commentaries on the ballad of Rei Ramiro (included in *Romanceiro*), the story of the Arch and José do U, the historical background of Gaia and the social function of the Bishop's annual visit, the childhood recollections that include the traditional clergymen's dance to São Gonçalo — all these provide antiquarian interest in Scott's manner, and the same may be said of the Manuscript of the Convento of Grilos as a pretended source for the novel; the processional visit to Gaia as well as the Prelate's final confrontation with the townspeople in the See are the subject of few but impressive descriptions. Garrett's *Romances reconstruídos* show that neither lack of ability nor lack of interest in medieval scenes can account for the limited touches of external local colour in *O arco*. It is thus arguable that Garrett, while recognizing the importance of description, historical detail and local colour, which he does not neglect, understands better than a large number of followers of Scott that they can only have an auxiliary role in the creation of historical atmosphere; he concentrates instead on Scott's essential technique of connecting the actions of his characters and historical personages with historical events, and of giving them an inner life, a psychology that is in accordance with the spirit of the age they belong to. Thus Vasco, though created at roughly the same time as Carlos, does not share the latter's Byronic characteristics, any more than Scott's heroes do. By and large —excepting Gil Eanes's jarring speech with its references to the present—, the behaviour of the figures in *O arco,* be they fictional or historical, reflects either the convictions and prejudices of the period or those reactions that are common to man at all times. Particularly remarkable is Garrett's study of the psychology of the populace and of the burghers in the fluctuations of the crisis, already discussed with enthusiasm by Fidelino de Figueiredo.[70] He creates an impression of historical authenticity by using dialogue and the minutiae of behaviour to show the people of Oporto in the relations between the different social strata and in the interaction of leader and led.[71] It is in his way of connecting the life of the individual and of the mass with the historical events, in the delineation and function of his characters, in his portrayal of the popular and the aristocratic elements that Garrett shows himself as a perceptive follower of some of the most significant aspects of Scott's achievement.[72]

Scott's presence is also apparent in *Viagens,* in the background information that runs through the work —in the passages on architecture, on

[69] Antscherl, p. 175.
[70] F. de Figueiredo, *História da literatura romântica,* p. 75.
[71] It is this very interaction of the different social layers that Garrett advocates for the drama and novel of actuality in *Memória ao Conservatório,* 1843, i. e. two years before the publication of *O arco* '(...) a sociedade que (lhe) está por cima, abaixo, ao seu nível (...)'.
[72] For a discussion of *O arco* as an historical novel see Maria Alzira Seixo, '*O arco de Sant' Ana* de Garrett — Marcas românticas numa atitude narrativa e num esquema romanesco' in *Estética do Romantismo em Portugal* (Lisboa, 1974), pp. 113-20.

historical details, in the story of 'O homem das botas', in the discussion of the ballad of Saint Iria— which is woven into the narrative as in the Scottish Novels. This feature of *Viagens* is significant for Garrett's understanding of the function of the antiquarian element in Scott, as a way to hold the reader's interest, and also as the expression of a nationalist desire to contribute to the history of the Border. In this respect *Viagens* is a continuation of *Romanceiro*, in the same way as *The Minstrelsy* leads into the later works. In this, as in other points dealt with above in which Garrett is inspired by Scott, he shows a keen perception of the methods of his model, and makes them his own, in an original and national manner.

V

STERNE

Sterne was one of the most popular writers in England and on the continent in the late eighteenth and early nineteenth century but despite this fact he does not seem to have attracted Garrett's attention until 1843, when he is mentioned in the two volumes published that year: *Viagens na minha terra* and *Flores sem fruto*.

His presence in *Viagens* has not gone entirely unnoticed by Portuguese and English criticism. Thus António José Saraiva and Oscar Lopes,[1] José Augusto França,[2] Jacinto Prado Coelho[3] and, more recently, Helder Macedo[4] have named *A Sentimental Journey* as a stimulus to *Viagens;* João Gaspar Simões does so too, while ruling out any link with *Tristram Shandy;*[5] and Norman Lamb probes the matter further, relating *Viagens* to Yorick's sense of humour and cult of sensibility, as well as to the form of *A Sentimental Journey* and of *Tristram Shandy.*[6] Curiously enough, Antscherl fails to show the perspicacity evinced in his study of affinities with Byron, and categorically excludes any connection with Sterne.[7]

It is my contention, however, that there is unmistakable proof of Sterne, both the creator of Shandyism and of the Sentimental Traveller, as an inspiration to *Viagens,* and a great deal more of it than has been shown so far.

In the study of the Byronic presence in *Viagens* we saw that it was associated with that of Sterne, in connection with travel books and with certain aspects of style. Byron himself derived much from earlier writers, and it is often difficult to know whether influences at work in Garrett were the result of first-hand readings or second-hand experience through Byron. In the case of Sterne, there is external evidence to show that Garrett had in fact read and appreciated him, and it is therefore possible to conclude that such features of Garrett's writing which remind one simultaneously

[1] A. J. Saraiva and O. Lopes, *História da literatura portuguesa* (Porto, n. d.), p. 722.

[2] J. A. França, Vol. I, p. 249.

[3] 'Garrett prosador' in *A letra e o leitor* (Lisboa, 1969), pp. 72-100 (p. 77).

[4] H. Macedo, p. 15.

[5] J. Gaspar Simões, *Almeida Garrett* (Lisboa, 1964), p. 134.

[6] N. Lamb, 'The Romanticism of Almeida Garrett's *Viagens na minha terra*', *Bulletin of Hispanic Studies*, 26 (1949), 104.

[7] Antscherl, p. 166.

of the humorous Sentimentalist and of the Romantic poet are the outcome of converging influences. Such a conclusion is confirmed by a few cases of association of Sternean with Byronic themes, as we shall see.

Like Addison and Byron, Sterne appears in *Viagens* explicitly and also in the way of intratextual influence. Like them, he is repeatedly referred to by name and several allusions are made to his writings. Thus, in the Prologue to the first and second editions he is included in the long and varied list of writers with whom Garrett professes to be well acquainted, as a scholar who is as knowledgeable of foreign literatures, from ancient to modern, as of his own:

> o autor das *Viagens na Minha Terra* é igualmente familiar com Homero e com o Dante, com Platão e com Rousseau, (...) Sterne e Cervantes (...) [8]

In Chapter XI Garrett declares his adherence to Yorick's attitude towards love:

> Estou, com o meu amigo Yorick, o ajuizadíssimo bobo de el-rei da Dinamarca, o que alguns anos depois ressuscitou em Sterne com tão elegante pena, estou sim.[9]

These lines, which show that Garrett appreciated Sterne's association of the Pastor-jester in *Tristram Shandy* with the fool in *Hamlet,* are reinforced by an overlapping of the two figures further on in the same passage, when he writes 'Yorick tem razão, tinha muito mais razão e juízo que seu augusto amo, el-rei da Dinamarca'.[10]

References to Yorick would not necessarily mean that Garrett had read *Tristram Shandy,* for Sterne was in such demand that extracts of his works were published not only in periodicals, but also in anthologies and in schoolbooks on the continent during the last quarter of the eighteenth century: however, Pastor Yorick's ancestry is not among the chapters usually quoted,[11] and this is a first inkling that will be supported by further evidence later in this chapter. From these quotations one can conclude that Garrett was aware of the fact that Sterne also related Yorick, in his quality as a fool, to the figure of *Don Quixote* [12] — an instance of the multiple allusive ramifications of *Tristram Shandy* that would not be without appeal to the author of *Viagens,* and which is not going to be discussed in the present work, but which may lead to the belief that Garrett discerned enough analogies between the two masters of digressive narrative to pair them off in his list in the Prologue.

The references to Yorick that I have mentioned are inserted in a passage in which Sterne is both translated and imitated, and which is

---

[8] *Viagens,* p. 2.
[9] *Viagens,* Chapt. XI, p. 77.
[10] *Viagens,* Chapt. XI, p. 78.
[11] J. C. T. Oates, *Shandyism and Sentiment, 1760-1800* (Cambridge, 1968), pp. 15-19.
[12] Laurence Sterne, *The Life and Opinions of Tristram Shandy Gentleman,* edited by Graham Petrie with an Introduction by Christopher Ricks, The Penguin English Library (Harmondsworth, 1967), Vol. I, xi-xii.

linked, not with *Tristram* as might be expected, but rather with *A Sentimental Journey*. It is as if Garrett was giving a clue, through the preliminaries of Yorick's jester tradition, of his concept of love as he was about to expound it, that is to say, as a duality of sentimentalism and of its mockery. Just as the resurrected, philandering Yorick makes his own the French officer's definition of the Sentimental Traveller,[13] so Garrett quotes Yorick's words to define the equation of love with kindness and generosity. The skilful translation he makes of a passage from the episode 'Montriul' [14] confirms the truth of his remark in the Prologue concerning his command of foreign languages. With a slight alteration at the beginning of the excerpt, for purposes of quotation, Garrett translates:

> Toda a minha vida tenho andado apaixonado já por esta já por aquela princesa, e assim hei-de ir, espero, até morrer, firmemente persuadido que se algum dia fizer uma acção baixa, mesquinha, nunca há-de ser senão no intervalo de uma paixão à outra: nesses interregnos sinto fechar-se-me o coração, esfria-me o sentimento, não acho dez réis que dar a um pobre... por isso fujo às carreiras de semelhante estado; e mal me sinto aceso de novo, sou todo generosidade e benevolência outra vez.[15]

The digressions from this translation, however, enlarge the original Sternean concept, so that in Garrett the passion of love appears not only as the source of good and benevolence, but is bound up with literary creativity. Thus the Byronian theme of the poet's freedom from the destructive passage of time, discussed earlier on, is interwoven with the Sternean praise of love:

> Este é o único privilégio dos poetas: que até morrer podem estar apaixonados (...) A mais gente tem as suas épocas na vida, fora das quais lhes não é permitido apaixonarem-se (...) Ora o que não ama, que não ama apaixonada-mente (...) Deus me livre dele. Sobretudo que não escreva: há-de ser um maçador terrível. Talvez seja este o motivo da indefinida permissão que é dada aos poetas de andarem namorados sempre. O romancista goza do mesmo foro e tem as mesmas obrigações.[16]

---

[13] Laurence Sterne, *A Sentimental Journey through France and Italy by Mr. Yorick*, edited by Gardner D. Stout Jr. (Berkeley and Los Angeles, 1967), p. 181.

[14] *A Sentimental Journey*, pp. 128-9.

[15] *Viagens*, Chapt. XI, p. 77. Sterne's original runs as follows: '(...) having been in love with one princess or another almost all my life, and I hope I shall go on so, till I die, being firmly persuaded, that if I ever do a mean action, it must be in some interval betwixt one passion and another: whilst this interregnum lasts, I always perceive my heart locked up — I can scarce find in it, to give Misery a sixpence; and therefore I always get out of it as fast as I can, and the moment I am rekindled, I am all generosity and good will again (...)'. Garrett's translation of Sterne's passage was first identified by N. J. Lamb, in 'The Romanticism of Almeida Garrett's *Viagens na minha Terra*', *Bulletin of Hispanic Studies*, 26 (1949), 104.

[16] *Viagens*, Chapt. XI, pp. 76-8. The association of the ideas of time, love and literary creation in terms that may be seen as a blending of Byron and Sterne also appears in the Preface to *Fls. s. f.*, O. A. G., Vol. II, 1843, p. 7: '(...) não há melhores nem mais nobres almas que as dos poetas: agora conheço bem, desde que o não sou, e que sinto a picada das más paixões e dos acres sentimentos da baixeza humana avisarem-me que está comigo a idade da prosa (...)'.

These digressions are followed by a confessional passage which bears the mark of Sterne's analysis of the vagaries of the human heart, and which brings to mind the episode 'Amiens' in *Sentimental Journey*,[17] describing Yorick's reaction to the invitation from the Lady of the Remise to visit her in Brussels. Conscience advises a sorely tempted Yorick to refuse it, reminding him of his vows of constancy to Eliza, at whose 'pure taper' he had last kindled his flame; the instability of his good intentions, expressed in a crescendo of effusions, is ironically exposed in the abrupt epigrammatic conclusion:

> I had sworn to her eternal fidelity — she had a right to my whole heart — to divide my affections was to lessen them — to expose them, was to risk them: where there is risk, there may be loss — and what wilt thou have, Yorick! to answer to a heart so full of trust and confidence, so gentle and unreproaching?
> —I will not go to Brussels, replied I, interrupting myself —but my imagination went on— I recall'd her looks at that crisis of our separation when neither of us had power to say Adieu! (...)
> And shall this tender flower, said I, (...) —shall it be smitten to its very root— and smitten, Yorick! by thee, who hast promised to shelter it in thy breast?
> Eternal fountain of happiness! said I, kneeling down upon the ground —be thou my witness— (...), That I would not travel to Brussels, unless Eliza went along with me, did the road lead me towards heaven. In transports of this kind, the heart, in spite of the understanding, will always say too much.

Garrett's own waverings between what was to become his consuming passion for Viscondessa da Luz, and the memory of his devoted companion, Adelaide Pastor, and the love for the child she bore him, form the veiled substance of a passage that may be regarded as a study in the techniques of Yorick's humour: in a clear instance of aposiopesis, that favourite figure of the Sternean style, Garrett flirts with the benevolent feminine readers, in a pattern of advance and retreat, whetting their appetite with the promise of the tale of a most mysterious and interesting love affair, and at the same time professing his fidelity to other bonds —'uma saudade e uma esperança, um filho no berço e uma mulher na cova!' — in a combination of sentiment, pathos, and intimacy, followed by the ironical hint of the triumph of fickleness over consistency. In these pages Garrett, like Sterne, presents sentiment as something inevitable and admirable —the crown of human glory— and, simultaneously, as a source of ludicrousness.[18] The fact that Byron, too, successfully imitated this aspect of Sterne in his apology for Juan's inconstancy, when he forgets Julia for Haidée, in Canto II, 209-10 of *Don Juan*, may bear no relevance to Garrett's passage, but one should not exclude the hypothesis that it may have worked as the reinforcement of a stimulus.

The importance of this chapter for a study of Sternean influences must be fully appreciated, for here we see Garrett's parallel to the English

---

[17] *A Sentimental Journey*, pp. 145-8.
[18] Alan Dugald McKillop, *The Early Masters of English Fiction* (London, 1956), p. 185.

writer as an ironist, a parallel he claims when he compares himself to Yorick-Sterne, in whom the pathetic and the comic operate at the same time:[19] we see Garrett's open profession as a humorous sentimentalist, wielding Sterne's technique of self-mockery. And here too one finds Garrett incorporating the innovations of his predecessors Sterne and Byron not only as an ironist but also in the technique of the convergence of the level of the narrator with that of the narrative —which, as we have seen, is Byronic, but is also one of the techniques in *Tristram Shandy,* where the real author, Sterne, is associated with the fictional one, Tristram, who, in turn, absorbs the function of one of the characters of his narrative, the dead Yorick.[20] But Garrett's experimentation with novel-writing in *Viagens* includes other fundamental aspects of Sterne, and to start with, one should consider the attitude of the writer towards his creation.

It will have become apparent in the chapter on Byronic influences that this question concerned Garrett right from the early days of *Dona Branca* onwards, and was expressed in references to the work itself alongside remarks and digressions on literature in general, and that this interest was pursued in *Viagens.* In all such points Garrett adopts, like Byron, the stance of a moralist. And, before proceeding any further, I must reintroduce the *caveat* of convergence in the analysis of influences at work in *Viagens.* However, it does seem correct to say that Garrett was attracted by Sterne's attempts at a novel form, in which the main objective was to examine the spontaneous act of creation of the book, with the active participation of the reader. Disruption of the structure, a new vocabulary, a full exploitation of punctuation and typographical signs coupled with the involvement of the reader were some of the techniques that Sterne experimented with to achieve his purpose, blazing a trail towards the modern novel.

Xavier de Maistre, who Garrett quotes in *Viagens* in the opening epigraph itself, as well as in the text, is one of the many who felt the challenge of Sterne's procedures, and it is not impossible that he should have led the Portuguese writer to Sterne, reinforcing the idea of a psychological journey. Be that as it may, it becomes clear from *Viagens* that Garrett read Sterne at first hand, and intelligently, and that he recreated those and other Sternean techniques in a talented and imaginative way. The result is that it is largely thanks to that background —no writing is done in the void— that *Viagens* achieves its prominent status in Portuguese romanticism, and that a modern Portuguese prose has come into being.

Among the most striking analogies between the two writers are such related matters as their attitude towards the reader and their supposed spontaneity, which are connected, in turn, with similarities in the spirit of exhibitionism and the cult of sensibility, with their humour, with the apparent haphazardness in the structure of the work and in the language itself.

Both Sterne and Garrett take pains, as I have said, to impress on the

---

[19] See Peter Conrad, *Shandyism. The Character of Romantic Irony* (Oxford, 1978), p. 106.
[20] Benjamin H. Lehman, 'Of Time, Personality, and the Author', in *Laurence Sterne. A Collection of Critical Essays,* edited by John Traugott, Twentieth Century Views (New Jersey, 1968), p. 32.

reader the casual nature of their creations. Thus, in the Prologue, Garrett insists that *Viagens* is 'Composta bem ao correr da pena' and that this, of all his works, 'é (...) talvez a que ele mais descuidadamente escreveu'.[21] The same wish to make the work appear as the result of the unguided, unchecked flow of thought and emotion emerges in the text of the book: 'Isto pensava, isto escrevo; isto tinha na alma, isto vai no papel: que doutro modo não sei escrever'.[22] Such lines reflect the artistic principle of casualness that dictates Tristram's 'Ask my pen —it governs me— I govern it not',[23] or 'I begin with writing the first sentence — and trusting to Almighty God for the second',[24] or again 'for I write in such a hurry, I have no time to recollect (...)'.[25] The instances in *Tristram Shandy* abound, and these remarks by Sterne and Garrett on their spontaneity are expressions of a common desire to elicit the reader's admiration: they stand as writers who rise above literary conventions and guidelines and are moved, unimpeded, by their creative instinct alone. Paradoxically, they resort to the artificiality of such remarks to impress its naturalness on the reader.

The narrator of *Tristram Shandy* makes ironical claims for talent and erudition, and the traveller of *A Sentimental Journey,* a man already assured of success, sets out to communicate with the reader as someone self-confident and civilized who cultivates sentiment as a source of moral and social improvement, as well as of enjoyment of life. Garrett reflects, to a certain extent, the attitude of both Tristram and Yorick the Sentimental Traveller. Thus, in the Prologue he presents himself as a public personality and as a fashionable figure in the literary and in the social world: it was pointed out earlier in the discussion of Byronic influences that such a depiction lent a cosmopolitan and sophisticated quality to the narrator of *Viagens;* but there is still another purpose in Garrett's self-eulogy, as a 'man of many parts'. A reflection of the combination of Tristram's exhibition of knowledge and of Yorick's stress on sentiment is found in the Prologue, where Garrett's erudition in the fields of art and science, old and modern, is complemented by qualities of the heart — an innate kindness and benevolence: 'e por fim de tudo, o natural indulgente e bom de um coração recto, puro (...)'. And all these faculties of heart and mind are reflected, not deliberately, but naturally, spontaneously, in the writings of Sterne and Garrett...

But their simulated spontaneity serves other purposes distinct from that of inflating the ego of the writer through the reader's admiration. It is consciously and carefully used to grasp the reality of the flow of thought and of the vagaries of sensibility in a liberated form, which breaks away from the conventions of narrative as observed by a Fielding or a Richardson. Sterne's spontaneity, associated with the chaotic form of *Tristram Shandy,* serves his purpose of startling the reader by exposing to him the mechanics

---

21 *Viagens,* pp. 3-4.
22 *Viagens,* Chapt. XXIX, p. 211.
23 *Tristram Shandy,* VI, vi, p. 403.
24 *Tristram Shandy,* VIII, ii, p. 516.
25 *Tristram Shandy,* I, xxi, p. 87.

8

of creation and involving him in the process.[26] Reflections of Sterne's disruption of the usual order in the narrative, which influenced Byron himself, are found in *Viagens*. Thus the dislocation of the Preface, which only appears in Chapter II, can be regarded as an analogy to Tristram's postponement of his own to Volume III, xx. Another striking instance of Sternean disruption and suspension is the way in which Garrett interrupts the tale of Carlos and Joaninha in Chapter XXVI:

—«Porquê? já se acabou a história de Carlos e de Joaninha?» diz talvez a amável leitora.
—«Não, minha senhora», responde o autor mui lisonjeado da pergunta: «não, minha senhora, a história não se acabou, quase se pode dizer que ainda ela agora começa: mas houve mutação de cena. Vamos a Santarém, que lá se passa o segundo acto.» [27]

and in Chapter XXXI:

Entraremos portanto em novo capítulo, leitor amigo; e agora não tenhas medo das minhas digressões fatais, nem das interrupções a que sou sujeito. Irá direita e corrente a história da nossa Joaninha até que a terminemos... em bem ou em mal? [28]

In fact —as is sometimes the case with Tristram— Garrett disregards his repeated promises, and he does not resume the tale until Chapter XXXII. In the above quotations one can see the association of suspension with the Sternean technique of dialogue with the reader and his involvement in the unravelling of the plot. The first quotation provides us with an example of the presentation of the narrative in theatrical terms — a feature of Sterne's bent towards dramatization that may well have appealed to Garrett. This instance of direct reference to the stage in *Viagens* has a few correlatives in *Tristram Shandy*, as 'in the chapter following (...), you shall step with me, behind the curtain, only to hear in what manner my father (...)',[29] or:

I beg the reader will assist me here, to wheel off my uncle Toby's ordnance behind the scenes, — to remove his sentrybox, and clear the theatre, *if possible*, of horn-works (...); — that done, my dear friend Garrick, we'll snuff the candles bright, — sweep the stage with a new broom, — draw up the curtain, and exhibit my uncle Toby dressed in a new character (...) [30]

The recourse to the technique of drama as shown above is yet another aspect of the process of involvement of the reader in the act of creation, in a deliberate breach of the convention of suspension of disbelief. It can also be seen as part of a common desire to present events not in reported form, but in their unfolding in the present. It is in the process of concurrent

---

[26] See Viktor Shklovsky, 'A Parodying Novel: Sterne's *Tristram Shandy*', in *Laurence Sterne. A Collection of Critical Essays*, edited by John Traugott, pp. 66-89.
[27] *Viagens*, Chapt. XXVII, p. 198.
[28] *Viagens*, Chapt. XXXI, p. 226.
[29] *Tristram Shandy*, XV, xvi, p. 420.
[30] *Tristram Shandy*, VI, xxix, p. 438. The examples are numerous; see also, for instance, IV, viii, p. 280, or II, xix, p. 159.

actions with time-shifts that Sterne can be considered the predecessor of the contrapuntal technique of the modern novel [31] and it is by learning this lesson, among others, from Sterne, that Garrett achieves modernity in Portuguese literature with *Viagens*. Though he does not adhere strictly to a dramatization of the tale of Joaninha —see for instance the reported flashback on Frei Diniz in Chapter XV—, Garrett resorts largely to a technique that is analogous to that of *Tristram Shandy,* when he causes the concurrent plots of the narrator's journey and of the love tale to break into each other in a number of deliberate interruptions, in temporal cross-sections which have their model in Sterne. Just as Tristram reassures the reader that the conversation on the staircase is not going to last as long as the previous one, or asks him 'to sit down upon a set' (of volumes) while he takes his time to digress, Garrett, too, keeps his reader waiting while he moves off in commentary:

> Benévolo e paciente leitor (...) acabemos com estas digressões e perenais divaga-ções minhas. Bem te vejo que te deixei parado à minha espera no meio da ponte da Asseca. Perdoa-me por quem és, dêmos de espora às mulinhas e vamos que são horas.[32]

And, like Tristram, the narrator in *Viagens* sets out to draw the reader's attention to such suspensions and interruptions. Thus he himself remarks on the maze of details and digressions in Chapter XXXII, when he is about to pick up the story interrupted seven chapters earlier:

> (...) não é que se quebre, mas enreda-se o fio das histórias e das observações por tal modo, que, bem o vejo e o sinto, só com muita paciência se pode deslindar e seguir em tão embaraçada meada.
> Vamos pois com paciência, caro leitor; farei por ser breve e ir direito quanto eu puder.[33]

This brings to mind Tristram's constant struggle with more material than he can cope with, which causes him to keep putting off the beginning of a promised tale, picking up threads of a story only to drop them again, and to write the 25th chapter of Volume IX before the 18th. No less striking a parallel is found at the end of Chapter IV of *Viagens,* where Garrett, imitating Sterne's advice to readers who are not curious to *skip* the end of a chapter, writes:

> A minha opinião sincera e *conscienciosa* é que o leitor deve saltar estas folhas, e passar ao capítulo seguinte, que é outra casta de capítulo.

This comes very close to being a translation of the lines in *Tristram Shandy*:

> To such, however, as do not choose to go so far back into these things, I can give no better advice than that they skip over the remaining part of this

---

[31] A. A. Mendilow, 'The Revolt in Sterne', in *Laurence Sterne. A Collection of Critical Essays,* edited by John Traugott, pp. 90-107.
[32] *Viagens,* Chapt. IX, p. 69.
[33] *Viagens,* Chapt. XXXII, p. 228.

Chapter; for I declare beforehand, 'tis wrote only for the curious and inquisitive.[34]

In the direct address to the reader, too, Garrett can be said to follow the Sternean manner, rather than the technique that was current in the eighteenth century. Sterne not only addresses the reader but establishes a stronger impression of intimacy by drawing him into a dialogue, revealing his devices, as seen above, and involving him in the act of creation; and time and time again a similar technique is to be found in *Viagens,* where the reader is explicitly made a participant in the development of the work. Thus, for example, Garrett involves the reader in a discussion on the discovery of the birth of a new love and the fading away of a prior bond, in an analysis that bears the hallmark of Sterne's sentimentalism, that is to say, in an analysis in which the reader is invited to compare his own feelings with those of the character, and, through that process, to feel sympathy and understanding for him.[35] The passage in question, on Carlos's fluctuations of feeling, is parallel to a previous one on the author's own vagaries of heart, discussed earlier on, and can therefore be read as an oblique form of the convergence of author and hero that has already been defined as Sternean-Byronian. It is too long for a complete quotation, but the following excerpt should suffice to show how Garrett masters the Sternean procedure of literary creation with the sentimental participation of the reader:

> O que lhe ela fora, assaz to tenho explicado, leitor amigo e benévolo: o que ela lhe será... Podes tu, leitor cândido e sincero —aos hipócritas não falo eu— podes tu dizer-me o que há-de ser amanhã no teu coração a mulher que hoje sòmente achas bela, ou gentil, ou interessante?
> Podes responder-me da parte que tomará amanhã na tua existência a imagem da donzela que hoje contemplas com olhos de artista (...)?
> E quando vier, se vier, esse fatal dia de amanhã, responder-me-ás também da parte que ficará tendo em tua alma essoutra imagem que lá estava antes e que, ao reflexo desta agora, daqui observo que vai empalidecendo, descorando... já lhe não vejo senão os lineamentos vagos... já é uma sombra do que foi (...)
> Leitor amigo e benévolo, caro leitor meu indulgente, não acuses, não julgues à pressa o meu pobre Carlos; e lembra-te daquela pedra que o Filho de Deus mandou levantar à primeira mão que se achasse inocente (...)
> (...) Chamava-se Georgina; e é tudo quanto por agora pode dizer-vos, ó curiosas leitoras, o discreto historiador deste mui verídico sucesso.[36]

The tone of Sterne's addresses to the reader —addresses which are frequent in *Tristram Shandy* but altogether absent from *A Sentimental Journey*— ranges from the conventionally impersonal or courteous to rebuke or near abuse, by way of mild flirtation and humour. Instances of this gamut are provided in Volume III, xxiii, p. 215, in 'What would your

---

[34] *Tristram Shandy,* I, iv, p. 38.
[35] John Traugott, 'Introduction', *Laurence Sterne. A Collection of Critical Essays,* p. 4.
[36] *Viagens,* Chapt. XXII, pp. 164-5.

worships have me to do in this case?'; or in Volume I, xviii, pp. 76-7, in the dialogue with 'the fair reader' on the delicious sentiment that mixes in the friendship between the sexes; or Chapter xx of the same volume, p. 82, in the dialogue beginning 'How could you, Madam, be so inattentive in reading the last chapter?' in which Tristram punishes the reader for her superficiality and makes her start the whole chapter all over again; or in the abrupt chiding in Volume III, xxxvi, p. 232, 'Read, read, read, my unlearned reader! read, — or (...) I tell you (...) you had better throw down the book at once (...)'. In *Viagens* the fully developed dialogue with the reader occurs only a few times in the passages on the oscillation between old and new love, or at the end of Chapter XXVI, p. 198, all of which were discussed above. But on the whole Garrett achieves the effect of a two-way dialogue through questions, exclamations and other devices of lively, direct speech, and his attitude to the reader closely reflects Tristram's, in examples like the following: 'Mas senhores, ponderem, venham cá: o que há-de um homem fazer?', [37] which may be compared to the first of Sterne's, quoted above; the admonishing 'espero que o leitor entendesse agora. Tomarei cuidado de lho lembrar de vez em quando, porque receio muito que se esqueça'; [38] or the more truculent 'cuidas que vamos estudar a história, a natureza (...)? Não seja pateta, senhor leitor, nem cuide que o somos (...)'.[39] Humour, too, is a tone used by Sterne and by Garrett in their dialogue with the reader, when referring half seriously and half jestingly to their scholarship, which they regard in an ironical light, as they do love. Thus the narrator in *Viagens* solemnly addresses the reader 'Saiba pois o leitor contemporâneo, e saiba a posteridade, para cuja instrução principalmente escrevo este douto livro (...)', just as Tristram warns him that 'without *much reading*, by which your reverence knows I mean without much knowledge it would not be possible to penetrate the moral of the next marbled page'.[40] The addresses in *Viagens* serve wider purposes than Tristram's: they also serve those of Yorick the traveller (though his methods are different), as was shown in the quotation of Chapter XXII above, which is to involve the reader sentimentally, to ask for his sympathetic participation.

While bearing in mind the fact that Addison and Byron are models followed by Garrett in the development of a conversational style of his own, what has been said in the present chapter about the dialogue with the reader and his share in the creation of the work places *Viagens* firmly in the Sternean tradition. Tristram's definition of his own composition could well be Garrett's motto:

> Writing (...) is but a different name for conversation (...) no author, who understood the just boundaries of decorum and good breeding, would presume to think all: The truest respect which you can pay to the reader's understanding is to halve the matter amicably, and leave him something to imagine, in his turn, as well as yourself.[41]

[37] *Viagens*, Chapt. VI, p. 43.
[38] *Viagens*, Chapt. II, p. 18.
[39] *Viagens*, Chapt. V, p. 34.
[40] *Tristram Shandy*, III, xxxvi, p. 232.
[41] *Tristram Shandy*, XX, xi, p. 127.

Furthermore, an explicit reference to some of the graphic devices of *Tristram Shandy* reveals Garrett's appreciation of Sterne's individualistic search for expressiveness in literature, which includes the representation of silence: [42]

> Onde a crónica se cala e a tradição não fala, antes quero uma página inteira de pontinhos, ou toda branca — ou toda preta, como na venerável história do nosso particular e respeitável amigo Tristão [sic] Shandy, do que só uma linha da invenção do croniqueiro.[43]

In practice, though without going to the extremes of fantasy displayed in *Tristram Shandy* and which are largely discarded in *A Sentimental Journey*, Garrett presents striking resemblances with Sterne in matters of punctuation and typographic presentation. Thus the use of the blanks between the paragraphs —like the early editions of the *Journey*—, the dotted lines, the colon and, above all, the dash, alone or combined with the colon and the semi-colon, to avoid the abruptness of a full stop, and marking pauses of different length, show Garrett engaged in an exploration of the means of expressiveness and communication afforded by the printed page that cannot but be related to Sterne. Punctuation and typographical devices play an eminent role in the fulfillment of their common aim: the shaping of a new language that conveys the accents and inflexions of the spoken word, and which is a sensitive tool for the analysis of emotion —the birth of a feeling, its subtle gradations— as well as of the process of thought in its unfolding. Ernesto Da Cal ascribes the revolution of punctuation in Portuguese prose to Eça de Queirós, but Prado Coelho has argued for Garrett's originality in this respect [44] — and it is more than likely that Sterne should have been the inspiration for the seminal breakthrough in *Viagens*. One innovatory aspect of punctuation that Prado Coelho claims as Garrett's, and not Eça's, is the frequent use of the conjunction *e* after a full stop, and he quotes the example

> De tanto não somos capazes nós. / E por isso admiramos tanto. / E perdoamos tanto. / E esquecemos tanto.[45]

A similar recurrent usage of the copulative *and* is to be found in Sterne, who may start not only a paragraph, but even a chapter in that way.[46] In view of the analogies already established it is not impossible that this stylistic feature of *Viagens*, too, should have been reinforced, if not prompted, by the reading of Sterne.

In both writers the effects of the disruption in punctuation are emphasized by a disruption in syntax, and the result is a prose that makes considerable demands on the reader's attention. This is more pronounced

---

[42] P. Conrad, p. 106.
[43] *Viagens*, Chapt. XLI, p. 292.
[44] 'Garrett prosador', note 1, p. 90. For a comparative study of the styles of Garrett and Eça see also Augusto da Costa Dias's Introduction to *Viagens*, pp. XLVII-LXIV.
[45] *Viagens*, Chapt. XXXV, p. 251.
[46] See for instance *Tristram Shandy*, IX, xxiv, p. 598, or IX, xxviii, p. 608.

in Sterne than in Garrett, and particularly true of the staccato style in *Tristram Shandy;* in the *Journey* the rhythm is much smoother and the language free from the eccentricities of the preceding work, but still the short broken sentences give the reader the impression that the focus of Sterne's interest flits about from one object to another far more quickly than Garrett's. Yet *Viagens* is clearly written in an oral style —an expert working out of devices to create the impression of the abolition of literature— a supple style that follows the poetics of spontaneity. 'Estilo solto, desarticulado, vibrátil' is how Prado Coelho qualifies it; [47] and, in a study on Eça, António Sérgio emphasizes the place of precedence that must be given to Garrett in the forging of modern Portuguese literature:

> Entre nós, o diálogo natural quem o criou foi o Garrett, pelo menos, o diálogo natural em português moderno. Aliás, a prosa do Garrett, ainda fora do diálogo, tem o dom de naturalidade do falar comum — com o ziguezague, o erradio, o modismo, o imprevisto, assim como nas *Viagens na minha terra* (...) [48]

Difficult as it is to establish stylistic comparisons in two languages as different as Portuguese and English, one cannot fail to be struck by the fact that the critics of Sterne and Garrett stress exactly the same features in their independent studies of these writers.

In *Viagens* as in *Tristram Shandy* the broken style is largely based on curt and loose periods, with abundant questions —often cumulative and addressed to the reader— as well as inversions of word order, frequent exclamations and points of suspension: in both works it contrasts with the Ciceronian period, with a variety of syntactic constructions. Profuse figures of speech like parenthesis, digression, repetition, paradox, antithesis and ellipsis, combined with aposiopesis and the dash are yet other features that *Viagens* has in common with Sterne, particularly with *Tristram Shandy*. Attempting to register the flow of thought by using the anti-Ciceronian style was not unique, but whereas most other writers before him have applied it to the portrayal of the authorial mind, Sterne employs it in relation to his characters [49] — and Garrett's analyses of Carlos's emotions, like the admirable passage characterised by Sérgio as 'conversa de Carlos com os seus botões', in Chapter XXIII, show him mastering the depiction of fragmented thought and emotion in true Sternean tradition.

In both works —and, once again, this is true to a greater extent in *Tristram* than in *Viagens*—, the preoccupation with expressiveness is not restricted to punctuation and to syntax alone, but extends to a highly imaginative use of vocabulary, with certain common traits. Among the most prominent are rich and picturesque vocabulary, abundant use of archaisms and neologisms, frequent Greek and Latin words and quotations, original metaphors. In Garrett's more sober, discreet and rhythmic prose,

---

[47] 'Garrett prosador', p. 87.
[48] António Sérgio, *Livro do centenário de Eça de Queiroz*, edited by L. M. Pereira and C. Reys (Lisboa, 1945), pp. 449-59 (p. 451).
[49] J. M. Stedmont, *The Comic Art of L. Sterne* (Toronto, 1967), p. 37.

the stimulus provided by *Tristram Shandy* can be seen in the creation of humour by means of lists of words, though they are never as long as Sterne's, like 'arraial de caleças, de machinhos, de burros e de arrieiros' (p. 18) and in rhyme effects, as in 'tanta degradação e derrogação!' (p. 19), 'os aperfeiçoadores, reparadores, fomentadores e demolidores das futuras civilizações' (p. 261), or 'uma roseirinha pequenina, bonitinha, que morreu, coitadinha!' (p. 25). Affinities with Sterne are particularly obvious in

> Francamente me confesso de sonâmbulo, de soníloquo, de... Não, fica melhor com seu ar de grego (hoje tenho a bossa helénica num estado de tumescência pasmosa!); digamos sonílogo, sonígrafo...[50]

or in the sentence that reminds one of Tristram's 'dioptrical beehive': [51] 'Volto já da digressão filológica: tornemos à óptica e à catóptrica'.[52] Such examples show Garrett juggling with words in ways that are also found in *Tristram Shandy*, creating humour through a combined scheme of word formation, or of rhyme with a display of learned and technical words, real or invented. Compare with:

> (...) for it was obstetrical, — *scrip*-tical, squirtical, papistical, — and as far as the coach-horse was concerned in it, — caball-istical — and only partly musical [53]

or with

> (...) our knowledge physical, metaphysical, physiological, polemical, nautical, mathematical, enigmatical, technical, biographical, romantical, chemical, and obstetrical, with fifty other branches of it (most of 'em ending as these do, in *ical*) have (...) been creeping up upwards towards that Αχμή of their perfections (...) [54]

In his lists of learned scientific terms, as well as in the use of Greek and Latin words and quotations, which, printed in Greek characters and in italics, are also used with an eye to typographical presentation, Garrett, like Tristram, introduces humour in a dual process of exhibition of erudition and simultaneous mockery of it — a ridicule of scholarship when it becomes formalism and pedantry. The comic intention is unmistakable in the following:

> e — *si parva licet componere magnis* (a bossa proeminente hoje é a latina) (...) [55]

> chamai-lhe *hoc*, chamai-lhe *hic*, chamai-lhe o *hic haec hoc* todo inteiro, se vos dá gosto... que em poucos anos veremos o estado de *acetato* a que há-de ficar reduzido o vosso carácter nacional.[56]

---

50 *Viagens*, Chapt. IV, p. 32.
51 *Tristram Shandy*, I, xv, p. 66.
52 *Viagens*, Chapt. XXXVIII, p. 276.
53 *Tristram Shandy*, III, viii, p. 178.
54 *Tristram Shandy*, I, xxi, p. 88.
55 *Viagens*, Chapt. VI, p. 41.
56 *Viagens*, Chapt. VII, pp. 54-5.

Native and foreign words, as well as neologisms — part of which are anglicisms and gallicisms— are also printed in italics, for emphasis, for irony, or in order to enhance the pose of cosmopolitan and intellectual affectation that he shares, respectively, with Yorick and with Tristram. *Parlour, étagère, ancle, stage, flirt, flartar* and *cru* (from the syntagm *raw weather*) appear in Carlos's letter, which, as one may recall, deals with his apprenticeship in English sophistication and etiquette; other examples, not in italics, but nonetheless revealing of Carlos's cosmopolitan-ism, can be gleaned from his epistle, like 'Inn' —which Garrett is careful to translate—, 'shake-hands' [sic], or the anglicism 'muito de mais', from the English 'much too much'.[57] The variety of the prose of *Viagens,* as of *Tristram Shandy,* is further increased by a number of lexical and syntactic archaisms, as well as fresh similes and metaphors — often used as a device for humour and expressiveness, as in 'Muitas hecatombes de mirmidões caíram no holocausto', referring to the mosquitoes drowning in the lemonade.[58] Such metaphors may appear in Garrett's description of gesture or posture, as so often happens in *Tristram Shandy,* with a comic effect: 'Bifurquei-me resignadamente sobre o cilício do esfarrapado albardão',[59] or 'o garbo teso e aprumado da perpendicular *miss* inglesa que parece fundida de uma só peça'.[60] The second example immediately brings to mind Trim's attitude when he is about to read Yorick's sermon: he stood '— stiff, — perpendicular —'.[61] Reinforcing the hypothesis that Garrett may have been stimulated by *Tristram Shandy* in his epithets, is the fact that here Garrett, like Sterne, is creating humour by presenting people in geometrical terms. But neither the metaphor nor the rare pun in *Viagens* —except for the mildly improper reference to Abelard[62]— bear the innuendos of indecency or obscenity that play such a large role in the humour of *Tristram Shandy.*

From what has been said above it seems possible to conclude that in *Viagens* Garrett adopts a number of the characteristic features of Sterne's style, particularly in *Tristram Shandy,* though avoiding its extremes. Roughly speaking, they seem to occur more often in the initial chapters, from I to XIII, in Chapters XXII-XXIII and the beginning of Chapter XXXII, as well as in Carlos's letter — that is to say, when Garrett puts on Tristram's pose of erudition and ridicules it, and when he analyses, like a true sentimentalist, the most subtle nuances of feeling.

Tristram Shandy also seems to have been a stimulus to Garrett when he associates in a single passage of *Viagens* ideas that appear in a fragmented form in different chapters of Sterne's book. In Vol. I, xx, p. 83,

---

[57] For foreign words, neologisms and archaisms, see J. Prado Coelho, 'Garrett Prosador', in *A letra e o leitor.*
[58] *Viagens,* Chapt. VII, p. 53.
[59] *Viagens,* Chapt. V, p. 37.
[60] *Viagens,* Chapt. XII, p. 85.
[61] *Tristram Shandy,* Vol. II, xvii, p. 138. According to the SOED the earliest recorded use of 'perpendicular' in a jocose sense to mean 'in a standing position' occurs in 1768; in fact, it appears that Sterne employs it in that way in 1759-67 (publ. of *T. S.*) and that that is the source of Garrett's borrowing.
[62] *Viagens,* Chapt. XII, p. 196.

Tristram warns the reader against the common malpractice of reading hurriedly for the sake of the plot, rather than of the 'deep erudition and knowledge' which his book, if properly read, would convey. Earlier on, in Vol. I, iv, pp. 37-8, he decides to let the readers 'into the whole secret from first to last', and justifies the need to consult all of them as a consequence of the wide appeal that his work will have:

> (...) As my life and opinions are likely to make some noise in the world, and, if I conjecture right, will take in all ranks, professions, and denominations of men whatever —be no less read than the *Pilgrim's Progress* itself—, and in the end, prove the very thing which Montaigne dreaded his essays should turn out, that is, a book for a parlour-window (...)

The matter of erudition is taken up in Vol. II, ii, pp. 106-7. Tristram writes as a man of erudition, he says, and 'even my similes, my illustrations, my metaphors, are erudite (...)'; this is followed by a paragraph on Locke's *Essay upon the Human Understanding*, 'a history-book (...) of what passes in a man's own mind', as he explains for the sake of those who have not read the book, or of those who 'have read it who understand it not'. A reading of the first two pages of Chapter II of *Viagens* suggests that these different passages were at work in Garrett's mind, consciously or not; some of these ideas appear as clear stimuli in Garrett's prose, others as more tenuous and indirect, but they are nonetheless recognizable in their allusions. Like Sterne, Garrett impresses ironically on the reader the fact that *Viagens* is a work of great knowledge, a masterpiece, 'uma obra prima, erudita, brilhante de pensamentos novos, uma coisa digna do século'; and after warning the reader about its merits, so that they might not be overlooked, Garrett, like Sterne, proceeds to let him into the secret of what it is about, contrasting the serious nature of the book with the light matter of French publications —he lifts the veil and explains that *Viagens* is 'uma coisa séria, grave, pensada como um livro novo da feira de Leipzig, não das tais brochurinhas de Paris'; all this is followed by a reference to a philosopher who wrote on the march of the intellect— 'o que diríamos, para nos entendermos todos melhor, o *Progresso*'. The elements of Sterne's passages are all there: the serious erudition of the work, its popularity, the fear that it might not be duly appreciated by the hasty reader, the need to disclose to him the real substance of the work and to explain it to him lest it might not be understood, the allusion to French books and to a philosopher; even the words *Progress* and the reference to man's intellectual process are brought in. Through the combination of these elements from Sterne with other ideas, some of them received —like the traditional opposition of Quixote and Sancho Panza, and their correlative, spiritualism versus materialism— and others that are the outcome of his own experience, Garrett writes the personal and original first pages of Chapter II, which contain the programme of *Viagens*.

As was said earlier in the chapter, *Viagens,* as a travel book, can be placed in the tradition of Sterne and Byron. The stimuli provided by both are sometimes combined, as was shown in the discussion of Garrett's comments on Yorick's creed of constant love. This phenomenon also occurs in the description of the town of Cartaxo, done in the Byronian manner, where the reference to Burgundy wines brings to mind Yorick's digression on the subject, at the outset of his journey. On the whole, the link between the manner of *Viagens* and that of *A Sentimental Journey* as travelbooks consists in the humorous way in which Garrett deals with some of the incidents *en route*, like the contests of merit between *ilhavos* and *campinos*, or the choice of conveyance in Chapter II. But from this it should not be inferred that Garrett lends to the treatment of such subjects the variety of tone that is found in Sterne: — the pathos and the sentiment that evoke a tear and a smile, and the humour derived from equivocal utterances, or from the ambiguous situations in which the Sentimental Traveller finds himself are absent from *Viagens*. With the exception of the passage in Chapter II, in which the narrator is confronted with the unattractive prospect of having to ride a lean mule rather than travel in a confortable caleche,[63] Garrett does not place himself in the frequent situations of vexation, in which the protagonist views himself as ludicrous. Yet this episode should be mentioned as a single instance in which Garrett practises this particular kind of Sternean humour. In it is to be found a combination of devices and attitudes that point to Sterne: the irony created in the description of an unimportant event in exaggerated, elevated terms of pomp and circumstance, the detail, the repeated rhymes, the interrogatory, exclamatory style, the punctuation — all inviting the reader to laugh at and with the narrator, in a laughter that is sympathetic rather than derisive:

> Togados manes dos antigos desembargadores, venerandas cabeleiras de anéis e castanholas, que direis, ó respeitadas sombras, se desse limbo onde estais esperando pela ressurreição do Pegas [sic] ... e do livro quinto — vedes este degenerado e espúrio sucessor vosso, em calças largas, fraque verde, chapéu branco, gravata de cor, chicotinho de cauchu na mão, pronto a cavalgar em mulinha de Palito métrico como um garraio estudantinho do segundo ano, e deitando olhos invejosos para esse natural, próprio e adscritício modo de condução desembargatória? Oh que direis vós! Com que justo desprezo não olhareis para tanta degradação e derrogação![64]

Again, unlike Yorick, who disregards monuments and objects of art to concentrate instead on the 'nakedness of the heart', Garrett, as shown earlier, not only visits them but does so until exhaustion sets in. But this is done in a way that bears no relation to the ordinary travelogue, as he insists in a paragraph in which he addresses the reader, like Tristram, and which is reminiscent of Tristram's style, after having affirmed the spontaneity of his writing:

> Muito me pesa, leitor amigo, se outra coisa esperavas das minhas VIAGENS, se te falto, sem o querer, a promessas que julgaste ver nesse título, mas que eu não fiz decerto. Querias talvez que te contasse, marco a marco, as léguas da estrada? palmo a palmo, as alturas e as larguras dos edifícios? algarismo por

---

63 *Viagens,* Chapt. II, p. 19.
64 Ibidem.

algarismo, as datas de sua fundação? que te resumisse a história de cada pedra, de cada ruína?

Vai-te ao padre Vasconcelos (...) [65]

A mitigated Sternean presence is found in the novel *O arco de Sant' Ana — Crónica do Porto,* published two years after *Viagens,* in such features as the colloquial manner and the attitude towards the reader. Once again the narrator sets out to win his sympathy and engages him in a dialogue meant to make him share his role of invisible observer of an action often presented in theatrical terms — a technique that enhances the dramatic structure of *O arco,* which may be roughly described as a sequence of scenes and which has been discussed in connection with Walter Scott. Thus Garrett writes in a way that is reminiscent of Tristram:

> Deixá-lo, deixá-lo e transportemo-nos nós, amigo leitor, para mui diverso posto que não mui apartado lugar. Façamos, com a rapidez com que em um teatro britânico se faz, a nossa mutação de cena; e deixar gemer as unidades de Aristóteles, que ninguém desta vez lhe acode.[66]

The variety of tone in Tristram's addresses to the reader, repeatedly recaptured by Garrett in *Viagens,* is replaced in *O arco* by a consistently courteous and friendly manner, established from the start with the heading *Ao leitor benévolo* to the Preface of the first edition and kept throughout the work. Indeed, whereas the reader was occasionally chided or dealt with in an abrupt fashion in *Viagens,* one finds in *O arco* that it is the narrator who is humorously rebuked for neglecting one of his heroines for too long:

> E Aninhas? (...) Que é feito dela, senhor historiador? Deixa-se assim por tanto tempo nas asquerosas enxovias de uma prisão a bela rapariga (...)? E passam-se capítulos e capítulos —o qual mais pequeno, é verdade, mas são muitos— sem nos dizer o descuidado cronista o que é feito dela? [67]

In fact, the relationship between narrator and reader evolves from *Viagens* to *O arco* towards greater identification: there is the suggestion that the reader is not only expected to act like the narrator, accompanying him up the staircase and through the Bishop's palace to peep through a door,[68] or watching the meeting of the burghers with their councillors from a gallery,[69] but also that he is expected to feel like him, sharing his concern and his feelings for the characters. Empathy is explicitly sought after, as well as sympathy, and the use of the possessive *nosso,* with its suggestions of affection and familiarity, paves the way for it, as can be seen from the following example:

> (...) e Vasco entrou em casa da nossa boa Gertrudinhas, de quem te confesso, amigo leitor, que já tenho saudades. Se te sucederá o mesmo?

65 *Viagens,* Chapt. XXIX, p. 211.
66 *O arco,* Chapt. III, O. A. G., Vol. 1, p. 238.
67 *O arco,* Chapt. XXVI, O. A. G., Vol. 1, p. 328.
68 *O arco,* Chapt. III, O. A. G., Vol. 1, p. 239.
69 *O arco,* Chapt. XXXII, O. A. G., Vol. 1, p. 357.

A ser assim, perto estamos de as matar, as tais saudades, porque no capítulo seguinte vamos entrar em sua casa também nós (...) [70]

On the whole one has the impression that, after the conscious experiments in *Viagens,* Sterne's presence in *O arco* is more general than specific, in all respects including language. A humorous and ironic conversational manner is maintained throughout the work, but without any of the idiosyncrasies or juggling with words of *Viagens.* One feels tempted to see in the greater sobriety of language, in its homogeneity and its smoother flow in *O arco,* in comparison with *Viagens,* a parallel with the evolution in style between *Tristram* and *A Sentimental Journey.*

The stylistic analogies that have been discussed by no means exhaust the diversity of style of *Viagens* — the verbal and structural elements of popular language, the innovatory quality of adjectives, or its poetic rhythm and quality, illustrated by Prado Coelho in his study of Garrett's prose, for instance, are nowhere to be found in Sterne. A study of Garrett's language would perforce show a wealth of riches that are totally independent of the English writer. Even in the affinities pointed out in this chapter it is necessary to remember that Sterne himself was part of a tradition, and in the debt of writers that Garrett also knew, like Rabelais and Cervantes.

Yet there must be no doubt that Sterne was ultimately one of Garrett's greatest models in the oral quality of his narrative and in the naturalness of his dialogue — lasting achievements which make of Garrett one of the most distinguished and seminal Portuguese writers. But Sterne, for Garrett, was more than a master of communication through words and non-verbal devices and of the portrayal of fragmented thought and emotion. He was also a master of depicting actions in counterpoint, of the paradoxical art of spontaneous creation whilst simultaneously revealing the artifice of creation, of conveying order under the semblance of chaos — of modernity in fiction. All in all, what Sterne showed to Garrett was liberation — liberation from linguistic and literary conventions, as well as from accepted values in life: love, learning, one's own self were not to be taken in deadly seriousness, but were to be refreshingly viewed in their duality, precious and yet at the same time ludicrous. The sustained parody in Sterne is part of an ironical, gently humorous acceptance of life which underlies his work — and Garrett, an ironist himself, senses this deeper significance and makes it his own.

[70] *O arco,* Chapt. XXII, O. A. G., Vol. 1, p. 310.

VI

SHAKESPEARE

Given Garrett's interest in English literature and the importance of Shakespeare in the Romantic movement, one would expect to find the English poet playing in his literary evolution a role comparable to those of Byron and Scott, with their wide and immediate repercussions. Shakespeare, as has been seen, was not unknown among the Portuguese pre-romantics. Yet the first references to him in Garrett's work —Preface to the first edition of *Catão* in 1822 and the accompanying *Carta a um amigo*— show no enthusiasm. Whether or not he had read him in the original, it is clear that he likes Shakespeare in the manner of his French contemporaries, that is to say, in the versions of Ducis, which were emasculated and expurgated adaptations rather than translations. As Van Tieghem writes,[1] Ducis simplifies the action and reduces the number of characters, transforms the catastrophe so as to obtain an edifying end, replaces the rich and varied language by monotonous, abstract and elevated verse, deprives the characters of their individual traits, turning them into flat, insipid figures, and suppresses the contrast in moods; the result is a stripping off of all the originality, depth and vigour of Shakespeare's plays, sacrificed to tame conventions in morals and literary taste. It is to such productions that young Garrett pays homage in 'Carta a um amigo', where he presents Ducis's *Othello* and *King Lear,* and not Shakespeare's, as examples of great art. A fragment from the same period in *Esp.*, MS 34,[2] corroborates this preference: the first twenty-four lines of a tragedy entitled *Othello* show that what Garrett proposed to adapt or to translate into Portuguese was not Shakespeare, but his admired Ducis.[3] The very choice of Addison as a model for *Catão* indicates how far Garrett is in 1822 from adhering to a Shakespearian concept of the theatre, and this is manifest in the prefatory writings to the play. Except for a quotation from Schlegel, there is no direct reference to Shakespeare himself, and when Garrett alludes to him, in connection with the Romantic genre, he does so in terms of qualified praise, which were not even his own, but were to be found in the majority of literary manuals, as he admits:

---

[1] P. Van Tieghem, pp. 117-18.
[2] O. P. Monteiro, Vol. I, p. 432.
[3] Fidelino de Figueiredo, *Shakespeare e Garrett*, pp. 23-4, and A. Crabbé Rocha, pp. 203-4.

O género romântico, filho de Shakespeare (...) suposto irregular e informe, tem contudo belezas próprias e particulares que só nele se acham.[4]

>tem grandes defeitos, mas grandes formosuras: falta-lhe a beleza da simplicidade e regular elegância, mas sobeja-lhe a do ornato e enfeites ingénuos, conquanto demasiados.[5]

In Ducis's adaptation of *Othello* the drama of jealousy is replaced by the tragedy of a disobedient daughter, and the author offers two alternative endings — the heroine is killed by her husband with a dagger (which is more elevated than being stifled with a pillow), or else her death is avoided by a timely explanation.[6] The playing down of violence, its dignification by the choice of a less prosaic instrument than a pillow and the propriety of avoiding the theme of marital infidelity in Ducis's adaptation all stem from a sense of decorum, which is shared by Garrett, and which is manifest in the amusing and light-hearted verses on Shakespeare and his *Othello* that he publishes in *O Toucador:*

>Ver agora sem vergonha
>O tal Inglês malcriado
>Jogar chalaça de arrieiro
>Sobre o trágico tablado!
>
>Ouvir o ladrão de um preto
>A bela infeliz amante
>Dizer finezas de Alfama
>Em linguagem de estudante!
>
>Ver o heroi, ardendo em zelos
>Mais negros que a sua cara,
>Afogar com um travesseiro
>A inocente a quem roubara!
>
>Se isto em inglês é beleza
>De expressão e de energia,
>Entre nós, os Portugueses,
>É nojenta porcaria.[7]

The lines that precede —'contentemo-nos de admirar o imortal Shakespeare, mas não o louvemos'— are yet another illustration of the difficulty in appreciating Shakespeare that he evinces in *Catão*. Eight years later, in the London edition of this play, when Garrett has finally ceased to subscribe to the concept of ideal beauty, when he had already written *Camões, D. Branca, Adosinda,* when he had progressed enough to view the classic versus Romantic antinomy as an opposition of art versus nature, he still refers to Shakespeare in somewhat lukewarm terms:

>nem caminhando de olhos fechados pelo estreito e alinhado carreiro de Racine —nem desvairando à toa pelas incultas devesas de Shakespeare—,

---

[4] Preface to the first edition of *Catão*, O. A. G., Vol. 2, p. 1610.
[5] *Carta a um amigo*, O. A. G., Vol. 2, p. 1624.
[6] P. Van Tieghem, p. 118.
[7] *O Toucador*, in Teatro, V.

procurou o autor conciliar (...) a verdadeira e bela natureza com a verdadeira e boa arte.[8]

There is a reserve in Garrett's acceptance of Shakespeare, in this text of 1830, that stands in marked contrast with his enthusiastic and immediate adhesion to Byron and Scott. The three were among the writers he 'discovered' during his stay with the Hadleys, and Shakespeare is the one he singles out when he digresses, in *Viagens,* on the effect of reading a work 'in loco', in the scenery that inspired it: 'Nunca tinha entendido Shakespeare enquanto o não li em Warwick ao pé do Avon'.[9] And yet in his work the external signs of his conversion to Shakespeare are few, in comparison with those of the two contemporary poets.

In his study *Shakespeare e Garrett* Fidelino de Figueiredo proposes to recognize Shakespearian influences in a certain number of points in *Camões.*[10] Thus he draws attention to the association of reminiscences of an English twilight with the death of Juliet, in Canto I, xv, which is indisputable; and with great perceptiveness he notes the similarity in the exhortative function of the appearance of the ghost in *Hamlet* and of the vision of D. Manuel. Fidelino de Figueiredo sees in *Romeo and Juliet* the model for the love plot, as for so many other stories of star-crossed love, and points out such clear similarities as the hero's banishment and return when his mistress is dead or believed to be dead. He also mentions other affinities, such as the opposition to the couple's love and the existence of a friar; they are, however, of a more tenuous nature, since the opposition to the lovers comes from one side only in *Camões,* and the two friars differ widely in role and character, as Fidelino de Figueiredo admits. In his quest for Shakespearian influences this critic presents Camões as another Romeo — a 'Camões-Romeu'; the identification, however, based as it is on external circumstances of the plot, without any psychological resemblance, can only be accepted in a very restricted sense. Camões is a Byronian hero by character and behaviour, as was shown earlier, and as Fidelino de Figueiredo himself recognizes. Despite this divergence one may conclude with the Portuguese critic, and with Kinsey before him, in *Portugal Illustrated* [11] —though the reasons are not the same— that *Camões* was composed under the inspiration of Byron, Scott and Shakespeare. It is however only right to add that Shakespeare's presence in the work is much less visible and much more superficial.

Turning to *D. Branca,* Fidelino de Figueiredo presents Shakespeare and Scott as the sources for its fusion of historical or semi-historical elements with the world of magic, ignoring Garrett's avowal of his debt in the matter to Wieland's *Oberon.* Filinto Elísio's version of this poem, published in his collected works in Paris in 1817-19, was certainly known to Garrett;

---

[8] Preface to the second edition of *Catão,* O. A. G., Vol. 2, p. 1614.
[9] *Viagens,* Chapt. XXVI, p. 195.
[10] F. de Figueiredo, pp. 27-34.
[11] Quoted in F. de Figueiredo, p. 34: 'Portuguese throughout catches the manner of Shakespeare, and sometimes reminds us of the flexibility of Scott, at others of the force of Byron.'

and, as Antscherl notes, in the composition entitled 'Filinto' (1819), written on the death of the exiled poet, Garrett refers to situations in *Oberon* which occur later in *D. Branca*.[12] There is no reason to doubt the veracity of his acknowledgement,[13] and there consequently seems to be no need to postulate a direct influence of Shakespeare in this feature of *D. Branca* as well as the indirect one through Wieland's own debt to *A Midsummer Night's Dream*.

A similar lack of precision can be objected to in Fidelino de Figueiredo's remarks on Garrett's use of native mythology in the same poem. Figueiredo quotes the well-known passage on the mythology of *D. Branca* from Garrett's letter to Duarte Lessa of 19 November 1824, and suggests that this is an obvious case of Shakespearian influence. The quotation is given out of context and on its own, without any accompanying reference to Scott or to Garrett's repeated admissions of inspiration from Scott; the reader is led to believe that Shakespeare is the sole stimulus for Garrett's novel use of *fadas* and *encantos*. Ambiguities such as this need to be clarified: Scott is the immediate inspiration for the native mythology in *D. Branca,* as has been established, and Shakespeare's influence though perceptible in the poem is less specific. This is not to deny that the fairies in Shakespeare did catch Garrett's imagination. They are mentioned, but only twice: Fidelino de Figueiredo quotes the passage in Carlos's letter, comparing Julia to the queen of fairies in *A Midsummer Night's Dream* (Chapter XLV, p. 318), and the lines portraying the heroine in *Helena:* '(...) Sílfide de Walter Scott não era; fada de Shakespeare não podia ser (...)' (Chapter VII, pp. 422-3). However, they belong to a later date.

Returning to the period of his early Romantic works, one finds a reference to Shakespeare in an article initially written for *Lyceu das damas* in 1823, but only published in *O Chronista* in 1827: [14]

> Hoje é moda o romântico, é finura.
> É tom achar Ossian melhor que Homero,
> Gabar Shakespeare, desdenhar Corneille (...)

> (...) Mas enfim, deixemos a cada qual com seu gosto. Em todos os géneros há belezas, e em todos muito que admirar. Kotzebue tem cenas de infinito preço; Shakespeare rasgos de sublime, que o talento humano dificilmente igualará jamais.

> Sejamos tolerantes; admiremos os grandes génios no que têm de admirável, seja qual for a sua escola ou sistema.

In the lighthearted manner that Garrett seems to favour when he writes for a feminine audience, he deals here, once again, with the controversy of classicism versus romanticism, taking an eclectic attitude: despite the fact that Garrett is favourable to romanticism, he chides those followers of the school who replace a servile imitation of the classics by an equally servile imitation of new models, and calls for an unprejudiced appreciation of art.

---

[12] Antscherl, p. 11. See also O. P. Monteiro, Vol. II, p. 241.
[13] In Note C to C. I of the first edition.
[14] O. P. Monteiro, Vol. I, p. 401, note 140.

9

In this passage Shakespeare is mentioned in a warmer tone than hitherto, but as an object of admiration, and not as a master to be copied — which is consistent with Garrett's message. Yet one senses that, quite apart from the restraint imposed by the nature of the article, there is something akin to a mental reservation in Garrett's praise of Shakespeare, which is similar to the reticent allusions in the Preface to the 1830 edition of *Catão*.

In this period Garrett seems to do precisely as he preaches: he admires Shakespeare without imitating him. The epigraphs in *Lírica de João Mínimo* and in *Adosinda*, both published in England in 1828, testify not only to his admiration but to the hours of reading fondly recalled in *Viagens*, and to the truth of his statement in 'Esquisse' quoted earlier on his acquaintance with the English poet. 'O amor maternal', 'O amor paternal' and 'O exílio' are the poems in *Lírica* which have epigraphs from Shakespearian plays: they are taken, respectively, from *King John*, III, i, *King Lear*, I, i and *Romeo and Juliet*, III, iii.[15] The aptness of such epigraphs, which are selected from the middle of speeches and not commonly quoted lines, reveals that Garrett was perfectly familiar with the Shakespearian texts. The epigraphs in the first two Cantos of *Adosinda* are taken from King Lear, Act II, iv,[16] and the last from Act IV, vii of the same tragedy; the third Canto has an epigraph from *Hamlet*, Act I, v. The fact that Garrett has chosen epigraphs from these two tragedies for *Adosinda*, with its theme of incest, has been interpreted by O. Paiva Monteiro as a sign that his interest in Shakespeare's theatre lies precisely in its violent passions.[17]

Shakespearian influences have been found by Fidelino de Figueiredo [18] and A. Crabbé Rocha [19] in Garrett's first stage production after his return from exile —*Um auto de Gil Vicente* (1830)— [20] with which he tries to revive the tradition of Portuguese theatre. Thus both critics, particularly Figueiredo, who discusses the matter in some detail, relate the use of the interpolated play in *Um auto* to Shakespeare. Figueiredo argues that Hamlet's alteration of the text of the itinerant 'troupe' has undoubtedly inspired Garrett to create a similar situation: Bernardim replaces another actor in order to substitute his own love lines for words of the text, and the ring given by the Infanta for the props of the play. Though the motivation is different —revenge for a father's death, and a plea for love— the device is put to similar use, writes Fidelino de Figueiredo, and brings both plays to a point of climax. Ingenious and fascinating as it is to relate Garrett's confessional stratagem to Shakespeare's device to catch a conscience, yet there is no conclusive evidence that *The Murder of Gonzago* is the inspiration —and even less the sole inspiration— for this feature of Garrett's *Um auto de Gil Vicente*. The idea of the play within the play, as Fidelino

---

[15] Here identified for the first time.
[16] In the identification of these epigraphs in O. P. Monteiro, Vol. II, p. 263, note 128, *K. L.* Act II, iv has been misprinted as *K. L.* Act III, iv.
[17] O. P. Monteiro, Vol. II, p. 263.
[18] F. de Figueiredo, pp. 39-41.
[19] A. Crabbé Rocha, 'Introdução geral ao teatro de Garrett' in *Obras completas de Almeida Garrett, Teatro I*, edited by J. Prado Coelho (Lisboa, 1972), pp. 12-14.
[20] Henceforth abbreviated to *Um auto*.

de Figueiredo is the first to admit, is already present in Gil Vicente's *Cortes de Júpiter,* on which Garrett bases his own work,[21] and it is not impossible that Garrett should have thought of Bernardim's device as a natural extension of the idea to make the text of *Cortes de Júpiter* —which he interweaves with his— a more integral part of the outer play; one should also consider the hypothesis that Garrett may have been inspired by this technique as found among writers from the seventeenth to the nineteenth century,[22] or very simply by the vogue of the double-plot among the Romantics. One must conclude that the Shakespearian influence in this aspect of *Um auto* is possible, but by no means certain, nor to be considered to the exclusion of other stimuli. Garrett's admiration for Shakespeare adds to its plausibility.

A. Crabbé Rocha also sees a Shakespearian influence in the story of the star-crossed lovers, which she relates in particular to *A Midsummer Night's Dream.* But this appears to be no more than a vague reminiscence, because the chain of unloved lovers in *Um auto* —Pero loves Paula, who loves Bernardim, who loves the Princess, who is going away to marry the Duke of Savoy— lacks the complexity and the usual happy ending of such Shakespearian situations. On the other hand A. Crabbé Rocha attributes to French influences what may well be regarded as a Shakespearian trait too: the combination of contrasting characters in *Um auto* — down-to-earth, jocular figures side by side with others surrounded by an aura of exquisite suffering. French or Shakespearian, it is an interesting point to note in a writer like Garrett, who hitherto had had difficulty in accepting the unevenness and contrasts of the Shakespearian theatre. His resistance to its freedom in the handling of the unities persists in his main stage productions, as Figueiredo writes, and *O arco de Sant' Ana* shows how Garrett's tendency to observe the unity of time spills over from the theatre to the novel. But if Garrett does not adhere to the form of the Shakespearian theatre, he seems to be affected by its spirit: in his masterpiece, *Frei Luís de Sousa* (1843), the conflicts of conscience that play an essential role in the tragic denouement are markedly Shakesperian, as Fidelino de Figueiredo remarks.[23] And in the *Memória ao Conservatório Real* that precedes the play Garrett regrets the fact that no Portuguese had so far done dramatic justice to Inês de Castro, a national theme that would take men of the stature of a Shakespeare or of a Schiller — playwrights who were beyond imitation but ought to be regarded as examples in drama on national subjects.

Viagens na minha terra, written in the same year as *Frei Luís de Sousa,* contains several references to Shakespeare. He is one of the writers with whom Garrett claims to be well acquainted in his display of erudition in the Preface; Hamlet's lines in Act I, v —'There are more things in Heaven and earth, Horatio / Than are dreamt of in your phylosophy [sic]'— are quoted in English (Chapter III, p. 24) and translated though

---

[21] Introduction to *Um auto de Gil Vicente,* O. A. G., Vol. 2, p. 1325.
[22] Robert J. Nelson, *Play within a Play* (New Haven, 1958).
[23] F. de Figueiredo, p. 43; in *Dois monumentos,* an Introduction to *Frei Luís de Sousa,* in O. A. G., Vol. 2, p. 1075, Teófilo Braga writes: 'A cena do retrato e do peregrino, que são shakesperianas (...).'

not faithfully in Note F; [24] in the passage on Cartaxo wine (Chapter VII, p. 55), in which there is a convergence of Byronian and Sternean traces, Shakespeare is named among those whose literary taste would be ruined by French viniculture. Further on, a reference to Hamlet's Yorick leads up to the pages in which he evokes Yorick and Sterne, and the longest passage, alluded to earlier, recollects his readings of Shakespeare in Warwickshire, the magic and power of his witches and ghosts, the figure of Falstaff, and the aroma of old-sack, about which he adds a vague note of supposed erudition. Such references reveal Garrett's knowledge of and liking for Shakespeare. But they are just some among the many allusions made throughout *Viagens* to a host of figures, mostly literary but not exclusively so, which are part of Garrett's vast range of interests. Among them Shakespeare occupies a prominent place. Yet unlike the other writers discussed earlier, from Addison to Sterne, Shakespeare's presence in *Viagens* is restricted to such references: he has no visible impact on the work itself.

A summing-up of the extent of Shakespeare's influence on Garrett's writings as a whole shows that, in terms of creativity, it finds little specific expression: apart from the few cases of assimilation discussed above, Shakespeare the playwright seems to have inspired Garrett in a general subjective way, and his gradual conversion and increasing admiration are mainly manifested in a number of external marks, like references, epigraphs and theoretical opinions. Nor is there any evidence of Garrett being affected by Shakespeare as a lyric poet. Restricted as such influences seem to be, Garrett is, nonetheless, a major precursor in the appreciation of Shakespeare in Portugal. His efforts to acquaint his contemporaries with Shakespeare's dramas include the organization of talks given by the playwright James Sheridan Knowles during a three-week stay in Lisbon, in 1845, as part of a series of lectures on English Romantic poetry, as well as poetry in fashion among the Romantics: Milton, Pope, Southey, Scott, Byron and Campbell. The gist of the lectures on Shakespeare may be gathered from the programme published in the press and quoted by F. de Figueiredo, [25] and from Garrett's work *Mr. Sheridan-Knowles*. [26] His account of the lecturer's dismissal of Aristotle's unities gives a measure, not only of the persuasive powers of the orator, but also of the aesthetic tolerance of the author of *Frei Luís de Sousa*:

> e com o exemplo de *Macbeth* —tragédia admirável que ele analisou rápida, mas profundamente— provou à evidência, demonstrou com toda a severidade da lógica, sem perder das galas da eloquência, que o verdadeiro drama trágico era impossível com as pretendidas três unidades de Aristóteles.

Another remark similarly shows how far Garrett had come from the days when he had admired 'le beau idéal', and reveals Shakespeare's liberating role:

[24] Garrett's translation is: 'Há mais coisas no céu, há mais na terra / Do que sonha a tua vã filosofia.'
[25] F. de Figueiredo, p. 51.
[26] Garrett, O. A. G., Vol. I, pp. 654-7.

mas bastariam decerto estas três lições para mostrar (...) que sem um longo, profundo e meditado estudo da natureza —de que ele [Shakespeare] foi o primeiro intérprete— não é possível fazer coisa alguma digna da arte, neste mais difícil de todos os géneros da literatura, o dramático.

Observations like these, even in 1845, must have had a ring of boldness and novelty for Garrett's Portuguese contemporaries. Of course he is not alone in admiring Shakespeare: in the regular attendance of a number of Portuguese at these talks, given in English, in Castilho's translation of *A Midsummer Night's Dream* in 1830, in Lopes de Mendonça's writings in *Revolução de Setembro*, reprinted in *Ensaios de crítica e literatura* (1849), in Ramalho e Sousa's abortive project to translate Shakespeare's complete works,[27] one finds varied instances of an active enthusiasm, which would be shared, too, by a silent group. But the Portuguese literary world had not fully accepted Shakespeare;[28] thus Fidelino de Figueiredo mentions how, as late as 1856, Rebelo da Silva still hesitated to give a faithful rendering of *Othello*, and how, in 1886, in a review of the translation of this tragedy by King D. Luís, Camilo Castelo Branco still confessed his inability to understand Shakespeare. Within the context of this general perspective one has a better understanding and appreciation of Garrett's response to Shakespeare. His introduction of the theatre of the Elizabethan dramatist to Portugal is one of his great contributions to romanticism.

[27] F. de Figueiredo, p. 59.
[28] This is not surprising, since he only became a well-established and popular figure in France from 1850. Apud Van Tieghem, p. 197.

CONCLUSION

What we have seen so far does not exhaust the study of English influences on Garrett's literary creations, where the presence of other authors is also apparent, though to a lesser degree. I have shown that Thomson's *Spring* is echoed in an early ode in *Lírica*, 'A primavera' (1815), which also has an epigraph from the same poem. Epigraphs from Milton head *O retrato de Vénus* (1818) and 'Melancolia' (1822) in *Lírica;* another poem in the same collection, 'A morte' (1819), bears an epigraph from Young. Garrett did not escape the vogue for Ossian, and in 'Oscar (Imitação de Ossian)' (182...) and in 'A caverna de Viriato' (1824), both in *Flores sem fruto,* he attempts to write in the manner of the Nordic bard; yet the last stanza of 'Oscar' reveals that Ossian's nebulous world is not congenial to Garrett, who declares his relief at returning to the sweeter climates of his native Elísia. Thomas Moore was a poet whom Garrett held in the highest esteem. This is revealed not only in his choice of an epigraph from Moore to precede 'A caverna de Viriato', but also in Note D to Canto V of *Camões,* quoted earlier, and in a note to Canto III, xvii of the first edition of *D. Branca,* when acknowledging the borrowing of an image from *Lalla Rookh:* after Byron's death Moore is, in Garrrett's eyes, the greatest living poet.[1] Garrett was particularly impressed by Moore's *The Loves of the Angels* (1823) and takes up its theme again and again: in fragments of a poem which constitutes MS 57 in *Esp.,* in 'As minhas asas' (184...) in *Flores sem fruto,* in 'O anjo e a princesa' in *Romanceiro.*[2]

A manuscript catalogue of Garrett's library in *Esp.* gives an idea of the extent of his reading in English and confirms the wide range of interest that he displays in his writings, from the reviews in *O Chronista* to the allusions in *Viagens.* Side by side with the *Waverley Novels,* already mentioned, one sees *The Minstrelsy* and Percy's *Reliques,* a life of Shakespeare and two sets of his complete works —one in English and the other in German—, the complete works of Byron and Moore with a separate translation of *The Lusiad* by the latter, Thomson's *The Seasons, The Canterbury Tales,* Dr. Johnson's *Dictionary, David Copperfield,* Washington Irving's *Tour on the Prairies,* works by John Adamson and Quillinan, and volumes of periodicals like the *Foreign Quarterly Review* and *The Spectator.* Such publications are found along with many other disparate works, ranging

---

[1] O. P. Monteiro, Vol. II, p. 134.
[2] O. P. Monteiro, Vol. II, p. 140.

from Bacon's *Essays* to Gibbon's *Decline and Fall,* and various volumes of English, Portuguese, African and ecclesiastical history, Blackstone's *Commentaries on the Laws and Constitution of England,* the *Lawyer's Cabinet, English and Jewish Tithe Systems Compared,* treatises on education and on economy, a cookery book, a classical dictionary, a Greek lexicon... It is thus evident that Garrett's English culture was extremely wide and varied. But, as we saw at the beginning of this study, he also had a thorough knowledge of and love for the literature of his country, which was one of the great and absorbing passions of his life. This is amply demonstrated not only in the Portuguese section of his library, but also in his early collecting of José Anastácio da Cunha's poems in Oporto, and in his reverence for Filinto, in works like his *Brief Review of the Literary History of Portugal* and *Bosquejo da história da poesia e língua portuguesa,* in his prefaces and indeed in the writings themselves, as well as in his multiple efforts to create a national theatre. He was familiar with the literature of Greek and Roman antiquity, he had some acquaintance with Italian authors —Alfieri and Dante, amongst others, left traces in his work—, and with Spanish literature; he even read some modern Germans in the original, like Herder,[3] Schiller[4] and Goethe, whom he admired exceedingly and from whose *Faust* he translates a passage in *Viagens.* Above all, he knew French literature, both classical and modern, very thoroughly, and, over and above that part of it which would naturally have been included in the standard equipment of an educated Portuguese at the beginning of the nineteenth century, he had come to familiarise himself with much more of it during his two periods of exile in France, from 1824 to 1826, and the two or three months in 1831-2. There is no doubt that his creative activities were very much affected by all these things, and if we are to assess accurately the importance of his debt to English literature, it is essential that we should also take account of the profit he may have derived from other external sources, which in this case means mainly French literature.

The French authors whom he seems to have known and liked best before his first exile were Racine, Voltaire, Ducis, Rousseau, Chateaubriand and Mme de Staël; Schlegel, though German, may be included in this group for the affinities of his thought with that of Mme de Staël. Racine gave him a model of a neo-classical theatre; the tragedies of Voltaire and Ducis showed him a more flexible yet still classical mode of dramatic writing which had considerable appeal for him. Rousseau with his individualism, his cult of nature and his mellifluous style, Chateaubriand with his extolling of the beauties of religion, his emphasis on the artistic inspiration to be found in Christianity and his glorification of melancholy, Mme de Staël with her defence of national differences in art and her discernment of the importance of historical and climatic circumstances in moulding culture, all helped to open new horizons to him. By the time he left Portugal, his

---

[3] Antscherl, p. 100.
[4] O. P. Monteiro, Vol. I, p. 512 ff., sees Schiller's influence in *Namorados extravagantes.*

into the prose of *Viagens na minha terra,* and he is undoubtedly a main source of inspiration for Garrett's decisive contribution to the transformation of literary Portuguese from a stiff and formal idiom to a flexible and natural language. No less important was Sterne's contribution to Garrett's search for freedom in form: in Sterne's ironical flouting of set values and of narrative conventions, and in his innovatory technique is to be found a major key to the modernity of *Viagens.*

Byron emerges as the most important and sustained English influence, a figure whom Garrett follows in his search for form, and with whom he has a parallel spiritual evolution, from the world of subjectivism and romance of *Childe Harold* and *Camões* to the final acceptance of the duality symbolized by Quixote and Sancho in *Don Juan* and in *Viagens,* by way of satires like *The Age of Bronze* and *Magriço.* In Byron's poetry Garrett found an echo of his own feelings of nostalgia and rejection in exile, of growing bitterness and disenchantment, and of awareness of life as at once tragedy and comedy. They were both taught by experience to see such primary motivations in their lives as love, politics, and literature, in terms of a mobility that was incompatible with one fixed system, and yet they both strove to reach an ideal harmony, Quixotes looking up despite the jostles of reality.

All this was transmuted in their work, in their rejection of schools, in the psychology of a Byronic hero which was part of themselves and which they learned to regard with humour, in the ambiguity created by the shift of voice and time, in these and other components of the irony that is their distinctive hallmark; it also showed itself in their struggle to make form, of which they both were loving craftsmen, a vigorous expression of their conflicting tensions. Because he recognized a kindred spirit in Byron, Garrett saw in his art a model of his own personality and experiences, and reflected its development, in form and content, in his own writings.

Byron and Scott complement each other as the fundamental formative figures of Garrett's romanticism. If in aspects of Byron's compositions Garrett had a poetical model for his own individual passions and preoccupations, in Scott he found the most important foreign inspiration for such main features of his work as nationalism and medievalism. Just as, in his own evolution, Garrett follows a course similar to that taken by Byron from *Childe Harold* to *Don Juan,* so does his *Romanceiro* occupy in relation to later writings, such as the theatre, *O arco de Sant' Ana,* and *Viagens na minha terra,* a position that can be compared to that of *The Minstrelsy* and of the early poetical works in relation to the Scottish Novels. Unlike so many other Romantics, Garrett appreciated Scott's medievalism not as a mere source of the picturesque but in its deep historical sense, and balladry and other forms of antiquarian interest were to him, as they had been to Scott, as valid a contribution to the reconstitution of the past as historical documents. Scott's original creation, based on a native tradition, could not fail to appeal to Garrett, who had himself, since his youth, aspired to create a national drama and who wanted to free Portuguese literature from indiscriminate dependence on others. Scott was an inspiring guide in leading Garrett along paths that he was anxious to explore.

To my loved ones

305.23
B665 y
1980

Brooks/Cole Publishing Company
A Division of Wadsworth, Inc.

Printed in the United States of America

10 9 8 7 6 5 4 3 2 1

Library of Congress Cataloging in Publication Data:

Bocknek, Gene.
 The young adult

  Bibliography: p.
  Includes index.
  1. Young adults. I. Title.
HQ799.5.B62 305.2'3 80-15148
ISBN 0-8185-0387-4

Acquisition Editor: *Todd Lueders*
Production Editor: *Stacey C. Sawyer*
Manuscript Editor: *William Waller*
Production Associate: *Jennifer A. Young*
Interior and Cover Design: *Ruth Scott*
Cover Photo: *Jerry Takigawa*
Typesetting: *Instant Type, Monterey, California*

PREFACE

This book examines the first stage of the adult life span—young adulthood—on the basis of the commonalities inherent in the human experience as a function of living out the life span. In the end, the vagaries of the adult span are neither so random nor so ineluctably complex as to be unknowable or unknown. In this book I have tried to assemble what is known, what has been studied, observed, and reported—from every available source—as it pertains to the period of young adulthood.

For almost ten years I have taught a course on the psychology of the young adult. As teacher, parent, advisor, and therapist, I have worked with young adults over a professional career spanning more than two decades. This experience has convinced me that the best path to understanding what is universal in adult development is through an understanding of the underlying psychological processes that all human beings share. That intrapsychic orientation pervades my approach, even when describing interpersonal or intracultural phenomena.

My interest in young adulthood dates from my first full-time work, in a university counseling center. I was struck by the differences between college students and other populations I had worked with in my training. Even when schizophrenic, the college students showed greater recuperative powers and more insight than older adults who were similarly disturbed. Later I found that this was also true of certain drug addicts and factory workers of the same age group.

I moved away from that period of exclusive interest in psychopathology and psychotherapy. I began to think of young adulthood as a normal developmental stage. The growth and development of adults attracted my interest. I rediscovered the truth that personality is an

iii

everchanging part of a dynamic life process. Students joined with me as co-learners as I began putting together a course to study young adults. From those beginnings emerged a succession of small studies, papers, and a few dissertations; this book culminates those efforts.

The book is written to, as well as about, young adults. It is designed to be a basic text in courses on post-adolescent development in departments of psychology, human development, education, and human services. I hope to inform readers about the young-adult life stage; I hope to make some of those readers more aware of themselves, as well.

Particularly in a first book, an author should acknowledge the contribution of those whose support, advice, encouragement, and help have sustained that literary effort. For me, that sort of listing would run on for pages. My students have been a constant source of stimulation, challenging and extending my thoughts. As an undergraduate, it was my undeserved good fortune to have been exposed to the seminal ideas of some great minds: Gardner Murphy's structural approach to the dynamic system that is personality; Kenneth Clark's insight into attitudes as a paradigm of prepotency; John Collier's profound understanding of cultural anthropology. Their impact has been indelible.

My family and friends have been unwavering in their support, a statement of faith that took a long time to justify. I can never fully acknowledge the debt of gratitude that is owed to so many, past and present. I want to thank the people associated with Brooks/Cole, including editors and staff, and the reviewers: James Brine, Southern Connecticut State College; Alan Hoffman, Wayne State University; and Kathleen White, Boston University. Their commentary, both professional and human, is much appreciated. My wife, Judy, provided invaluable intellectual, technical, and emotional support.

For me, this book is the opening of a door too long left sealed. As a teacher, I can hope that it will stimulate others; as a lifetime student, I have enjoyed the education I received by writing it.

Gene Bocknek

CONTENTS

1

THE APPROACH

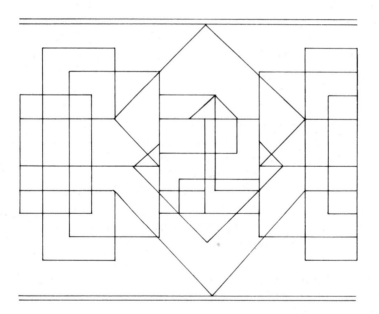

DEVELOPMENT AS NATURAL HISTORY

Psychologists are increasingly turning their attention to the adult life span. During the 1970s they focused on developmental theory and adult behavior. An emerging interest in adult development is the result. In part, this interest may be an offspring of the human-potential movement of the 1960s; in part, it may result from the post-World-War-II generation, which spotlighted child and then adolescent development and now is looking into full adulthood.

In essence, developmental psychology concerns the natural history of human evolution; what is more fundamental to an understanding of human nature than the understanding of the history of human growth? This book explores one segment of human natural history—young adulthood. Of all the periods in the life span, from birth to death, the first half of adulthood—young adulthood—is probably the least understood from a developmental perspective.

Across various cultures, the rites of passage into adult status, as noted by Van Gennep (1960), have taken place most commonly at puberty and occasionally several years later when a couple joined to produce children. From the perspective of cultural self-maintenance it may be adequate to define adulthood in such fundamental biosocial terms. For the psychologist, however, there can be a wide gap between the interpersonal and intrapsychic competencies of people at the two different life periods of puberty and childbearing.

Nevertheless, it is still common to find writers who speak broadly of *youth* as the interval of time between puberty and coming to maturity. In this book I will detail several important ways in which psychological differences between the two periods outweigh the observed similarities. Thus, a major purpose of this book is to make the case for understanding young adulthood as a time-limited stage of life characterized by distinctive, identifiable properties. In particular, I plan to differentiate clearly between young adulthood and what has become recognized in Western civilization as adolescence.

To accomplish this task it is necessary to establish a frame of reference. As I implied in the opening paragraphs of this chapter, my approach is that of applied developmental psychology. Consequently, the initial chapters of this book will describe the developmental perspective as it is being employed here. Although developmental theory denotes a normative approach, it concerns not only actuarial data but also the

potential inherent in human growth. Clearly, no developmental psychology can ignore the evidence of what people actually do, as a manifestation of human evolution. But it seems equally vital that the conception of human development not be circumscribed by what is apparent and/or typical. Both the actuarial and the potential approaches are rooted in systematic observation and study of human behavior. Both approaches have generated useful constructs and theoretical models. Indeed, there is ample reason to believe that in the future the two positions can and will be reconciled into more comprehensive theories of development.

ADULT DEVELOPMENT AS PROCESS

In this book we will view adult development at the level of psychological process. Overt behavior is seen as only a manifestation, and not the full extent, of underlying developmental processes. The concept of *process* (Bocknek, 1977) will be elaborated in Chapter 2, The Developmental Perspective. However, a few basic observations concerning the process model and adult development belong here.

Most theorists acknowledge an early adult life stage covering the first third of the adult life span; however, they often fail to distinguish between late adolescence and young adulthood. My position is that young adulthood represents a qualitative departure from adolescence. The term *youth*—so often used to describe similarities in behavior style of some adolescents and young adults—obscures subtle but important differences between these groups. In contrast, the differences between adults in the other life periods, from established adulthood through senescence, can be clearly distinguished.

The differences between adolescents and young adults represent changes that develop in the organization and operation of various psychological processes. To describe these changes one must infer the existence of underlying, or genotypic, phenomena capable of generating a variety of behavioral, or phenotypic[1], manifestations. The particular manifestations are a function of the interaction of the genotypic process with other intrapsychic processes (such as defense mechanisms) and the several environmental conditions prevailing at the time. Thus, a person who is developmentally ready to act in an altruistic fashion may or may

---

[1]*Genotype* is used here to mean the construct that is the source of different but psychologically connected behaviors. The observable connected behaviors are the *phenotypes*. For example, *rigidity* and *prejudice* are phenotypic manifestations of the genotype *authoritarian personality*.

not do so, depending on the opportunities and risks prevalent at that time and place. Also, whether a behavior *is* altruistic must, in the present framework, be determined by an examination of the intrapsychic events (intentions, objectives) of the doer, not simply by an "objective" analysis of overt behavior.

In short, the developmental approach used in this book is rooted in a process model in which the significant features of its data base are inferred rather than observed. It may be said that human development proceeds from the inside out, in that it is the evolutionary status of these psychological processes that ultimately defines the limits of observable behavior.

THE NEED FOR BETTER DEFINITIONS OF ADULT LIFE STAGES

The traditional description of adulthood lists three stages: early, middle, and late. Contemporary students of child development (for example, Mahler, 1968; Piaget, 1963) identify three, five, or more stages in the first decade of life. In adolescence, another two or three periods are commonly noted (Blos, 1962; Lidz, 1976). Is it possible that the next 50 years of life can be described by only three life stages? Is the adult span of years really that stable? Or are the lenses through which we view the adult life cycle still relatively unrefined? The research of Lowenthal and her colleagues (1975) and Levinson and his associates (1977) indicates that a more precise view of adult life periods may be warranted.

Unfortunately, the extent of knowledge in the field of adult development is still quite limited. Major personality constructs such as self-concept, ego, morality, and cognition have been studied longitudinally over the earlier years but rarely through the adult periods. Cognitive processes such as learning (Knox, 1977) and intelligence (Labouvie-Vief, 1977; Wechsler, 1958) have received attention as have some interpersonal and self/other attitudes (for example, Peck, 1968), but their implications for the study of life stages have not been explored.

It may well be that any attempt to comprehensively document all the stages of the adult life span is premature and approximate at best; certainly it is beyond the scope of the present volume. In the subsequent chapters I will present the case for a more restricted, but better delineated, psychological description of one of those adult life stages—young adulthood.

TOWARD A BETTER DEFINITION OF YOUNG ADULTHOOD

How does one define a life stage? The position adopted in this book is that developmental periods are both age related and sequentially fixed. Age-relatedness is adapted from the usage described by Neugarten and Datan (1973). These authors distinguish between life time (chronological age), social time (societal age grading, as in rites of passage), and historical time—when particular periods of life (for example, childhood) gain general recognition. Elsewhere, Neugarten (1975a) identifies the psychological perception of time as a form of phenomenology of aging. For example, in middle age, people deemphasize years lived and think in terms of years left to live. Thus, developmental periods are not independent of chronological age but are also affected by personal experience, social pressures, and human history in the macrocosmic sense.

Young adulthood typically occurs in the third decade of life for people living in the industrial world of the 20th century. Unless the human life span becomes radically shortened or extended, young adulthood would be expected to occur at approximately the same part of the life span in other societies and centuries as well. However, the duration of young adulthood as a life stage might well vary considerably—say, from two or three years to a decade—depending on sociocultural and historic conditions.

Even less flexibility exists relative to the sequential placement of young adulthood in human natural history. It will always follow adolescence and precede established adulthood. It will always be the first adult life stage. These assertions are not arbitrary; they derive directly from the logic of developmental theory subscribed to by writers such as Erikson (1959) and Loevinger (1966). Development proceeds sequentially, building on earlier functions, structures, processes, and events.

But the most important defining features of a life stage are not its chronology or sequential location. The essential point, which will be discussed in a later chapter, is that each life stage has *distinguishing psychological characteristics*. Such characteristics may be functional consequences of structural changes in the organism, or they may be themselves structural changes in the psychological organization of the individual. The former case can be illustrated by the confidence experienced by young adults that is due, in part, to physiological stabilization after the rapid physical growth of adolescence. An example of the latter

instance is the differentiation and integration of the ego that is also seen in young adulthood.

If it seems tautological to define a life stage by properties that are themselves apparently hypothetical, I would ask that you defer judgment until the evidence has been presented. Most people accept the reality of an adolescent life stage even while debate rages about the defining characteristics of adolescence. The tautology that seems so apparent may prove to be nothing more than an instance of hypothetico-deductive reasoning. To study developmental processes necessitates a focused search with specialized lenses; one needs to know what one is looking for and how to find it. Bacteria have always existed, but it required the use of a microscope to "discover" them.

This is perhaps the most appropriate time—before delving into the details of my presentation—to acknowledge the role, and bias, I bring to the task of defining young adulthood. Having spent the great bulk of my professional life working with young adults, as teacher, therapist, researcher, and parent, I cannot claim a position of totally objective detachment.

My view of young adulthood can be compared to that of a serious reporter investigating an area of chronic unemployment. What starts out as a dispassionate fact-finding tour gets subtly enmeshed with very human but "unscientific" sorts of side issues: What is the relationship between this group and the larger society? Is the group unfairly stigmatized? Advantaged? How does it impact on time and culture? As the reporter stays with the subject, learning more and more about it, there is a tendency to identify with it. Gradually there occurs a perceptible shift: discrete observations become elaborated descriptions; to make the descriptions more comprehensible to the reader, some interpretation of overt events is necessary; sometimes the interpretations border on justifications; some events are selected for interpretation, and others are relatively neglected. And, as the reporter gets ever closer to the story, description becomes tinged with advocacy.

The relative paucity of hard data on young adulthood further confounds the most scrupulous efforts to remain objective. For these reasons I shall attempt to make clear my theoretical orientation, my conceptual framework, the assumptions I have chosen to accept, and the data sources that have been available. At this writing, there is no other book on young adulthood. There is scarcely a literature worthy of that name, so scattered and fragmentary is its content.

But neither adult development nor young adults would be well served by a political propaganda piece. My purpose in writing this book is similar to that of the investigative reporter: to bring to the awareness of a community of readers a credible description and reasoned examination of an issue of interest. As much as possible I have endeavored to hew to the line of neutrality, detachment, objectivity. But that commitment assures only sincerity of purpose, not success of outcome.

The ultimate value of this book, I believe, will lie not in the irreversibility of any of its findings but in the extent to which it contributes to the expansion of knowledge in an important phase of the adult life span. I hope it will challenge and stimulate others to investigate young adulthood and report their findings.

OUTLINE OF THE BOOK

To the extent that existing knowledge and theory permit, I will identify the salient, distinguishing features of the young adult. The context of that description is the framework of developmental psychology, and the description relates closely to two essential points, which will be elaborated:

1. There are at least four adult life periods. Two of them, young adulthood and established adulthood, occur in the first half of the adult life span. For comparison purposes there will be some description of established adulthood, but most of the subsequent chapters will focus on young adulthood.
2. Those observable phenomena that phenotypically resemble extended adolescence turn out to be genotypically different when viewed at the level of psychological processes. Important qualitative differences separate young adults from both adolescents and established adults.

In Chapter 2, The Developmental Perspective, I make explicit the assumptions underlying developmental theory and discuss its applications and implications. The respective applications and limits of the various current models of development are also considered.

As related, in this book, development is conceptualized in terms of psychological processes. Chapter 2 includes an elaboration of the concept of process and a discussion of life stages: how they are conceived and what they imply in a psychology of developmental processes. Out of this emerges the rationale for a model of adult development.

Chapter 3, Models of Adult Development, examines and compares

major adult-development schemata. From these considerations the concept of a categorical-evolution model emerges. This model incorporates both life-span and stage features. It forms the basis of adult development to be used throughout the rest of the book. The idea of interrelated areas of evolution underlies this conception of human development.

The remainder of Chapter 3 is devoted to an overview of the life span from adolescence through senescence. Young adulthood is thus located in its larger developmental context.

Chapter 4, The Acquisitions of Adulthood, indicates those features that young adults share in common with other adults. To accomplish that purpose, the chapter examines historic definitions of adulthood across time and culture. Next, the distinguishing sociopsychological features of adulthood are identified. Finally, the broad sweep of change over the adult life span is described.

The legacy of adolescence is the theme of Chapter 5. The adolescent stage itself has been recognized only in fairly recent times. It is commonplace in the literature to find differences between adolescents and young adults obscured. Typically, phenotypic similarities have outweighed the genotypic differences. Because young adulthood develops from the achievements of adolescence, it is necessary to examine what qualities distinguish the earlier period.

Chapter 6, The Young Adult: A Theoretical Overview, provides a review of the contemporary literature. This summary has two purposes. It offers a perspective on the areas of agreement and dispute among writers in the field. It also creates a backdrop of data for the formulations of young-adult psychology that are presented in the ensuing chapters. With the conclusion of Chapter 6 all the information has been presented to permit an informed examination of young adulthood.

Chapters 7, 8, and 9 are devoted to an intensive look at those evolutionary categories of the young-adult life stage that were identified in the developmental model.

Chapter 7, Intrapsychic Issues, has two major sections. In the first, a number of intrapsychic characteristics are identified and described. I also show how the phenomenology of entry into young adulthood sets the stage for these features. As they are identified, comparisons with the earlier, adolescent, stage are almost inevitable. This is especially true in the discussions of idealism, activism, and self/world orientation.

The second section of Chapter 7 is concerned with the subtle transformations that take place in ego development. Although this mate-

rial is highly theoretical, its importance cannot be minimized. Perhaps no area of developmental theory is in greater need of systematic study. This section deals with self-particularization and ego integration, which are seen as evolving out of adolescent resolution of the identity crisis. Serious students of ego development in adulthood will find this section of particular importance.

Chapter 8, The Peer World, explores the fundamental developmental changes that occur in interpersonal relationships. The key concepts of this chapter are *partner* and *competitor*, which are treated as psychological processes rather than behavioral roles. Their evolution is traced, as is their dependence on other facets of development.

In Chapter 9, founding a family is examined in some detail. An unusual amount of attention is given to the place of love and marriage in founding a family in our own culture. Cross-cultural references are available for comparison, and my orientation remains focused on experience and process, rather than overt behavior. It can be argued that, in contemporary North America, founding a family begins, and sometimes ends, with the couple. But the psychological impact of parenting is also profound. Both components, therefore, receive consideration.

After much deliberation I have decided not to discuss the other broad area of intracultural expectation, building a career. Although there is an extensive literature on that subject, vocational development in this society is in the throes of major change. With the possible exception of specialists, few observers seem able to capture the essential ingredients of a rapidly and erratically shifting aspect of life. Women are increasingly entering the job market; jobs are shrinking as automation reduces the need for labor; leisure and part-time activities are more widespread. There is increasing specialization within fields. Alongside the obsolescence of some established trades, such as linotyping, is the accordion-like expansion and contraction of other jobs, such as comptometry. Technology, education, politics, and economics interact with social and psychological forces. The resulting uncertainty leaves unclear what is culturally expected. There are North American families who have not earned salaries for two generations. This group includes rich and poor, White and Black, male and female. Perhaps I cannot write about intracultural expectations relative to building a career because a dependable set of expectations no longer exists.

Chapter 10, Transition: Tension and Challenge, has a number of thrusts. The concept of *transition* is fundamental to a developmental

approach. Thus, entry into and exit from young adulthood must necessarily receive consideration. That discussion is encumbered, however, by the
paucity of data differentiating adolescence, young adulthood, and established adulthood. Part of the challenge in describing developmental
transition involves being clear on what the dependable, cross-culturally
valid features of each stage really are. In particular, the literature on
established adulthood is terribly sparse. Despite the centrality of this life
period for cultural survival, it has received very little attention in the
newly burgeoning field of adult development.

In this chapter I also outline more fully the longitudinal sweep of
development across the critical decades, from leaving childhood to
becoming a bulwark of society. In the process, I point toward identifying
some of the psychological variables that may characterize some future
developmental psychology of adulthood. This area is speculative at the
present time, yet quite important.

The last chapter, Some Reflections, appropriately returns to the
focal topic of young adulthood. My intent is for you to gain some clearer
sense of the impact and import of this life stage. The book begins with
making a case for understanding young adulthood as a discrete stage. It
concludes with making a case that young adults are essential within the
social fabric.

In a rapidly changing world, knowledge expands at an explosive
rate, contributing to what Toffler (1970) calls "future shock." It will take
all of humankind's talents to cope with the new knowledge and the
changes. Young adults can play an important role in that work. The
distinctive potentialities of young adulthood constitute a rich human
resource to be identified and used.

2

THE DEVELOPMENTAL PERSPECTIVE

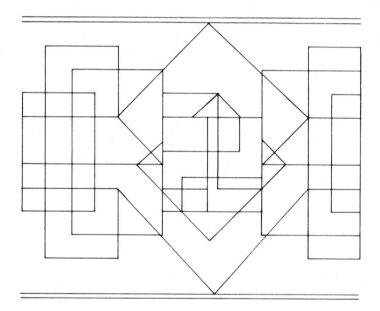

This chapter will place the young adult within a larger context of understanding. For this purpose it is necessary to understand young adulthood as a life stage from a developmental perspective. In particular, we will view development in the context of life-span psychology, following the person from birth to death. The sections that follow will delineate the implications of such an approach. Knowing these implications, you will be more alert to my points of reference and theoretical biases.

YOUNG ADULTHOOD AS A LIFE STAGE

If we view young adulthood as one segment in the life span, we automatically think of it as a transition—that is, not a fixed state but rather one period of an individual's life. During this period one's potentialities are distinctively different from what they were before and equally distinguishable from what they are to become. From this larger, life-span perspective, one can see the precursors to young adulthood in earlier life periods. For example, young adult activism develops in part from the gradual evolution of ego control over impulses. Similarly, one discovers features and qualities emerging in the young adult that will become important in the evolution of subsequent adult life stages. Recognizing young adulthood as a delimited period thus enables us to distinguish both the continuous features and the briefly emerging trends inherent in human life history.

At the same time, this orientation need not obscure the many individual variations that also enter into personality formation. Despite developmental similarities, many other factors—external and internal— influence growth, so that each personality evolves its own idiosyncratic character. To describe a particular stage of life as prone to impulsiveness does not in itself predict how this impulsivity will manifest itself— whether in social, political, interpersonal, or sexual behavior. Nor does such a description indicate the absolute intensity of a characteristic within any individual's total psychological integration. Nor does it even guarantee its immediate visibility in the person's day-to-day behavior. As is true of all psychological characteristics, its emergence into recognizable behavior depends on an appropriate set of environmental conditions. But it is also necessary that there be intrapsychic compatibility with its emergence at that particular time.

Thus, young adults may be characteristically oriented toward active involvement in their society. In a particular nation at a particular time in

its history, however, a climate of repression and fear may occur, as it did during the McCarthy era of the 1950s or the Nixon era of the 1970s. This social climate produced overt behavior suggestive more of apathy and silence than of activist concern. Thus, although the intrapersonal preconditions for certain behavior may be present, the entire psychological field of events must be considered before one can make predictions about observable behavior. Only as we recognize that there are intrapsychic processes "under the skin" can we consistently approach accurate appraisal, measurement, and prediction of their characteristics.

THE DEVELOPMENTAL APPROACH: PREMISES

Any theory of psychological development is based on premises. Our exploration of young adulthood and its adjacent life stages will be aided by a description of the premises of developmental theory.

1. Development represents a thrust. Undergirding all developmental theory is some concept of movement and change. The inevitability of change and the inexorable pressure toward it are indigenous to all human experience. The extension of this basic principle from childhood to the adult years lets us discard anachronistic notions of adulthood as a stable period of five decades, with rapid deterioration and decline at the end as the only variation. The discovery of growth characteristics throughout the adult years requires that psychological theorists and practitioners reexamine and redesign their approach to adulthood.

As one case in point, the concept of fixation is commonly defined as a state of arrested development, a cessation of growth. From the perspective evolving here, fixation is more aptly defined as a deceleration, or slowing down, of the developmental process.

2. Growth is the law of life. People change as a function of time and place, but mainly by virtue of their nature as living organisms in a finite evolutionary span from birth to death.

Although the rate of growth is most rapid in the earliest years, significant changes occur over the 50-year adult period of life. Levinson (1974) suggests that a new stage of development emerges every seven years. Buhler (1935) indicates three major adult stages. My own research has identified four stages: young adult, established adult, middle adult, and senescent adult. However such periods are conceived—as milestones

(Loevinger, 1966) or as stages—qualitative changes have been noted in time sense (Kimmel, 1974; Neugarten, 1968), cognitive function (Perry, 1970), personal orientation (Gould, 1972; Levinson et al., 1974), and ego development (Loevinger, 1966; van den Daele, 1975).

3. Development is directional. The onward thrust of life is neither random nor haphazard. The natural history of psychological evolution is sometimes continuous, often cumulative, frequently sequential, and always productive of new qualities or combinations. It is in the adult years that social skills, rudimentarily developed during the first two decades of life, are refined into the ability to make subtle distinctions (for example, between friend and partner) and to integrate more complex social relationships into one's self-image (for example, parent/breadwinner/mate).

The direction of developmental thrust is often quite predictable: simple to complex, differentiated to integrated, egocentric to allocentric. However, we do well to heed Loevinger's (1966) caution that growth does not always imply improvement. The discernible shift toward conservatism with age is inherently neither good nor bad.

4. Growth unleashes new potential. Each new period, each subtle restructuring of personal qualities, brings with it resources not previously available to the person. The reverse side of the imperative to change is the discovery of new capability or potential. This may emerge through a change in self-image: "I really am responsible!" "I'm not only older, I'm better." It may occur from an awareness of the changing reactions of others: "She called me 'sir'!" "They really respect my opinion." It may evolve as an aggregate effect after years of experience: "I am truly my own person." "My methods do get results."

An important corollary of finding new potential with adult development is that, as growth continues, the person may acquire inner resources to attack problems that previously had resisted solution. An important change in the transition from adolescent to young adult, for example, is the acquisition of the capacity for personal perspective or insight. This has obvious importance in counseling strategy, inasmuch as personal perspective is necessary for insight to occur.

5. The adult life span contains its own challenges and resources. Each period brings changes in the person's intrapsychic organization: a new level of self-awareness; a refined interpersonal sensitivity; a differ-

ent sense of one's relatedness to the world. In turn, these changes evoke needs, strengths, and vulnerabilities previously suppressed, unnoticed, or nonexistent. One's sense of mortality, and all that death implies, is obviously affected by one's own place in the life span. The vague future becomes the imminent present, depending on whether one is 25 or 45. The historical perspective one has attained at 65 is noticeably absent at 20. But the innovative, activist capacities of young adulthood are never again repeated *as a stage characteristic* in the adult life span.

6. *Development is irreversible.* The capacity for certain kinds of psychological growth (for example, intimacy) is predicated on the prior acquisition of other psychological properties (for example, identity formation). Even in regression people cannot reverse their developmental experience. The adult acting like a child, or reverting to earlier modes of gratification, does so with the experience and behavior patterns of an adult life incorporated into those actions. Grandpa can neither crawl nor experience crawling the way his year-old grandchild does. Nor can one leapfrog over developmental steps without suffering significant decrement in the process.

7. *There is a developmental imperative.* As personal qualities evolve and change, the person, of *necessity*, is confronted with an urgency to respond to this internal demand for change. The urgency may be experienced as challenge, opportunity, threat, or vague unease. Whether it is clearly recognized or only dimly perceived, the imperative to respond is like a demand from within oneself. Many people request counseling precisely because of their inability to cope with this felt need to change or because a mode of functioning that was previously acceptable has been rendered obsolete by their own growth.

Cultural expectations and demands on the individual undergo parallel changes. Society's tasks and attitudes vary according to one's perceived status in the adult age structure. The bearded young adult is asked "When are you going to settle down?" The white-haired old man is asked "When are you going to retire?"

Social definitions of developmental maturity may be quite different from psychological ones. Indeed, as we learn more about psychological development in adulthood, we discover that cultural demands to adapt are sometimes at variance with the felt imperatives of personal development. Some young adults may need to "retire" for a while. Some senescent—that is, aging—adults are far from ready to retire.

Indeed, environmental pressures toward foreclosure of one's identity development (Marcia, 1966) are so powerful that most adults "adapt" to the roles expected of them (Trent & Medsker, 1969) rather than opting for autonomous growth. We shall return to this topic in detail later.

THE DEVELOPMENTAL APPROACH: ORIENTATION

The developmental approach is a longitudinal view of human functioning. Its essential feature is the examination of people over time and, usually, during periods of rapid growth. Human development is concerned with the natural history of human beings, the ordinary course of events that characterizes the unfolding of a human life. Its focus is on what is common to people in general, rather than on what is unique in the individual case. Its emphasis is necessarily on determining what changes are typical over time and growth, rather than what is unusual or exceptional. As Loevinger (1976) points out, development therefore deals with abstractions. Observations serve as the source for generating or supporting hypotheses about human nature in general. Although developmental theory does not ignore individual differences, its preoccupation is with finding points and patterns of similarity among people.

As one ascends the phylogenetic scale, behavior is observed to become more complex, more varied, and more flexible. In human beings, behavior in a fixed situation is less predictable than that of pigeons or even rats. The behavior of *Homo sapiens* is a function not only of physiological equipment and instinctual reactions but also of experience. In humans, as in no other creatures on earth, development involves not biological maturation of genetically coded directions and actions but the interaction of learning with inherited predispositions. Even so fundamental a feature as one's gender identity depends on learning in order for maleness or femaleness to develop (Money & Ehrhardt, 1972).

Thus, the development approach is tied to human natural history—that is, the interactions of biological maturation with learning that produce similar patterns of readiness to react in people at similar periods in their passage through the life span.

THE DEVELOPMENTAL APPROACH: AN ABSTRACTION

To speak of development implies a unity, an internal consistency, within the organism. But the organism is composed of organs and systems, each of which develops according to its own schedules, which are

often unrelated. A child can be intellectually slow in developing yet socially precocious. At birth the infant's head is much closer to adult size than are its legs. Growth typically does not occur in smooth, equal units.

In the earliest months of life physical growth occurs at a tremendously rapid rate, whereas for most of the adult years physical change is at a minimum. By contrast, sexual maturation is very slow during the first decade, then surges forward, and eventually follows a pattern of gradual decline. Thus, any overall estimate of developmental status is necessarily an abstraction attempting to encompass widely divergent data for the purpose of providing a more systematic understanding of human function.

Quality of Change versus Quantity

Because development involves change over time, the ways of assessing change require attention. In physical science the standard measurement techniques are quantitative, and precise mathematical formulae are often developed to describe these relationships. The sophistication of physical science is attested to by its ability to measure and predict both infinitesimal fractions and astronomical distances. All too often, behavioral scientists have shared the view of their colleagues in physics and technology that quantitative accuracy is the hallmark of scientific achievement.

Yet biology, the basic science of life, employs primarily qualitative methods of observation, study, measurement, and prediction. The shape of a leaf or the presence of certain neural structures can be the definitive criterion for assessment, classification, and precise prediction. Darwin's theories of evolution are a testament to the power of qualitative methods of scientific inquiry.

It is particularly important to stress the salience of qualitative change for developmental theories. Growth often involves major shifts in the *locus* of experience (for example, from parent-centered to peer-centered) or the *kinds* of experience (for example, from need for food to need for group membership). Loevinger (1966) convincingly argues the case for assessing milestone[1] sequences (qualitative change) as against polarized variables (quantitative change). In the case of conformity to social standards, for instance, she notes an increase up to a point with increasing maturity. Beyond that point, conformity becomes less important but does not necessarily change to nonconformity. That is, the

---

[1]Loevinger's concept of milestones is discussed in Chapter 3.

opposite of conformity may be either nonconformity *or* not conforming (where one is indifferent to, rather than opposed to, conformity).

In addition, quantitative methods of appraisal may ignore qualitative differences in the meaning of the behavior. How easy it is to mistake legitimate criticism of parental behavior for blind adolescent rebellion. Similarly, the relative absence of a characteristic can be significant in quite different ways.

> A useful purpose will rarely be served by classing together in regard to conformity those who have not yet grown into it, those who are not willing to conform and those . . . who are able to conform but do not need conformity to insure impulse control [Loevinger, 1966; p. 203].

MODELS OF DEVELOPMENTAL CHANGE

If development is best conceptualized through qualitative change, some structural model must be invoked as a framework for understanding the change. Two of the models currently in use are the embryonic and the hierarchical (Loevinger, 1976).

The embryonic model is rooted in biology. It reflects the coming to prominence of different organ systems, each of which goes through a critical period in its ascendance when it is most susceptible to the impact of life experience. Erikson's (1950) theory of psychosocial development uses an embryonic model. Each of his eight ages of life "comes to its ascendance, meets its crisis, and finds its lasting solution during the stage indicated" (p. 271). Each succeeding stage is affected by the solutions reached in the earlier stage(s). But stages do not build systematically. In Erikson's terms the critical issue of the fourth stage, Industry versus Inferiority, will come to ascendance during the latency period irrespective of the resolution of the third-stage issue, Initiative versus Guilt. The hierarchical approach presupposes an invariable sequence of developmental stages, each building on and affected by the prior stage(s). Implicit in the hierarchical model is a belief that the organism advances as it achieves higher developmental levels. Maslow (1954) and Piaget (Tanner & Inhelder, 1957, 1958) both exemplify this construction in their theories of motivation and of moral and intellectual development, respectively. In Maslow's theory, for example, higher-level needs such as beauty and knowledge will have little motivating effect if lower-level (earlier-evolving) needs such as belonging are unsatisfied. In the area of cognitive development it has been found that many people do not reach

Piaget's level of formal operations. Instead, they continue to think at the level of concrete operations (Loevinger, 1976).

We can also distinguish developmental models that emphasize longitudinal features from those that are more cross-sectional in nature. The ongoing research at the Berkeley Institute for Human Development, originated by Macfarlane (1939), epitomizes the longitudinal view that personality change over time defines development. Sanford (1956) studied personality development in the college years. And more recently, Vaillant (1977) published the findings of the Grant Study, conducted over a period of 30 years. The cross-sectional model studies a particular age, period, or stage relative to its own features and characteristics. Development in this model is defined by those features of personality observed when time is held constant. Abraham (1927) studied character structure at the anal stage of psychosexual development, which is said to occur around the age of 2. Neugarten (1963, 1968) and her associates have conducted numerous investigations focusing exclusively on the psychology of middle-aged adults.

Longitudinal models tend to emphasize the flow of developmental processes, whereas cross-sectional models focus on those features that are distinctive of particular life stages. Loevinger (1966, 1976) has attempted to bridge these two models by designing a developmental paradigm based on milestones. She rejects the critical-period belief inherent in the embryonic model and explicitly denies that developmental progress is either age related or an improvement on earlier levels. People whose level of ego development is self-protective may be of any age, may be with or without psychopathology, and may not necessarily be more or less psychosocially effective than people who are at impulsive or integrated levels of development. Her conception of development is structural, in that she is specifically concerned with ego organization and its relative stability.

The developmental model used in this book emphasizes evolving processes that coalesce into discernable life stages. It is eclectic in that it endeavors to synthesize components of existing developmental schemata into one more suitable to an understanding of adult development. This model will be described in detail in Chapter 3.

ADVANTAGES OF A DEVELOPMENTAL APPROACH

Conceptualizing human behavior as an evolving, directional, ever-changing process has certain advantages and limitations. First, let us examine the advantages. The idea of a sequential unfolding of processes

assumes that there are broad normative trends to which people conform. Consequently, it should be possible to systematize observations of human behavior relative to these trends and to note the various traits, characteristics, functions, and other properties of such behavior. One use of this information is as a foundation for making predictions about individual behavior. A second way of using these data is to establish a baseline against which to better understand individual variations. But one need not assume that variations from the standard baseline are automatically abnormal or pathological. Rather, by recognizing a particular sequence and anticipating it, we can examine ways in which individual variations of all kinds can and do occur. This, in turn, gives us a better appreciation for unique variations while simultaneously providing further support for the broad general thrust of human behavior.

From the viewpoint of scientific methodology, the systematic basis for understanding human behavior is broadened and solidified by postulating a dependable and predictable sequence of events. A developmental schema allows for more objective investigation and study, a wider range for generalization of inferences, and more empirically verifiable modes of testing hypotheses. It also lets us isolate component patterns of human behavior. For instance, what is the natural history of idealism as the person grows from adolescence through young adulthood and into established adulthood? In addition, we can better distinguish those phenomena inherent to the species on a biological level from those that may be more dependent on cultural or experiential variations.

As perceived from a developmental point of view, human behavior is placed in a sequential context relative to time and function. We have the opportunity to observe the relationships between the advent of certain functions and the development of capabilities over time. We can observe these ongoing relationships to distinguish between which are necessary and which may be more accidental, which lead to the unfolding of certain processes and which are incidental. This sequence of emergence, in turn, can be related to what the person's *necessary* equipment is for adequately functioning in life. On a more basic level of research the developmental context provides a basis for comparing our species with the evolutionary development of other species. For example, it becomes possible to relate human behavior to primate behavior. The famous studies by Harry Harlow (1958) involving the response of infant monkeys to various kinds of mothering models would have little significance

were it not for the comparability of the developmental patterns of monkeys with those of human beings.

Finally, our concern for human development has a broader application to the larger issue of social evolution. Human beings create social clusters and social units—be these families, clans, or whole societies—and it has long been observed that the evolution of social forms often runs parallel to that of individual human experience. Consequently, increasing knowledge in either area may have important implications for the other within the context of a developmental schema; that is, understanding the early modes of perception and experience of a child growing to maturity can provide models for insight into the developmental processes and modes of functioning in newly forming groups, organizations, or systems.

A promising area for further study has to do with applying the insights of anthropology and sociology into social behavior to a more refined understanding of individual human behavior in terms of a developmental sequence of events. Are there parallels to be drawn, for instance, between those conditions that lead to the deterioration and destruction of cultures and the conditions that may lead to deterioration and psychological disruption of individual lives? The concept of alienation as applied to individual behavior is one instance in which this parallel has already occurred, as witness Emil Durkheim's (1951) concept of *anomie*. Anomie, the alienation caused by social disorganization and isolation, finds its psychological counterpart in Erich Fromm's (1947) theory of neurosis as an alienation from oneself involving internal disorganization and isolation.

Additionally, understanding how group or individual development can be enhanced and strengthened has very important implications for therapeutic or educational procedures designed to maximize human potential.

Finally, the developmental approach contributes valuable insights to the study of psychopathology. Contemporary psychoanalytic ego psychology is founded on the premise of an early developmental sequence. Specific psychopathological syndromes (for example, borderline structures) are aligned with specific developmental periods (for example, separation/individuation) (Kernberg, 1972). Apart from psychoanalytic theory, an appreciation of the demands precipitated by developmental change helps us understand how some seemingly well-functioning peo-

ple become severely disturbed. Personality characteristics or defensive responses that are suitable during one life period may be maladaptive or unacceptable when the individual encounters a different life stage with different expectations or requirements.

LIMITATIONS OF A DEVELOPMENTAL APPROACH

A truism of scientific inquiry holds that as soon as one adopts a point of view—whatever its advantages—one inherits, as well, a set of disadvantages. It is therefore advisable to be aware of these limitations.

Insofar as the developmental point of view denotes an irreversible, directional sequence of events, it suggests that development is biologically determined and that human behavior is primarily inherited or instinctual—that is, unlearned and unaffected by environmental contact. Indeed, this is one of the major criticisms leveled at Freud's theories. The approach adopted here, however, is similar to that of Super (1957) who indicates clearly that human development necessarily includes a predominant place for environmental experience. In general, the genetic component in development is inversely proportional to the biological complexity of the organism. The higher up on the evolutionary scale, the larger the role of experience in the organism's maturation. Human development is the result of the interaction of a multiplicity of variables, among which experiential learning occupies a prominent role.

This assumption of multiple factors deals also with a second criticism of developmental theory—namely, that it implies a universality of traits and characteristics. Although it is true that certain predispositional tendencies are implicitly considered to be universal to the species, a large amount of variability is still possible. For example, the predisposition to physical height limits human beings to a definite range of vertical growth. Yet within this range some people are less than 4 feet tall, and others have exceeded 8 feet. But a human being 20 inches or 20 feet high would be considered an impossible biological mutation. Moreover, there is no evidence to suggest that development is ever reversed, that tall people can "grow" shorter.

Developmental theory has also been criticized for implying a discontinuity of personality structure or function. The concept of stages may suggest that the individual is a different kind of person depending on the particular life stage. In its extreme form it would suggest that an adoles-

cent girl is more similar to another adolescent girl than she is to the girl she was during her latency period. In this sense personality is described as having no continuity, as though each stage produced its own personality, housed in the same body. The work of Arnold Gesell (1946) has been challenged on this basis. At times his descriptions of child development seem to imply that every child on his or her second birthday suddenly acquires negativism, temper tantrums, and the need for a daily nap at 3 o'clock in the afternoon. Three hundred and sixty-five days later the outbursts cease, and the child begins to play amicably with other children. This sort of interpretation results from the same kind of "averaging-out" process that describes the U.S. family as having 2.1 children. As Jones (1943) and others have noted, certain personality traits (for example, docility or aggressiveness) may remain with the person through several developmental stages, if not throughout an entire life span. But their overt manner of expression may vary greatly, partly as a function of situation and experience but also as a function of the relevance of the trait to particular developmental needs.

Hence, although the developmental approach is not without its drawbacks, there is, on balance, ample justification for its use in attempting to understand human behavior.

FACTORS INFLUENCING DEVELOPMENT

Precisely because human development is so complex an interaction of maturation and learning, we must modify any developmental schema to acknowledge the factors that contribute to individual variations around the abstract model. Indeed, these influences can be so profound as to restrict, delay, or even block the emergence of developmentally prepotent features.

Cultural mores and traditions, such as child-rearing practices or attitudes toward women, exercise a determining influence on factors vital to personality development. Environmental conditions can and do play a significant role. The survival-based ethos of a Nazi concentration camp or an urban ghetto provides a different view of the world from that experienced in the plush surroundings of Beverly Hills, California. The sociopolitical climate of the United States during World War II had an impact on young people that can be markedly contrasted to that of the Vietnam War.

Familial experiences play a major role in a child's development. The

family's socioeconomic status, the quality and amount of parenting, and the child's birth-order position are all of demonstrated significance in subsequent behavior.

Finally, personal talents or liabilities—whether intellectual precociousness or physical deformity—condition one's encounter with the outside world and the internal changes one undergoes, and affect both interdependently.

It may seem from even this brief recitation that factors of such magnitude can outweigh the impact of more intrinsic developmental features. In many instances this may indeed be the case. But even these potent forces have a differential effect, depending on the developmental maturity of the person involved. The impact of parental divorce is quite different on children at 2 and at 22. If humankind cannot be extricated from its environment, neither can it be separated from its psychobiology.

IMPLICATIONS FOR ADULT DEVELOPMENT

There is now an extensive literature in developmental psychology. Most of the material in this chapter is distilled from that knowledge. Unfortunately, the great bulk of research and theory deals with childhood and adolescence. Whereas the adult segment covers about 70% of the life span, probably 10% of the literature is concerned with adult development.

Most of the literature on human development has been confined to the first two decades of life. The reasons for such an emphasis are readily understood. Among humans the most rapid growth and maturation takes place during the 20 years after birth. And whatever the biological species, its most dramatic changes occur during the period of most rapid growth. Next, what happens to the organism during its formative period has far-reaching consequences. As a purely practical matter, moreover, infants and children—those under closer societal supervision—are more accessible to observation and study by behavioral scientists than they will be during more autonomous developmental periods. It is largely by virtue of this accessibility that infants, college students, and white rats have provided so much of the data for academic researchers. Finally, as students of human development became increasingly involved with personality development, they turned to the pioneer contributions of psychoanalytic theory, which places primary emphasis on the early years of life. As Erikson says:

Psychoanalysis has consistently described the vicissitudes of instincts and of the ego only up to adolescence, at which time rational genitality was expected to absorb infantile conflicts or irrational fixation to preserve them for repeat performances under manifold disguises [1950, p. 237].

One of the costs of Freud's contributive genius has been a serious retardation of research into the developmental psychology of adult personality. This has come about partly because of a glib acceptance by some that most adult behavior could be explained by the psychoanalytic concepts of repetition-compulsion, transference, identification, and primary-drive derivatives. Vaillant (1977) continues that tradition of describing adult behavior in the language of child-based defense mechanisms.

The major thrust of theory and research into adult thinking and behavior, however, has not come from psychoanalysis or traditional channels of academic psychology. For the delineation of periods of adult life and for the conceptualizing of vital dimensions for comparison, one must turn to the practical contributions of vocational psychology. In particular, the works of Ginzberg, Ginzberg, Axelrad, and Herma (1951), Super (1957), and Havighurst (1952) have been of signal importance. In the course of exploring the determinants of occupational choice and vocational behavior, these investigators have found it expedient to evolve adult developmental models. One consequence of this approach has been Havighurst's notion of developmental tasks (1952). Another has been the previously mentioned extension of the concept of development from the childhood years to include the entire life span.

Pressey and Kuhlen's (1957) work is probably the classic of its kind, providing a lasting source of empirical data on dimensions of change in psychological attributes over the life span. Within the field of education, meanwhile, there has been an increasing interest in explicating the issues and problems specific to adult-education programs (Knowles, 1974). From this concern has arisen the impetus to develop more knowledge about the psychological characteristics of the adult as a learner and student (Knox, 1977). Thus, it has been largely from applied areas of behavior science that the first systematic efforts have come. If the notion of a young-adult period is to be fully explored, it will need to be reconciled with preexisting data in child development. Equally important, a developmental model capable of reflecting the various stages of the adult life span will have to be utilized.

It may be well at this point, therefore, to clarify certain concepts as they will be used in the developmental model. In addition, some review of the criteria for establishing a developmental stage is in order.

DEFINING TERMS

Development—that is, psychological development—proceeds as a function of the interaction of experience, physiological status, and readiness for learning. The status of each of these components at any point in time/space directly affects the status of the other two. Psychological impact (effect) depends on the particular characteristics of the combination of components at that time. It is the combination, as a Gestalt, that is the psychologically effective unit.

Experience requires both the occurrence of particular events and the person's presence at the time of occurrence. Few of us have experienced earthquakes because, although earthquakes have often happened, we were not at the right place at the right time. Similarly, few of us have entertained Martian visitors in our living rooms, despite extensive experience with living-room entertaining.

Physiological status refers to the range and level of function of the body and its parts. Factors such as disease, age, exercise, heredity, and nutrition can be responsible for wide variations in maturation of the body's apparatus relative to development.

Readiness for learning is a concept familiar to most educators. There are points at which maturational and motivational influences coalesce relative to specific activities. At these times the individual is particularly susceptible to acquiring that particular skill or knowledge. Reading readiness, for example, refers to that period when the child's physiological equipment and curiosity have ripened so that he or she is optimally susceptible to learning how to read. In biologically primitive species, where maturation and motivation are largely determined on a genetic basis, certain kinds of learning occur only at these periods of readiness. The associative learning that takes place is called imprinting, and it is an irreversible, one-shot event. Because of the human being's endless capacity for learning, people can unlearn or relearn at periods beyond the point of readiness. It would appear, however, that belated learning—or unlearning and relearning—is an appreciably less effective way of learning.

Development can be considered a continuous process. A man becomes bald by continuously losing his hair; rarely does baldness happen

overnight. Height and hunger both develop by degrees, bit by bit. Normative charts show typical heights and weights plotted against chronological age. The changes, moreover, occur in measurable units of inches, pounds, and years. Yet despite the undeniable accuracy of this method, we often prefer to describe these same characteristics in nonnumerical, or qualitative, language. Someone is *short* or *tall, thin* or *fat, young* or *old.* Similarly, we are able to differentiate a smile from a grin qualitatively without invoking a unit of measurement. Indeed we are able to communicate such distinctions as *cute* and *lovely* with even greater accuracy by *not* having recourse to quantitative comparisons.

Thus, although development is a progressive, continuous *process,* it is especially useful at times to view it in a qualitative, or discontinuous, way. Hence we speak of developmental stages.

A developmental stage is characterized by certain qualitative differences that distinguish it from the periods before and after it. It represents a period of life during which a number of processes coalesce to form a distinguishable matrix or constellation. This particular constellation of psychological events will never again recur spontaneously in the life of the individual. But one can observe this same constellation of processes consistently in other individuals at about the same period of the life span.

This matrix of processes that identifies a life stage is best understood as a readiness to respond—a set of susceptibilities, or potentialities. Whether it is manifested in overt behavior—or in what form—will be determined by environmental opportunity interacting with this readiness. It must be emphasized that the interaction between organism and environment is itself part of the potentiation process. The person who is ready to laugh finds more environmental opportunities to do so.

The terms *process* and *structure* occur repeatedly in this book. *Process* refers to psychological events, or aspects of those events, that are ongoing in time and space. *Structure* refers to qualities of organization, stability, and strength of a psychological construct. Thus one can view ego as a process that is changing and growing and/or as a structure that organizes and controls certain personality functions.

3

MODELS OF ADULT DEVELOPMENT

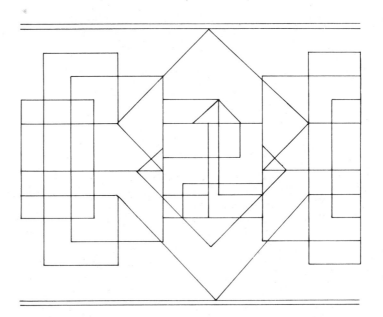

Research in adult development has produced several different theoretical models. Each of these models attempts to deal with major problems in studying the adult life span. Although it is necessary to recognize some of the methodological problems in this area of knowledge, I will not venture deeply here into those large issues. You are referred to sources such as Bayley (1975) and Neugarten (1975a) for a more extensive inquiry into the problems of research design that are particular to life-span psychology. The purpose of this chapter is to examine the existing models and the information they have generated. From these findings will emerge the schema I have found most useful in conceptualizing the adult life span and, within that context, the place of young adulthood.

LIFE-SPAN MODEL

The most comprehensive of the models is the *life-span* schema. Investigators within this framework present dimensions of human development as they evolve from infancy through old age.

The earliest life-span study was done by Charlotte Buhler (1935). Buhler collected 300 biographies, including in her survey the external life events, the subjects' internal reactions to these events, and their objective accomplishments during the course of life. These data were then combined with a biological life curve. Within this framework, life is divided into five stages. The first stage, from birth through late adolescence, is centered on home and school activities. The second, or preparatory, stage involves entry into self-chosen and independent activity. The third stage begins around the end of the third decade. It is characterized by a final choice of vocation and establishment of a home. The fourth stage is one of psychological crises—deaths (of parents and relatives), discontent, a sense of weakness, and general restriction of the dimensions of living. The final stage is entered in the early 60s. Physical decline is more conspicuous. One experiences retirement, sickness, and the death of associates.

Carl Jung (1969) offered a more simplified, four-stage depiction of the life span. From a contemporary perspective, it is unique in its emphasis on the adult years. Jung's theory was based on his extensive readings and clinical observations. The first stage, childhood, is concerned with learning about the world. The second stage is youth, which extends from puberty to around age 40. This period is seen as a coming to terms with what is attainable in life. Middle age is characterized by the reversal in dominance of one's masculine and feminine qualities. The

scope of life also undergoes contraction at this time. In old age, extending
through the 80s, people are the keepers of the laws and "guardians of the
mysteries" of life. It is the old who seek the meaning of life.

Havighurst (1952) uses the concept of developmental tasks to
identify the attitudes and behaviors that people are expected to master as
they progress along the life span. In turn, these changing tasks define the
six life stages he identifies: infancy and early childhood; middle childhood; adolescence; early adulthood; middle age; and later maturity.

Erikson (1959) constructed a life-span schema that has been the
most influential model of its type. He associates each of eight life stages
with a particular polarized psychosocial crisis: trust versus mistrust;
autonomy versus shame and doubt; initiative versus guilt; industry versus
inferiority; identity versus identity confusion; intimacy versus isolation;
generativity versus stagnation; and integrity versus despair.

Characteristic of the life-span approach is the identification of a
particular concept or dimension (for example, crisis, task) that organizes
the developmental process at each successive stage of its unfolding. The
more recent investigators who outline only the adult years from a life-
span perspective tend to follow a similar format. Vaillant (1978) describes the development of defenses, viewed on a dimension of maturity.
Levinson and his colleagues (1978) attribute to each adult stage a particular issue or task (for example, "becoming one's own man"). Whitbourne
and Weinstock (1979) view adult development as an extension of the
Piagetian processes of assimilation and accommodation. Ongoing experiences are assimilated into the existing personality structure, or else the
personality changes to accommodate new events.

Methodologically, the life-span approach would seem ideally suited
to the study of human development as it unfolds. Human longevity,
however, raises a number of problems for longitudinal research. Baltes
and Schaie (1973) and Wohlwill (1970) treat the design problems extensively. In general, measures used by early investigators (for example,
Macfarlane, 1939; Vaillant, 1977) tend to be less sophisticated than those
currently available. Alternatively, life-history data reported in retrospect
are subject to distortion, repression, and selective forgetting.

CROSS-SECTIONAL MODEL

As its name implies, the cross-sectional approach examines the
features of a particular time period or developmental stage. Comparisons

between stages are of subordinate or neglible interest. Neugarten's historic investigations of middle age provide data on time perception (Neugarten & Datan, 1973) and attitudes toward menopause (Neugarten, 1963) as well as the general world view of people in middle age. White (1975) describes "growth trends" of young adults (see Chapter 6) and does not relate his findings to preceding or subsequent life stages. Other investigators have studied the last half of adulthood (Peck, 1968), the disengagement theory of old age (Cumming & Henry, 1961), emotional patterns of the elderly (Gitelson, 1977), and parenthood (Gutmann, 1975).

The cross-sectional method permits more intensive study of features unique to a particular life period. But the evolutionary aspects of development from stage to stage may be ignored and must be subordinated in the cross-sectional approach. As the Schaie, Labouvie, and Buech (1973) investigation of intelligence has demonstrated, intrastage variations can be as wide as those between stages when studied over a 14-year period.

MILESTONES MODEL

A different approach to the psychological study of the life span has been described by Loevinger (1966): the identification of developmental milestones. Although this approach is also longitudinal, its thrust is to describe the qualitative evolutionary changes in fundamental aspects of personality development.

Perhaps the preeminent example of milestone research is Piaget's (1963) work on cognitive development in children. Perry (1970) has extended this research into the college years. Kohlberg's (1964) theory of moral development is also designed as a milestone model. Isaacs (1956) formulated the concept of relatability to describe the evolution of interpersonal relationships. Most recently, Loevinger (1966, 1976) has published a model of ego development. The findings of these investigators will be discussed further in Chapter 6.

The advancement of developmental theory has been appreciably enhanced by the identification and description of those basic psychological ingredients that continue to evolve over the life span. Unfortunately, an exclusive preoccupation with only one or two dimensions of personality development characterizes the milestone approach. The theories of both Loevinger and Kohlberg are also vulnerable to another criticism.

Neither model attempts to locate the later-evolving milestones in the adult life span. A person could, in these models, attain the highest levels of development at either the beginning or end of the adult years.[1] Consequently, one is left to infer that decades of adult experience have negligible impact on the psychological processes of ego or moral development. Alternatively, one would seemingly be faced with the conclusion that the adult years are static and devoid of all but the most accidental of changes. Finally, the milestone approach fails to relate the several developmental curves to one another. It is as though moral, social, intellectual, and ego development were independent.

In point of fact, most theorists would agree that there is a close and ongoing interdependence among the various developmental ingredients. Intellectual development permits certain moral issues to emerge, and interpersonal growth depends on the integrity of the individual ego processes. Because these evolutionary forces do affect one another, their patterns of interaction are of vital importance to the overall developmental process. From the perspective of holistic Gestalt psychology, a more parsimonious explanation would be that people develop as whole people. Ingredients such as ego, morality, intelligence, and the like have no life history of their own, independent of the total person. Whether one bakes a pie or parents a child, the structure undergoes change in its entirety.

One can identify components in the structure or stages in the process, but the frame of reference is always the whole. The model to be presented here subscribes to this holistic viewpoint. In developmental terms it is called the principle of categorical evolution.

CATEGORICAL-EVOLUTION MODEL

According to the approach suggested here, development is an organismic process, more than the sum of its parts. One can identify central components of this process, but they are understood to be in constant, mutual interaction. From the interactive process there emerge certain recognizable patterns, called *stages*. Stages, in turn, generate certain features distinctive to their constellation. A set of properties, or features, thus identifies each stage. In turn, each new constellation modifies the previous patterns of interaction and sets new directions for the developmental process.

As a conceptual model, the categorical-evolution principle acknowledges the importance of both longitudinal components and cross-

---

[1]Kohlberg (1978) is now moving to study the effects of aging on moral development.

sectional stages. Both of these sets of categories are conceived as interdependent constructs in a holistic model of development in which change—rather than static states—is the natural condition. One important element that the categorical-evolution model shares with its predecessors is in the highlighting of qualitative over quantitative changes. Finally, because an evolutionary reorganization is necessary at each stage of adult development, a number of milestone changes can be expected to emerge. These changes in fundamental areas of development distinguish and identify the several stages.

Consistent with the qualitative approach adopted here, explicit reference to chronological age has been omitted. The weight of increasing evidence seems to indicate that great variations occur in the chronological emergence of psychological characteristics. These differences are a direct function of variations in the precise timing of psychological experience. Because of the endless variety of cultural patterns, chronological time may be expanded or reduced drastically, relative to developmental stages.

It is the relative location in the life span, not fixed chronological age, that distinguishes a developmental stage. Consequently, a focus on psychological variables—apart from temporal considerations—emphasizes the essential sequence of events for cross-cultural comparisons. Nevertheless, in our own society, chronological age has a variety of psychologically significant meanings. Age, therefore, cannot be entirely ignored without neglecting an important variable containing relevant data. In an attempt to satisfy both objectives, the chronological definition of the young-adult period *in our society* is discussed elsewhere (see Chapter 1) as it relates to certain basic issues. From this background, we now proceed to an examination of the developmental model used here.

CHARACTERISTICS OF THE DEVELOPMENTAL MODEL

The developmental model presented here is founded on the following assumptions.

1. Psychological changes occur over the entire life span.
2. These changes can be qualitatively distinguished as developmental stages.
3. To qualify for status as a distinct and separate developmental stage, these changes must involve psychological functions rather than physical, hormonal, or situational modifications.
4. The psychological features of a developmental stage should be clearly distinguishable from those in the preceding and subsequent stages.

It is anticipated that various parts of the model presented here will enjoy only a short life in their present form. Systematic knowledge about the adult years is in a rudimentary state. As investigation and study proceed, a more highly refined understanding will emerge. In this connection, it is worth noting that most adult-development theorists—Buhler, Neugarten, and Erikson, for example—list only three adult stages. Although other investigators, including Super (1963) in a vocational adaptation of Buhler, continue to identify three stages—early adulthood, middle age, and old age—there is a trend to partition these periods into substages of different kinds. The model presented here lists four stages: young adulthood, established adulthood, middle-age adulthood, and senescent adulthood.

Before we proceed to an examination of the developmental stages, some clarification of nomenclature may avoid later confusion with related terms. In selecting names for the stages, I tried to use terms having broad acceptance in the behavioral-science community. In a developmental schema omitting chronological age referents, it is particularly important that the stages be recognized with a high degree of consensual validation. The model is outlined on Table 3-1. The adolescent stage is included for comparison purposes.

Reading the column headings horizontally, you will notice a progression from Intrapsychic Issue through Interpersonal Focus to Intracultural Expectation. Each of these requires elaboration. At the outset, it should be noted that, whenever we deal with psychological factors within an organism, these variables exist in constant dynamic interaction with one another. What goes on inside people is only for conceptual purposes separate from the others with whom they are in contact. And no one can be understood without reference to cultural milieu, ethos, and expectations. Thus, the idea of a normal boy's trembling with fear at the prospect of going to the beach on a hot summer day is puzzling until we learn that the boy is Black and the beach is populated by a notoriously violent anti-Black group.

Nevertheless, there is value in separately listing the component ingredients in order to differentiate important facets of psychological functioning.

Intrapsychic Issue

The column headed Intrapsychic Issue might as easily have been called Ego Task. The essential concept here is that throughout life the

Table 3-1. A Model of Adult Development

Stage	Intrapsychic Issue	Interpersonal Focus	Intracultural Expectation
EARLY ADOLESCENCE	Identity crisis Reactivation of earlier issues	Opposite sex and peers generally	Development of interests and abilities Initiation to heterosexual behavior
LATE ADOLESCENCE	Reintegration— "I am"	Leadership models	School and work choices Emotional independence
YOUNG ADULTHOOD	Self-particulari-zation: "What and who I am" Ego integration	Partners and competitors	Founding a family Building a career
ESTABLISHED ADULTHOOD	Consolidation and effectuation	Everyone (peers primarily)	Sustain society Contribute to psycho-social growth of family
MIDDLE-AGED ADULTHOOD	Self-confrontation	Personification of principles	Provide for own sustenance and eventual retire-ment
SENESCENT ADULTHOOD	Death	Remembered persons	Self-maintenance.

organism confronts internal issues with which it must come to terms. Whatever their immediate origin, these issues have far-reaching implications for the way the person thinks and reacts within. As natural outgrowths of the person's experience with self, these issues are not necessarily problems to be solved or conflicts to be terminated. Instead, they can be thought of as facts of intrapsychic life to be lived with, assimilated, and understood. Intrapsychic issues must be dealt with in appropriate ways so that one can recognize, come to terms with, and master the feelings or impulses aroused by them. This permits the person

to incorporate the potentialities inherent in them into ongoing ego functions.

The intrapsychic issue is the least overt and most universal of the components listed. Ego functioning is inferred rather than observed. By defining the process, we can recognize the way it is manifested. But the specific behavior may vary from culture to culture or across periods of history. Helplessness, for example, can be demonstrated quite differently depending on the person, place, and circumstance.

Interpersonal Focus

The next column acknowledges the crucial importance of human interaction at virtually every stage in the life span. As the person evolves psychophysiologically, the kinds of interpersonal experience that are needed developmentally also undergo change. The people in the individual's human environment may remain constant over a considerable time. General social and human needs may be reasonably satisfied. But at different times in the life history each individual requires certain kinds of personal contacts as a function of his or her developmental level.

As these needs evolve, appropriate persons are selected out of the human environment for participative exploration. For the infant, it may be a mothering figure; for the adolescent, a peer. In addition, the same person may serve quite different developmental functions at different times. Such is the case, for example, when an older sister serves as a mothering figure in early childhood and as an object of sexual or romantic fantasies in adolescence. Even though the person is the same older sister, she is seen differently as a function of what is developmentally significant for the subject at that time.

Thus, it is postulated that there is a natural history of interpersonal evolution over the life span. In adult development this consists of a progressive refinement, elaboration, and utilization of previously acquired skills in gender and generational differentiation. Learning to relate to both sexes, to one's own sexual and gender identity, and to people both older and younger is a necessary part of the life course for adults in any culture. For this reason it seems likely that interpersonal development would be a central ingredient of human natural history. What the present model makes evident is that this process continues throughout the life span as a necessary component of the developmental experience.

Intracultural Expectations

As used in this context, *intracultural expectation* diverges substantially from the term *developmental task* used by Havighurst and others. In its more generally recognized form, the developmental task is an *activity* appropriate to the person's age or vocational status. It may originate from physical maturation, cultural pressure, or the person's own values and aspirations. The developmental task is specific to the individual's cultural or subcultural group. It arises at a time when the individual is said to be ripe for that sort of learning experience. It involves developing specific attitudes and skills. Successful completion of the task brings happiness and a readiness to move on to the next level. Failure leads to difficulty in subsequent tasks (Havighurst, 1952).

By comparison, an intracultural expectation is basically a *psychological function* or capacity that is to be met and mastered. It is less specific than a "thing-to-do" conception would imply; it is, rather, a process to be engaged in and assimilated. Although such expectations may often seem to originate with the person, society would in any event expect or require their successful attainment.

The intracultural expectation represents not society's highest aspirations for the individual but rather the way it defines psychosocial competence for any given stage. Finally, as defined here, it is expected that the intracultural expectations will have an appreciable cross-cultural applicability. Many of the tasks are fundamental to the continuation of any cohesive social order.

Thus, the intracultural expectations in this model refer specifically to our time in North American history. In other cultures or in other eras, some or all of these expectations might be quite different. However, cross-cultural consistency is more likely to occur when one focuses on processes rather than behaviors.

Referring to the developmental chart in Table 3-1, along the left-hand margin, there is a vertical listing of the several adult developmental stages: Young Adulthood, Established Adulthood, Middle-Aged Adulthood, and Senescent Adulthood. For purposes of contrast, Adolescence (early and late) is included as well.

It should be emphasized again that development proceeds gradually, if unevenly. The shifting orientation that is characteristic of adult life stages evolves over years. One does not become an adult the way one becomes a college student. There are no formal rites as the person leaves

one stage and enters the next. Developmental stages tend to overlap and merge. That a new stage has been engaged becomes apparent only when the various component features have matured and come together so as to gain visibility. The person whose intrapsychic development is advanced may still be struggling to resolve intracultural expectations of an earlier stage. Many adults seem never to have resolved certain adolescent facets of development. But these matters accentuate the value of a developmental model, in that they serve as a standard by which to evaluate and clarify a given individual's developmental status and needs.

Finally, psychological development proceeds at a different pace in the adult life span than it has earlier. A single developmental stage may extend over a decade or longer. In those areas where prior development has been incomplete, progress may be even slower. An established adult may exhibit remnants of adolescent peer relations with business associates, yet be an effective parent at home.

THE LIFE STAGES

Adolescence

Articles are written about children; books are written about adolescents. Or so it seems. For the present purposes adolescence can be thought of as being composed of an earlier and a later period. We are by now familiar with the facts underlying the description of early adolescence as a tumultuous age (for example, see Lidz, 1976) in which hormonal activity and rapid skeletal growth conspire with social change (in this culture the period of entering junior high school) to create a mélange of psychic distress, confusion, and excitation. Maturation of the gonads brings with it a major shift of interest from same-sex activities to a heterosexual orientation. At the same time (perhaps because sexual maturation conveys a sense of coming of age), earlier issues incompletely dealt with become reactivated. Small wonder that intrapsychic confusion is the rule rather than the exception at this time!

Identity crisis is the normative experience. Strain is severe on the ego's organization of integrated functions. Rorschach studies of early adolescents reveal an intrapsychic distress similar to that found in women undergoing their first pregnancies and in people with incipient psychosis (Huntington, 1968).

The most significant interpersonal figures become one's peers. This is a major shift, even though its onset can be traced back to the earlier

juvenile, or latency, period. Despite a continuing need for parental support and reassurance, early adolescents give primary interest and attention to their age cohorts. Separation from the family and parental authority, rather than rebellion, is at issue. Assimilating the attitudes and values of peers is of great importance. At stake is the evolution of emotional independence from one's family of origin. It is also eminently practical, in that fellow teenagers constitute the generation with whom adolescents will spend the bulk of their productive adult years. Finally, it is consistent with the sense of impending maturity that early adolescents endeavor to discover and develop their own interests and abilities.

In the later phase of adolescence, the primary issue is the person's reintegration of a sense of self. Whether this resolution occurs through identity formation (Erikson, 1966) or foreclosure (Marcia, 1972), the central ingredient is the coalescing of a sense of ego integrity in a notion of "I am." At this time, the adolescent's needs for a significant figure are directed to someone who can serve as a model to emulate. For this reason the significant figure may be someone who symbolizes a value (such as success), or the model may be as concrete as the young married woman next door. By this time, too, it is expected that the person will have sufficient self-clarification to begin vocational planning. Not infrequently, the pressure to make schoolwork choices helps to integrate hazy or partially formulated aspects of identity formation.

Whatever the sequence, when these steps are taken, the passage through childhood is complete, and the person stands on the threshold of adulthood. This sketchy outline of adolescence will be amplified in Chapter 5. But an extended treatment of adolescence cannot be attempted here. You are referred to Blos (1962) for a classical psychoanalytic approach and to Douvan and Adelson (1966) for a more generic psychological understanding.

Young Adulthood

As we have seen, the central issue of late adolescence involves coming to a sense of "I am." This conception is understood to reflect a sense of personal wholeness, of being intact. In young adulthood, the issue is one of *self-particularization.* Young adults seek to define themselves more specifically: "What am I?" Having attained a measure of confidence in their fundamental psychological integrity as a self-in-being in some global sense, they now move to identify the self's components— attitudes, interests, skills, values, beliefs, wishes, and aptitudes.

At this point it is not necessary for a crystallized, fully articulated self-concept to be "discovered." Although many concerned parents would feel grateful relief at the evidence that their progeny had "found themselves," most educators and psychotherapists would view final stabilization in this period as premature, a rigidification of the personality. Self-particularization means a coalescing of the vital concerns that affect and influence the person. These concerns may not be resolved, or even resoluble (as in the case of a commitment to human welfare). They may be only indirectly or partially conscious. Indeed, it is typical for the self-particularization process to occur primarily as a subliminal or preconscious experience, punctuated by instances of conscious awareness. This is not surprising, inasmuch as most human thinking is not at a conscious level.[2]

The process involves an ongoing series of experiences, ideas, emotional associations, memories, and experiments. They are broadly, rather than specifically, interconnected, but the underlying genotypic consistency becomes increasingly more apparent even though the overt phenotypic behavior seems diverse. Thus, young adults may discover that they enjoy sharing affection and long-term, more than short-term, relationships. Yet they may be only vaguely aware that these traits reflect a preference for intimacy over conquest and make no connection at all between this constellation of attitudes and a philosophical commitment to humanitarian beliefs. Whether or not such a matrix of attitudes, actions, and ideas ever becomes conscious, it serves importantly as a unifying, directional, and motivational aspect of the personality—much in the same manner as Allport's (1937) idiographic trait.

Whatever the content, longevity, and degree of conviction or articulation of such a construct, its sheer existence serves to identify and specify the internal dimensions of the self-concept. A set of internal reference points is established that helps give young people their self-directed and self-controlled *adult* character. Self-particularization and ego integration will be explored further in Chapter 7.

As further evidence of their adult status, young adults find the most significant people in their lives to be other adults who are their peers. Although sexual distinctions are, of course, still prominent, there is now to be found a growing attitude of partnership that tends to transcend

---

[2]If you question this statement, consider how much conscious thought you give to such complex voluntary actions as walking or planning the exact wording and vocal inflections of your everyday conversation—or even how you are going to spend your money for the next two months.

gender. There is a distinct sense of being "co-venturers." Sexual conquest for its own sake gradually begins to give way to a notion of sharing experience. This is an essential precursor to the development of a heterosexual loving relationship. Sexual selections are increasingly made from a partnership orientation that differentiates degrees and kinds of affiliation.

The interpersonal focus that is complementary to partnership in young adults is that of competitor. A competitor orientation enables people to distinguish their thoughts and needs from those of significant others and retain a critical degree of autonomy within an affiliative relationship. Both partnership and competitor relationships demand a degree of maturation not usually found in adolescents. As will be seen in Chapter 8, both features are interlaced with the achievement of a firm ego identity. Moreover, partnership and competitorship both involve a process of interpersonal differentiation that develops from the kinds of peer relations established in adolescence.

In this as in most other cultures, founding a family and building a career are the requirements for being accepted as an adult. Viewed solely from the perspective of intracultural expectations, the span of the young-adult period can be described as progressing from the initiation of sex and work objectives to the solidifying of these plans in decisive actions. By any standards those people who have set about creating a family and are constructing a stable base for providing for their own material needs have made a place for themselves in adult society. In addition, the psychological impact of these tasks is associated with a marked change in people's thinking. Several interrelated departures from previous attitudes take place at once. One of the most important of these is the ability to make personal commitments. Thus, as the character of thought and central concerns change, the individual moves out of the young-adult stage and into established adulthood.

Established Adulthood

According to Super and his colleagues' (1963) data, this period is the most productive part of the life span. For the great majority of people, founding a family and embarking on a reasonably well-articulated career tend to structure both the perception and the objective reality of life. Through these two channels are directed most of the energies of most adult people. Indeed, the central tasks of adult life viewed from the societal perspective are defined with cross-cultural universality as providing for economic security and social preservation and growth.

As breadwinners, established adults determine for their family (or primary group) the material conditions under which they will live. They may dedicate their efforts to the acquisition of wealth or may be indifferent to it. In either event, spouse and children will adjust their lives in response to that decision. Throughout history, the very survival of the family's constituent members has been dependent on the attitude and action of the breadwinner/parent. It is no coincidence, therefore, to find that many societies have invested the head of the household with the power of life and death over other family members.

At the same time, established adults are charged with perpetuating the species by producing progeny and with protecting their relatively helpless offspring. They are thus quite literally the anthropological pillars of their society. They not only care for their own families but in so doing also help to sustain and continue the growth of their sociocultural unit.

Established adults represent, in addition, a vital identification figure for children in their years of most active growth and change. By virtue of children's need for identification in their psychological growth process, the established adults' sheer presence or absence is a vital issue of demonstrated effect. As active participants in children's education, moreover, they can powerfully affect psychosocial development. For most children, the encouragement or criticism of adults is a central motivating factor influencing what, when, and how they learn. The more significant the adult is to the child, the greater is the influence. Thus, established adults are not only responsible for societal maintenance but also have a major role in the kind and quality of growth likely to be found in the upcoming generation.

For most adults in this period, the central intrapsychic issues are *consolidation* and *effectuation*. Having largely identified their own strivings, talents, beliefs, and aspirations, established adults need first to solidify these features alone and in relation to one another as well as to relate them to their goals in life. By this time they are typically past the point of familiarization with career, family, and other personal objectives. Their increasing experience enables them to refine, modify, or refocus these objectives as they become more sophisticated in their activities. Their technical skills—as a worker, parent, spouse, human being—are reaching a peak attainable only through extensive experience with the consequences of actions or decisions made at a time when they were living as mature, responsible adults. This longer-term perspective

enables established adults to make more confident predictions about the relationships between events. With this impetus and the support and encouragement of society, they are excellently situated to put into practice their thoughts and beliefs. Thus it is that most men have their greatest career growth in this time span. This is a period when opportunities are presented for responsible action and when reward and promotion quickly follow and support successful decisions.

The woman is not less fortunately placed. If she is primarily involved in a career, her pattern will probably parallel closely that of her male counterpart. In addition to her work, she will probably have discovered sources for affectional expression. She will have come to some resolution concerning marriage and sexual activity. Whatever the decision, she is usually freer and more comfortable with her sexual life. As the data of several studies of sexual behavior (Gagnon, 1973; Kinsey et al., 1953; Masters & Johnson, 1970) suggest, both single and married women seem to have difficulty unshackling themselves from the sexual mores of this society before their 30s.[3]

The married woman who does not have a career benefits both materially and vicariously from her husband's establishment in a career. Greater job security and increased income provide her with more latitude for a variety of plans and purchases. She may also share the pleasure of being the unseen partner in her husband's accomplishments. The growth of the marriage and the children provide another tangible source of pleasure for husband and wife. At the same time, the wife/mother experiences an increasing autonomy as her children become less dependent on her for constant care and attention. For many women this period coincides with the initial emergence of thoughts about a "second career" when the children are grown. Unlike the anxious concerns of earlier stages, however, her sense of competence as wife and mother provides a source of security.

For the dual-career woman, management of home and paid employment will often impede progress in one or the other area. But there is no evidence that psychological development is impaired or that the evolution of effectuation is in any way delayed. Nevertheless, personal stress may well be increased by the extensive demands on her energies.

The interpersonal world of established adults excludes virtually no

---

[3]Despite the evidence of much greater sexual freedom among people in the teens and 20s, my clinical experience with women in these years still indicates a significant amount of sexual inhibition, which limits sexual satisfaction.

one and includes virtually everyone. As the vital growth force in society, they interact with all ages and kinds of people.

Middle-Aged Adulthood

Middle age corresponds to the fourth stage of Buhler and Frankel's life-span schema (Buhler, 1935). It is during this period that people become aware that the anabolic, or building-up, phase of life is over. Whatever they were to become, they either are or are not. With rare exceptions (such as national politicians), they are at or near maximum attainment. Youth is gone; decline lies ahead. Parents and some older siblings, relatives, and friends may be dead or gone. Children have families and careers of their own. Thus is the stage set for a critical psychological issue—*self-confrontation*. At this point, when the future is no longer tomorrow, one comes face to face with oneself and one's life. The menopausal reaction of women differs from men's experience only in its physiological component. For both sexes, the sense of loss of potency can be acute. For both, the question "What have I done with my life?" is poignantly and overridingly salient. Some people attempt to deal with the issue by demonstrating their continuing prowess with a flight into sexuality. Some react with severe depression. It has been contended that the high incidence of fatal illness at this period (for example, heart disease and cancer) is in many instances a reaction to involutional self-confrontation.

Much has been written of the pain and pathology of middle age. Arthur Miller's *Death of a Salesman* and Neil Simon's *Plaza Suite* provide excellent literary examples of the power of self-confrontation in middle age. But much less attention has been given to growth in middle age. Rubin's (1978) study of 160 middle-aged women contradicts popular mythology in that her most common finding was not depression over the "empty nest," but relief. This finding parallels those of Neugarten et al. (1963), whose menopausal subjects were generally free from symptoms of physical or emotional distress.

With middle age comes a relaxation of the demands of parenting. There is also a progressive shift in responsibility from sustaining the culture and its subgroups to maintaining oneself. Thus, a tremendously liberating period can ensue as middle-aged adults come to terms with themselves. With fewer external demands on their time and energy, they are able to explore or extend their personal lives in greater depth.

At middle age the intracultural task for North American adults is

providing for present sustenance and future retirement. One discovers a marked reduction in material needs with children married, indigent relatives deceased, and one's own preferences in food, clothing, and shelter simplified. More money is available for investment and recreation. This is the age at which many people undertake their first extended vacation, begin second careers, or just start to accumulate surplus funds. Interpersonal interests tend to become more abstract—to be reflected in contemplation of human nature and concern with principles rather than persons. A gradual process of disinvolvement with individuals begins to take place at this time. As a result, petty interpersonal irritations are reduced, because people do not matter quite so much. This may partially account for the benign, "grandfatherly" quality that so markedly overtakes many middle-age adults after the initial shock of transition has passed. Having come to an acceptance of themselves, they are able to live genially with others and to find new dimensions for exploration and satisfaction.

Senescent Adulthood

The senescent adult confronts mortality. At this stage of the life span one becomes increasingly aware, personally and experientially, that one must die. True, death itself may be years or even decades away—particularly as nutrition and medical technology continue to extend life expectancy. It is also true that the septuagenarian of today often looks ten years younger than did his counterpart a generation earlier. Nevertheless, with aging come unmistakable signs of greater infirmity. The person can become aware of progressive physical decline many years in advance of total incapacity or death. A lessening of psychomotor and cognitive functions adds further to a sense of decline. Memory for recent events tends to blur, and new learning becomes more difficult.

At the same time, there is a reduction in the number of familiar faces in the person's immediate environment. Progressively fewer friends, immediate relatives, and other associates remain alive. A growing sense of social alienation develops as more and more strange faces appear. It is not surprising, therefore, to find an increasing interpersonal preoccupation with the past and with the remembered people who inhabited it. This concern also provides the important opportunity to review one's life and weave it into some meaningful sense of history and tradition. This integrative process is probably responsible for the evolution of what Peck (1968) calls a transcendent attitude, in which the

person transcends mortality and relates self to some cosmic understanding of the universe, usually through philosophy or religion.

Additionally, senescent adults are freed from responsibility for most of the activities that structure life. The subsequent loss of authority further tends to increase a sense of weakness and lack of value. Our society does expect them to care for themselves, physically and materially, to their maximum ability. It is refreshing to note that geriatric workers have reported a close correlation between self-maintenance and social involvement. One is tempted to suspect that many of the signs regarded as characteristic of advanced age—invalidism, loss of reality contact, and regressive behavior—may be largely a function of senescent adults' sense of alienation and self-devaluation, so that they cease caring for or about themselves. Although death is inevitable, misery and degeneration need not be. It is hoped that future generations will devote enough attention to the terminal life stage to better integrate it into the developmental fabric of the entire life span.

Thus, in synoptic form, we have spanned that bulk of the life span, beginning with adolescence and encompassing the various adult stages. The categorical-evolution model applied here permits an examination of some of the most widely acknowledged, global dimensions of development. From this model it can be seen that the adult years are years of identifiable change. In truth, significant segments of this model are hypothetical, even speculative. The model presents an expectable version of the life span, not necessarily one that is always attained. But the principles set forth earlier have been maintained. It is possible to describe an evolutionary pattern of growth covering the most central areas of human development, which represent the adult life stages.

It may well seem that too much has been covered too glibly—that it is presumptuous to attempt to describe the adult life span in a book and absurd to attempt it in a single chapter. I plead guilty on both counts. What has been presented above constitutes not coverage but an outline of psychosocial development in order that this examination of the young adult be undertaken in some meaningful context. If it is feasible to talk of a distinguishable young-adult period, its proponents should be able to describe characteristics of this stage that are distinctive yet embedded in the larger adult span. It is beyond the scope of the volume—and in advance of the necessary empirical data—to present a more detailed position at this time.

4

THE ACQUISITIONS OF ADULTHOOD

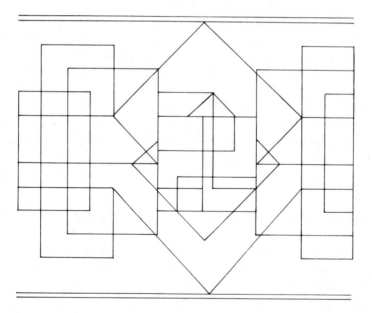

DEFINITIONS OF ADULTHOOD

When the question "What is an adult?" is posed, the answers are likely to be as diverse as the persons who might raise it. The term *adult* derives from the Latin *adultus,* the past participle of *adolescere,* to grow up. Adult, therefore, implies a developmental sequence in which the growth process has been completed. Consistent with such a formulation, the most common conception of the adult relies extensively on physical attributes. Those who have attained adult size are more likely to be considered adult. Height, girth, and strength are prominent features of a first impression and set up a chain of associations related to the growing (child)/full-grown (adult) dimension.

Age as a determinant of developmental status has a long history. Ancient Hebrew law designated the 13th birthday as the specific point of transition from religious immaturity to responsibility for one's own actions (*bar mitzvah*). Legal definitions of adulthood almost always include age specifications. It is interesting to observe the wide variations in age-based statutes, depending on locale, sex, and subject of regulation. Within the Commonwealth of Massachusetts, for example, one is legally old enough to drive at 16½, drink in public at 20, commit adult crimes at 17, marry at 21 or 18 (depending on one's sex), and run for an elective state office at 21.

Although physical size and chronological age narrow the range, neither adequately defines adulthood.

Maturity

From biology derives the tradition of defining *adult* as meaning mature. In biological language maturity denotes ripeness, or full development within the genetic and ecological limits established by the species in its particular locale. The organism's various substructures have evolved to their natural point of completeness, so that the critical functions of maintenance and propagation of the species can be best executed. The mature rose has green leaves open to the sun; a sturdy stem is spiked with thorns to ward off animals that might trample it; and its petals are fully spread, releasing its attractive scent and exposing its pollen to contact with the insects, who are enticed to feed but depart as unwitting agents of fertilization.

Happily for the biologist, maturity can be measured by directly observable structures and characteristics of the organism. *Adaptive* func-

tioning, however, is viewed independently of maturity. Neither the dinosaur nor the American bison is considered biologically immature despite an inability to ward off extinction. The shark, despite its primitivity, has survived for eons. Ecological success—the ability of the organism to adjust to its environment—is quite a different issue from maturity.

For the behavior scientist, however, human beings' inextricable involvement with the world prevents any such dichotomy. Most major personality theorists—for example, Freud (1938), Lewin (1935), Murphy (1947), Murray (1938), and Sullivan (1947)—include environmental adaptation as a central aspect of human functioning. Necessarily, therefore, human ecology is part of the assessment of psychological maturity. A strong, intellectually gifted person whose adult life is spent in the chronic ward of a mental hospital would scarcely be considered mature.

Maturity as psychological health. Heath's excellent review of the literature in human maturity (1965) reveals both the methodological issues and the findings that have emerged from previous investigations. Heath differentiates his use of the term *maturity* from conceptions of *normality, adjustment,* or *age.* He reserves the definition of *maturity* to uses synonymous with *psychological health,* with both concepts described as idealized end states. Using a research strategy of selecting the criterion groups, Heath was able to define mature and immature male college students according to judges' evaluations. These subjects were then interviewed and tested extensively to measure such variables as stability, integration, allocentric organization, autonomy, and symbolization. When all the data were analyzed, Heath was able to conclude that

> A mature person . . . does seem to be a more stable person who masters disturbing information more efficiently; he is a more integrated and allocentrically organized, i.e., realistic person, though he is also able to use regressive or autocentric types of thinking more effectively than the immature person. He may have more memories available to awareness, particularly those organized around his self-image which is more accurately symbolized. While his cognitions are less dominated by more primitive motives it is still not clear just how autonomous he is of the influence of coercive external information. . . . The capacity for involvement and commitment, the strength of a person's purpose, may be a missing dimension. But creativity does not seem to be a centrally defining dimension of maturity [1965, p. 340].

It should be remembered that Heath's concern is with personality

development toward an "ideal end state." Although this conception of maturity bears some positive relationship to life-span development, in the latter case the end state is literally the end state of death. Another, more fundamental, limitation of Heath's data is inherent in his population sample. A study confined to selected late adolescents cannot deal with issues of psychological maturity that are not yet ready to be encountered—especially matters such as commitment or personal involvement. Few college underclassmen are confronted with a need to make a long-term interpersonal or professional commitment. Consequently, these involvement/commitment issues did not enter into a definition of who was mature and who was not.

Other investigators have examined maturity in more familiar but also more general terms. Freud is said to have defined maturity as the capacity for working and loving. For Gordon Allport, maturity is "the ability to view oneself with complacency" (1961). Erikson's formulation of maturity specifies the capacity for intimacy and generativity. Intimacy is used to mean the ability to enter a deep, close relationship without fearing loss of identity or destruction of the other person.[1] By generativity, Erikson means the ability to foster the development of a new generation. Emphasis is placed on such psychosocial functions as parenthood and teaching (1950).

Maturity as self-actualization. Abraham Maslow (1954) abstracted case analyses of a variety of fictional and nonfictional figures and evolved his classic listing of the properties of self-actualization as an optimal state of psychological development. These properties are described as follows:

1. More efficient perception of reality. The person is more comfortable with reality and less frightened by the unknown.
2. Acceptance of self, others, and natural events, processes, and needs.
3. Spontaneity and zestfulness in living.
4. Ability to concentrate, persist, and work on objective tasks.
5. Capacity for detachment, privacy, and self-sufficiency.
6. Autonomy from mass opinion and an independence of culture and environment.
7. A continued freshness in appreciating the uniqueness of similar events.

---

[1]James Baldwin's *Another Country* (1962) is an exquisite treatment of the many variations on this theme.

8. Appreciation of the limitless horizons of reality.
9. Compassion and concern for human welfare, individual and collective.
10. Deep, selective, and persisting social relationships.
11. A democratic character structure of respect and tolerance for others.
12. Ethical certainty, so as to persevere in one's convictions.
13. A sense of humor not basically hostile in intent.
14. Creativeness as an individualistic way of approaching any situation.

A functional definition. Goodenough and Tyler (1959) offer what is perhaps the most functional description of the qualities of maturity:

1. Looking toward the future in one's perceptions and thoughts.
2. Abiding by the realistic choices and decisions one has made.
3. Involving oneself in permanent relationships.
4. Acting on plans rather than on impulse.

What these definitions of maturity share is an approach based on observation and insight into the optimal or ideal functioning of the human being as a psychological entity. Implicit is an acknowledgement that chronology bears some relationship to the eventual attainment of adult maturity. Maslow is said to have asserted that self-actualization rarely peaks before middle age. Yet it is also true that *maturity* is often used as a relative term: "He is immature for his age." It is readily apparent that there are mature and immature young adults, mature and immature middle-age adults. Thus, although psychological maturity bears some relationship to the life span, the qualities that distinguish a mature person are probably not confined to one segment of the adult years—or, necessarily, to adulthood.

Attributes of Adulthood

What, then, are the attributes of adulthood? Generally speaking, they take into account, first, the reality of the person as a culturally embedded creature. Consequently, adult attributes are defined, at least in part, by the society in which the person dwells. Because humans have founded a great variety of societies, however, it is also necessary to define adult status universally—that is, independent of its particular form in any one society.

In some cultures a person attains adult status when he or she reaches a certain age. In rural Japan, womanhood was attained only by producing

a child. Although marriage is generally acknowledged to be the province of adults in North America, other societies arrange and conduct marriage between prepubertal children. It may be that a strictly sociocultural definition of adulthood can state only that people are adult if and when they can perform those role functions established as adult patterning in their society. To that extent, the developmental tasks described by Havighurst (see Chapter 2) may provide an appropriate basis for intra-cultural comparison of people who are labeled adults by other means (such as statutory). The psychological definition of *intracultural task* set forth in Chapter 3 may offer yet another dimension for this kind of comparison.

To understand adult processes across different cultures and historic periods requires some understanding of psychic functioning. Granting the pervasive impact of acculturation on personality development, it is nevertheless reasonable to assume that those biological maturational features that distinguish *Homo sapiens* must have some psychological counterpart. Furthermore, even the most dissimilar societies bear some structural resemblance to one another (Levi-Strauss, 1963) and have certain myths and mores in common. It seems reasonable to suppose that these general requirements would also indirectly militate toward the evolution of similar human characteristics to serve the sheer organic survival needs of the culture. The survival, proliferation, and biosocial growth of human society over the past 100,000 years or more, under wide variations of climate and geography, effectively argues the case for at least certain dimensions of interpsychic similarity.

With the progressive sophistication in psychological understanding of cross-cultural observers, the argument for a universalist definition of adulthood appears to be gaining support. Rudolph and Rudolph (1976) reported on their studies of adulthood in India at the turn of the 20th century. Indian culture was, and is, centered on an extended family structure and system. Yet, despite the distance in space and time separat-ing that culture from ours, Rudolph and Rudolph conclude that

> becoming an adult involves detachment and differentiation from a diverse set of parental models and a distinct sense of self . . . . We do not mean to suggest that becoming an adult in an extended family is just like becoming an adult in a nuclear family, but we do find that it is not so different . . . as much of the literature dealing with it depicts it to be [p. 163].

Option in adulthood. As I noted in Chapter 3 on adult development,

complexity is a major difference between the child and adult segments of the life span. In addition, one of the primary rewards for accepting responsibility as an adult is that one acquires a greater measure of freedom and power. This combination of greater complexity and increased power confers on adults one of the most critical of psychological attributes—the capacity for option.

At the level of ego development viewed alone, the capacity for option emerges early in childhood. Once a human being has evolved the ability to delay response and can differentiate between environmental features, the capacity for choice comes into existence. But, given the limits of children's experiential repertoire and the regulatory rights of the adults in their lives, their options are, in actual practice, quite limited.

In adulthood a significant measure of personal control evolves. There is wide experience with one's own needs, wishes, and desires. Adults can differentiate urgent needs from passing whims. They have learned quite a lot about behavior and its consequences. Decades of everyday living experience have taught them what to expect in the way of costs and, especially, benefits accruing from their actions. Adults' personal perspective further contributes to control by providing awareness of the inventory of skills, abilities, limits, and risks that will be available when engaging the world.

At the same time, adults are conversant with their environment. They are familiar with the social structure's traditions and degrees of freedom. They know the physical limits of their world. The longer they have lived in a stable environment, the more expert they are about its dimensions.

Finally, their own status as adults in their social context assures that some measure of autonomy will be accorded them by peers and others in the human environment. Consequently, all the necessary ingredients are present to permit the exercise of competent choice. When McLeish (1976) adapted Peck's adult data to describe a Ulyssean adult, he implicitly addressed this aspect of adult life. He distinguished between those people who actively interact with the life process and those who resign themselves to accommodating to basic needs and role demands.

One of Levinson's singular findings was that his subjects had a growing awareness of their essential aloneness, a realization that their lives were fundamentally in their own hands. The power of this concept—of the capacity for option—is only beginning to be fully appreciated by those who work to foster adults' development.

Adult Characteristics

As one surveys the mass of data from other times and cultures and from various segments of our own society, certain adult characteristics emerge that appear to have broad application.

Paradigm. Adults are, first, the *paradigm* of their species or culture. They represent and symbolize their culture. To use a biological metaphor, they are the ripened specimen—what the society produces—at its developmental peak. As such, they serve as models of what the species is, what its young can become. They embody not only the appearance but the customs and beliefs that make up their culture. Despite its vagaries and vicissitudes, the adult segment of the life span is the most stable period. Although change is a constant feature of life, the rate of change as a function of time is much reduced compared with childhood and adolescence. In addition, and perhaps as a verification of the preeminence of the adult period, it is by far the longest segment of the life span. Childhood and adolescence together occupy not more than the first two decades. Using current actuarial estimates as a guide, adulthood covers a 50-year period, or better than 70% of the total sentient existence. For purposes of evolutionary and ecological efficiency, therefore, it is certainly appropriate that the least varying and most extensive period of life should be its most representative as well.

Responsible. Adults are also the *responsible* members of their society. They are the decision-makers, the ones with the widest range of options and opportunities, and the ones who select—for themselves or others—courses of action, plans, and directions. They are the acknowledged power, the real and symbolized authority, in the community. Although their strength is originally a direct result of superior physical status, sheer size and musculature would not guarantee adults their position as the responsible members of the culture. Adults are responsible because they can function autonomously. Their knowledge, skills, and judgment equip them to be competent and reliable, able to handle their own lives.

Important in this regard are the aggregate experiences compiled over the years of living and integrated into a source of knowledge and skill. It is the accumulated social intelligence, born of multiple practical experiences, that is fundamental to being accorded responsibility and

being competent to function responsibly. Another aspect, however, is dependability. By virtue of being more stable and less variable, adults are more predictable. Consequently, they are the people who can be counted on, and, in turn, held accountable. They inspire the trust and confidence of others.

Sustainer. Finally, adults are the *sustainers* of the society and of the species. Biosocially mature adults are successful procreators who bring forth a new generation. So fundamental and so universally valued is this function that it is celebrated in the customs of every society and practiced in the most hostile environments. Babies were conceived and born even in the Auschwitz and Dachau death camps of Nazi Germany. While thus ensuring continuity into the future, adults simultaneously bring forward the past by continuing to activate traditional mores, traditions, and values of the culture.

More basically, they provide physical security by building and maintaining structures that protect against adversities of climate and natural enemies. They are directly or instrumentally the ones to ensure food, clothing, and shelter. They nurture and protect the weak and helpless members of the group. They heal and they rule so that the culture and its members can endure.

In return they acquire the privileges of freedom and power in the society. They make or enforce laws—not only to regularize the society but also to enhance and protect their own privileged position. They are usually accountable to other adults and to their own conscience, but sometimes to neither when they can claim divine powers. Thus, human society is crudely dichotomized into "can" and "cannot" segments, composed of adults and children, respectively. The implications for intergenerational conflict can therefore be profound. The unequal distribution of burden and privilege across generations is a universal fact of life.

DEVELOPMENTAL CHANGES IN ADULTHOOD

Although psychological change is much more gradual in the adult years, the seeming stabilization of characteristics is largely due to the long period over which change occurs. It may seem that after many years of sameness an adult's personality undergoes rapid change in its last years. Actually, change is ongoing throughout the adult span.

Thanks to the work of a relative handful of investigators, extremely

valuable information has been collected. One of the intriguing variables studied is that of *time perception.* Neugarten (1975b) reports that by middle age people view time by the years that remain, rather than by their chronological age (years expended).

My own preliminary data suggest that the fantasy projections of established and middle-aged adults are more likely to be located in the immediate future than those of young adults and adolescents. Older adults seem to show greater interest in past events. Young adults appear to have a more substantial sense of future time than do adolescents.

Expansion and Defense

Two major trends have been identified in adulthood. Labeled *expansion* and *defense,* these features seem to emerge and develop at different periods. Kuhlen and Murphy (1955) describe expansion as an orientation toward the achievement of positive growth or productivity goals. This would include raising a family, building a career, and developing friends, competencies, hobbies, and the like. Activity directed at fulfilling one's potentialities (perhaps similar to Maslow's self-actualization) would relate to the need for expansion. It is felt that the need for expansion is strongest up to middle age and diminishes thereafter.

The need for defense emerges later in life for most adults. It is viewed as more negative, in that it is oriented toward protecting the individual against loss and conserving the status quo rather than advancing beyond it. With aging comes a sense of loss—of physical skills, competencies, and abilities. The defensive orientation attempts to protect the person from threat and anxiety engendered by this sense.

Consistent with this premise is the finding of Neugarten (1975a) that advancing age brings major psychological changes, including a decrease in available ego energy, reduced cognitive acuity, and less flexibility in attitudes generally. It is increasingly difficult to manage the inner life. Thus, it may be necessary to invoke more protective procedures in order to maintain optimum functioning. Although sexual interests and activities persist throughout the later years, there is evidence of a shift in sex-role behavior patterns, especially as regards the dominance/submission continuum. Gutmann (1975) reports cross-cultural data indicating that, as both sexes age past the parenting years, women become more aggressive and dominant, whereas men become more dependent and hedonistic.

The Role of Time Sense

In their modes of thinking and perceiving, adults function in ways that are qualitatively different from those of children and adolescents. Buhler (1935) speaks of a "need for ongoingness," which denotes both the significance of the content of life and an awareness of the passage of time.

Adult thinking is conditioned by two to six or more decades of experience. Over this period thinking becomes more patterned to the individual's own needs, attitudes, and beliefs. The functional, pragmatic aspects are of more interest and concern than are purely theoretical, abstract, or ideal concepts. The adult's thoughts are thus more closely bound to reality and to practical objectives (Whipple, 1974). Events and experiences are interpreted in terms of their implications for the individual, both at the level of sensory data and at the level of cognitive integration, or understanding. By virtue of this predisposition the adult mode of mental functioning is more self-directing, because it does examine incoming data against a large background of patterned experiences.

In the subtle realm of time perception, differences are also apparent. The child's view of the future is vague, hazy, indefinite. During adolescence a growing awareness evolves, but the future tends to be envisioned as rosy and of infinite duration. By contrast, the past is ignored or depreciated. It is in adulthood that the future becomes finite and that progress is measured on a time/age dimension. The future has a more immediate meaning. With progressive aging, future and present blend into each other, and concern with the past increases. One of the major differences between the young and the old is that the former value the past negatively, whereas the latter tend to reminisce with satisfaction.

Many reasons can be found for these qualitative differences. To the young the prospective privileges—real and fantasied—of adult freedom and power are far more appealing than the helpless, indentured state of childhood. To many young children, being an adult means "you can do what you want," as compared with the view of childhood as "you hafta go to school" or "you hafta do what you're told." Childhood is rarely left with reluctance, although some anxiety often accompanies the transitional points. Growing up, *Peter Pan* notwithstanding, is generally regarded as something eagerly anticipated. Conversely, "being a kid" evokes more negative associations or simply blank areas of memory suggestive of repression. The past takes on new value as the future unfolds. When bright hopes recede, as the future becomes an increasingly shorter time

span, thoughts return to other significant events—those that have gone before.

In addition, with experience comes the inevitable human need to seek meaning and system in life's events. A sense of history evolves and, with it, the desire for a retrospective survey in order to weave past and present into a continuous whole that represents the span of a life's experiences. An appreciation of causality, with the perspective of many decades of raw data to analyze, often leads to rich insights into one's own life and into human nature as well. One of humankind's most frustrating paradoxes is its vast capacity to teach information while remaining so inept at using the insights and mistakes of personal experience to avoid the repetition of error and pain.

Nevertheless, the ability to find continuity, order, and meaning in life affords a sense of closure, of completeness, that helps make the inevitability of death a reasonable part of the life span. It is worth recalling that concern with the past does not automatically harbinger flight from reality or impending senile dementia. Similarly, optimism about the future is no sure sign of either health or immaturity. Both characteristics are inevitable concomitants of life-span evolution. *The way they are handled by a given individual may, however, yield valuable insight into that person's effectiveness or, conversely, psychopathology.*

The Second Half of Life

Robert Peck (1975) has presented the most succinct integrative depiction to date of the later adult years. After age 30 there are only two major stages, middle age and old age, according to Peck.

Middle age versus youth. With the advent of middle age and a noticeable decline in physical prowess there is an increasing reliance on acquired wisdom, knowledge, and experience. According to Peck, "Most [people] reach a critical transition point between the late thirties and late forties" (1975, p. 613). Even in the most physical of occupations, professional sports, the successful athletes are those who have substituted experience and knowledge for sheer physical talent. The football quarterback has learned how to "read" the defensive alignment of the opposing team; the veteran baseball pitcher outwits the batter now that he can no longer over-power him.

In everyday human relationships another kind of change is evident:

away from sexual and toward social relationships. During young adulthood personal relations tend to be competitive within the sexes and sexually oriented between them. In both cases heterosexuality tends to polarize reactions. As sexuality becomes more regularly institutionalized—usually through marriage—it is less an issue and more a part of one's way of life. A broader awareness of others is fostered as the orientation to sexual partners and sexual competitors is diminished. The distinctively human qualities of generosity, shallowness, humor, or kindness become more visible when erotic interchange is less important. The capacity for intersexual friendship based on personal and social values and interests reaches a high point during middle age, according to Peck.

Middle age versus old age. Middle age can also be contrasted with old age. The middle-aged person retains more emotional flexibility than the older person. Unlike the fixed emotional investments (cathexes) of older people, middle-aged adults' feelings and concerns can be focused to keep them in closer touch with major changes in the world.

Paralleling this cathectic flexibility is the assertion of greater mental flexibility. Middle-aged adults can more readily consider and adapt to new ideas; they are less committed to a fixed point of view independent of changing times and circumstances.

With entry into old age, the adult's functioning is progressively more withdrawn from day-to-day interaction. The central psychological issue concerns the quality of that withdrawal from mundane life. If it is a withdrawal into self-preoccupation, it will probably result in deterioration. If it is to be adaptive—enabling the person to function with maximal effectiveness and meaning—the withdrawal of energy will lead to a transcendent attitude. Self-occupied people exhibit the overt manifestations of senility, concerned primarily with sheer bodily functioning and disorder. Transcendent people (Peck is here relying heavily on Erikson's conception) go beyond somatic limits to relate themselves to the cosmos.

Preoccupied people generally manifest all the qualities of narcissistic withdrawal. They focus their attention and energies on their immediate experience and emphasize the minutia of personal awareness defensively, forever vigilant to signs of impending threat or stress. Their preoccupation is defensive in that it serves—however ineffectively—to protect them from the anxiety worked by the aging process and the inexorable approach of death.

A transcendent orientation, by contrast, helps elderly people relate

to the world, to history, to humankind, to their god. Confrontation with impending death is a confrontation with one's insignificance as a mortal structure. Transcendence is a way of finding relevance in one's existence and, therefore, a way of accepting inevitable death as a part of life.

Thus, both the stable and changing characteristics of adult life can be described and listed. Adults provide the standard of developmental maturity, biological ripeness, economic competence, esthetic excellence, and psychosocial autonomy. The adult is the reigning generation. If this status provides great freedom and power—which it undoubtedly does—it also exacts heavy tribute for these privileges. The adult is the responsible member of society, upon whose knowledge and decisions the fate of social grouping rests. Finally, the adults are the sustainers of culture—providing for physical security, protecting the less capable, maintaining a social structure, and bringing forth and nurturing those who will eventually supplant them.

The Growth/Decline Interaction in Adulthood

The biological model of the life cycle—growth, maturation, and decline—proves to be an ineffective paradigm for understanding adult development in psychological terms. In an organism as complex as an adult human there is a constant interplay of coexisting processes, some emerging, some at full power, some diminishing. Idealism, pragmatism, and disengagement—characteristics of different adult stages—may all be discernible even though they may be at different points in their respective developmental curves of emergence and disappearance. If growth, maturation, and decline are presented as simultaneous rather than consecutive, a more useful picture of the adult life span emerges.

To consider young adulthood exclusively in terms of growth, for instance, would misrepresent the fully matured innovative potential and the declining remnants of adolescent narcissism that are likely to be present. To view senescent adulthood strictly as a period of decline would ignore the position of social primacy held by the elders in almost every society known to humankind. Growth and decline, birth and death, are a daily part of each person's life.

A number of writers have fastened on polarities in discussing adult development. Erikson's entire schema (1959) is based on polarities (for example, intimacy versus isolation and integrity versus despair). McLeish (1976) cites Peck's distinction between the fulfilled (still in motion) and the unfulfilled (no longer in motion) life. Rappaport (1972) identifies

attrition and meaning as the vital poles of adult experience. Active/passive role reversal characterizes the description of the later years by Gutmann (1975). Expansion and defense are used by Kuhlen and Murphy (1955) to conceptualize the sequence of adult development. Implicit in many of these formulations is an implication of positive and negative or, more particularly, a sense of deficiency or debilitation at one of the polar points.

By contrast, Riegel (1975) urges that such developmental "contradictions" be seen as the "very basis" for growth. From his perspective, these polarities can be understood as imperatives to change that inevitably confront people. Growth and decline interact rather than oppose each other. And both are ongoing.

Development as encounter. Thus, it may well be that the direction adult development takes depends on how the individual encounters the emergence and diminution of prepotent qualities inherent to each life stage. The developmental clock mediates potential, or readiness; the culture (including significant others) determines its form; the individual person assimilates (usually), integrates (often), or repudiates (sometimes) that psychological experience. It is this interaction—between developmental potential, cultural mediation, and individual reaction—that ultimately determines the person's adult life patterning. It is within these flexible constraints that growth and decline occur.

Physicians and physiologists are now of the opinion that much of what has been subsumed under normal aging is traceable to more pathogenic sources, such as poor diet, bad health habits, and social alienation. A number of clues suggest that psychological growth and decline may, similarly, be less a function of normal aging than of the quality and character of life experience. Evidence of the relationship between mental health and economic conditions is so strong that the sociologist M. Harvey Brenner could inform congress that a "one percent jump in unemployment could quite predictably be linked to a loss of some 50,000 lives" due to alcoholism, homicide, suicide, and related causes (Brenner, 1978).

Hindrances to growth. More subtly, growth can be inhibited or perverted by the interaction of environmental pressures with human response. As Haan (1977) points out, anxiety can activate fragmentation responses or defense mechanisms. Fragmentation responses are autistic

reactions that distort or debilitate growth and learning. Defense mechanisms, by focusing on anxiety reduction, impede understanding (and resolution) of the conditions that give rise to the anxiety. But perhaps more important for the population at large is Marcia's (1967) concept of identity foreclosure.

Marcia describes identity foreclosure as a process in which a person (usually late adolescent) uncritically complies with the vocational and ideological urgings of significant others rather than confronting the stress and conflict of making commitments out of personal conviction. According to Trent and Medsker (1969), more than 75% of the 10,000 high school graduates they studied had dealt with their identity crisis through foreclosure, rather than resolution. If these data are at all representative, it is small wonder that most adults seem to fall far short of optimal development!

Finally, my own clinical experience over two decades as psychotherapist, career counselor, and industrial consultant suggests that the development of most adults is to some degree impaired by anxiety-binding defenses, areas of identity foreclosure, and other growth-impeding processes.

Human potential. To fully comprehend the power of the developmental perspective, therefore, is to seek the potential of what can be and not to be constrained by the limits of what is currently normative. We can learn much about human development by reviewing past discoveries and by studying what is happening currently. But, given the demonstrable impediments to growth that are themselves normative (for example, how different are foreclosure pressures from ordinary socialization activity?), it is imperative that development be defined to include the study of prepotency, of the readiness and susceptibility to act in certain ways. I am speaking of something much more specific than human potential or self-actualizing trends. The orientation reflected here attempts to locate, identify, and describe particular potentialities inherent in each life stage.

A universalist approach to development holds that one theory can account for all human development, over time and culture. Those who criticize such an approach point to the impossibility of adequately collecting data on people in inaccessible cultures, to say nothing of the problems of studying people who lived thousands of years ago. But the most important contribution developmental psychology can make is in uncovering what can be learned of human capability. To that end, there is an

advantage in studying developmental processes in people and places where conditions have produced the most growth. In a world where half the inhabitants go to bed hungry, there may be real merit in studying those who rarely have to confront survival issues such as hunger, if the concern is with the upper reaches of human capability.

At the same time it has been shown by Garmezy (1976) and others that adversity can elicit maximum potential, even as chronic affluence can focus the quest of other people to revert to the most rudimentary levels of hedonistic pursuit.

Thus, although it is tempting to argue for locating developmental research in the most affluent societies, one must also seek the furthest reaches of human growth where people have been able to meet and master significant adversity. Moreover, different environmental conditions may impact selectively on the several life stages. The social disruptions of post-World-War-II Japan and the relaxed standards of the 1960s in our own country may have facilitated growth for young adults in both nations; but it is equally probable that they provoked defensive reactions among senescent adults in the two societies.

Transitional periods. Following the precedent set by Buhler and Jung almost 50 years ago, most adult development theorists identify three life stages: early, middle, and late. Early adult life is conceptualized as a period of entry and exploration, middle adulthood as entrenchment and maintenance, and late adulthood as retraction and retirement. But contemporary research makes it increasingly difficult to sustain the position that there are only three adult life stages. Both Super (1963) and Vaillant (1977) find that males encounter other life periods. The investigations of Loevinger (1976) and the Levinson group (1978) seem to indicate that transitional periods between stages have profound effects equivalent to the stages themselves. It is evident that our understanding of the acquisitions of adulthood is far from complete. Indeed, one of the important motivators that goad people into psychotherapy is their inability to apply the adaptive reactions of an earlier period of life to the changing, transitional, circumstances of the adult experience.

5

THE LEGACY OF ADOLESCENCE

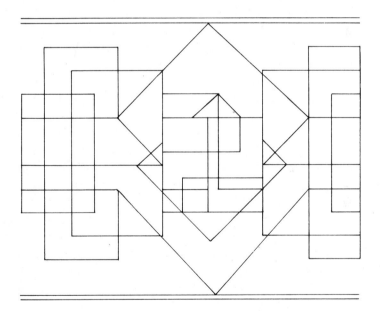

Adolescence is unquestionably one of the most tumultuous, anxiety-ridden, disturbed, and disturbing parts of the life span. It is also one of the most exciting, exhilarating, joyful, and thrilling periods of life. Tears and toughness, anger and laughter, seclusiveness and spontaneity, infantilism and maturity—all jumble together in endless mixtures and sequences, consistent only in their unpredictability.

Beginning around puberty and ending with the achievement of a sense of identity, adolescence usually coincides with the teen years. Within this span occurs the last major spurt of physical growth. Boys commonly add a foot or more of height—an increase of 20%! The rate of growth is not smooth and continuous but, more typically, uneven and dramatic. I well remember a friend who grew 6 inches over a ten-week summer vacation. The disproportionate sprouting of arms, legs, and noses contributes to the awkward, gangly look so frequently seen in the early teens.

With puberty, of course, comes sexual development. By 14 or 15, the great majority of adolescents is capable of producing children. Concomitant with gonad maturation is a marked intensification of interest in the opposite sex, varying from idyllic romantic reverie to explicit sexual arousal. Heterosexual interests can be expected to develop from fantasy to flirting and then to dating, kissing, petting, and eventually coitus. The advent of sexuality is a great source of pride and of pleasure—a sure sign of getting older and the fun that comes with it. But what a source of consternation, even mortification, to the girl whose swelling breasts seem to call attention to her in the most gross, boastful way. Another girl, meanwhile, waits agonizingly for the day she can legitimately wear a bra. And what of the boy constantly terrorized by the unpredictability of his voice box? Will his voice crack in mid-sentence as he asks *that girl* to go to the school dance with him? Or will his penis, which affords him so much secret pride, suddenly bulge his pants in the middle of a two-minute speech to his English class?

It is perhaps paradigmatic of adolescence that the best and worst of what lies ahead should occur as briefly exalting or terrifying vignettes for which there is little warning or preparation.

CROSS-CULTURAL PERSPECTIVE

The recognition of adolescence as a life stage is primarily an outgrowth of Western industrial civilization. It came in response to the

complexity of demands made by this cultural pattern. Whereas other societies recognize the biological coming of age with some formal *rite de passage,* life in the Occidental world seems to require a more extensive period for the transition from child to adult.

As Ruth Benedict observed many years ago (1934), life in other societies flows more smoothly from stage to stage. In most preindustrial cultures children are gradually trained for their eventual adult roles. Although there are formal rituals to initiate people into adulthood, children have received extensive preparation before their change in status. Thus, they have ample opportunity to adapt to the future demands that will be made of them. Contrast the Eskimo child's early training in hunting and fishing with the Western child's games of cops and robbers. Or the Hopi gradual initiation into sexual activity with the now-you-can't, now-you-can sexual mores in the United States.

Whereas other societies begin early to train children for adult roles, our society has evolved a series of developmental jumps that sometimes requires the reversing of attitudes in a single step. From hide-and-seek to cowboys and Indians to baseball, high school, career choice, and marriage, a boy's evolution into manhood can only appear fortuitous. The little girl who plays house is daily confronted with television scenes recounting the drudgery of housework. She takes academic courses but is socialized to prepare for domestic life. She is lured to paid work but told it is unfeminine. She is trained to puritanical sex codes but expected to become a passionate lovemate on the day she marries. It is perhaps understandable, therefore, that it has been found necessary to prolong this difficult transition over a period of years. Time is needed to adjust to these severe and often inconsistent demands.

Double Pressure: Sex and Career

Perhaps the greatest paradox of our society, however, lies in the way we impose an alien set of tasks on human beings who are preoccupied with fundamental psychobiological concerns. There are three times in the life span when the person's attentions are crucially focused on physical condition. During early infancy the child's physical helplessness necessitates an orientation toward sheer survival. Physical decline in later years confronts the individual with the aging process and ultimate mortality. And sexual maturation at puberty introduces the person to a whole world of mystery, delight, challenge, and conflict.

The transcendent fact of genital maturity overrides and infuses all other matters in the life of young people. To casual observers, dedicated investigators, or the young themselves, this fact is self-evident. Its impact and its implications are tremendous. Yet at this point our society acts to inhibit and constrict sexual exploration. And it simultaneously places ever-increasing pressure on people—especially males—to make decisions and undertake commitments that may determine the course of their vocational development for the next 40 years. Instead of studying and discussing sex and family living they must choose a high school program, grind out good grades, and study and discuss colleges or careers.

The blatant irrationality of this situation is only partially modified by its being spread over a five- to eight-year period. It may help to explain why so many marriages are unhappy, why vocational dissatisfaction hovers at the 75% level, and why adolescence sometimes lasts for a decade or longer. How can a society expect incompletely developed young people in a period of rapid physical and psychological change to evolve the capacity to make the two most profound decisions that the culture will demand of them? Mohr and Despres (1958) correctly identify three chief preoccupations of adolescence as peer status, vocational potential, and sexual feelings. How unfortunate that our society does not provide the structure and climate most conducive to resolving these issues without first confounding them.

Conflicting Signals from Society

If further evidence is needed of the debilitating discontinuity of our social pattern, the study by Mussen and his colleagues (1963) may be illuminating. They found a basic consistency from adolescence to early adulthood in attitudes, beliefs, and behavior patterns indicating that masculinity is an enduring personality characteristic. But the investigators found that, whereas high masculinity was related to good adjustment in adolescence, it was correlated with poor adjustment in adulthood. Those features suitable for effective functioning as a male adolescent were found to be less appropriate for a male adult.

Of course, some discontinuity is inevitable, perhaps salutory, in normal development. But Mussen's data suggest that consistent characteristics of the person—for example, masculinity—are responded to by the culture in ways that make yesterday's asset today's liability. Small wonder that the adolescent transitional years are replete with turmoil and

confusion. Precisely for this reason, the overriding psychological imperative of adolescence is that of consolidating some sense of identity or ego synthesis (Adelson, 1964). Erikson's cross-cultural observations led him to conclude that the identity crisis is common to adolescents everywhere. In our society, the task may be particularly stressful.

How Western Adolescents Adapt

Adelson's data from interviewing 3000 adolescents stand in revealing contrast to attempts to stereotype the North American teenager as a dopey Dobie Gillis, an insight-ridden, victimized Holden Caulfield, or a predatory, leather-jacketed hoodlum. Instead, he describes modal adolescents as ones who respond to the multiplicity of pressures by trying to make some order out of psychological chaos. This they accomplish—when successful—by fleeing into the security of peer culture and by achieving some sense of selfhood. Most adolescents, he observes, resist conflict, crisis, and change. They are more concerned with self-consolidation than self-exploration.

These findings appear to be at variance with theoretical formulations derived from intensive psychotherapy with intelligent upper-middle-class adolescents. However, they are consistent with some findings about the structural and dynamic personality characteristics of adolescents in general. Ames's normative study of adolescent Rorschach responses (1959) suggests that teenagers are more withdrawn and preoccupied, more anxious and impulsive, and less mature than adults. These data indicate that adolescents are more concerned with keeping their heads above water psychologically than with self-actualization or even self-discovery.

Peter Blos (1962), whose *On Adolescence* is the definitive psychoanalytic position on the subject, describes a recrudescence of unresolved Oedipal and pregenital conflicts. Thus, he stresses yet again the tumultuous, problem-ridden nature of the adolescent experience.

Cole (1970) differs widely from these writers in her view of this period:

> In the normal growth of a typical individual, childhood fades, adolescence advances, and adulthood arrives in a gradual, smooth series of small changes and with only temporary and incidental difficulties and disturbances [p. 5].

Offer and Offer (1970) cite data that appear to support Cole's thesis. But their studies seem less concerned with psychological processes and more with overt behavioral reactions.

Whatever the viewpoint of the individual theorist, it seems quite clear that the two central issues in adolescence are (1) emancipation from childhood ties and (2) handling the time gap between biological and sociological maturation.

ROLE OF PEERS

Probably the most important vehicle for dealing with these issues and bringing about the transition from childhood to adulthood is the peer group. This social structure performs a variety of functions vital to the development of adolescents. As we noted in Chapter 3, the peer group is the mode through which adolescents transfer their point of orientation from the older generation to their own. Although this process begins to occur gradually during the latency period, it is in adolescence that one sees most clearly the peer group joining the parents as a vital source of authority. By affiliating themselves with the peer group, adolescents more effectively separate themselves from their parents. The peer group is thus an alternative source of security and structure, another reference point, that helps to evolve an independent sense of direction and purpose. Yet, even though adolescents seek autonomy and separation, they continue to need the support and reassurance provided by parental structure.

Peers also serve more specifically as aids in learning the skills and techniques appropriate to dealing with one's own generation. These include relating socially, psychologically, and sexually. In particular, peers bring one to a closer contact with the functional issues around which sexual development takes place—masturbation, menstruation, erotic fantasy and excitation, and genital exploration and contact. Fellow adolescents also provide reinforcement for experimentation with ideas, mores, and manners. In addition, they encourage or condone departure from behavior patterns favored by the adult generation.

In turn, these departures and individual experiments help adolescents evolve a sense of themselves as distinctive from the preceding generation. This separation serves to offset the obvious continuity of their lives as children and family members. The purpose here is nothing less than driving enough of a wedge between adolescent and family so that one can see oneself as a person apart from familial context, yet not

cut off from it. In this respect the peer group, with its distinctively different identification model, provides a necessary training ground. It may be disconcerting for parents to discover that the values and attitudes of other equally inexperienced young people seem to carry more weight than does their own loving concern. Nevertheless, learning to live with one's own generation is a vital need for the individual and, indeed, for society as well.

Immersion in the peer group further enhances one's self-identification as an incipient adult—that is, one who is quite literally "growing up." Within one's own generational milieu, one is treated as an equal—as a full-fledged, fully enfranchised member of a particular society. To this extent, individuals are encouraged to think of themselves as being, in some very vital, personal ways, adults, matured members of their own group.

Despite their seeming lack of concern for the feelings of their parents, most adolescents experience considerable conflict or guilt. This is partly because of their overt rejection of parental and family standards. It is partly because they are physically pulling away from those who have raised them. And it is partly, perhaps, because they fear rejection as well. The peer group, by providing a forum for sharing these experiences—for recounting and comparing common difficulties, concerns, fears, and resentments—provides a significant buttress against the onslaught of guilt and anxiety. Even though the sharing is often a comparison of rationalizations, even though the hurts and points of issue may be more fancied than real, or more provoked than imposed, for the adolescent the need is central and acute. Whether the peer group is embodied in a clique, a couple of friends, or one intimate companion, the young person desperately requires the support and reassurance that only an age cohort can provide.

To the observer the mores and standards of adolescent peer culture commonly appear to be even more slavishly ritualized than those of the larger society. Yet from the point of view of the adolescents themselves, the origin of these standards in their own generation means that there is an opportunity to test out a new set of standards, roles, behaviors, and attitudes. Although these attitudes and roles may be just as confining as were the previous models, they at least have the virtue of being a different set, and, to this extent, they provide an alternative against which adolescents can measure themselves through their own experiences.

Finally, the attitudes and values of peers not only replace the

temporarily rejected family values but also reflect more closely the existing psychological needs of the adolescent. To parents, on the one hand, the teenager is too much caught up in running around in frenetic and often seemingly wasteful expenditures of time and effort. Peers, on the other hand, are better able—albeit unconsciously—to recognize the need to burn off great surges of energy. Parents bemoan the sexual concerns reflected in dancing, conversation, reading interests, and the like—as well as in habits of dress and general behavior. The peer group, in contrast, responds to the commonly felt concern with sexuality—with coming to understand sexual attraction, handle it, and master it. Parents have difficulty in adjusting to the adolescent's impracticality and radical shifts in attitude. But the peer group's concern for loyalty and literal honesty may come closer to the adolescent than the hypocrisy that is part of adults' way of compromising between desires and everyday realities.

It is important to note that the "peer group" is not a single entity—except insofar as adolescents have made a transition of allegiance from the parental generation to their own. But within this shift of allegiance one commonly observes adolescents moving from one peer subgroup to another, to a recirculation of friendships. Their interpersonal ties change to reflect the events occurring within themselves. Thus, although peers exert a very powerful influence on adolescents, the changing of subgroups means that no single one will exert the long-term influence that parents or other stable figures in the social environment do.

The tremendous social pressure toward conformity to peer-group standards is certainly an outstanding phenomenon. The seeming trivia of wearing exactly the right color of dress or the precise type of hairstyle assume major importance—especially in early adolescence. Clique formation and the specific activities of in-group and out-group members become matters of central significance. Much alcohol and drug abuse can be traced to response to peer pressure—to showing that one is "with it" (Wittenborn et al., 1969). Personality organization at this time adheres closely to Loevinger's (1976) description of the conformist level of ego development.

Status consciousness is probably at no point more acute than during adolescence. As teenagers pull away from the adult-dominated past and move into a new environment of peers, their standing within that environment becomes part of the definition they seek of who they are and who they are trying to become. Thus, peer-group formation takes its place as a necessary step in the sequence leading to the most fundamental

of needs for adolescents, the search for a sense of identity. From a point of view of psychological development, this quest for identity is truly a critical issue. It is in this sense that Erikson's (1959) term *identity crisis* achieves its exquisite appropriateness. In a subsequent chapter we will examine more closely the nature of this search for identity and also the form it takes in young adulthood as the need for self-particularization and ego integration.

Having acknowledged the well-recognized features of adolescence discussed thus far in this chapter, we can now relate these data more directly to the psychology of the young adult. The adolescent experience evolves psychological characteristics that provide the background from which young adulthood will emerge.

PSYCHOLOGICAL CHARACTERISTICS IN ADOLESCENCE

At the outset, I should distinguish between the notion of psychological characteristics of adolescence and the idea that there is a universal adolescent personality. The psychological characteristics I speak of refer to internal events in the structure and orientation of the individual. These events are a consequence of, among other things, the developmental period in which the individual is engaged. How the individual deals with these internal events (such as separating from parents) in the light of previous experiences and in the context of other needs and desires (such as wanting parental support) will determine his or her specific personality structure. To understand how personality changes, however, we do need to understand the significant features that change as people develop from one life stage to another.

Thus, the personalities of adolescents are as varied and distinctive as those of people in general. But certain underlying characteristics are specific to the adolescent experience itself. For example, narcissism and idealism need to be understood in terms of the impact they have on the particular individual's perception of everyday experiences, how life events will affect their manifestation, and how they in turn lay the groundwork for the person's emergence into young adulthood.

Sexual Preoccupation

Just as one of the prime facts of adolescence is the advent of biosexual maturity, so one of its prime psychological characteristics is

sexual preoccupation. A large part of the adolescent's inner life revolves around issues related to the biological fact of gonad maturation. As with any other major adjustment to internal events, individuals devote much of their energy and thought to the significance of its impact. Sexual fantasies, sexual wishes, and the desire for sexual experience permeate awareness or activate defenses to repress that awareness. In turn, this leads to activities and experimentation involving the genitalia and a concern for sexual interaction—particularly with members of the opposite sex.

Throughout the adolescent period there is progressive experimentation and initiation into direct sexual contact. Cross-cultural data (Money & Ehrhardt, 1972) indicate that for the great majority of people sexual intercourse first occurs during this period. In addition, a vast array of incidental skills are being tried out and developed. These range from the simple ability to conduct everyday conversation with the opposite sex to being able to develop relationships on a social and personal level. For people of homosexual or transgender orientation, adolescence often brings their dawning awareness of self into poignantly sharp focus.

Even where sexually oriented behavior is minimal or nonexistent, it can be safely asserted that considerable amounts of effort and energy are being expended by the individual in containing, blocking, inhibiting, or channeling sexual expression. In the case of the male, the most celibate inevitably have sexual dreams including nocturnal emissions—even where such ordinary forms of sexual discharge as masturbation are proscribed. From a psychological viewpoint the primary issue here is not what the person does in overt behavior. Rather, it is the fact that so much of mental life and feelings is taken up with sexual matters. And, irrespective of what the person is actually doing, he or she is, to a very considerable degree, involved with developing or preventing from emergence this consistent preoccupation with sexuality.

Narcissistic Orientation

A closely related attribute of equally far-reaching significance is the narcissism of adolescence. Narcissism refers to the investment of energy in oneself as the focal source of interest and concern. Indeed, one's interaction with the world is largely of meaning to the extent that it relates to this pervasive self-involvement. In this sense adolescents can truly be described as self-oriented people caught up in their own experiences.

The more popular definition of narcissism connotes self-love. Thus, it appears to the observer that the adolescent studying pimples in the mirror, combing hair, or debating endlessly over which sweater to wear is engaging in blatant self-indulgence. Yet, as adolescents ruminate during these activities, most of their comments are of a self-deprecatory nature. Anguish, more than adoration, seems to be the dominant theme.

In both senses of the term, *narcissism* has to do with adolescents' preoccupation with any issue relevant to their self-image. This narcissistic concern also affects their perception of how the world sees them. It is as though a hair out of place or a casual snub were of the utmost significance for their well-being and stature. As Freud originally noted, narcissism is not so much a matter of self-love but rather of deep self-concern. Behavior that appears to be selfish and egotistical, therefore, usually betokens the anxious shortsightedness of narcissistic self-preoccupation.

Ego Fluidity

To understand ego fluidity, it is necessary to go back to the basic fact that the adolescent is not an adult but in transition from childhood. Along with incomplete physical and social development goes incomplete intrapsychic development. In particular, we are concerned with the matter of ego development. The ego, the person's regulative system of personality functioning, has not yet achieved the integrity and solidity of adulthood. This incompletely developed set of processes then comes under the tremendous stresses already described as accompanying the onset of puberty and adolescence.

One consequence is that the ego functions in a highly unstable fashion. The person becomes unpredictably vulnerable, so susceptible to stresses that seemingly small incidents can be rapidly magnified into events of major importance. The individual is subject to wide variations of mood and temperament. Happiness and tears seem virtually to coexist at times. The person can be readily brought to a state of fury, depression, or exultation by ordinary events. Sometimes the reactions are so inappropriate that they seem pathological. But, unlike pathology, these lapses in ego effectiveness occur as brief episodes. It is common to observe periods when control over emotions and behavior is less dependable than might otherwise be expected. Adolescents at one point can function with the maturity of an adult and seconds later act in the most childlike ways.

Happily, most teenagers enjoy a high recuperative power. That is,

the ego processes that are so vulnerable to pressure are also highly resilient. Rapid recovery from psychic insult is the rule rather than the exception. It is this ability that most differentiates typical from disturbed adolescent reactions (Erikson, 1963).

Over the course of adolescence one can observe the process of maturation as a function of the firming up of the ego. The ego evolves into a consistent, dependable set of regulatory functions that is able to control and integrate reactions to the environment as well as input from the environment. Mood swings reduce in intensity, and the individual's responses become more moderated. But even in later adolescence this variability in response can make adolescents difficult people to live and work with—for the parent, the teacher, the counselor, the friend, or the passer-by. Consequently, the evolution to maturity of ego functions is central to the transition from adolescence to eventual adulthood.

Impulsivity. One aspect of ego fluidity is so important as to merit special consideration as a separate issue in understanding adolescence. This is the characteristic of *impulsivity.* By this term we refer to the almost immediate, reflex-like, direct spilling over into behavior of feelings, wishes, and urges that may affect the person. Impulsivity is marked by its immediacy of response and its unreflective quality. There is no consideration or deliberation—or even integration into cognitive functioning—from the time of the input of stimulus until the activation of response. In general, impulsivity is due to an extremely intense urge to react that overwhelms ego controls, a weakened or inadequately developed set of ego functions, or some combination of the two. Because adolescents are beset by a variety of unfamiliar and intense urgings, feelings, and wishes at a time in life when ego functions are incompletely developed, it is easy to see why they are particularly susceptible to impulsive reactions. The capacity for delayed response and the ability to check out reality—qualities gradually acquired during childhood—give way to the intrapsychic erosion and external pressures of adolescent life. Immediate need overwhelms the ego organization, and an impulsive act results.

It is not only teenagers, of course, who are subject to impulsive reactions. Children in general have an incompletely formed or simply unlearned ability to integrate stimulus materials, to define appropriate ways of responding, and to delay reactions. In addition, impulsive behavior is characteristic of certain psychopathological reactions.

The tendency to act unreflectively on wishes and feelings, however,

is important in understanding adolescence when we delve into how this life period differs from the one ahead. A reaction process that would be indicative of aberrant or disturbed behavior in an adult is commonly part of the normal adolescent response. We will soon examine the young adult's activist orientation, which in itself implies a tendency to translate wishes into actions. The important distinction here, however, is that in young adulthood the decision to act is based in part on an ego-mediated, volitional choice rather than the overwhelming of ego controls, resulting in impulsive behavior. This point will be discussed more fully in Chapter 7.

Absolute Idealism

Throughout the recorded history of ideas it has been observed that idealism is the province of the young. The biblical story of David and Goliath and the feats of Joan of Arc are two of the more flamboyant examples of a quality whose occurrence is far more common during this segment of the life span than at other times.

Whatever its roots in human nature, idealism depends on maturation and experience as much as it does on youthfulness. During early childhood the person learns to distinguish between self and environment. Through identification and education the individual gradually incorporates a capacity for moral judgment. As Piaget has convincingly demonstrated, however, the child's concept of morality is strikingly different from the adult's. Sheer morality—the literal goods and bads, rights and wrongs incorporated during the first dozen or so years of life—begins to share the stage with values early in the second decade. Values, which involve goals and purposes, are also endowed with moral judgment. The advent of formal operations in thinking enables the person to manipulate abstract ideas, independent of concrete reality. Finally, the maturation of metaphysical interests—in truth, God, rightness—prepares adolescents for the first explicit encounter with idealism.

As with other kinds of new learning, the complexities of idealistic thinking tend to be condensed into simple forms at first. Given adolescents' limited world experience and core preoccupation with self, it is not surprising that their approach to idealism should be oriented to establishing clearly marked guideposts. They can hardly be expected to be sensitive to nuances and exceptions when their first contact is conditioned by the need to translate knowledge into immediately relevant terms. Thus, we

find the adolescent's idealism to be polarized into values that are both abstract and absolute. Truth, purity, loyalty, trust, beauty are treated as though there were a perfect set of standards for measuring these qualities. For the teenager, moreover, the idealized quality is either present or absent. One tells the truth or one lies; a person is beautiful or ugly; one is saint or a sinner. During the period of hottest furor over the Vietnam war, it was not unusual to see a sample of adolescents swing from avid approval to fervent opposition to U. S. involvement—within a 12-month period. A similar phenomenon was observed 8000 miles away. The Chinese Red Guard, composed primarily of teenagers, renounced previous values in a "Cultural Revolution" precipitated by the statements of Mao Zedong. In both cases, the concern was typically not with underlying issues or reasons but rather with the necessity for applying a sweeping, unequivocal judgment to which one could attach oneself (with one's peers).

If this description of behavior appears also to fit many adults, it is because chronological age offers no guarantee that psychological development has reached maturity. Relatively little is known about the natural history of idealistic attitudes and the factors that affect their evolution.

Idealism, the espousal of the highest human values, appears for the first time during adolescence. The particular form it assumes is absolutist. That is, the qualities are seen as dichotomies rather than as continua. There are no grays, only blacks and whites. Trust must be total. To veer from absolute fidelity is to be a hypocrite. The idealism is also abstract, an idea more than an action. Events and behaviors exemplify the concept. Not until further maturation occurs will ideals become principles that guide and direct behavior.

This rigid polarization of thinking about ideals tends to be used as a way of structuring the world, assigning a category or a label to persons and things. Thus, idealism is of help to adolescents in their efforts to order the world. In addition, idealism provides a basis for making their first independent, calculated efforts at affecting the world through their own efforts. This is distinct from the spontaneous acts of love or generosity one observes in younger children. It is even different from the conscious act of doing a "good" deed known to be approved by significant elders. The evolution of idealism permits the adolescent to make an independent judgment based on a broad principle of value that may well transcend direct personal experience or that of family and associates. Perry's (1970) data indicate that even late adolescents who are in college

manifest the same absolutist, abstract kind of thinking. Neither intelligence nor verbal fluency seems capable of modifying this aspect of the developmental process.

Nevertheless, the emergence of idealism is a significant step forward in adolescent growth and development, however limited the understanding may be at this time. When we examine young adult idealism in the next chapter, we will notice that it is both strikingly similar to and different from adolescent idealism.

6

THE YOUNG ADULT: A THEORETICAL OVERVIEW

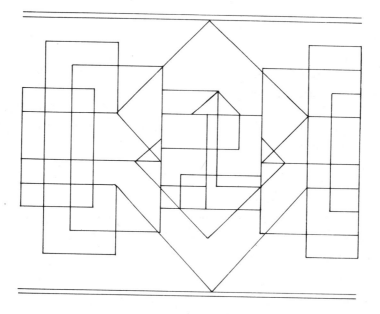

Over the course of several decades a small but significant body of literature related to young adulthood has begun to emerge. Before 1959, *Psychological Abstracts,* the annually published compendium of professional literature in the field, did not even have an index listing for the young adult. Even today most of the available literature on young adulthood is based on unsystematic clinical observation and theory. And the more rigorously designed studies have been concerned not with young adults but with dimensions of personality stability and change over time. Fortunately, some of those studies report data for a time span that overlaps the period when young-adult functions are likely to evolve and operate. Although not designed as studies of young adulthood, these data contribute significantly to the limited pool of information available.

This chapter has two major segments. The first part covers those theorists who have explicitly acknowledged young adulthood as a life stage. The second part includes the work of those longitudinal research workers whose writings contain material relevant to young adulthood.

FOUR THEORISTS

Happily, there are theorists who do recognize a distinct stage of young adulthood. These writers have provided valuable insights into the period. I will not attempt a comprehensive review of each; their writings extend well beyond the subject of young adults. What follows, then, is an examination of that part of their work that is most germane to the study of young adulthood.

Erikson

Artist-*cum*-psychoanalyst, disciple of Freud, exposed to the foremost anthropologists of his generation, Erik Erikson was one of the first writers to use the term *young adult.* He remains one of the few psychoanalytic writers to conceptualize development over the life span. Paradoxically, he considers his major effort to be a contribution to the understanding of childhood.

Erikson's development theory is patterned on the biological evolution of certain critical stages, thus modifying rather than departing from Freud's model of psychosexual development. What is truly "psychosocial" in this concept is his assumption "that society, in principle, tends to be so constituted as to meet and invite this succession of potentialities for

interaction and attempts to safeguard and to encourage the proper rate and the proper sequencing of their unfolding" (1963, p. 270).

Just as individuals are pressed to adapt to societal needs, Erikson asserts, societies are constructed so as to adapt to the developmental imperatives of their members. In deriving these conclusions, Erikson draws actively on his first-hand observations of several different cultures, including preindustrial and technologically sophisticated societies. These cross-cultural observations powerfully affected Erikson's psychoanalytic grounding when he shifted from the traditional psychosexual model of development to the psychosocial model.

His conception of the life cycle reflects the importance of these influences. Following Freud, he retains the notion that conflict is at the core of personality development. The eight critical periods that define the life cycle are explicitly structured in terms of opposition: basic trust versus basic mistrust, autonomy versus shame, initiative versus guilt, industry versus inferiority, identity versus role confusion, intimacy versus isolation, generativity versus stagnation, and ego integrity versus despair. His "predetermined steps" are crises that identify each life stage and that must be encountered at their point of emergence. The outcome of each encounter determines whether the person will experience progress or regression, integration or retardation. Unlike Jung, who viewed polarities as necessary ingredients of the personality, Erikson contends that opposed forces exist only because of the person's inability to completely resolve the crises of each developmental stage. Such a failure can significantly affect further growth.

In the Eriksonian scheme the vital transition from adolescence to young adulthood is, for the first time, identified in strictly psychological terms. The critical developmental issue of adolescence is identity versus role confusion (1963). Identity is the aggregate of past experiences, endowed abilities, and social-role opportunities, matched by the recognition of significant others in one's environment. In role confusion the adolescent "overidentifies" with heroes or cliques "to the point of apparent complete loss of identity." If identity crisis is the hallmark of adolescence, identity formation indelibly marks the end of adolescence and entry into young adulthood (1968). Successful resolution of the identity crisis thus paves the way for major adult tasks.

For Erikson the core issue of young adulthood is the conflict between intimacy and isolation. Intimacy covers a variety of experiences,

ranging from "physical combat" and "close affiliations" to orgasm and "intuition from the recesses of the self." Isolation implies a readiness to see others as alien and dangerous. All too often the same people can be objects of both intimacy and isolation. This is most likely to occur when the individual cannot differentiate between intense feelings, such as passion and combativeness.

The next adult stage is generativity versus stagnation. Generativity is "the concern with establishing and guiding the next generation," including a broader definition of caring for the creatures of the world. Stagnation, a deep sense of personal impoverishment or pathological self-concern, is the result of the failure to attain a nurturant, generative orientation.

Of particular importance for present-day understanding is the underlying assumption of *ego boundaries,* a concept Erikson (1968) acquired from his teacher, Paul Federn. The concept of *identity* connotes a structural integrity, not simply a grouping of ideas and attitudes about the self. Intimacy implies a sense of security about one's ego boundaries, such that "fusion" with another person does not risk the loss of one's own identity. The conceiving of identity development in structural terms is, as we shall see (Chapter 7), a critical insight for understanding the young adult.

Somewhat ambiguously, Erikson links intimacy to genitality and thence to six corollaries, which may be taken to encompass a utopian view of the "healthy personality." These are (1) mutuality of orgasm (2) with a loved partner (3) of the opposite sex (4) with whom one shares mutual trust (5) and with whom one regulates work, procreation, and recreation (6) so as to secure a satisfactory development for one's offspring. Inasmuch as Erikson appends this section to his discussion of intimacy versus isolation as a young-adult indicator, it is unclear whether he views these features as criteria of an optimum, ideal, or usual outcome of young adulthood.

In any event, Erikson's enduring contribution centers on his application of an intrapsychic approach to a sociocultural context, primarily through his notion that the two find common ground in the process of identity development. The dominant feature of a life stage is the specific psychosocial issue encountered by individuals in the continuing evolution of their identity. Erikson's concern with adolescence and youth has had profound implications for understanding the transition into young adulthood.

Havighurst

While teaching human development to his students at the University of Chicago, Robert Havighurst evolved the concept of *developmental tasks,* "those things that constitute healthy and satisfactory growth in our society" (1952, p. 2). Like Erikson he uses the biological model of embryology, which emphasizes critical periods of growth as well as the direction and sequence of development. If the task is not achieved at the proper time, it will not be achieved well. Failure in this task will cause partial or complete failure in the achievement of other tasks to come. His thinking also parallels that of Erikson in that development is seen as social and psychological—a learning experience. Developmental tasks are "bio-socio-psychological tasks, midway between an individual need and a societal demand" (1952, p. 3).

Havighurst identifies the "early-adult" period as between the ages of 18 and 30. He sees it as made uniquely stressful by the varied and important tasks it contains. These include (1) selecting a mate, (2) learning to live with a marriage partner, (3) starting a family, (4) rearing children, (5) managing a home, (6) getting started in a career, (7) taking on civic responsibility, and (8) finding a congenial social group. Havighurst is, therefore, one of the early writers to locate young adulthood in the life span and to offer a systematic method of identifying its features. In his writings, moreover, there is an empathic awareness of the difficulties confronting those trying to enter adult society.

Both the strengths and the limitations of the Havighurst model lie its dependence on the concept of *developmental task* and all that it denotes. Developmental tasks serve to define one's status in a life stage. They accomplish this by providing a framework within which individuals and their culture can attain some mutual sense of need satisfaction and reward. But developmental tasks are rarely universal. As Havighurst notes, his definition is culture specific, based on North American middle-class values. It also assumes, tacitly, that even in a rapidly changing society the mainstream attitudes and expectations are only gradually modified.

Built into his model is an acknowledgement that upper- and lower-class values are often at variance with the middle class in significant ways. But time and events act to reshape the values of any social class. The sexual mores of 1952 bear little resemblance to those of 1980, especially in the middle class. Even within unchanging developmental tasks, such as managing a home, changes in sex-role expectations can radically alter

those definitions. Developmental tasks are therefore useful only as an index of specific groups at designated periods of historic time.

The construct of *developmental task* would probably have wider general application in more stable societies. Havighurst's model relies heavily on observable social behavior. The listing of specific tasks allows for them to be readily identified as common social expectations. For the individual, the meaning of task achievement is presumed to be social approval, personal satisfaction, and growth. In this respect, Havighurst anticipated Erikson's emphasis on the power of social recognition. One wonders, however, whether individual life needs are routinely in such close harmony with cultural expectations. Do North American middle-class expectations in the 20th century provide an optimum model for human development? Is the person who fails to conform to these tasks doomed to dissatisfaction, failure, and unhappiness? Finally, by his own standards of establishing a biological and psychological basis (as well as the documented social basis) for developmental tasks, Havighurst provides little evidence that these tasks are essential to individual development.

The concept of *developmental task,* in some form, is likely to be an enduring contribution. It is difficult, moreover, to conceptualize a society in which stage expectations do not exist. It is probable that certain cultural imperatives are, indeed, universal and invariant. In the case of young adults, for example, attaining the tasks of providing for oneself and ensuring a new generation are of Darwinian magnitude. Perhaps by attempting to be too extensive in its detailing of developmental tasks, Havighurst's theory is vulnerable to the criticism of overreaching itself.

White

Perhaps best known as the translator of complex psychological literature into lucid textbook form, Robert White has also done extensive clinical and theoretical research with young adults. Although he can be conveniently classified as an ego psychologist, White's interest in personality development is eclectic. Accomplished in the literature of both "natural growth" and psychopathology, White draws on social, familial, biological, and developmental sources in formulating his discoveries.

White's description of the psychological attributes of the young adult was first published in 1952. It received important empirical support from Nevitt Sanford's (1956) research to be reported later in this chapter.

White's later (1975) revisions of his thinking have not substantially altered the earlier formulation. The "growth trends" identified by White are five in number: (1) stabilizing of ego identity, (2) freeing of personal relationships, (3) deepening of interests, (4) humanizing of values, and (5) expansion of caring.

Stabilizing of ego identity. White adapts Erikson's concept of ego identity to mean "the sense of being a distinct individual within a social framework" (1975, p. 326). More succinctly, identity refers to a sense of self. In young adulthood White observes a greater stability and consistency in this self and greater freedom from transient influences.

Experience in living various social roles helps define a clearer sense of ego identity. The person's inner consistency permits a fuller "realization of capacities for development." Finally, as the young adult becomes more familiar with self-determined attitudes and preferences, this generates a "greater capacity to exert an influence on the surrounding world" (1975).

Freeing of personal relationships. Young adults develop the ability "to respond to people in their own right." This implies a more realistic, in-the-present assessment of personal relationships, less colored by events in the past history of the perceiver that might otherwise prejudice or distort the experience. By becoming less tied to their personal history in relating to others, young adults can be more responsive to the current relationship. A greater sensitivity to the other person develops. In turn, this aids the learning of new social skills and a wider variety of ways of interacting. "The person moves in the direction of increased capacity to live in real relationship with the people immediately around him" (1975, p. 345).

Deepening of interests. White attaches particular significance to the role of interests in shaping the enjoyment of life. Although interests are not static, they do tend to stabilize aspects of the personality over time and experience. The deepening of interests implies "progressive mastery of the knowledge and skill that is relevant to a sphere of interest." Interests are thus tied to both competence and commitment in White's thinking. In both of these respects, the deepening of interests plays a vital role in young-adult development.

Finding realistic pathways of living is a central part of young

adulthood. When young adults can identify clear and dependable areas of stable interest and ability, they have taken a major step toward solidifying natural directions for their future growth.

Humanizing of values. Young adults discover human and social purpose in hitherto abstract value constructions. In part, White conceives of this as "a continuation of moral growth." Young adults increasingly find personal relevance in moral issues, translating them into terms that can be understood and affirmed in their own expanding lives.

What White calls values correspond closely to what I will later refer to as ideals. He is among the first theorists to distinguish between the abstract morality of adolescence and the more functional morality of young adulthood. More particularly, he correctly identifies the evolutionary process that underlies the development of idealism from adolescence to young adulthood. He also anticipates by almost 20 years Perry's discovery of the evolution of relativism in the structure of ethical thinking among college students. In young adulthood values become incorporated into the person's identity, rather than existing as abstract ideas external to belief and action.

Expansion of caring. White's fifth "growth trend" partakes of a number of related concepts. It includes Adler's "social interest," Allport's "extension of the sense of self," Angyal's "trend to homonomy," and Erikson's "generativity." As White uses *expansion of caring*, it seems to denote an extended social conscience—a concern to help those in need. This quality brings the young adult more in contact with idealistic service to the world community. It also denotes an expansion of one's own sense of self through nurturing others. For White, the "increased caring for the welfare of other persons and human concerns" is "a growth trend that comes into its own during young adulthood."

In some respects, expansion of caring seems located developmentally earlier than related concepts cited by White. Erikson, for example, clearly puts generativity at a stage beyond the intimacy of young adulthood. Similarly, the constructs advanced by Adler (social interest), Allport (extension of the sense of self), and Angyal (homonomy) are commonly taken to be indicators of full psychological maturity rather than the first stage of the adult life span.

White's work is notable for its emphasis on personality attributes in

the growth process. His formulation incorporates a number of variables central to personality development: identity, values, interests, interpersonal relationships, consistency, and differentiation. Kimmel (1974) questions whether White's data can be applied to other than the college students he studied. It may also appear that the findings are neither specifically nor necessarily associated with young adulthood. (White himself notes Sanford's findings that college senior women, presumably young adults, manifest less ego stability than they did as freshmen.) The empirical test is yet to come. Whatever that outcome, White has provided a model of personality development in adult life that is grounded in the individual rather than in societal demand. Thus, it speaks to what people are like, and can be like, during a particular period of the life span.

Wittenberg

Psychoanalytic theorists have long been criticized for attributing little to adult development beyond a recapitulation of preadolescent experience and conflict. Rudolph Wittenberg's small volume *Postadolescence* (1968) is an outstanding exception. He explicitly asserts that "postadolescence represents a specific phase of growth in the life cycle" (p. iv). That he fails to identify postadolescence as an explicitly adult stage is, by comparison, a small point.

Wittenberg identifies five "metapsychologic characteristics" and three "socioeconomic factors" in young adults from their late teens to early 20s. The metapsychologic characteristics are

1. A self-image crisis, in which the person alternates between responding to superego demands (parental/authority standards) and adhering to one's ego-ideal (becoming one's own authority). Moving toward autonomy is the central task of postadolescence.
2. Brief states of depersonalization, in which the person experiences a loss of sense of identity. The young adult may feel temporarily disembodied, isolated, estranged.
3. End of role-playing. The experimentation with life roles seen in adolescence gives way to more reality-based awareness, often with accompanying depression.
4. Awareness of time continuity. The postadolescent sense of the passage of time becomes more acute, particularly as it relates to present and future commitments. It includes developing the ability to allocate and utilize time in one's activities, plans, or defenses.

5. Search for a partner, in which the young adult chooses a love object for a "permanent affiliation." Wittenberg cautions that one must distinguish this activity from a defensive flight into marriage. In the latter case, marriage becomes a way of avoiding the anxiety of identity resolution, role experimentation, and time's continuous passing.

The socioeconomic factors are

1. The economic bind, in which "young adults want to pay their own way" but society actively keeps them from participating in the labor force. This is tantamount to social rejection, because it comes at a time when young adults are striving for autonomy.
2. Group formation, which is used to personify the young adult's ego-ideal. In adolescence the group functions as a protector or as a means of providing oneself with an identity. For the young adult, membership in a social, political, or religious group becomes part of one's role and self-definition. Social isolation in young adulthood tends to be indicative of psychological disturbance, according to Wittenberg.
3. Evolving a *Weltanschauung,* or philosophy of life. The character of this philosophy depends on the success the young adult has had in coming to terms with all the above-mentioned pressure. One's *Weltanschauung* provides the basis for an internalized heirarchy of values, a means by which one can deal with oneself in encountering and adapting to the outside world and its value structure. However, Wittenberg ironically observes that, the more seriously postadolescents subscribe to their emerging philosophy, the greater likelihood of encountering the moral contradictions in society.

Wittenberg's theoretical formulations reflect their source—psychoanalytic work with 50 young adults, most of whom were his patients. The extension of psychoanalytic insights into the adult years has required more than a quantitative extrapolation of earlier theories of child development. Throughout, Wittenberg makes clear the qualitative changes that occur in the transition from adolescence to young adulthood. Identity development and psychological autonomy characterize postadolescence, rather than the taming and neutralization of drives that is the task of earlier periods. As psychoanalytically-oriented developmental theorists move into the adult years, Wittenberg's contribution can be expected to gain greater attention. He is among the first of that group to describe adult forms of individuation and "real object" (Blanck & Blanck, 1979) relationships.

LONGITUDINAL RESEARCH FINDINGS

The empirical research data relevant to young adulthood tends to be adventitious more often than intentional. Rarely have young adults been studied systematically, in whole or in part. Most of the studies to be reported here originate from the more general concerns of personologists and developmental psychologists. The former tend to be concerned with systematic change or constancy of the personality over time. The latter focus on the evolution of specific psychological functions or structures over time. Among the personologists are Symonds, Sanford, Levinson, Lowenthal, and Vaillant. Developmental research has come from Kohlberg, Isaacs, Perry, and Loevinger.

Personologists

Symonds. Percival Symonds (1961) was one of the early psychologists to apply projective techniques to the study of normal personality development. In a 13-year longitudinal study he sought to learn more about the continuity of personality from adolescence into adulthood. Symonds studied a group of 40 adolescent volunteers, male and female, using picture-story and interview measures. Only 28 of the original sample were available for reexamination 13 years later, and his comparisons are based on these data.

For our purposes, Symonds's data offer a rare opportunity to study developmental differences in intrapsychic functions between adolescence and young adulthood. Although there are methodological problems with some aspects of the research design, comparisons can be legitimately drawn in certain areas. Symonds categorized the types of stories his subjects created for the test pictures. When the two sets of stories were analyzed statistically, significant differences were found in the contents of the adolescent and young-adult sets. "The themes that showed a decrease [in the later administration] are the ones that . . . make clear the essential characteristics of adolescent fantasy" (1961, p. 31).

These characteristics of adolescent fantasy include crime against property, criminal death, accidental death, hostility, and being aggressed against. Symonds ascribes this violent content to the eruption of aggressive impulsivity in adolescence. A second thematic cluster includes mystery, tricks, and magic, which are interpreted as covert sexual references.

Themes of disobedience and rebelliousness, interestingly, showed no significant change.

As young adults, the subjects showed significantly more depression, many fewer happy outcomes to their stories, but more wishful thinking. Symonds ascribes these findings to the "disillusionment that has set in" among the subjects 13 years later, in 1953. Thus, even as he concludes with evidence for the persistence of personality trends, it is clear that patterned differences between life stages are also in evidence. Hostile urgings seemingly give way to depressive thought (self-directed anger?) and disillusion.

Sanford. Following World War II, the educational benefits awarded returning veterans triggered an unprecedented demand for college education. This, in turn, focused attention on the college experience and its impact on personality. During the mid-'50s a research group headed by Nevitt Sanford tested and interviewed a group of students as they progressed through Vassar College, at that time a liberal-arts school for women from predominantly wealthy families. Sanford's findings are reported (1956, 1962) as they relate to the impact of college education. To the extent that the college years (from 17 to 22) in our society correspond generally to the transition period from adolescence into young adulthood, his data may illuminate developmental changes as well. It should be noted, however, that Sanford consistently refers to his subjects as "late adolescents." From his perspective the research was not a study of change in developmental status. Rather, it was designed to shed light on how colleges could enhance the growth needs of their consumer population. Nevertheless, by describing the consistent features of freshmen and the changes observed when they were seniors, the study does provide useful information about this transitional period.

Freshmen women were described as having strong impulses that were opposed by an "alert, rigid, punitive conscience." They manifested stereotypic thinking, a deferential attitude to authority, and dependence on external sources for their values. They showed a need for "moral heroes" to follow and a need to be perfectionistic in their standards and expectations. They were quick to label imperfections as evidence of hypocrisy and phoniness. In self-esteem these socioeconomically advantaged women displayed instability, simultaneously experiencing over- and under-estimations of self. They sought external sources for evaluating self-esteem.

Change in personality features was measured by Sanford (1956, 1962) and Webster (1956) along the dimensions of "social maturity," "impulse expression," "developmental status," and "masculine role." Positive changes in these areas led Webster to conclude that Vassar students, like those in a parallel study at Bennington College, became "less conservative" and showed "increased tolerance for individual differences" and "more freedom to express impulses." In addition, seniors gave evidence of "greater openness to experience" by virtue of a greater awareness of instability. Data from other women's colleges were consistent with these findings.

Extreme caution is clearly dictated in generalizing from the results of a sample of affluent college women during the 1950s. Nevertheless, one cannot fail to note certain similarities between Sanford's description of college freshmen and Wittenberg's comments about the characteristics of his patients. Where Sanford describes a late-adolescent punitive conscience, stereotypic thinking, and deference to authority, Wittenberg finds adolescents manifesting a morally prohibitive superego, polarized thinking, and conformity or opposition to authority. Parallels between Webster's findings and White's description of young-adult characteristics are also striking. The openness and increased tolerance for individual differences noted by Webster in college seniors is reminiscent of aspects of the humanizing of values in White's language. Both White and Sanford describe a more differentiated ego in their respective groups as well, although terms such as *ego, self,* and *identity* are used somewhat loosely. White and Sanford tend to define *ego, self,* and *identity* in perceptual and experiential terms. By comparison, Wittenberg and Erikson refer more explicitly to formal organizational properties, such as ego-ideal and identity structure. Ultimately, developmental theory must include both experiential and structural components in its formulation of the dynamics of growth processes. The next theory to be considered does contain some of these elements.

Levinson. A research group in Connecticut headed by Daniel Levinson (1978) has studied the adult development of 40 men, mostly college graduates in the corridor from Boston to New York, using interview and TAT material. The group sought to discover "relatively universal, genotypic, age-linked, adult development periods." It has identified a postadolescent period of early adult transition, beginning at 16 to 18 and ending at 20 to 24. This period involves learning to separate physically and

differentiate psychologically from one's family of origin. The next period, entering the adult world, starts in the early 20s and extends until 27 to 29. During this time the young man explores and makes tentative commitments to a variety of adult roles and relationships. He develops an initial definition of himself as an adult and establishes a link between valued aspects of the self and the world at large. Age 30 is seen as a critical point relative to the next stage, one of "settling down" to a more ordered and stable period of life.

Central to this formulation is the concept of *life structure*. This is a pattern for living that is evolved during the period of entering the adult world. It must be stable yet allow the person to keep options open without making strong commitments.

The ambitious scope of the Levinson group's effort has produced a theory remarkable for its age-linked specificity. Critics challenge whether his sample is representative for a universalist theory of male adult development. Vaillant's findings (1977) question the accuracy of recall after a lapse of 10 or 20 years. Levinson's description of the period of novice adulthood, from 17 to 32, is based on the recall of men between 35 and 45. Although some age linking of development to the life span is probable, Neugarten and Datan (1973) indicate that time is measured socially, historically, and psychologically in people's lives and is not determined strictly by chronological age. It remains a tantalizing question whether an adult developmental scheme can be both *universal* and so specifically age linked as their data suggest.

At the same time, aspects of the Levinson group's findings are reminiscent of the findings of other writers. The concepts of *life structure* and *the dream* are similar to the *Weltanschauung* of Wittenberg's young adults. The dynamics of the early adult transition—leaving the family of origin—resonate well with Ausubel's (1977) concept of *desatellization,* which is discussed in Chapter 10.

In sum, Levinson's theory commendably attempts to incorporate dynamic, experiential, and structural components. It overreaches itself largely in its claims to age specificity and universality of generalization.

Lowenthal. A research group interested in adult development is conducting a longitudinal study of four life periods. Its sample, located in the San Francisco Bay area, includes male and female high school seniors, newlyweds, middle-aged people, and preretirees (Lowenthal, Thurnher, & Chiriboga, 1977).

The aim is to provide data on age and sex differences as people encounter the stress of periods of change in their lives. The subjects are, therefore, not necessarily representative of the general population or of a particular life stage; that is to say, all young adults are not newlyweds. In addition, the inquiry is directed at reactions to the presumed life stress of transitional periods and not at overall developmental functioning. Finally, many of the research parameters are socioanthropological (for example, social activities) rather than psychological (for example, self-image) in character. Nevertheless, the baseline information provides useful resource material if approached with these constraints in mind.

Of the four age groups the newlyweds had the lowest socioeconomic status, despite a relatively higher level of education. They also had the widest and most frequent activities of the different groups. The marital relationship was characterized by a convergence of social roles, in that both men and women worked and participated in shared social activities. Yet, in spite of the contemporary rhetoric about changing roles, both sexes reported that the male was the dominant authority in the marriage! In their interpersonal relations, though, the focus was less on role and status and more on the personal qualities of their spouse and on the sense of mutuality in their relationship. Projective testing of newlywed husbands reflected positive attitudes of "loving, caring and intimacy." Wives showed more nurturant themes, suggesting a response to their husbands' covert dependency needs.

In the area of self-concept newlywed men seemed less constrained and more action-minded, daring, and innovative. By contrast, women seemed less energetic and more possessive. Compared to high school seniors (the closest age comparison) they had a much more favorable self-image. The newlywed group reported the fewest emotional problems and fewest visits to a doctor and presented themselves as being the most happy. They were also seen as "the most open to new experiences."

Intelligence testing provided interesting data. Of the four developmental groups the newlyweds ranked third in vocabulary (*verbal* intelligence) but first in block design (*performance* intelligence). The action orientation of the group was thus reflected in their generally active life-style and also in their intelligence function.

The emergence of both similarities and differences between men and women was matched by sex differences in the other three groups as well. These data amplify the need for a life-span psychology that accounts for those developmental differences in which gender is an interacting

variable. Results suggest that the self-image of men becomes increasingly crystallized as they move through life, whereas among women uncertainties continue (1977, p. 80).

Of particular concern in the Lowenthal group's data is a depressive quality hinted at in the newlywed female group. Self-chosen statements indicating low energy or maintaining that "life is meaningless" may either be specific to their sample or show some general postmarital letdown. It is notable, however, that Symonds (1961) reports increased depression among young-adult men, and Rappaport (1972) considers disillusionment to be endemic to that period of the life span.

Vaillant. Back in 1935 Harvard College sponsored the Grant Study. A team of psychologists and psychiatrists recruited mentally healthy students to participate in a long-term study of their adult lives. About thirty-five years later, George Vaillant (1977) concluded the investigation and published his findings. The 95 subjects were evaluated relative to their "psychological well-being."

Qualities originally thought to be indicative of mental health— "vital affect," "friendliness," and "humanism"—were later discovered to be evidence of a developmental period. "Such 'virtues' seem to have been more associated with a transient phase of development than with enduring character" (p. 211).

Features of personality structure, not traits, were more predictive of later satisfaction. In particular, those young adults who were "well integrated" and "practical and organized" seemed to show the highest adaptation levels during later years. Paralleling Wittenberg's findings, Vaillant describes adolescent friendships as determined by the need for comfort and support. Young adults choose relationships that respect individual differences, a finding that jibes well with the Lowenthal group's data just reported.

However, the Grant study data fail to support the Levinson group's contention that developmental change is highly specific to chronological age. According to Vaillant, subjects at age 50 repressed or denied events they had described to investigators while in their 20s.

Vaillant's data underscore the importance of the transition from adolescence to young adulthood. In particular, they emphasize the saliency of two factors in fostering development through the adult life span. These are the structural integration of personality (presuming resolution of the identity crisis of adolescence) and interpersonal compe-

tence with peers (implying progress beyond the comfort and support level of interaction).

However, Vaillant cautions that "the sociocultural narrowness of the Grant Study sample severely limits the conclusions" (1977, p. 236).

Developmental Psychologists

Kohlberg. In longitudinal research there is a group that prefers to study the evolution of more-circumscribed areas of development. Lawrence Kohlberg's work on moral development (1964, 1969) is a classic example. Like Piaget in his thinking on cognitive development, Kohlberg conceives of morality as a psychological restructuring that evolves in a predictable direction and sequence. He has constructed a natural-history model of moral development. It begins with punishment and obedience as the first moral determinants and proceeds through hedonism, approval, law and order, democratic contract and individual principles. Law and order, Type 4 in Kohlberg's model, is usually attained by adolescence. Few people—25% or fewer—develop beyond this point.

Type 4 moral development is characterized by conforming to law and sustaining the authority of the social order. Personal responsibility is typically equated with social responsibility. Deviation from social norms is to be punished. Type 4 differs principally from Type 3 in that fear of disapproval, loyalty, and idealization of authority was the rule at that lower level.

Type 5 features the primacy of democratic process. Justice is based on community welfare, democratically arrived at. Authority is determined by social contract and is not defined by the person holding that position. Laws presume universal human rights.

Type 6 emphasizes adherence to principles of personal morality. Individual conscience and responsibility underlie morality and action at this level. Respect for the individual and for the sacredness of human life are intertwined. Universal values are presumed to issue from attainment of this level of conscience. Kohlberg cites rare individuals, such as Mohandas Gandhi or the Reverend Dr. Martin Luther King, Jr., as examples of Type 6 moral development.

Gilligan (1977) contends that women's moral development differs from this model, in that relatedness rather than individuation is at the highest levels. Others, myself included, dispute Kohlberg's (1978) contention that structural change in personality ceases before adult develop-

ment begins. Despite 20-odd years of empirical research, Kohlberg's measures have rarely been applied to people beyond college age.

The natural history of adult development, as part of a true life-span developmental psychology, must incorporate both sex differences and the full range of the adult life span. Whatever their limitation, Kohlberg's contributions to understanding moral development are historic.

Isaacs. Within a framework closer to ideal development, Isaacs (1956) has offered a description of how the capacity for interpersonal relationships evolves. This capacity he conceptualizes as *relatability,* defined as "a sequence of levels of increasing differentiation of the self from others, and the increasing affective appreciation of the delineation of others" (p. 12). Thus, progressive complexity in differentiation and affective awareness characterize the development of relatability.

Six relatability developmental levels are identified by means of TAT fantasy stories; they are identified by the Greek letters zeta, epsilon, delta, gamma, beta, and alpha. The evolution of relatability is said to occur along the dimensions of basis for self-control, concern for others, method of understanding others, and object-relations capacity. At the first two levels (zeta and epsilon) the person is unaware of another, separate human being in the relationship. At the third level (delta) the person acts on another, but without any real understanding of the needs and feelings of the other person. The fourth level (gamma) is typical for society. The person can acknowledge the needs and feelings of another person. Waiting to receive, sharing, cooperating, and giving are all evidenced.

At the fifth level (beta) there is an increasingly more realistic perception of self and others. Differentiation of one's own feelings from those of another is accompanied by "being able to stand off and view the activity around one's self." The self/other delineation is now complete.

The sixth level (alpha) represents interpersonal maturity. Secure ego boundaries and highly differentiated affective awareness permit extending oneself toward the other freely; neither guilt nor threat intrudes. One can receive and give with consideration for short-term and long-term implications for one's individuality.

Isaacs's schema is intriguing in that it approaches interpersonal development from an exclusively intrapsychic perspective. His levels refer to cognitive/affective fantasy; they have no parallel behavioral referent. The model speaks only to the evolution of intrapsychic organization relative to interpersonal functioning, not to that functioning itself.

Its structural orientation—emphasizing ego boundaries, differentiation, and affective and cognitive aspects—joins with ego psychology in a manner similar to that which I espoused in the early chapters. Both approaches subsume that development, and all human behavior, proceeds from within the person outward to the interacting environment.

Loevinger's (1976) criticism of Isaacs—that he fails to include fantasy material as behavior—does not take full account of the important differences between inner experience and overt reaction. However, she does find useful comparisons between Isaacs's levels and those in her schema. These will be examined shortly.

Perry. Piaget's work on intellectual and cognitive development ranges from early childhood into adolescence. William Perry has extended that area of research into the college years. Relying on interviews and student diaries and journals in the personal document research mode popularized at Harvard by Gordon Allport (1937), Perry (1970) found characteristic growth stages in the cognitive development of Harvard students. Nine "positions" of intellectual and ethical growth are encompassed by three major stages: dualism, relativism, and commitment.

Dualism is characterized by bifurcated thinking, in which "we" and "right" are joined against "others" and "wrong." Authority, in these positions, is always perceived as definite and certain, whether one's own belief adheres to or opposes it.

Relativism involves a major developmental step. It acknowledges degrees of correctness, but also a pluralism of points of view: there is no one right answer. Equally important is a shifting in perception of authority. Even where authority retains its status as possessor of rightness, there is an awareness of a part of the world in which opinions can vary, both in kind and in degree.

Commitment affirms the person's own position in a relativistic world. As Perry uses it, *commitment* is "a conscious act or realization of identity and responsibility" (1970, glossary). It makes the person active and affirmative. And it includes an awareness that authority, as part of the pluralistic world, has no special access to rightness.

Perry's findings offer striking parallels to Sanford's data collected ten years earlier. Students at both Vassar and Harvard are considered to be distinctly advantaged in wealth, social class, and intellectual endowment. Yet both sets of freshmen manifested simplistic, authoritarian

modes of thought at the outset of their college careers. Only toward the later years of college was there a consistent tolerance for new ideas and a corresponding ability to think in terms of relativism and pluralism. Commitment-level thinking typically is seen in the years after college graduation.

Perry acknowledges three alternatives to developmental growth: temporizing, escape, and retreat. *Temporizing* is described as a suspension of growth (for a year), but without lapsing into escape. This sounds like a behavioral analog of Erikson's psychosocial moratorium in the adolescent identity crisis. *Escape* involves avoiding coming to terms with relativism. It is reminiscent of Marcia's concept of *foreclosure,* which I discuss in Chapters 4 and 10. *Retreat* is a rejection of growth "by entrenchment in a defensive position" of dualism. More generally, Perry intends it to mean a regressive reaction to developmental pressures.

Perry's work suggests that cognitive and linguistic development play an important part in the transitional period between adolescence and young adulthood. The structural changes in thought processes that he describes have relevance beyond intellectual and ethical development. In particular, they relate to an understanding of ego development and to the work of Loevinger and others.

Loevinger.   Among contemporary developmental theorists Jane Loevinger ranks among the most erudite. Her examination of developmental models (1966, 1976) has already been discussed in Chapter 2. Her work on ego development (1976) stands at the juncture of developmental psychology with personology. Eight major "milestones" of ego development are identified: presocial, impulsive, self-protective, conformist, conscientious, individualistic, autonomous, and integrated.

Loevinger (1966) earlier disavowed any direct correlation between developmental ontology and chronological age, asserting that both 40- and 14-year-olds could be at a Conformist stage of ego development. Nevertheless, her more recent work comparing various theorists (1976) at least tacitly acknowledges a convergence of various developmental strains, such as morality, ethic/intellect, and ego. This convergence suggests that there *is* some relationship between life-span location and chronological age. For example, her description of the Conformist stage sounds suspiciously like the adolescent style described by other investigators. "The Conformist obeys the rules just because they are the accepted

rules. . . . Disapproval is a potent sanction for him. . . . The person tends to *perceive* himself and others as conforming to socially approved norms" (1976, p. 18). She goes on to portray a "rigid adherence to stereotyped norms." A simplistic tone is found, evidenced in moralistic clichés and banal descriptions of inner feelings. Interest in appearance, social acceptance, and reputation are paramount. Many of these aspects replicate features that other investigators have identified in adolescence.

Between the conformist and conscientious stages is a transitional self-aware level. There is an inherent paradox in referring to this period as a transition, inasmuch as "it is probably the modal level for adults in our society" (p. 19). The self-aware level is characterized by increased consciousness of self and one's inner life. There is also an awareness of "multiple possibilities in situations," rather than holding to a belief that there can be only one right answer.

At the conscientious stage one finds the ability to design long-term goals and ideals, the internalization of rules, and the capacity for "differentiated self-criticism." Rules are no longer absolute, and social conformity gives way to social concern. "A rich and differentiated inner life characterizes the Conscientious person" (p. 21). Perceptions are more vivid and realistic and are better expressed. The ability to perceive from an observer's viewpoint is noted. Comparisons between this stage, Perry's relativistic positions, and White's qualities of young adulthood (for example, deepening of interests, expansion of caring) leap to mind. The conscientious person shares the democratic view of rules held by Kohlberg's Type 5 individuals. Isaacs's beta level of relatability seems comparable to the conscientious stage in the level of differentiation present and the capacity for taking others' perspective and sharing in their feelings.

Between the conscientious and autonomous stages is another transitional period, the individualistic level. Here the person accommodates to individuality in self and others. Differences between people are accepted and tolerated. In addition, there is greater tolerance for paradox and contradiction. There is a reduced need for achievement and a less moralistic sense of personal responsibility. Although this period fits logically into Loevinger's schema, it resonates less with other developmental theories.

The autonomous stage is characterized by conceptual complexity, including the ability to cope with conflict and ambiguity. Self-fulfillment and a parallel appreciation of the autonomy of others are notable compo-

nents of this stage. While aspiring to be realistic, the autonomous person adheres to abstract social ideals as well.

The integrated stage is Loevinger's highest state of ego develop-ment. It is seen as an extension of the autonomous stage, including all its components. In addition, there is "consolidation of a sense of identity," a phrase that is unfortunately not further defined. The integrated stage of ego development most closely approximates Maslow's self-actualizing person, as discussed in Chapter 4.

Loevinger readily acknowledges the interaction of ego development with cognitive, interpersonal, and moral development. In view of her holistic approach to human growth, an assumption that lines of develop-ment are interdependent seems entirely warranted. Conscientiousness virtually requires the ability to think in relativistic terms. It also denotes a recognition of freedom in relatability, which, in turn, suggests that moral development is at a level of democratic contracting. This kind of develop-mental coherence is, in fact, at the heart of Loevinger's thinking. "The central claim of this book is that many diverse aspects of thought, interpersonal relations, impulse control, and character grow at once, in some more or less coherent way" (1976, ix).

Although Loevinger correctly refuses to assign precise chronologi-cal ages to these psychological stages, their emergence can reasonably be assumed to be linked to other human experiences over the life span. A young person contending with puberty can hardly be expected to be conscientious, empathic, and relativistic. Within the longitudinal per-spective adopted by Loevinger an awareness of the linkage of psychologi-cal development to location in the life span is inherently recognized. "At the Conscientious Stage, the major elements of an adult conscience are present. . . . Few persons as young as thirteen or fourteen years reach this stage" (1976, p. 20).

Loevinger's description of the conscientious stage has many fea-tures that seem to correspond to what is identified in this book as characteristic of young adults. (My own preference is to emphasize the developmental readiness inherent in life stages, whether or not poten-tialities are commonly actualized in a culture at a particular time.) Loevin-ger includes in the conscientious stage the capacity for "self-evaluated goals and ideals," "differentiated self-criticism," "responsibility for other people," "conceptual complexity," "mutuality in interpersonal relations," "longer time perspective," and "the ability to see matters from other

people's view." These characteristics approximate closely what White (1975, pp. 336–361) calls growth trends of young adulthood. The capacity for self-evaluation and self-criticism are parts of a "stabilizing ego identity"; social responsibility is clearly implied by his "extension of caring"; interpersonal mutuality is a necessary component of "freeing personal relationships." Finally, I must acknowledge that for the last dozen years I have been teaching psychology of the young adult to graduate students. The characteristics of young adulthood that I have described (and that are presented in Chapter 7) closely correspond to the attributes of the conscientious stage in Loevinger's research. Is it sheer coincidence that three independently derived theories converge? The law of parsimony suggests a more rational explanation.

THE BEGINNINGS OF CONVERGENCE

The professional literature concerning young adulthood is probably comparable to that in any newly emerging field of inquiry. The sources are diverse, a mixture of theoretical backgrounds and the findings of researchers and practitioners. Yet there are certain threads of commonality, one clue that substantial findings are emerging from the confusion of methods, models, and assumptions. Table 6-1 compares a number of theorists and researchers and the particular dimension of development each emphasizes. They are arrayed relative to each other, but also relative to the model of adult development I presented in Chapter 3. This comparison suggests that there is a substantial literature up to and including the early years of transition into adulthood. As one examines the content of the several theories, it becomes apparent that it is neither capricious nor arbitrary to speak of convergence.

Kohlberg's Type 5 person can differentiate between authority as status and the person in an authority position. Isaacs's beta person can delineate and differentiate between people, attitudes, and feelings. Relativism, in Perry's terms, requires the ability to differentiate in a pluralistic world. Erikson's concept of intimacy presumes the ability to differentiate ego boundaries in order to link them. A differentiated inner life is central to Loevinger's concept of the conscientious person.

In life stages prior to young adulthood a similar kind of convergence of findings can be demonstrated. As Table 6-1 suggests, however, beyond young adulthood there is a striking paucity of systematic theory and data.

Table 6-1. A truncated comparison of developmental theorists

LIFE STAGE	ERIKSON (Identity)	LOEVINGER (Ego)	KOHLBERG (Moral)	PERRY (Intellectual)	ISAACS (Interpersonal)
EARLY ADOLESCENT		Conformist	Approval	Dualism Multiplicity	Delta
LATE ADOLESCENT	Identity versus role confusion	Conformist or conscientious	Law and order	Prelegitimate multiplicity	Gamma
YOUNG ADULT	Intimacy versus isolation	Conscientious	Democratic contract	Relativism Commitment	Beta
ESTABLISHED ADULT	Generativity versus stagnation	Autonomous ——→ Integrated ——→	Individual Principles ——→		Alpha ——→
MIDDLE-AGE ADULT					
SENESCENT ADULT	Integrity versus despair				

But, for the purpose of studying young adulthood, there is sufficient material to pull together a coherent picture. The next three chapters are devoted to examining young adulthood using the developmental model outlined in Chapter 3. They investigate, in succession, intrapsychic issues, interpersonal focus, and intracultural expectations.

7

INTRAPSYCHIC ISSUES

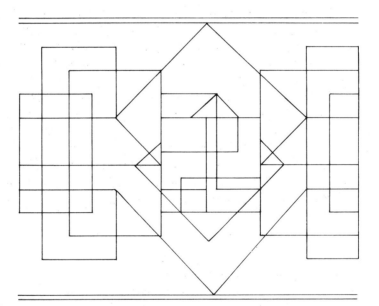

As we have seen, a developmental stage is usually precipitated by important changes in the growing individual's life situation. These changes may be intrapsychic, interpersonal, or impersonal, as in a change of social status. In the case of the young adult, physiological, societal, and psychological development come together to produce a unique state of affairs. The complex interaction of these processes results in a new Gestalt for the person, characterized by specific psychological properties.

After examining some of the conditions that give rise to these changes, this chapter will take up two major topics. The first section, Young-Adult Characteristics, is concerned with the *content* of the emerging developmental potentialities. What are the typical characteristics, and how are they likely to be manifested? The second section, Ego Development, is concerned with structural aspects. What is the organization of ego and identity in young adulthood?

PRECURSORY CONDITIONS

With the end of the second decade of life most of the *physical growth* process has completed its urgent pace, and the individual becomes relatively stable. The endocrine glands have moderated their activity and achieved a balance among the various hormonal secretions. Unpredictable episodes of sweating and blushing give way to more elegant emotional responses. Skin eruptions disappear, and the limbs become more proportional as other body parts catch up in growth. For the first time in the life of the young person a period of relative physical stability has been attained. Young adults also find themselves at or near maximum physical vitality by most physiological measures. And they are at a high point in neuromuscular integration and competence. They are literally at the top of their form from a physical standpoint. The result is that young adults are better coordinated, more graceful, and more physically comfortable with themselves. They are alert, vigorous, and resilient. Their bodies have finally become solid and dependable structures.

From a *societal point of view* important changes have also occurred. The person looks like an adult to others and receives multiple cues of that social recognition so important to a sense of self. The attainment of legal majority provides access to most of the everyday rights permitted to adults, such as voting, drinking, marrying, and signing documents. Young adults have thus acquired many of the exclusive in-group privileges of the adult world. For the first time in their lives society formally agrees with

their own perception of themselves as adults. Indeed, even if they were not aware of themselves in this way, the granting of these new privileges and prerogatives would inevitably confront them with the change in their social status. Socially, they have gained entry—but not full status—as adults.

On a *psychological plane* the gains in physical stability and social enfranchisement are alone sufficient to bring a different kind of self-awareness. On a conscious level this may be experienced as a satisfying sense of acceptance. On deeper levels it can be felt as a new integration of self. This awareness is in turn supplemented by the impact of a clearer internal definition of self—a greater sense of self-regulation and of moving toward personally defined objectives. Many young adults report a feeling akin to invulnerability, as though immune to illness, accident, or disability. There is a feeling of being better "put together." On a psychological level, then, there is a counterpart to one's sense of physical coherence. Resolution of the adolescent identity crisis leads to a sense of wholeness about oneself. Whether or not that holistic identity is esteemed, it is at least a relief from the confusion or unknowns that preceded it in adolescent self-awareness.

The cumulative impact of these discoveries is an unmistakable awareness that one has entered a new period of life. Despite the absence of any explicit cultural procedure designating a *rite de passage,* this entry almost invariably produces an excitement and a sense of beginning. Remember, too, that for most of one's life adulthood has meant something prized—a time of greater freedom, privilege, and capability. Consequently, common emotions at this time are eagerness, enthusiasm, and cheer. Even when there are strong feelings of anxiety, doubt, or insecurity, one can usually discern the evidences of excitement over arriving at this point in life.

YOUNG-ADULT CHARACTERISTICS

It is as a result of these developing conditions that those characteristics distinctive to young adulthood make their presence known.

Sens de Pouvoir

The young-adult *sens de pouvoir* is a sense of strength and vigor, ultimately a *sense of one's own capabilities.* This sense of capability is experienced as a feeling of inner power, at times felt consciously but more

often subliminally. In either case it can be described as an attitude of "I can do," "I am capable." This attitude derives partly from physical matura-tion, partly from the development of increasing sophistication with the world, and partly from a successful assimilation into the society at large. One discovers that one can satisfy important personal needs. Young adults have increasing evidence of their ability to form relationships, to get established on an emotionally independent basis, and to feel prepared to meet the world in direct confrontation.

As one emerges from the teen years, the adolescent indices of competence form an important basis for self-appraisal: feeling self-directed, being sexually experienced, possessing sociolegal freedom and privilege. By these standards most young adults are aware of successful achievement. One is given advice, not orders; one's wishes are accepted, whether or not approved. One has experienced sexual intimacy and at least some degree of fulfillment. Moreover, society has formally acknowl-edged the right to engage in activities restricted to adults.

Consequently, the *sens de pouvoir* is rooted in tangible personal experience. This experience is real and immediate. Whatever feelings of dismay one may have are largely overshadowed by a sense of excitement and readiness to encounter what lies ahead. Finally, a clearer sense of self prepares young adults to begin to think of themselves as a resource, as a source of strength in dealing with that which surrounds them. They are more than ready. They are, in Erikson's words (1963), "eager and willing" to apply themselves to the most challenging of tasks.

World Consciousness

Young people from earliest childhood are apt students, ready to learn about themselves and the world that surrounds them. The earliest periods are primarily concerned with collecting experiences: assimilating the fundamental bits of knowledge that affect immediate survival, identi-fying the central rules of living, and relating to the main cast of characters in one's immediate life. With adolescence (see Chapter 5) there comes a sharp focusing on oneself and the narcissistically experienced impact of that self on others.

It is from the context of being open to self-experience that young adults undergo a major change, in which they now become aware of the issues of the world at large. Suddenly, world events have personal signifi-cance. Less preoccupied with themselves, they are better able to see the

relationship between national and international events and the course of their own lives. Although the capacity for this level of understanding had been present at least potentially for some years, they are now ready to deal with this larger scale of impact and occurrence. No longer as caught up in self-preoccupation, the young adult discovers both an ability and a willingness to examine the complexities of interaction between people, places, and events. Sanford's (1962) study of college senior women found that, compared with freshmen, they "took in" more of the world and had a broader contact with events outside their personal lives.

But quite apart from their own readiness, the world at large also begins to impinge upon them much more directly. Familiar abstractions now become concrete realities. Unemployment, birth control, legal rights—all of these become matters having implications for one's own action and well-being. From this it is not difficult to take the next step toward understanding those world affairs that give rise to the need for armies, dictate economic conditions, and control the social or political climate. It is a common source of consternation to young adults to discover how government, religious institutions, and other impersonal structures have direct impact on the most private details of their own lives. Consequently, they come to realize that they must be aware of these structures. They quickly learn to appreciate the importance of labor unions and legislators' voting habits. Industrial waste disposal and cultural taboos both have an immediate impact on the kind and quality of life one leads.

Having responsibility for one's own life dictates that one must plan. And planning, in turn, requires that one be aware of the central events and issues in the world that can enter into one's plans. World consciousness, as it is being defined here, requires not so much an ability to name figures and current events as it does an awareness of the relationship between factors in the immediate world and one's own functioning. This is an essential step in what White (1975) calls the humanizing of values in young adulthood. Like world consciousness, it involves the individual's conceptualization of self in a larger framework of relationships. Young adults come to see that the type of community they inhabit is important in the evolution of their personal life-style. They realize that working conditions and salaries in another industry affect their own economic well-being. In short, the narrowly limited sense of the cosmos typical of childhood gives way to a wider definition of one's sphere of awareness.

Activist Orientation

Activism refers to a tendency to put into practice one's ideas and objectives, as opposed to thinking or talking about them. Activism resembles impulsivity in that both entail direct, visible, often dramatic behavior. It is important to distinguish the two, however. Impulsivity refers to a state of affairs in which emotions or urgings overwhelm the individual's control and spill over into behavior. It involves either impaired or underdeveloped ego processes. In either case, individuals have difficulty in controlling their affective response to stimuli.

Activism, by contrast, is a volitional opting for activity or for putting ideas and wishes into application. Whereas impulsivity discharges tension for immediate gratification, activism is goal-oriented, purposeful, planned behavior. Even when the response is seemingly immediate, as in verbal repartee or a table-tennis rally, it is organized and directed, not uncontrolled. Yet it is in areas such as this that the young adult's behavior may seem almost identical to that of the adolescent. The essential difference between adolescent impulsivity and young-adult activism is on the level of psychological process. Unfortunately, these differences are not apparent to the casual or uninformed observer and must be carefully studied to be differentiated and understood. Young-adult activism is thus a volitional action orientation. Better-developed ego functioning, in concert with a sense of capability, disposes young adults to act by converting feelings and associated thoughts into deeds.

At the other end of the developmental stage, when young adulthood begins to give way to established adulthood, one finds activism yielding to a more reflective orientation. Increasingly, as the adult years progress, people are inclined to consider issues ideationally and are less oriented toward taking vigorous, dramatic action. It is certainly true that many older adults examine issues from a wider array of points of view, and particularly from a longer time perspective, giving them a greater awareness of the issues' complexity. From this awareness may logically follow the conclusion that simple direct action will probably not provide a remedy.

However, it is also true that many seemingly logical arguments are really little more than sophisticated rationalizations to avoid taking action because of the risks that are perceived to be involved. Other older adults, adopting an attitude that "you can't fight City Hall," invoke the

defenses of avoidance, detachment, apathy, and denial as a way of ducking any kind of imperative to take action. By contrast, it is typically during the young-adult period that people will do more than pay lip service to the beliefs they presumably espouse. Consequently, they are the most dependable group of adults when it comes to getting a job done quickly. Once involved in a project, there is no more willing or vigorous worker than the young adult. Because of their action orientation and high level of coordination in psychological and physiological activity, young adults are probably the most effective workers in an intensive, time-limited, direct-contact task.

Capacity for Personal Perspective

One of the characteristics that most distinguishes the evolution from adolescence into adulthood is the capacity to stand back and take a look at oneself from a spectator's point of view. This is a characteristic that is distinctive of most adults and almost entirely absent from those people who are not adults. To view oneself from outside, one must have successfully attained a sense of closure about one's *identity*. People who are still involved with completing a sense of wholeness (the major intrapsychic issue of adolescence) are obviously not in a position to detach themselves from that work. The capacity for personal perspective thus requires that people have resolved the identity crisis. In addition to some holistic sense of identity, the ability to conceptualize objectively is essential to personal perspective. The evolution of formal thought operations, in which the person can reason logically and impersonally (Piaget, 1963), is the process that enables objectivity to evolve. Piaget locates this development in early adolescence.

Thus, personal perspective depends on the evolution of two processes—formal operations and identity resolution—that are usually not complete until the end of adolescence. With young adulthood, it becomes possible for the person to distinguish between individual (part) characteristics and overall (whole) self-appraisal. The adolescent's typical inability to accept criticism commonly results from the perception that any flaw in part of the self diminishes the entire person. To tell an adolescent that she is shy is to say that she is a lesser person. If he discovers a pimple on his left nostril, he is likely to think of himself as being an ugly person.

As self-particularization beings, young adults, in contrast, become aware of individual characteristics distinct from the self as a totality. They

are able to acknowledge limitations, faults, and problems. Even though these qualities may be humiliating, even though they may not want to acknowledge them, they are seen as parts, not the whole, of the personality. Rather than fleeing from ego-alien properties, young adults are much more likely to look at them and take steps to resolve them. This is one reason why many a problem first seen in adolescence or earlier is openly acknowledged, and becomes the basis for self-referral to therapy, at the time of young adulthood. The capacity to acknowledge problems and work on them gives young adults in general a favorable prognostic picture as candidates for therapeutic intervention.

The evolution of personal perspective also enables important areas of growth to occur. Personal perspective is basic to self-understanding and insight. With the ability to view themselves and their actions, young adults can not only acknowledge limitations but also discover assets and strengths. Personal perspective allows them to get to know, utilize, and accept themselves. One is reminded here of Gordon Allport's shorthand description of the mature person as "one who can view himself with complacency."

Reservoir of Confidence

The young-adult years are not particularly tranquil or happy. Symonds (1961) and Rappaport (1972) suggest that depression and disillusionment are common at this period. In view of the tremendous frustrations of this life stage and considering the weighty decisions that are being made, such a finding is not surprising. It is perhaps fortunate, therefore, that one characteristic of the young adult is the existence of a reservoir of confidence. People who attain young adulthood retain a basic sense of trust in themselves and their own potential. Even after the most painful confrontations and greatest disappointments they are typically able to pick themselves up, pull themselves together, and prepare to try once again.

One probable source for this reservoir of confidence lies in the psychological and physiological resiliency and vigor of young adults. Their overall neuromuscular maturation endows them with a sense of well-being about their physical self. The inner feeling of being attuned to one's body gives rise to a sense of command over oneself. Some people actually develop an attitude of invulnerability—a feeling that they can readily bounce back from illness or injury or that they may indeed be less susceptible to disability than are other people. This may explain why

young adults so commonly engage in what seems to others to be hair-raising entertainment, such as parachuting, scuba diving, surfing, skiing, mountain climbing and the like. Because they feel capable, vigorous, and strong, they are more likely to undertake strenuous and risky activities; because of their physical condition and confidence, they are also more likely to be successful. The willingness to take chances and the frequent record of success, in turn, reinforce their reservoir of confidence. Clinical experience suggests that the person who began serious drug use in young adulthood is a better rehabilitation prospect than the one who began as an adolescent.

An apparent corollary of self-confidence is optimism. Thus, it is reasonable to inquire whether a more positive, favorable, or cheerful outlook toward life is also characteristic of young adulthood. Symonds (1961) followed a group of adolescents into young adulthood. His interview and testing data argue against optimism as a distinctive feature of this life stage. Young adults may have an idealistic view of what the world should be like. They may be endowed with a sense of their capability and possess the confidence to act on behalf of their beliefs. But these attributes do not imply an optimistic faith that the world will be responsive or even sympathetic to their views. On the contrary, young adults tend to be poignantly aware of the often harsh impersonality of the world. Much of the cynicism of later adulthood is rooted in the disillusionment of thwarted young-adult efforts. It may be true, however, that young adults are optimistic about their own capabilities but pessimistic about the world's reaction to them.

The reservoir of confidence implies that young adults are more likely to trust their own capacity to extricate themselves from difficulty and to master personal challenges. Thus, they may be better able to marshal their energies to succeed in this regard and thus justify their own sense of confidence.

Outrageous Idealism

One of the more intriguing aspects of the young-adult experience is the subtle changes that take place in idealistic outlook. It is often said that young people in general are the repository of idealism in a society. But only recently have we begun to understand the developmental changes that occur within this idealistic orientation. As children become cognizant of reality and begin to comprehend relationships, they are able to turn

their attention to more-abstract notions. Piaget (1963) and others have described how thought proceeds through a series of changes in late childhood and the latency years. Thus it is that, in adolescence, thinking moves into issues of values, ethics, and philosophy—the first manifestations of the evolution of idealistic thinking. As we have seen, adolescent idealism tends to be highly moralistic, abstract, and polar. Consistent with the adolescent orientation, idealistic thinking reflects an essentially inward-turned point of view. Thought is more philosophical and therefore more concerned with the symbolic meaning of the ideal than with its reality-based counterpart. For the teenager, idealism is a larger-than-life conceptualization of a personally felt good.

With the advent of young adulthood a change occurs in the quality and nature of idealistic thinking. We have discussed how young adults are more aware of world events around them, how they are oriented toward taking an active part, toward finding practical expression of their thoughts and feelings, and how they have confidence in themselves and in their ability to make things happen. One consequence of this constellation of characteristics is that young adults retain a belief in their ideals and a readiness to put them into practice. For them it is not enough to espouse a virtue. More important is the necessity of finding ways to implement it. Perry (1970) found an increasing relativism in the morality of his students as they entered young adulthood. This finding parallels the earlier research done on the Vassar College group by Sanford (1956) and Webster (1956). White's (1952, 1975) idea of the humanization of values in young adults also speaks to the tendency to apply idealistic beliefs in the real world.

A subtle feature of the modification of ideals into more relativistic language may be that it facilitates the ability to translate abstract values into do-able objectives. If we recall that almost simultaneously young adults are developing a greater awareness of their environment and being less caught up in themselves, we may understand how idealistic concerns move from personally meaningful abstract symbols to externally directed opportunities. It is precisely that willingness to dare to act on idealistic thinking that leads to the rubric *outrageous idealism.*

In ways both large and small, young adults have regularly applied themselves to a variety of activities aimed at human betterment. When a car pulls over to the side of a highway to help the occupants of a disabled vehicle, notice who the rescuers are. During the great power failure over the northeastern region of the country in November 1968, what hap-

pened to all those young adults whom society expected to exploit a crisis with games? Undoubtedly there were some who frolicked. But it was young adults who risked personal safety by directing rush-hour traffic at major intersections when all the lights went out. It was young adults who took to the streets to reassure and guide elderly people. And it was they who took an active leadership role in preventing panic and contributing some order to a nearly paralyzed region.

On a much wider scope of affairs one recalls the Hungarian freedom fighters who led the revolt against Soviet control of their country. These were primarily young-adult workers and students, in a coalition that history has seen repeated many times in the past. The original Peace Corps and its national counterpart, Volunteers in Service to America, were primarily populated by young adults. The reaction against the Vietnam War was spearheaded, directed, and given its fullest impetus by young adults. But perhaps the picture on the opposite page showing young East Berlin men throwing stones at Soviet tanks during the June 1963 uprising epitomizes what is meant by outrageous idealism. Across time and culture, radical political and social movements tend to be powered by young adults. And these people are most often motivated by the desire to restructure the society for general human betterment rather than direct personal profit.

On February 23, 1967, the front page of the *Boston University News* featured an editorial calling for the impeachment of President Lyndon B. Johnson. In an open letter to the Speaker of the U. S. House of Representatives it documented charges against the president based on his involvement in the Vietnam War. So shocking was this attack that both the president of the university and the Speaker of the House—himself a Massachusetts citizen—felt impelled to offer public apologies for this outburst on the part of "irresponsible" students. Yet by April 1968, 14 months later, Johnson announced his decision to retire from office— primarily because of general protest against the Vietnam War.

The specific qualities of outrageous idealism are (1) at the outset, a commitment to important humanitarian causes; (2) the impetus to act—to find some way to implement this sense of moral purpose; and (3) the courage or confidence to dare to believe that some of these beliefs can actually be brought to fruition. Of course, the fact that certain socially beneficial actions would appear to be connected directly to this kind of idealistic pursuit in no way guarantees that all young adults act this way. Nor is it certain that, once young adults are motivated to act in the

FIGURE 7-1. Outrageous idealism: East Berlin, 1963. (Photo courtesy Wide World Photos.)

interests of outrageous idealism, the results of their efforts will necessarily prove beneficial in the long run. Implicit in the notion of outrageous idealism is its extremist quality. Consequently, it is certainly possible that this capacity can be mobilized in the service of ends that may have other than socially redemptive consequences.

An anguished population of young adults can be exhorted into action against a perceived social ill as defined within their own culture or circumstances. The young adults who apparently formed the backbone of Adolph Hitler's storm troopers early in his rise to power were undoubtedly convinced that they were acting on behalf of a mistreated, economically impoverished Germany. They believed they had a leader who would cure the ills inflicted on the Fatherland and in this way serve the most idealistic of national purposes. Polling and voting data from the 1968 U.S. presidential election indicate that much of segregationist George Wallace's strength also came from young adults. These people may have been responding to the racial bigotry of a demagogue. More probably,

they were reacting to the attraction of a populist leader offering a solution to the problems that affected their part of the country.

A final issue in this discussion is the distinction between capacity and overt manifestation. A capacity for outrageous idealism in no way guarantees that such attitudes and behaviors will manifest themselves. Many circumstances may act to suppress or dilute these tendencies. The society may discourage or even prohibit the participation of segments of its membership. In some societies all decision-making responsibility rests in the hands of the older members of families or tribes, and dissenters are exiled. In individual cases various intrapsychic problems may inhibit or blunt the expression of idealistic concern. The person may have an inability to be assertive. Or hostile or antisocial urgings may predominate. Or the individual may still be functioning on an adolescent or preadolescent level of development in regard to the evolution of idealism.

Some broader implications of the relationship between changes in idealism and psychological development can also be derived from Perry's theory (1970). As the person's development proceeds, relativism gives way to a third stage, that of commitment. According to Perry, the young adult identifies self with a particular set of beliefs, recognizing that other beliefs are also possible. Young adults' commitment to a set of values occurs as a part of their affirmation of their identity. It seems likely that practical implementation of one's ideals also plays a role in the evolution of mature ego functioning, as part of the process of self-particularization (see page 124). In any event, one important avenue for an emerging commitment of self would appear to be through the enactment of one's values and beliefs—that is, ideals. Thus, outrageous idealism, apart from its immediate personal and social impact, may figure into the person's ego development as well.

Innovative Potential

An important aspect of young adulthood is the individual's openness to experience and change. Young adults are ready to use the combination of experiences and competencies already evolved, trying them out in new situations. Unlike adolescents, who tend to be conventional, young adults are open to ideas and alternatives that may be unconventional or untested. Their reservoir of confidence seems to provide a willingness to try new things, to experiment—indeed, to hope. In addition, the sense of

entry into a new period of life may predispose them to encountering and espousing that which is new. Finally, the *sens de pouvoir* may augment a readiness to be innovative.

Whatever the origins of this innovative potential, a common consequence is that young adults bring to familiar situations an enthusiasm, an energy, and a confidence that enhance and strengthen their freshness of approach. In contrast to older adults, young adults have not already encountered the frustrations and disappointments of unsuccessfully trying to solve complex problems of daily life. They see not an old, chronic problem but one for which new ideas and new developments may bring new avenues of hope and new modes of attack.

For young adults, time perspective centers on "now." Their sense of capability, their sense of arrival, their world consciousness are all recent acquisitions. To the perpetual irritation of their elders, they tend to see situations and problems as though they also were recent developments. In this respect young adults have been justly criticized for being ahistorical. All too often, neither the problem nor the obvious strategies for resolving it have gone unnoticed. More commonly, the difficulty was recognized but resisted existing methods of solution. Conversely, the perspective of previous disappointments may serve to discourage older people so that they are reluctant or pessimistic about expending further effort in a direction that has produced only failure in the past. The lessons learned from history may thus be counterproductive. Leonardo da Vinci tried to fly, and failed. Only because later experiments were made (based on new discoveries and equipment), only because innumerable other people approached the challenge as something that could now be mastered, did two young brothers finally succeed.

In more recent years, when conservative U. S. automobile companies were losing out to foreign imports, they turned in desperation to a young new breed of people—particularly men and women under 30—to inject some vitality and originality into their production plans (*Parade Magazine,* 1966). Out of this came a radical change in the idea of what kinds of automobile the American public is most attuned to purchasing. The result was the smaller, sleeker, sportier cars that became a standard for the industry in the late '60s and the '70s.

To repeat a previous injunction, these characteristics must be viewed as tendencies rather than generally observable traits. Innovative potential is best understood as an openness to change, a susceptibility to

new ideas, a readiness to challenge conventional mores and methods. It can be thought of as a response set, or an attitude. Unlike the antiauthority reactions one observes in adolescence, it is not necessarily oppositional or rebellious. Frequently, the person's motives are exploratory, examining alternatives or searching for commitments. Unfortunately, parents and other older adults may interpret the challenge as an attack or criticism. When this happens, open discussion can degenerate into mutually defensive controversy.

For the individual young adult, evolution of this innovative potential lays the groundwork for making a significant positive contribution. The incorporation of this attitude sets the stage for thinking about existing conditions, newly emerging problems, or plans for the future. As we shall see in Chapter 11, this quality can be of particular significance during the present era of human history.

Summary

It is thus theoretically feasible to distinguish the qualities that differentiate young adults from adolescents. These are the psychological characteristics of *sens de pouvoir,* world consciousness, activist orientation, capacity for personal perspective, reservoir of confidence, outrageous idealism, and innovative potential.

Under optimum psychological development one would anticipate that all seven of these characteristics could be observed by the trained investigator. Unfortunately, there is no guarantee that physiological evolution will bring with it psychological development into maturity. For all too many people the attitudes and characteristics of adolescence are adapted, and sometimes twisted, to conform to the realities of adult social roles. For these people the individual's own inner maturation only slowly proceeds beyond adolescence. In general, however, the adult in the third decade will probably show some characteristics of adolescence, many features of young adulthood, and perhaps the beginning of those qualities we will come to identify with later adulthood. As a further precaution we should also note that at this time there are few theoretical or empirical data to help us distinguish those characteristics distinctive of established adulthood. Further comparisons of young adults with older ones are therefore limited. The tentative material available on the transition into established adulthood will be presented in Chapter 11.

EGO DEVELOPMENT IN YOUNG ADULTHOOD

The study of intrapsychic development mirrors the psychological understanding of human behavior just examined. Much that is significant in adult personality has been recognized and identified, such as the motivational role of needs and attitudes and the centralizing tendencies of personality into the organizing structures of ego or self. However, much still remains to be learned about the evolution of personality structure that occurs within the four or five decades of the adult span. Too often, adult personality is viewed as relatively fixed and unchanging. There is a tendency for theorists and therapists alike to pay lip service to "dynamic change" but in practice to view the last 50 years of personality organization as static. In childhood and adolescence, by contrast, personality is generally recognized as being in a constant state of change.

Investigative research has paid primary attention to the evolution of needs, conflicts, and self-concept—the dynamic content of personality growth. Although structural components of adult personality development have been actively studied, relatively little attention has yet been given to describing the *development* of personality organization as such. When one endeavors to study the transitional period of personality development from childhood to adulthood, therefore, one soon finds oneself sailing sketchily charted seas. In particular, the structural aspects of personality change are probably the least understood. Contemporary theorists such as Haan (1977) and Blanck and Blanck (1979) clearly identify organizing processes as the structural core of personality. And it is precisely the structural, or organizational, aspects of personality that most significantly differentiate immature from mature functioning. Adults with higher levels of perceptual organization show less psychopathology (Hurwitz, 1954; Kruger, 1954), greater visual/motor efficiency (Lofchie, 1955), and more social effectiveness (Lane, 1955). This section of the chapter will attempt to clarify certain aspects of that structural transition.

Theoretical Antecedents

The several personality theorists have described adult personality structure as highly differentiated (Lewin, 1935). It is depicted as comprising dynamic substructures variously identified as instincts (McDougall,

1921), traits (Allport, 1937), canalizations (Murphy, 1947), thema (Murray, 1938), and defenses (Freud, 1937). These components are centrally integrated by regnant processes (Murray, 1938), or ego (Fenichel, 1945). Ego development is said to follow the evolutionary principle of change from simple to more complex forms (Menaker & Menaker, 1965). In addition to the general consistency among theoreticians, there is clinical support for conceptualizing adult personality structure as an organized, integrated, centrally coherent system of functions. The Rorschach Psychodiagnostic, probably the best measure of personality structure available, consistently portrays that quality of organized coherence when it is applied to effectively functioning adults (Beck, 1960).

How does such a structure come to be? Perhaps these integrative, organized qualities are true of personality functioning at every stage level. If not, are there necessary and sufficient precursors to adult maturation?

It is doubtful that these questions can be fully answered at the present state of knowledge. Enough is known, however, to permit development of a general outline and to indicate some reasonable directions in which exploration takes us. The basic framework for understanding the intrapsychic structure of young adulthood is thus directly linked to larger issues of personality development. For an understanding of the general principles affecting the development of personality structure, the work of Gardner Murphy is indispensable. With regard to the peculiarly delicate transition from adolescence to adulthood, Erik Erikson's insights are particularly relevant. That the works of an academician/scientist and a clinician/theorist should independently converge at a common point is itself suggestive of a rich payload.

Murphy's Three Stages of Personality Development

Following Werner's (1940) general theories of psychological development, Murphy (1947) has postulated that personality development—in whole and in part—moves continuously across three stages, or levels. Stage 1 is referred to as a period of diffuse, undifferentiated structure and function. The organism reacts globally to issues in its life space. It does not distinguish between major and minor events, between central or peripheral response systems. Such behavior is observed most commonly in humans during early infancy. The neonate—be it hungry, cranky, or colicky—responds to these different discomforts with the same cry and

the same reaction. The nature of the discomfort, as the new mother soon discovers, cannot be distinguished by the kind of cry, at least during the first few months. In addition, it is apparent that crying is not a lungs/throat/mouth activity. The face reddens and contorts; the back arches; the entire body stiffens; the arms thrash; the legs kick. Crying is thus a total, massive reaction—global, diffuse, undifferentiated.

In Stage 2 specific skills and abilities and an awareness of details emerge. Stage 2 is characterized by differentiation of wholes into parts by a focusing, or localization, on specifics. Rorschach research (Hemmendinger, 1951) finds that children see fewer whole-blot responses at this time and that the number of detail responses increases. In everyday behavior the child learns to use parts of the body—for example, arm and hand for catching a ball—and to coordinate these parts and functions—for example, throwing, catching, and batting a ball. The whole is subordinate to its constituent parts at this stage.

Stage 3 involves relating the differentiated parts or units to one another. This is the level of integrated wholeness, of organized unity among diverse components. Athletic skill is seen in relation to intellectual competence, value structure, and self-concept. According to Murphy, Stage 3 is the most developed and, so, the most mature level of personality organization. But at what point in the life span does Stage 3 emerge? Does structural development of the personality leap from the differentiated development of Stage 2 in childhood to the mature integration of Stage 3 in adulthood? Murphy's own writings (1947) indicate that the three stages also occur on a microcosmic level, especially when changes are being experienced by the person. Entering a crowded room, engaging in a new relationship, or encountering a developmental stage can elicit the sequence of diffuse → differentiated → integrated response.

The developmental process of personality growth does not occur smoothly or in sudden quantum leaps. Rather, it is an ongoing function of an everchanging, evolving, complex human being. The personality interacts on many hierarchical levels, within itself and with field forces that are themselves in constant flux. Once again, it is evident that human natural history—even on so fundamental a level as core personality development—is the product of many interacting forces. Even as we identify central ingredients of personality development such as ego structure, we must acknowledge the impact of culture, history, and individual experience on the evolution of that general pattern.

Erikson's Identity Development

Erikson's approach to intrapsychic development emphasizes the evolution of one's identity. This evolution occurs partly as subjective awareness; most profoundly, it is a structural reorganization of the personality.

According to Erikson (1956, 1968), identity evolves over eight crises of life. The person's experiences in meeting each of these psychosocial crises plays a vital role in the evolving sense of self. The onset of puberty sets the stage for the identity crisis. At this point in adolescence the stakes are nothing less than identity formation versus identity diffusion, maturation versus psychopathology. Resolution of the identity crisis paves the way for identity formation. This marks the end of adolescence and the person's entry into young adulthood.

By identity formation Erikson means the "comprehensive gains which the individual, at the end of adolescence, must have derived from all his pre-adult experience in order to be ready for the tasks of adulthood" (1956, p. 56). Erikson would thus appear to be describing a personality structure based on differentiating, integrating, and synthesizing parts into an organized whole. In Murphy's terms, this is a Stage-3 phenomenon. Yet in speaking of the resolution of the identity crisis, he seems to stress the new sense of ego integrity, *of wholeness itself,* rather than its internal composition as a conglomerate of parts. To this extent, the personality is more reminiscent of Murphy's first developmental stage of diffuse wholeness. In fact, Erikson seemingly goes on to say precisely this: "The final identity . . . includes all significant identifications but *it also alters them in order to make a unique and reasonably coherent whole of them* [italics mine]" (1956, p. 113). Because Erikson is not primarily concerned with identity formation as a structural concept, a number of questions remain unanswered.

Must one conclude that identity formation is complete at the end of adolescence? Does this relatively stable, recognizable sense of oneself imply functional integration as well as structural wholeness? Murphy's opinion (1972) is that each new developmental confrontation involves all three stages. Erikson's conceptualization of ego would seem to argue for an executive, hence integrative, definition of identity. Because he views the ego as an integrative, centralizing system, it would appear most unlikely that identity formation is seen in exclusively static terms. Moreover, given his life-span perspective, it would be of dubious logic to

expect Erikson to view identity as a static construct, formed to conclude adolescence and unchanging thereafter. More likely, his concern with other issues has left unfinished the matter of changes in identity structure over the adult span. A more reasonable guess is that identity formation is conceived much as Maslow conceives self-actualization: as an ongoing, never-ending, ever-deepening process of potentiation.

Ego Organization

These past years of study make it clear that two sets of events can be observed in young adults. There is, on the one hand, a sense of wholeness—of integration—about themselves. Young adults know who they are. The groping and confusion of adolescence is behind them. On the other hand, they remain clearly exploratory, even experimental, about themselves. If there is a casual or confident air, it is not a smug, stand-pat attitude. There is a lot more to know and understand about oneself, even when one is reasonably knowledgeable and relatively secure. The "coherent wholeness" that Erikson ascribes to resolution of the identity crisis aptly depicts the psychological solidity that distinguishes young adults from adolescents, even when they are experiencing difficulty:

> It is too much . . . you are expected to cope with it all and to integrate it into some cohesion. And you do, somehow. Somehow, you prevail. [A Black woman's journal, Goethals & Klos, 1970, p. 152.][1]

By contrast, the adolescent experience and self-concept tends to be of two varieties. At times it is vivid and assertive but simplistic—as though one or two adjectives could account for the whole personality. At other times it is vague, blurred, unsure, tinged with confusion or anxiety:

> My thoughts are always so clear inside but when they're out they're just all a mistake. Do you understand what I'm telling you? Do I sound as mixed up as I feel? [Journal of a 15-year-old girl, anonymous and unpublished.]

These excerpts from personal documents illustrate presence and absence of those qualities of integrated, organized wholeness, which is a necessary

---

[1]This and all other quotations from this source are from *Experiencing Youth: First Person Accounts,* by G. W. Goethals and D. S. Klos. Boston: Little, Brown and Co., 1970.

condition for attaining adulthood. But it is not sufficient for attaining maturity. True ego integration also demands articulation and refinement of the subsystems that make up the whole. The exploratory quality in young adulthood seems directed at just this task of expanding, elaborating, and deepening one's awareness of the components of the self. This is the process called self-particularization.

Self-Particularization

Young adulthood is a period of refined examination, of further differentiation of the components of one's self. It is distinguished by a focusing on the specifics of personal experience. Details, nuances, variations, and alternatives take on a particular importance in personality function. Unlike the latency-age child, who acquires specific knowledge and learns localized skills as the basic ingredients of a self-concept, the young adult's self-particularization is directed at refining and expanding the self. Self-particularization is, therefore, a deepening—a qualitative enrichment—of the personality. From this process there evolves a more highly differentiated, more complex self.

A critical aspect of this enrichment derives from the ongoing experiences of the person. Young adults' activist orientation impels them to enter situations and deal with them, using their confidence, energy, beliefs, and past experience. With each new encounter there is significant new learning. But, whereas in the past such learning provided raw material for building self-concept or self-esteem, now its role has changed. Because young adults have already evolved a sense of identity, the new experiences interact with preexistent expectations. These, in turn, further the development of self-understanding and a general enrichment and sophistication of the quality of that awareness. It is this intangible quality of depth that most impresses the observer as maturity.

Subtly, often unconsciously, young adults change in the very character of their thought process. But what is experienced as an expansion of the *content* of the self is actually due to greater differentiation in the *structure* of the personality. Self-particularization, then, depends on an earlier coalescence of personality components into a unity such that the individual is free to explore and experiment with life for its own sake, not for basic self-definition. As a result, experiences can be encountered and related to components already present within the personality. By virtue of this, significant personal growth takes place.

Again in contrast to childhood learning, the primary changes are

qualitative rather than quantitative. In the example of the woman quoted on p. 123, note the complex awareness of herself, organized around being a Black female—a fundamental aspect of her identity:

> If you as a woman attempt to assert yourself . . . you are undesirable. You are left alone. And you are lonely. Because you are also intelligent. You have ideas. . . . You have a mouth. And you must decide which is more important to you. Do you want a man, or do you want to use your mind? . . . But you cope. It is too much to be a teacher-educator, . . . revolutionary, woman, girl, student, . . . and black. . . . You are expected to cope with it all and to integrate it into some cohesion. And you do, somehow. Somehow, you prevail [Goethals & Klos, 1970, p. 152].

That deepened, complicated, expanded organization of personality is self-particularization. And with it comes an augmented sense of one's own capability. Despite the obstacles and the contradictions one can, indeed, prevail.

Ego Integration

Ego integration can be understood best as a multidimensional process. For Lidz (1976) it includes an autonomous ethical system, greater ego control, consolidated gender identity, capacity for commitment, and secure ego boundaries. Structurally, it corresponds to Murphy's (1947) third stage of personality development, integrated wholeness. It includes coordination of functions and consolidation of structure within the personality. It involves a centralized organization of intrapsychic processes, which provides for the unity and regularity of personality. Implicit in this formulation is a hierarchical principle, as well; that is, the regulatory system necessarily involves establishing priorities, of structure as well as content. Indeed, the most fundamental component in such a priority arrangement is the predominance of structure in personality organization. Effective functioning requires interrelating social activity with emotional need, career behavior with value orientation. Especially, one must be able to organize issues in some hierarchical order of importance.

Thus, in both conceptual and practical terms, ego integration must be acknowledged as a vital stage of maturation. Not only must structure take precedence over function; the essential feature is that the whole must predominate over its component parts. However strong particular motives, drives, or values, the overall organization of the personality must take precedence. Otherwise, both developmentally and functionally,

a lower level of effectiveness will result. There is extensive and historic support in the research literature (Health, 1965; Hurwitz, 1954; Kruger, 1954; Lane, 1955; Lofchie, 1955) for the proposition that psychological maturity is associated with this holistic type of personality integration.

The attainment of ego integration is subjectively experienced as a transcendent sense of wholeness, even in the face of adversity. Quoting again from the personal journal of the Black student:

> How many times did we tell ourselves those first few weeks [at college] "I am me, myself first. And then a Black woman, second." Somewhere, the two things can no longer be dichotomized. . . . Somewhere, you and your blackness meet and you come to terms with it. . . . And it is a positive joy to be discovering your power and your relationship with the world, no matter how hostile that world is to you sometimes. You . . . will be carving out your place in the world you are going to make. You will grow. . . . And this is what this is all about [ibid., p. 153].

MODELS OF INTRAPSYCHIC TRANSITION

But now we have come to the end of the "known world" as far as ego development is concerned. We have Murphy's developmental levels, the Eriksonian description of the end of adolescence, and clinical observations distinguishing young adults from adolescents. What is the actual progression of events as the developmental transition continues?

As one reviews the first dozen or so years of life, it is not difficult to discern a general trend of function. The child moves from diffuse and overgeneralized reactions to the development of specific skills and parts and the coordination of these into patterns and subsystems. By the end of latency, children have distinctive personality characteristics. As they enter puberty and adolescence, they have had the benefit of a relatively stable, albeit evolving, personality coalescence. Then, sometime during adolescence—earlier more usually than later—the structural disruptions of which we have spoken begin to occur. These reactions to the radical psychophysiological changes going on in the body weaken and strain the structural integrity of the personality itself.

Thus, while adolescents struggle to adapt to changes within, it is even more fundamental to their survival to assure that some modicum of ego integrity be maintained. The structural unity of the personality is more important than its component qualities or manifestations. It is for this reason that some adolescents seem not at all perturbed by puberty. In

many such instances the psychological impact of the endocrine change has been warded off with defense mechanisms. Rather than face the threat of change, the organism devotes its energies to maintaining an internal constancy. In other instances adolescents get into manifestly psychopathological, destructive patterns that they adamantly refuse to alter. Etkind (1979) describes these as patterns of withdrawal or attack, which have in common an unsuccessful effort to master the challenge of adolescent development.

It may be that a great number of these seemingly self-injurious patterns serve the deeper need of providing a focus for personality reorganization away from an internally unacceptable pattern of previous functioning. Many acting-out adolescents find their present style of function (including destructive, illegal behavior) preferable to their earlier, socially approved, but intrapsychically damaging mode of living.

> Alan was the youngest child and only son of overprotective parents. Under their anxious tutelage he was a good student, more comfortable with adults and babies than with his peers. He was dependent, shy, and relatively passive. A few months before his sixteenth birthday his school grades dropped sharply. It turned out that he had also been frequently truant. He began getting into interminable arguments with his parents: first undermining, then challenging, finally defying their authority. He ran away from home on several occasions, engaged in petty theft, experimented with drugs and alcohol. Efforts to intercede, even on the part of those he liked best, were met with diffidence. Alan was unconcerned about his behavior or its attendant risks, even though he could offer no explanation other than "I want to do what makes me happy." Professional help was rejected, and it became clear that Alan was determined to pursue his course of action, no matter what the consequence [case history, author's file].

Because the subject was not psychotic, and indeed seemed content when not guilty or frightened, it became apparent that some fundamental developmental needs were being met that took precedence over the real dangers he was provoking.

Translating Erikson's emphasis on the adolescent need for wholeness into Murphy's developmental framework yields a provocative thought: is the adolescent identity crisis resolved by a structural regression to the diffuse wholeness of Stage 1? If this is the case, self-particularization can be understood in part as a Stage-2 type of differentiation, identifying parts of the whole as they relate to one another. Ego integration (Lidz, 1976) would correspond to a Stage-3,

integrated-wholeness, level of development. That is, the turbulent strain of adolescence on personality structure at Stage 2 may induce a temporary regression to a more simple kind of personality organization, diffuse wholeness. When intrapsychic reorganization can occur using diffuse wholeness—usually around some generalized notion of who one is—there is resolution of the identity crisis.

> So that's the way it was the last half of junior year [of high school] and pretty much all of senior year. It was one big isolated depression. It seemed like no one would recognize me as a person. For me this had a lot to do with acknowledging the fact of my feelings—*affirming that I was sensitive. I was never sure just what being sensitive entailed but I knew that it was very important* [Goethals & Klos, 1970, p. 135].

Being "sensitive" served to provide this young man with some diffuse sense of identity. Attaining that level of identity formation marks the end of adolescence. Next comes the task of particularizing the components of the self, identifying and articulating existing features and seeking to discover new qualities and experiences. In this respect self-particularization can be seen as a more sophisticated version of Stage 2. Finally, as both new and old components are related to one another and to the whole—for example, as one's musical skills are related to family needs and esthetic values, all of which are related to life goals—the person has evolved into ego integration, the Stage-3 personality organization. The integration and synthesis of components with wholeness is now the dominant principle.

Continuing into later adult periods, one can assume that optimal adult development will require continuing integrative efforts in other, more complex matrices of components. Or perhaps the aging process eventually leads to combining components into larger, simpler units that are more readily coordinated with organismic purposes. In Figure 7-2 an attempt has been made to represent these alternative models schematically. In the first instance, self-particularization would be a process unique to young adulthood or only evoked by unpredictable circumstances during the rest of the adult span (Model A).

The second theoretical model (Model B) would continue to view ego integration as unique to the most developmentally mature level of organization. Self-particularization would still be seen as a special, more advanced sort of Stage 2, in that it goes beyond developing and identifying parts and into their refinement, elaboration, and ramification. Thus, a

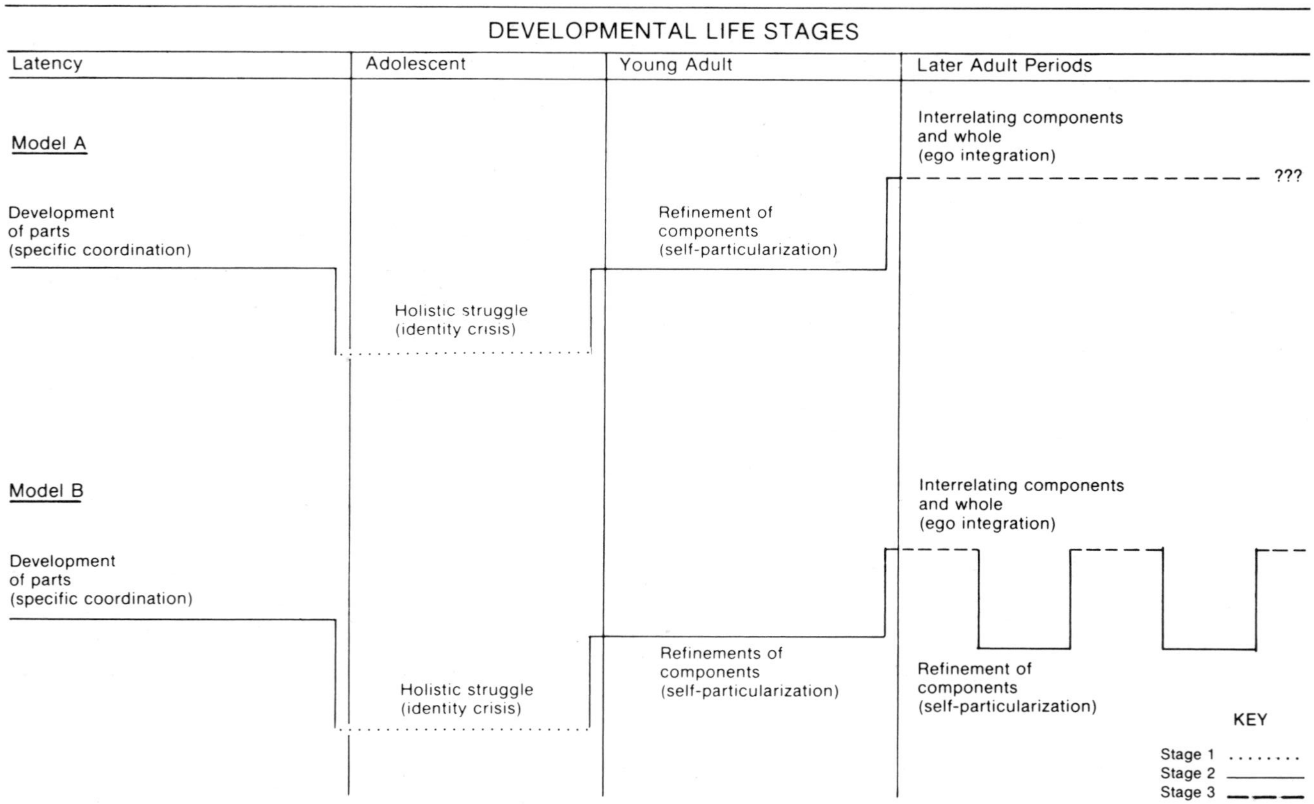

FIGURE 7-2. Two models of ego development

well-established interest in music may become particularized to involve less experimentation with musical performance but a deepening interest in early church music. Self-particularization is thus conceived as an ongoing, lifelong process, operating in complementary relationship to ego integration. This model of personality organization would see Stages 2 and 3 in constant interaction. Stage 3 is dominant over the long term but is punctuated at different points along the way as emerging issues command attention, are particularized, and are eventually integrated into the whole.

This conceptualization would identify young adulthood as the period during which these complementary processes first emerge. Self-particularization and ego integration would then be considered as serving each other while evolving within themselves over time. Implied here is a reciprocal relationship between stages, rather than what is typically described as the inexorable thrust of maturational trends.

Although much of the previous material is based on clinical and theoretical data, some experimental findings do seem to be relevant and supportive.

In one of the earliest studies of this period in the life span, Sanford (1956) described the changes observed in college women as they moved from late adolescence as freshmen to entry into young adulthood as seniors. The women manifested simplistic, rigid, overgeneralized values as freshmen. These values gradually became more *humanized,* by which Sanford meant more related to specific conditions and, ultimately, tied to social purposes. The progression appears remarkably parallel to the generalized-whole → specific-part → integrated-whole developmental sequence we have already described. Another major change, the *stabilization of ego identity,* is suggestive of what has here been called self-particularization: "Seniors are striving to include more in—they are on the road to becoming richer and more complex personalities" (1956, p. 76).

A study done 15 years later suggests further support. Perry's studies of intellectual and ethical development of college students (1970) examined 140 Harvard and Radcliffe undergraduates. The student interviews were analyzed structurally. That is, the method the students used to organize knowledge and value, rather than the actual content of the data, was the focus of the investigation. Perry's structural approach to cognitive processes is directly pertinent to the structural approach to personality advocated at the beginning of this chapter. Because cognitive

processes are part of ego operations, the developmental evolution described in his findings has relevance for a more general understanding of ego development in the transition from adolescence to young adulthood.

As we noted in Chapter 6, Perry distinguished three major stages of intellectual and ethical development in his research sample: dualism, relativism, and commitment. Basic dualism occurs before college, clearly in the adolescent period. It is described as a mode in which "the person construes all issues of truth and morality in the terms of a sweeping and unconsidered differentiation" (1970, p. 59). One notes a tendency to confuse moral judgments with intellectual decisions. This fragmented, simplistic view eventually gives way to relativism, which permits a deepened understanding of gradations, nuances, and varieties and acknowledges the possible correctness of more than one view. Thought and reasoning are thus enriched both qualitatively and quantitatively. In one subject's words, "You find yourself thinking in *complex terms;* weighing more than one factor in trying to develop your own opinion" (p. 113).

Finally, one enters the period of commitment—"an affirmatory experience through which man continuously defines his identity and his involvements in the world" (p. 135). Commitment requires that one integrate ideas and commit oneself to a position based not necessarily on the discovery of an ultimate truth but, more likely, on personal relevance. "I sort of see this now as a natural thing—you constantly have times of doubt and tension—a natural thing in existing and being open, trying to understand the world around you, the people around you" (p. 165). For the most part, Perry's subjects were unable to function in the commitment mode until they were into their 20s—that is, at or en route to young adulthood. These data would seem to suggest the progression of development processes we have been speaking of, from simplistic concepts through more complex ramifications to ultimate integration by way of a committed position.

Clearly, much more investigative work is necessary before drawing firm conclusions about the evolution of intrapsychic development from adolescence into young adulthood. Moreover, it is painfully evident that there are virtually no hard data to describe phases of ego development from young adulthood into the established-adult period. The challenge to the venturesome researcher is as enormous as the opportunity.

This has been a difficult chapter for me as well as you. It attempts to

capture both the content *and* structure of the intrapsychic processes of young adulthood—no small task. For a psychologist oriented as I am to an intrapsychic approach, this is one of the most important chapters in the book. However, following the tortuous pathways of intrapsychic development can strain even the most credulous minds. But if development is to be understood as a universal phenomenon, it is at the level of intrapsychic structure and function that people are (psychologically) most alike. Culture and climate are powerful influences on the shaping of overt behavior. As a result, one cannot hope to find many developmental similarities among people from different groups if the investigation is confined to the most visible behavior. The power of the intrapsychic approach lies in its ability to study those levels of human behavior most protected from the adaptive demands of society and geography.

I have tried to portray here those prepotencies, ready to emerge, that are distinctive to the young-adult life stage. They are not always visible; they are not always present; but they can be recruited, if what I present here is accurate.

8

THE PEER WORLD

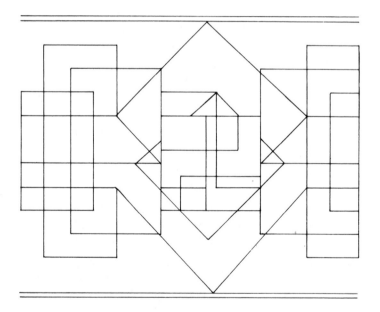

The transition of social locus from family to outside world, begun in childhood and emphasized in adolescence, becomes complete in young adulthood. Individuals make permanent the change in their focus from nuclear family to an immediate peer culture and finally to their generation. It is within this peer world that young adults will have to make their place, because this generation will eventually inherit control over the society and, indeed, the earth. But who are the young adult's peers? For many people, and especially in the popular media, young adults are members of a generation of youth. To discuss the peer world we first have to examine the concept *youth*.

Earlier (Chapter 4) I spoke of the comparative meanings of psychological adulthood and psychological maturity. There is a curious discrepancy between the way older adults view young adults and the way teenagers and children view them. To adolescents, as to children, a huge gap exists between them and young adults. People in their 20s are clearly "grownups." But to the average over-30 adult, the young adult is most commonly thought of as a "kid"—that is, some form of young person-still-growing. The term that most clearly epitomizes the ambiguity surrounding designation of young adults as either full-fledged adults on the one side or advanced adolescents on the other is the label of *youth*.

YOUTH—THE YOUNG ADULT AS SUPERTEEN

As the term is generally applied in our society, *youth* refers to people between the approximate ages of 16 and 25. These young people are characterized by their energy and vigor, by their relative freedom from responsibility, by their concern for heterosexuality and mobility, and by their lack of commitment and experience. They are said to be physically attractive and hedonistic by orientation. They are frequently thought of as naive, impulsive, and without serious purpose.

Although it is apparent that the term *youth* has gained wide social and professional acceptance, it is equally clear that many different age ranges are subsumed under that name. The Chinese Red Guards, ranging in age from 10 to 18, were called youth, just as are most adolescents and many young adults.

Keniston (1975) would prefer to categorize certain people over 21 as youth. He identifies certain "major themes" of youth: tension between self and society; pervasive ambivalence toward self and society; wary probing; alternating feelings of alienation and absolute freedom; refusal

of socialization; specific role identities; preference for movement over stasis; and banding into countercultures. Youth is seen as a self/society issue from Keniston's perspective. It is unclear whether he makes a distinction between single and married people within this designation. What is clear is that for most teenagers the young adult is the culmination of adolescent aspirations. When asked what age they would most like to be, both adolescents and young adults tend to identify the young-adult years. Thus, a great many adolescents look up to young-adult figures they know as ego-ideals. And many young adults are tempted to think of themselves as being a kind of superteen—that is, a person who has really made it, the epitome of the teenage ethos.

The reasons for this consensual admiration for the young adult among both groups are not hard to find. Now at the peak of physical development, young adults have a coordination that adolescents admire and so often have not attained. Young adults are usually more sexually experienced and accomplished; they have a social savoir faire that adolescents with their sexual preoccupations can only gawk at with envy. The sophistication they have gained over the years of experience since their own adolescence is coupled with developmental and cultural maturation. They drive cars, travel independently, mate, have their own money. They buy their own clothes, live in their own apartment, and function independently of traditional parental jurisdiction. These accoutrements are representative of the values and goals given highest priority by teenagers. But young adults are more than superteens. They are qualitatively different: in maturity, idealism, and knowledgeability.

Maturity

Young adults have had more time and experience in dealing with the world. Thus they have had more opportunity to grow and refine their personality and perceptions. As a result, young adults tend to be more mature than their adolescent counterparts and more mature than they themselves were as adolescents.

The essentially self-preoccupied, narcissistic involvement of adolescents limits their ability to cope with another individual with any detachment. By contrast, young adults are more capable of a true interrelationship—one based not on reflected self-adoration or on immersion of oneself in the other person but on appreciation of the other individual for his or her own characteristics and features. Better-

organized psychologically themselves, young adults are more able to see the other person as an individual, rather than solely as an object or instrument for personal need satisfaction (Lowenthal et al., 1977).

In terms of ego development, the profound differences between adolescents and young adults were detailed in the last chapter.

Idealism

The catch phrase "idealistic youth" often blurs the distinction between adolescents and young adults. As we saw in Chapters 5 and 7, the idealism of the young adult is less abstract and more related to real-world circumstances. Although it may be no less extreme in content than adolescent idealism, it is more consonant with the context of world events. Strict fidelity to abstract moral constructs such as peace or justice, unrelated to existing conditions, is more typical of adolescent thinking.

Knowledgeability

In a broader sense, young adults are better informed, more knowledgeable, and in general more concerned with everyday realities and events. They are aware of their ultimate involvement with many aspects of the environment that do not directly affect them at present. More conditioned by reality, they are therefore more aware of the absence of black and white absolutes in the world. And they are better able to acknowledge the complexity that makes simple opinions naive opinions.

Young adults have a greater capacity to consider the future relative to the present—that is, to plan ahead and to organize life. Thus, although they may be just as much given to action, their actions are likely to be less impulsive and better considered in terms of consequences. Despite common opinion to the contrary, young adults are *in truth* more like an established adult in psychological functioning than like an adolescent. The quality of their thoughts, attitudes, and concerns reflects much more the maturity that one associates with adulthood than it does childish thinking. *Even though many of young adults' concerns are typical of adolescence, the way they deal with those concerns reflects qualitatively different psychological processes.*

Labeling a significant part of the population *youth* because of certain similarities in dress and behavior contributes little to an understanding of developmental stages. Indeed, the concept of youth seems to obscure important differences in psychological features of adolescents

and young adults. Society tends to perpetuate this condition by equating youth with a pleasure-bent lack of responsibility. It compounds the problem by making it frustratingly difficult for young people, particularly young adults, to gain access to meaningful participation in adult roles of governance and power. The cultural cost, as we shall see in Chapter 11, can be considerable.

Now that we have distinguished young adults from the general peer group *youth,* we can go on to examine the evolution of their interpersonal relationships.

PEERS AS PARTNERS AND COMPETITORS

There is a major distinction between how adolescents and adults interact with their peers. As we saw earlier, adolescents immerse themselves in an all-pervading peer culture. Their thoughts, beliefs, interests, and tastes, as well as a wide array of everyday activities, are conducted in the context of whether peers are likely to disdain or approve. Young adults, by comparison, begin to function much more autonomously in their reaction to their contemporaries. As Erikson (1968, p. 137) has noted, young-adult peer behavior is characterized by a concern for partnership and competition. Instead of totally binding themselves to peer relations and standards, as they had been doing, young adults now begin to separate themselves from group thinking. Instead, they individualize their actions. The ethic of blind loyalty to a clique gives way to a more selective evaluation of individuals and circumstances. They begin relating to *people in situations,* depending on whether affiliative or assertive reactions are called for. The differentiation of partnership and competitive relationships is fundamental to most mature interpersonal contacts.

Peers As Partners

The roots of a partnership orientation derive from the earliest periods of life. Indeed, without some of these developmental precursors, it may be that a capacity for partnership is severely inhibited or never becomes part of a person's psychological repertoire. The roots of partnership probably develop from the infant's confrontation with its helplessness. The experience of being cared for, protected, and given fundamental nurturance provides the person with a basic affiliative orientation toward the world. A secure relationship with a mothering figure provides the basis for an attitude that people can be engaged in enduring relationships

based not on destruction of the other but on enhancement of felt needs.

If infants learn to receive and trust during the first period of life, early childhood provides them with the opportunity to discover the safety and value of giving to another person. They come to relinquish some of their needs for mastering in the face of the necessity for an accommodation with the adult world. Latency brings with it the opportunity for experiencing the first true partnership arrangements in teamwork and collaborative activities, both at play and at school. These in turn are elaborated on, somewhat at least, in the affiliative relationship of the peer culture during adolescence.

In other aspects, however, the self-centeredness of the adolescent acts as a significant impediment to the establishment of true partnership relations. The adolescent typically enters into relationships that are fundamentally exploitative, in that the other person provides an immediate gain or benefit for the individual. Adolescent love is permeated with intensity of feeling for the love object because (a) the object loves the adolescent, (b) satisfies the adolescent's needs for prestige or status, or (c) represents some aspect of the adolescent's own idealized ego, either in fact or in aspiration. Economic determinants notwithstanding, a primary reason for the 75% failure rate in teenage marriage—and, parenthetically, an important reason why so many adult marriages based on an adolescent conception of love also fail—is precisely because narcissistic aspects prevent the partnership interaction fundamental to a lasting relationship between two persons.

Requirements of partnership. From an intrapsychic perspective, partnership involves the ability to include another person within the limits of one's own ego boundaries. However, in partnership one does not incorporate the other person figuratively within these boundaries but rather expands them to encompass that which the other person is and represents. Thus, partnership involves the extension of one's self (and the capacity to tolerate such strain). Also implied here is the assumption that this process is reciprocal. The partnership relationship can vary from one of extreme intimacy to that of a more short-term, narrowly based contractual agreement. In either event there is involved the ability to give, take, and share oneself with another person without loss of one's self. Partners are able to sustain joint activity toward a common goal in a climate of cooperation and mutuality.

Inherent in sharing part of oneself is sharing part of one's life span. That is, partnership should be conceptualized as a voluntary affiliation over an extended period. Although the objective limits of the time commitment are indefinite, perhaps it is the very uncertainty that makes the commitment psychologically most meaningful. It is precisely the indefinite duration that makes the partnership very appealing for some and quite threatening for others.

For example, the individual with strong security needs may view the commitment to a long-term relationship as a way of immediately resolving problems in the area of closeness to people for all time to come. The partnership thus conceived is one in which at least one of the members flees from uncertainty and anxiety into a larger relationship and consequently uses it in a defensive rather than a constructive way. This is the sort of psychodynamic posture referred to by Erich Fromm in *Escape From Freedom* (1941) when he speaks of dependent people's submerging themselves in some autocratic or hierarchical social or political structure. In *The Art of Loving* (1956), Fromm explores the issue as it relates to the more intimate kind of interpersonal experience. In both cases the individual can use the alliance as a means of avoiding reality rather than extending it and growing within.

For others, the prospect of an indefinite involvement implies an extension of commitment that is intolerable—too binding, too restrictive, too limiting. For these people the partnership is seen not as an opportunity for a special kind of growth but, for whatever unresolved reasons within, a limitation on their ability to grow. Between mature people a partnership arrangement above all implies mutual respect. Such respect recognizes the individuality of each member. It acknowledges further that the partnership is designed to constitute not a haven or a refuge so much as an opportunity for mutual enhancement and development. One does not expect to be gobbled up by the other or to lose oneself in the other. Rather, it is expected that there are some central issues and points at which the two intimately intermix. At other points the individuals embark on their separate, parallel, or even divergent pathways.

Partnership means a sharing of oneself, not a loss of identity. It means committing or giving up some, but never all, of one's autonomy. It recognizes that, whereas one relinquishes the orientation to a simplistically egocentric "me-alone" attitude, this does not give way to an automatic "you-first" attitude. Thus, partnership requires that each individual

has a well-enough-developed sense of self to retain his or her individuality and to maintain respect both for self and for the partner. Ego integrity is a vital precursor of partnership.

Ingredients of partnership. Only when these conditions are met can one proceed further into an explication of the content of this kind of relationship. Therefore, one of the most frequently assumed corollaries of an affiliative relationship—the affectional component—is relevant only after respect for ego boundaries exists. It could probably be argued that meaningful, effective partnerships can and do exist in the absence of any basic affectional feeling between the members. Nevertheless, most partnerships involve the capacity for some affectional relationship. In this context we understand that partnership can include a love relationship but has applications that extend well beyond that specific kind of affiliative alliance. Many other forms of close, ongoing involvement are also possible, indeed necessary, in a complex society.

As Ellis (1962) has repeatedly pointed out, an obsessive need to convert all relationships into love relationships is more characteristic of neurotic behavior than of mature functioning. Although the subject of love is dealt with in a later context (see Chapter 9), it can be said here that a constructive working relationship is undoubtedly fostered if there is some sense of personal warmth between the members. At the same time, both partners must have the capacity to recognize and order their own value system such that what they aspire to within the context of the partnership is that which can be accomplished in that relationship. For example, it may be necessary to jeopardize the security of the relationship if contradictory points of view on an essential issue are to be confronted and resolved. Important philosophic or other value judgments about which there are major disagreements may need to be subordinated at some point or even for the duration of the relationship. Some of these issues may not be necessary to the purposes of the affiliation and would only serve as disruptive forces were they to be the issues constantly brought up for discussion and review. The ordinary business partnership does not require that its members come from the same religious background. Psychotherapists do not have to love their patients in order to feel concern, compassion, and warmth for them.

A vital ingredient in effective partnerships is the ability to tolerate varying degrees of closeness and to be able to distinguish different kinds of closeness. Two people may be cordial without being friends. Partners

can disagree without destroying the partnership. At the same time, partnerships that do not permit the expression of honest emotion are necessarily limited in their ultimate effectiveness. The partnership relationship involves being able to moderate a variety of feelings without carrying emotions to extreme points. In this manner, feelings can be openly expressed within a range of intensity that is not disruptive or corrosive. The expression of emotion thus serves to strengthen the relationship rather than jeopardize it.

If it seems that this description presents a model of partnership that is more ideal than evident, the impression is not accidental. It is most probable that a great number of relationships fall far short of that described here. It is for this very reason that so many partnerships fall far short of the expectations held out for them by their members. At the same time, not all partnerships demand the stringent level of mature functioning I have described. The optimal condition has been emphasized simply because we too often equate the semblance of psychological process with its actual occurrence. The external trappings of a partnership need not imply that a mature involvement of the members exists. It is the underlying nature of the relationship—the processes of interaction that we are attempting to describe here—that determines its true character and quality.

Peers As Competitors

The intrapsychic rudiments of competition probably date back to the earliest periods in ego development. One of the first distinctions made by the infant is between "me" and "not-me," separating self from the world. The ability to distinguish between self and others is a fundamental component of the competitive orientation. A second component evolves from the experience of the child with frustration. The development of a tolerance for delay or disappointment, particularly when other people are involved, aids self/other differentiation. Later in childhood, rivalry experiences emerge within the family itself. The child discovers that not all members of the family receive equal treatment. For reasons sometimes clear and sometimes unknown, certain members—indeed, certain of his or her siblings—receive more or less affection than others. The experiences of coming out ahead or of feeling left behind—that is, winning and losing—commonly make their first appearance in family experiences.

It must be apparent that this psychological definition of competition is different from the usual cultural or economic definitions with which you are familiar. In this psychological context *competition refers primarily to the constructive use of aggressive feelings in activity relative to self or other people.* The key notion here is the management of aggressive feelings as the essence of a competitive orientation. In this sense, competition is viewed as being much akin to what others have called an urge to mastery (Adler, 1927) or desire for competence (White, 1975). All these terms refer to a constructive utilization of assertive energy. Thus, in any society the ability to be assertive—to use initiative in formulating ideas and actions, to cope constructively with problems—involves this fundamental competency. In industrial societies particularly, the motivation to achieve becomes a matter of special importance (McClelland, 1961).

As Atkinson and Raphelson (1953) have refined the notion, achievement motivation depends on the existence of both an opportunity and an expectancy of success in expending effort toward a particular objective. Bocknek (1959) found differential academic performance in college students to be a function of reliance on or susceptibility to internal or external motivational incentives. Competition, then, becomes an important index of the individual's ability to mobilize and invest energies in pursuing one's interests vis à vis the surrounding world.

Competing effectively. In order for people to function effectively, they must develop a tolerance for both success and failure. It is axiomatic that one can attain success only by risking failure. The risk engendered by striving often involves much more than the obvious objective task of reaching a goal. To commit one's energies toward an explicit purpose implies that one values the achievement. It assumes that one has the necessary abilities to complete the task. And it acknowledges that one has needs requiring particular fulfillment. To risk failure, therefore, can potentially cast doubt on one's judgment, competence, completeness, and value. Ultimately, one's feelings of worth become involved with experiences of personal accomplishment. Conversely, attitudes about achieving—or even thinking about achieving—may be interpreted as reflections on one's sense of worth. Succeeding, or winning, may be taken as evidence of one's prowess, virtue, and value. Failing, or losing, can similarly be translated into signs of weakness, stupidity, incompetence, or undesirability.

In our own society, the social implications of being called "a winner" or "a loser" are universally recognized. Thus, the associated meanings attached to striving can actually outweigh the significance of the objective task in many instances. The fellow who won't ask a woman for a date may fear the humiliation of refusal more than the lost opportunity to be with that particular woman. The golfer who shoots a hole-in-one enjoys a moment of exhilaration over her incredible feat that temporarily overrides the knowledge that she is still just an average player. The ability to incorporate both success and failure depends on an inner security that transcends the impact of individual experiences. One's self-concept requires a firmer base than the inevitable ups and downs of daily living.

Striving—that is, competition—must also be possible for the individual in situations where victory or defeat is irrelevant. In many life activities construing the situation in terms of success or failure can interfere with the actual intent of the effort. People who make everyday social contact into a game of "who is wittier" or "who is smarter" debase and dehumanize those relationships. Nevertheless, it goes without saying that many situations require the full use of one's wit or one's intelligence, and people must be free to expend their effort at these times. Conflict or anxiety over the spontaneous use of one's energies can be a crippling limitation in meeting the demands of everyday life.

A central feature of effective competition is the ability to differentiate between aggressivity and hostility in one's own responses. Aggressivity involves assertiveness, the ability to use one's energies spontaneously and responsibly in thought, action, and deed. It is also the capacity to stand separate from others, so as to center on one's own needs and objectives. Hostility has an inherently destructive purpose. That is, the hostile intention is one of inflicting hurt and pain, or obliterating the object toward which it is directed.

A common underlying cause of the failure of many talented people to achieve commensurate with their abilities has to do precisely with the fusion of assertiveness with hostility in their thinking. This equation of two qualitatively different impulses can result in an immobilization of constructive aggressivenes for some or a useless cutthroat orientation toward any sort of comparative effort for others. It has become increasingly apparent from interviews with professional athletes that many find competitive sport to be a socially acceptable method for venting raw desires to inflict pain and punishment on others. At the other extreme, one finds many young adults unable to select or pursue a career or a mate,

because this would involve an assertive expression of their own impulses. To express assertive impulses would threaten to release hostile feelings they are striving to control.

An optimal utilization of competitive feelings probably involves developing a transcendent attitude toward accomplishment. This transcendent mode would enable individuals to pursue their ideals and to relate themselves to certain objectives by nonhostile, nondestructive, assertive competition. These efforts are based on utilization of their own abilities and talents in striving toward objectives they have established or identified. The concept of transcendence is used here to indicate that the objectives are based not on a need to prove oneself, but rather on the expression of one's capabilities and desires. In another sense transcendence implies having disassociated hostility from aggressiveness such that one can freely and spontaneously engage tasks and other people without fear of doing harm or provoking attack. The destructive aspect of competition can often be avoided by setting up goals based on one's own needs, rather than on a reaction to another person.

Overemphasis on winning. An unfortunate fact of life in our society is the emphasis placed on competitive success. We are raised to value success as though it is an end justifying any means of attainment. We marvel at the business executive who achieves great wealth from humble beginnings and choose not to inquire into his scruples en route. Fame is so overvalued that we seem ready to believe that a great military leader in war will naturally be a great political leader in peace. The sad examples of Generals Tyler, Grant, and Hayes did not deter the U. S. electorate from twice rejecting for president a political statesman, Adlai Stevenson, in favor of a war hero, General Dwight Eisenhower.

A more insidious result, however, is that focusing on the visible evidence of success ignores the substance that makes accomplishment truly valuable. To strive—and, by doing so, to apply and extend one's abilities—is conducive to psychological growth and well-being. To attain an objective builds confidence and a sense of security about oneself. But to center on victory irrespective of methods, means, or essential value of the objective frequently has adverse effects on one's sense of worth, social perception, value structure, and ego identity. To pursue goals lacking inherent worth is ultimately to demean one's own sense of purpose or value. The person who does worthless things ultimately feels worthless. To be accorded praise by others for these efforts, in turn, reduces one's

esteem for society and promotes the growth of cynicism about society and those within it. Similarly, one's own values are eroded by social reinforcement of norms that are publicly derived rather than developed personally. Finally, the schism created by the difference between personal goals and publicly acclaimed ones inevitably leads to alienation and self-estrangement, with resultant damage to one's own ego integrity. An increasing number of theoreticians (Fromm, 1947; Marcuse, 1955; May, 1967) cite this estrangement as a fundamental cause of human misery and discontent.

Once again, as with partnership, one needs sophisticated observation to distinguish between cultural behavior and psychologically based origins. The internal processes that motivate the overt behavior are the proper concern of this chapter. It is obvious that people behave competitively in many different ways and in many different areas. And probably, the more mature kind of competitive functioning is less common when society so insistently expects on material results for competitive effort. Too often, people are drawn into rivalries based on common culturally defined values rather than those that have evolved out of the person's own mature decisions.

Peer relations in young adulthood are, in sum, best understood by the manner in which those relationships are engaged. One can have both partner and competitor relations with the same person. Partnership and competition are really ways of describing the increasing sophistication in interpersonal relating that becomes possible in young adulthood.

9

FOUNDING A FAMILY: INTRACULTURAL EXPECTATION

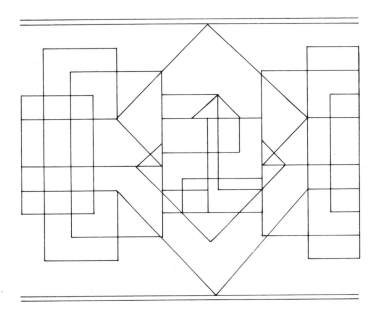

THE INSTITUTION OF MARRIAGE

Whenever human beings cluster into groups, one finds a system for pairing and procreating. If nothing more were involved, the sheer primordial urge to survive would dictate that such arrangements be universal. In fact, as we shall see, founding a family serves more than this intraspecies biological function. In Western civilization, particularly in North America, the custom of monogamous marriage is deeply rooted. True, both divorce statistics and the frequency of extramarital sexuality indicate that total fidelity to monogamous marriage is hardly a universal practice. Nevertheless, it is equally true that the North American ethos prizes marriage even without children and, moreover, extols the virtue of marriage based on love or romantic attachment. This chapter, unlike most of the others, is written from the perspective of cultural expectation.

Society as a whole has a vested interest (relative to its own survival) in seeing to it that marriage occurs as a necessary precursor to raising a family. Consequently—and nowhere is it more evident than in North America—the concept of marriage is impressed on the child at an early age. Thereafter, it becomes increasingly evident through the growing-up period that young people are expected to eventually select a mate and marry as the first step toward starting a family and thus perpetuating the society. The 1960s and 1970s witnessed a spate of experimentation with alternative forms: group marriages, communes, voluntary childlessness, gay marriage, living together. But history offers no reason to suspect that any of these forms will replace or outlive the cultural imperative to found a family.

Arranged Marriage

The contemporary standard for marriage in North America is in marked contrast to the folkways and traditions of other cultures and, indeed, of early American tradition. Most commonly in the rest of the world over the course of recorded history, formal coupling was felt to be too important a matter to be left to the young. Instead, the power or responsibility for arranging marriages resided with the parents. Primary consideration in such marriages was given to practical matters such as social standing, economic benefit, lineage, and supply and demand. The essential function of these marriages was to bring forth a new generation in a viable familial context. In certain instances, another important

motivation was political. Two major families or monarchies might mate their young as a way of binding factious groups together in the interests of peace, or at least more amicable economic relations. The arranged marriage absolves the couple from any responsibility for the selection of a mate. That choice of mate is delegated to the hands of other people, who must bear the full burden for the ultimate decision that is made.

The central concept in arranged marriage is that of duty. The young woman and man implicitly acknowledge the obligations each has to fulfill the marital contract. That responsibility is carried out not as a matter of individual choice but as the enactment of what is expected by the society (or, more specifically, one's clan, tribe, or family). And one is expected to fulfill those obligations faithfully. The rewards to be gained are those of social approval, establishing one's place within the social order, and deriving what pleasure one gets from the rearing of children or a new line of descent. In addition, there may be some expectation of improved socioeconomic status by virtue of the specific terms of the marriage contract.

But such embellishments as affection, love, happiness, and pleasure are not assumed or expected to be available within the marriage context. Traditionally, if these satisfactions are to be obtained, one assumes that they would be available through extramarital relationships. Indeed, one suspects, it is for this very reason that concubinage, polygamy, and the variety of other extramonogamous liaisons are so well established in societies where arranged marriage is the rule rather than the exception. Although these arrangements typically empower men with sexual freedom, women have often constructed their own channels for satisfaction when conventional marriage fails to provide it.

Marriage Based on Love

The modern notion of marriage as primarily a love relationship, providing a sense of closeness, intimacy, and affectional satisfaction, is comparatively new on the scene. Although love has throughout recorded time been a legitimate basis for the coming together of two people, this theme appears almost as counterpoint to the more prevalent exercise of pragmatism in the arrangement of marriages. The biblical story of Jacob and Rachel and the romance of Romeo and Juliet are noted for the rigorous and tragic qualities of the couples' relationships in the face of traditional institutional methods for matching people. Even in the con-

temporary *West Side Story,* the couple's relationship is destroyed by traditional problems.

One thing is certain, however, in today's society: a marriage based on love and affection is taken as the model rather than the exception. Yet as Lidz (1976) points out, there is little evidence to suggest that love marriages are any happier than arranged ones. The romantic marriage offers no assurance that the affection will continue and grow. At the same time, the arranged marriage has survived centuries of practice. Although arranged marriage is based on the concept of duty rather than wish, there is good evidence that deep affection and contentment can arise out of the working toward a common goal. The contemporary obverser cannot escape wondering, moreover, if many North American marriages presumably consummated out of love are not in fact motivated as much by practical considerations of economic and social standing. The ideal of "getting ahead" for many women has meant finding an attractive, ambitious, and successful husband.

At the same time, racial and ethnic factors play a very important role in weeding out many potential mates. People also tend to marry those who live relatively close to them. Because families tend to segregate themselves along cultural, economic, and religious lines, the available pool of possible mates is reduced for these reasons as well.

The marriage based on love also presents certain distinct psychological hazards. The opportunity to choose a mate carries with it a much greater burden on the partners to live with their decision and their choice. Having made the decision, they are expected to accept responsibility for a long-term commitment to another person and to a set of objectives and goals. And, they expect to be happy.

One little word. Love continues to resist precise definition, despite the apparently wide frequency of its occurrence and the untold amount of time and effort devoted by writers, philosophers, and sages to clarifying its nature. One difficulty, of course, is that love has so many different applications. There is the affection one feels toward a benevolent older person. There is the churning pride and satisfaction in beholding one's offspring. There is throbbing, mind-numbing erotic passion. And there is the deep satisfaction and tranquility of an intimate, longstanding, and voluntary relationship. The two people who meet, "fall in love," become betrothed, marry, and live a full, rich life in love with each other typically report that what they called love in the first months of their attraction has

little or no relationship to their emotions shortly after marriage. In turn, those emotions have little similarity to the feelings they share after 10 or 20 years of marriage.

Is this evanescent set of emotions, then, the basis for a lasting contract—one that will include the sharing of material goods, social relationships, attitudes, and responsibilities? Despite the apparent irrationality of such a position the popular verdict nevertheless seems to be overwhelmingly in favor of just such an arrangement!

As one tries to probe into the nature of that which is called love, it is possible to discern a variety of components, most of which are noncognitive and nonrational and many of which are largely unconscious. In a mature relationship, love is an amalgam of affection, intimacy, and shared concern.

Affection. Underlying any discussion of affection or intimacy in marriage is the relationship these experiences have to sexuality. So closely have sex and love and sex and marriage been associated that something must be said to indicate where they do not overlap. Fundamental here is the recognition that sexual satisfaction depends on neither love nor marriage. It is obviously possible to experience exquisite sexual delight without being in love or married. Conversely, love—and, even more so, marriage—offers no assurance of sexual satisfaction. These facts notwithstanding, it can also be postulated that the most profoundly moving sexual experiences occur in lovemaking between partners who possess the ingredients of mature married love. Thus, while sexual gratification is a natural sequence separate from personal involvement or social convention, its deepest fulfillment is often found in the presence of these other considerations.

Affection betokens a sincerely felt sense of caring. It is a spontaneous concern characterized by a feeling of pleasure. By contrast, concern without pleasure usually results in anxiety, worry, or criticism. Real affection brings with it a warm glow and the desire to give to or share with the object of one's feelings. Generous impulses and the desire to impart pleasure are a natural consequence of this experience. Although it can develop quickly, affection tends to evolve and deepen with time and familiarity. It is affection that evokes tolerance or amusement in response to the other's habitual idiosyncrasies. Affection is a placid, gentle emotion. As such, it provides an effective counterbalance to raw passion. The two affects combine to produce some of life's most compelling experien-

ces. By itself affection is somewhat sensual but not specifically sexual. It is therefore able to enhance or heighten sexuality but also to provide warmth in the absence of sexual passion. In this respect affection is an emotion that can be directed at a wide variety of people without encountering cultural taboo or personal conflict. Unfortunately, many people who lack experience in sharing affection confuse this emotion with sexual feelings. Much human misery has resulted from such confusion.

Intimacy. An immediate distinction should be drawn between psychological and physical intimacy. One need not presuppose the other. Clinical work with prostitutes indicates that promiscuous sexual intimacy can lead to withdrawal and alienation—distance rather than closeness. Conversely, two persons can be deeply involved with each other— completely attuned to each other's thoughts, habits, and beliefs—without sexual attraction or contact. Although there can be no doubting the beauty and power of sexual and romantic experiences, the intensity of these temporary experiences should not be confused with the depth of a more long-lasting contact. At most they only touch the edge of intimacy.

True intimacy begins with self-definition. Some psychological integrity is necessary before a person can share with another. The oneness of an intimate relationship should never occur because one of the participants gives up his or her own identity. At the same time, the readiness to open oneself to another is critical to the evolution of intimacy. Likewise, one must be able to tolerate the advances and exploration of the other. Intimacy thus depends on the preexistence of a sense of one's own individuality. Included here is a secure notion of one's sexual identity, of course. But intimacy rests most heavily on one's identity as a person. All the factors previously discussed in relation to psychological development are obviously involved in coming to this point. This relationship between intimacy and sense of self would appear to be in conformity with Erikson's developmental theory (1959), which puts identity as an adolescent issue and intimacy as the psychosocial crisis in young adulthood. However, Goldin's studies of development in college students (1977) are more in support of the view that intimacy engenders individuation and a sense of identity. The issue clearly merits further study.

To be really close to another person, one must be willing to feel and understand that person's point of view. In an intimate relationship much that occurs between the participants is nonverbal. A glance, a gesture, a frown can communicate as precisely as a spoken sentence. More subtle

yet, a good deal of communication takes place subliminally, through small acts or expressions of which one or both of the participants are unaware. One common characteristic of an intimate relationship is the ability of participants to perceive and respond to these unconscious cues—for example, when two people intently watching a movie seek and find each other's hands without realizing what has taken place.

Finally, intimacy implies physical closeness. To accept another person within one's own psychological space; to share an embrace; to expose one's nudity to the sight and touch of another; to relinquish the protection of delicate, sensitive tissue to the aroused passions of another; to join flesh, abandon constraint, and flow into the other. This, on its most fundamental level, is intimacy.

Shared concern. Early researchers in marriage put too much stress on common interests and similar background as important factors in a successful union. Although ample statistical data support such an emphasis, it now appears that other explanations can be given. Considering the difficulty in obtaining a divorce in most of the United States until recent years, a broken marriage was most likely to occur among those who could either circumvent the laws or disregard them. The former category included those who had the money to go to "divorce mills" in Nevada or Mexico or whose background less stringently demanded a permanent marriage. This group included primarily the newly rich in business and entertainment. Among families of established wealth it is customary to preserve the marriage while pursuing separate lives. The other group, who ignored the laws, contained largely those most likely to find all laws oppressive, the underclass segment of society. Less socially enfranchised and more unstable by their heritage, lower-class people were thus less likely to feel bound to societal expectations or to value stable relationships. These people might also be less bound by cultural convention in selection of a mate.

But it does not follow that those couples who stay married are necessarily happier or more successful in their matrimonial experience. Rather, experience suggests that, for many couples who remain married, religious conviction, fear of embarrassment, and a need to conform are the primary motives.

More recent research on happy couples suggests that permanent love evolves from the experiences that are shared together in the marriage. The mutual concerns of any relationship—small events and large,

happy or calamitous—become part of a unique experience for those two persons, their own private history. Out of these shared experiences can emerge an awareness of their interdependence and an appreciation of the concern each invests in the other and in the marriage itself. It is precisely this shared concern, evolving over time and experience, that endows married love with one of its most sublime qualities. Contrary to common belief, neither premarital experiences nor the commitment implied by a marital contract provides the most binding ties. Rather, the willingness to build together seems to be the most enduring basis for a successful marriage.

Pearl Buck's *The Good Earth* depicts traditional peasant marriage in rural China as a procedure in which husband and wife meet for the first time at the wedding ceremony. Yet it becomes evident that a deep, abiding love can grow between two strangers who depend on each other's cooperation, endure hardship and privation together, and share the pleasure of joint accomplishment. In fact, *The Good Earth* is more than a novel about peasant life in a remote place and time. The relationship described is probably far more typical of human experience than is the North American love-before-marriage expectation. Undeniably, it is easier to put up with adversity or irksome habits when there are strong positive feelings for one's spouse at the outset. But "being in love" is no guarantee that problems will be faced together or that happy experiences will be shared. Especially if "being in love" is inculcated as some stress-free romantic idyll is married life likely to seem a major disappointment. There is perhaps no greater misconception about marriage than the emphasis on premarital romantic love over commitment to the relationship itself as the primary ingredient for success.

Premarital Contact

Most societies provide for contact between the marital partners before the nuptial ceremony. This contact varies from almost totally free to strictly proscribed and closely supervised. The Spanish dueña was devoted to ensuring that the relationship between the betrothed couple was almost exclusively verbal and cultured. Among certain Nigerian tribes the bridegroom is permitted no more than an occasional peek at his intended during the last months before the wedding. In the former instance, it would appear that a sexually repressive premarital tradition demanded that the couple relate in other than erotic ways. In the latter,

sexual privation seems related to enhancing the erotic anticipation of marriage.

Take the high level of sexual excitation in adolescence and young adulthood. Add the physical intimacy necessary for sexual contact—the sheer closeness of the two bodies and the amount of touching and feeling involved. Combine these with the exquisite pleasures of sexual satisfaction. Is it any wonder that sexual relationships are so easily confused with love relationships? Even the euphemism *making love* implies that coitus means something more than a sexual experience. When sexual pleasure is culturally proscribed, it can be expected that other functions of that society will be subverted to sexual purposes. Conversely, an acknowledgement of the natural necessity for sexual contact among adults should permit more fluent functioning in other respects. It is no accident that the maturity of personal contact between the sexes among young people today should parallel a period of unprecedented sexual freedom. One also observes among these more naturally functioning young adults a much reduced tendency to equate sexual satisfaction with a love relationship. It remains to be seen whether better, more viable marriages will result from this greater understanding. Certainly, a more solid foundation for mature relationships has been laid down.

In general, of course, the premarital courtship period is intended as a time for preparing oneself for marriage. Rapoport (1961) identifies both intrapsychic and interpersonal components of this preparatory process. The individuals examine (or are confronted by) their own readiness to marry. Ego integrity, sexual identity, and the ability to love, share, and acknowledge one's needs—these are some of the concerns within oneself. The greatest interpersonal task is to begin to function as a partnership—discussing, planning, experimenting as a couple.

Why People Marry

Motives of the sexes. In the historic analyses of why people marry, it has been customary to ascribe differing motives to men and women. One of the most commonly offered reasons for why men marry is their simple need for a dependable sexual outlet. Yet this explanation hardly suffices to explain the existence of marriage. Even in the United States, for all its puritanical traditions, the best estimates are that at least 80% of men have sexual intercourse prior to marriage. Moreover, opportunities for sexual expression increase throughout the sexually active years. Besides,

sexual outlets have been available in addition to marriage or instead of marriage since time immemorial. Man's domestic needs—for a cook, housekeeper, general keeper of the hearth—have also been cited as important motives. In addition, nurturant/succorant needs have been acknowledged as a factor. Under this last category are included the raising of children, caring for the sick and crippled, and, particularly, men's own needs for support and nurturance (Lowenthal et al., 1977).

It has been traditionally assumed, of course, that woman's instinctual inclination is toward marriage. Originally her physical inferiority was offered as the reason for her economic dependence and, hence, her need for a spouse. Hence also the justification for said spouse to dominate the relationship as the stronger person. Further, the maternal instinct presumably drives women inevitably to marriage so as to have a family. Meanwhile, women over the last century have been making steady progress toward legal and social parity as human beings. With this development has come a parallel realization—that marriage too often has been a prison rather than a partnership.

For Western women the traditional motivation to marry stemmed from the need for financial security. Secondly, being unmarried carried with it the stigma of being unwanted. With increasing freedom for women, however, marriage is coming to be seen more as a genuine option. The feminist movement that arose before World War I was rekindled at the close of World War II. There are those who argue that a postwar shortage of men does more to stimulate women's-rights groups than does any issue of ideology. But whatever its origin, the trend toward increased education and professional training for women, plus the reduced time necessary for household maintenance (due to the advent of automatic appliances, frozen dinners, disposable diapers, and the like), has created a situation in which women are much less confined to a domestic role. The large-scale mechanization of industry further promotes vocational equality in that sheer physical strength is still a factor in only a small proportion of jobs. With these changes a corresponding increase in sexual freedom for women has also been noted by many writers. Interestingly, despite increasing access to contraception and abortion, childbirth rates continue high.

In any event, marriage optimally provides more than security for women or sexual outlet for men, or the reverse. Marriage should be an opportunity for two persons to live together and complement each other's interests and needs by virtue of both similarities and differences.

Satisfying needs. One of the great errors of early marriage counselors, as I have noted, was to assume that matching overt signs of compatibility (interests, social class, religion, and so on) would increase the likelihood of marital happiness. More recently it has been discovered that an exact correspondence of interests and attitudes between partners may be more conducive to boredom than it is to contentment. In strictly sexual attraction, the initial erotic resonance that fires two people with romantic passion may quickly disappear if it is based on physical characteristics that are unlikely to endure once the first bloom of youth has passed. When the attraction is due to the capacity of each other to fulfill deep-lying needs, however, the prognosis for long-term satisfaction may be much more hopeful.

Two young people meet. Their religious backgrounds are similar, both are rich, and both are college educated. They express similar social and political beliefs. Although they are highly compatible on all the traditional indexes, their marriage may lack intimacy, purpose, and even a real compatibility of fundamental attitudes and aspirations.

In another instance a young woman with aggressive qualities is shrewish and dissatisfied with docile men. The men she relates best to are confident people with a facility for taking charge in everyday social situations.

An attractive man dates women of varying intelligence, beauty, race, and religion. The one quality that consistently attracts him is the woman's spontaneous response to his need for physical closeness and affection.

It is not uncommon for intense needs to draw a couple together into marriage. With aging, new experience, or simple satisfaction of needs, however, the motivational basis for the marriage may change in a few years. Because of these changing needs in marriage Margaret Mead (1966) has suggested that more than one marriage per couple may eventually be necessary. The first marriage may satisfy companionate or sexual needs without any long-term implications. The second may fill the need for family rearing and sharing of affection. The increasing body of literature on the life stages of marriages (Duvall, 1967) indicates that it may be necessary for married people to evolve new bases for sustaining the relationship. Whatever the original motivations were, the character of a marriage changes so drastically over its natural history as to require comparable adaptive changes on the part of the couple.

Drawbacks of marriage. Whether the dominant motive for a marriage is economic or involves a need for status, love, security, and private

or pathological gratification, the persons involved have committed themselves to live with each other, create a family, and provide for themselves. In the traditional roles the husband is breadwinner and decision maker. He is sexually dominant and more worldly wise. The wife is cook and housekeeper. She is sexually submissive and deferential if not passive. If these are accepted as legitimate roles and tasks, one accepts the obligation to perform with competence in these areas. One's success in this venture relies on readiness and ability to adapt to these cultural standards. Once adopted, they provide explicit objectives designated by the culture as signifying a good marriage.

Ironically, and sometimes tragically, the successful performance of one's marital role may also result in the smothering of important personal needs. The man whose career interests are in economically unrewarding directions must choose between failing his family as breadwinner or stifling his own fulfillment so as to earn a better salary. The woman who thrives on competitive interaction with peers must confront a career of supportive, nurturant response to little children. Small wonder that marriage provokes drabness or despair, guilt or disappointment, for a significant number of people.

Given this tremendous potential for disillusionment, an observer might ponder the ubiquity of marriage, especially monogamous marriage, across time and culture. Can a social structure that has proven so durable have survived only because of cultural pressures to maintain it? Marriage exists in societies where extramarital liaisons are normative as well as in social systems where adultery is punishable by death. It is found where survival is a daily concern as well as where nature is bountiful. Can there be any doubt that, despite many flaws, the marital relationship serves fundamental human needs?

Rewards of marriage. One such need is *acceptance.* Whether the relationship is dull or tempestuous, loving or critical, the marital partners realize that they are known and accepted by each other. If only by the sheer fact that the marriage is not dissolved, it acknowledges some rudimentary degree of mutual acceptance. One has been exposed, observed, and—whatever else—endured. The great arbiter of all marriages is time. Passions and depression ebb and flow. Little habits infuriate or endear. Moments become days; weeks become years. No matter what else is said or done, each partner knows that there is one person in

the world who has seen the best and the worst in one and that—at some level—one is accepted by that person. On its soaring occasions marriage brings love, contentment, fulfillment. But day in and day out, over the long pull of time and experience, acceptance also means acceptable.

Another basic need is *relatedness*. Frieda Fromm-Reichmann (1967) lists loneliness as one of the most encumbering sources of anxiety. The need to belong, to relate oneself to something or someone, has been widely recognized as fundamental. Even in the absence of sexual love the innumerable intimacies of marriage create ties between the partners that bind them in ways that are unique to each relationship. Arguments, emergencies, happy times, moments of ecstasy elicit a multiplicity of investments of oneself into the relationship. The longer the relationship is maintained and the more personal the experiences, the deeper and greater is the involvement of self in the total process. Out of the time, energy, and experience shared and invested evolves a subtle sense of purpose, of relevance. The patterning of one's expenditure of effort becomes, in Allport's phrase, functionally autonomous (1937). That is, the marriage acquires its own motive strength. One experiences a sense of relatedness not only to a person but also to a purpose. The sustaining of the marriage becomes a meaningful activity in itself.

One's spouse, therefore, is but part of a larger relatedness. Thus, even where the partners do not relate well to each other, the greater objective—the marriage—may justify continuing the partnership. Nor is this distinction as fanciful as it may seem. Over time the marriage may accumulate a stable residence, a community, neighbors, friends, status, reputation. These, in turn, become part of that relatedness. As many divorced people have learned, to end the marriage is to relinquish that totality.

Maslow's (1954) basic need for belonging pertains here. To feel oneself a part of something, to be connected to someone, is—at minimum—to avoid the awful feeling of isolation and loneliness. The companionate relationship so much a part of long-lived marriages satisfies these basic needs. "It's 5 o'clock; Joe will be home soon" relates the individual to person, system, and world. In his profound book *Escape From Freedom* Fromm (1941) details humans' historic need to involve themselves in something larger, even dictatorship, to escape the dread feelings of alienation.

Acceptance and relatedness may seem small benefits for the costs of

marriage, particularly to young people savoring the taste of autonomy and minimal restriction. Before too long, however, the most self-sufficient discover in themselves the need for a close, dependable relationship. For most people, it is the commitment to permanence that is objectionable. Such a commitment is often repugnant to people who value honesty, who are aware of their own recent history of personal change, who prefer to live in an extended *now* time dimension, and who are therefore understandably skeptical of the legitimacy of permanent commitments. The more fixedly monogamous the society, the more restrictive and encumbering marriage seems. Yet it is the very locked-in character of the marital contract that demands that the couple confront each other at all points and examine each other anew. Almost always after the fact of formalizing the contract, each partner views the other in terms of making a lifetime accommodation—a very different issue from "do I love (like) him (her)?"

Marriage also affords partners the opportunity to fulfill a variety of wishes and fantasies—those developed in early life as well as those more recently acquired. It is probably characteristic of most successful marriages that the partners at different times play different roles—at one point an older sibling, at another point a sexual partner, at a third point a parent, a child, and so forth. Consequently, each partner at different times in the marriage is called on to be nurturant, dependent, assertive, submissive, affectionate, and protective. Unfortunately, certain wishes and fantasies may be destructive to an effective marriage relationship. The man who needs to enact and satisfy all his hostile and sadistic wishes toward a domineering mother, for example, may choose the kind of mate whom he can provoke to play the part, or who naturally plays the part, of his mother. This will recreate the destructive relationship between mother and son, which was never satisfactorily resolved. It is typical of these pathological relationships that one characteristic mode of interaction, which is a repetition of earlier disturbing experiences, tends to dominate the relationship. Because of that need, the more beneficial components of the marriage are either obliterated or subordinated to the major neurotic interaction. The fear of discovering such pathological needs in the relationship may be an important deterrent to some people, keeping them from making a lifetime commitment to a marital partner.

Yet despite all these individual misgivings marriage has proven to be a remarkably durable social structure in human cultures. In the last

analysis, the most potent reason for marriage is probably the desire to found a family. For all the discussion about freedom to choose one's own mate, the role of love, commitment, and intimacy, marriage in most instances still becomes primarily a matter of the availability of options at the time the person is ready to marry.

HAVING CHILDREN

The desire to procreate emerges from many different sources. Producing children is for some the *raison d'être* of getting married. For others it is the way in which the marriage can be maintained when the relationship seems shaky. For others still it becomes a way of avoiding a confrontation with the intimacy required of a mature heterosexual relationship. In an optimum relationship the opportunity to bear children develops as a climactic culmination of a meaningful heterosexual love relationship. Nevertheless, the bearing of children necessarily brings the marriage into a new status with its own set of expectations, rewards, and requirements.

The woman is partially disabled by the impact of pregnancy and birth. A stable source of nutrition and support is vitally important to the health and welfare of both mother and fetus. Thus, a supportive relationship is of utmost importance to ensure the proper development of the conception, birth, and nurturance of a child. The marital contract, therefore, has significant psychobiological underpinnings quite apart from whatever romantic or social conventions may dictate its existence. Although adult status in a society is often linked with entry into marriage, social acknowledgement of maturity is reserved until the time of childbearing. In rural Japan, as we have seen, a female is not considered to be truly adult until she has borne a child. Similarly, Helene Deutsch (1944) states that a woman who has not borne a child is not complete. For men, the situation is quite comparable. Gutmann's cross-cultural data (1975) indicate that fathering a child has explicit personal and social value for males.

Importance of Children

The siring of progeny in itself has a variety of psychological meanings for the parents. With the attainment of parenthood comes a sense of arrival as a full-fledged adult. The wonder of birth never ceases to lose its

impact as the parents are confronted with that which they have wrought. This fundamental participation in the life process confers an unparalleled sense of one's potency. To be a mother or father, much more surely than being a husband or wife, means that one has attained fundamental membership status in one's culture. Producing a child is a statement of commitment that another generation will perpetuate the society.

At the same time the demands of parenthood are considerable. At issue immediately is the ability to accept responsibility for the care and protection of others, particularly those unable to care for themselves. Feeding, clothing, and housing a set of small mouths at the very minimum entails accepting a broadened economic responsibility. For the breadwinners, the idea that other people's very lives may depend on their ability to provide can indeed be an immense burden. For the nurturing one, the awareness that the health and safety of the children rest in one's hands is a responsibility that can seem awesome at times. The sheer physical and material demands of parenting are extended by the emotional demands the child makes for care and attention. Children change so rapidly and vary so widely that it is virtually impossible for any parent to constantly feel a sense of love and warmth. A colicky baby or negativistic child can test the patience and forebearance of the most loving and gentle parents.

The child's needs for attention inevitably impinge on the interests and available time of the parents, in this way restricting their own lives and activities. To cope with these demands requires a tolerance, and often brings out a maturity, from individuals who previously had not quite arrived at such a point. Thus, bearing and rearing children offer great potential as a growth experience for some parents. For others, the experience can be a breaking point.

Parenthood also demands that one evolve the ability to share love among several people. Children desperately need love and affection and most of the time are capable of eliciting it to some degree. For the parent, however, there remains a task of distributing love and affection among very different kinds of people in ways that are appropriate to them and yet consistent with the parent's own needs for both giving and receiving love. The kind of loving one bestows on a daughter is different from that one bestows on a wife. Social mores, moreover, may dictate different ways of expressing affection, depending on the sex of the child. Finally, unconscious personal needs may affect the parent's ability to express love and affection.

Chapter 9

Satisfactions of Parenthood

At the root of any consideration of parent/child interaction is the irreducible fact that the child is a product of the parent's own body and therefore an extension of the parent's own self. In psychoanalytic terms the child is an externalized narcissistic object. As Freud (1938) sees it, a major reason for parental love is precisely that the child is an externalized representative of self. One loves one's self through loving one's child.

Another reason for parental involvement with the child is that the parents are able to relive their lives vicariously. Parents many times try to fulfill their own ambitions or act out their own secret wishes, by either tacitly accepting (and thus permitting) what the child does or overtly directing the child into certain kinds of behavior. Parenthetically, it has often been observed by those who work with juvenile offenders that the delinquent child's actions are found to be related to a secret wish that the parent had when he or she was a child. More generally, the child's life cycle recapitulates the parent's own childhood, and, for many parents, this is an opportunity to relive the past. Some parents try to achieve their own idealized image of childhood experience in the life of their child. However altruistically this effort is conceived, one invariable result is that the parent's needs are imposed on the child, and the child becomes servant to the parent's personal gratification.

On a broader plane of reference children are the individual's link with immortality. It is written somewhere that one who bears children never dies. In the most literal sense the maxim is entirely correct. One's inherent genetic attributes are passed down to one's child. More than that, all the attitudes, values, and beliefs that one can inculcate are transmitted to the future through one's children. But perhaps the most compelling impact of parenthood is the discovery of one's linkage with history and tradition. At one level there is the biblical injunction to populate the earth with one's seed. At another level, and perhaps more personally, there is the sense of continuity with one's own history and tradition through continuing the family name, propagating one's ethnic group, and participating in the propagation of humankind. By extending their values into another generation, parents realize how they are tied to their own history, which in turn is part of a continuity that stretches both backward and forward in time. This revelation of one's sense of place is perhaps even more poignant today when the traditional institutions that have rooted people in their society—family structure and organized religion—are so disrupted.

Parenthood and Development

David Gutmann (1975) had advanced the proposal that parenthood is not only a life stage but also a key to studying the life cycle cross-culturally. Gutmann asserts that parenthood is the ultimate Darwinian imperative. Human evolution could not proceed in the absence of a sociobiological institution for fostering the growth of offspring. The variety of tasks mandated by the need to produce and protect children necessitates that there be a division of labor between two parents.

Over the course of evolution, Gutmann asserts, one type of parent has been selected out to provide nurturance and emotional security. The other type of parent evolved to provide physical security, as a wide-ranging hunter of food and protector from natural enemies. Male dominance and aggression and female nurturance and docility are thus seen as evolutionary responses to the "parental emergency." When childrearing is over, cross-cultural studies indicate, women become more assertive and dominant and men become more docile and hedonic. Having fulfilled evolutionary requirements as parents, the sexes are able to reverse roles: "Thus, neither sex is the final custodian of the qualities that we choose to call 'masculine' and 'feminine.' These qualities tend to be distributed not only by sex but also by life period" (p. 181).

Both parenting and the socialization of children in traditional sex roles may be in the service of important evolutionary requirements, according to Gutmann's formulation.

Patricia Self (1975) questions the inevitability of traditional sex-role assignments, however. She notes that the traditional division of labor along sex lines shows little evidence of being innate. In contemporary society men and women seem capable of reversing many parental roles. Men can perform primary caretaker functions, and women can function as breadwinners. Species survival in technologically advanced societies appears to be increasingly less dependent on traditional sex-role assignments.

Self goes on to criticize the data that suggest sex-role reversal in middle age. She notes that most of those studies are cross-sectional, not longitudinal. They may, therefore, reflect generational differences rather than personality changes. Finally, as the number of years required for full-time, home-based parenting decreases, she anticipates "that we will see parents responding to infants and children more on the basis of their behaviors and needs, rather than on the basis of expectations of sex-appropriate behavior" (p. 187).

THE FAMILY AND SOCIETY

The successful accomplishments of marrying and founding a family meet the culture's expectation of the young adult. By virtue of this success, young adults gain credence as full-fledged members of their society. The consensual recognition thus achieved, in turn, affects the person's self-concept, enhancing growth and development. Unlike legalistic credentials (such as attaining age 21) that formally alter the person's social status, founding a family in itself demands that the individual possess in at least some minimally adequate supply, the psychosocial qualities of adulthood. To put the matter more succinctly, it takes an adult to love, marry, and rear a family. The very process by which one gains the social credentials of an adult elicits those abilities germane to adult functioning.

Through this process, society not only serves its own self-preserving needs but also contributes to the growth and development of its members. It is axiomatic that any society that fails to accomplish both of these purposes must eventually decline. Although societal demands shape the competencies of its constituency, society must also satisfy basic human needs if it is to survive. Ultimately, people and society must make some fundamental accommodation to each other, rather than being antagonists. The intricate psychosocial process of founding a family is a truly marvelous ecological phenomenon, because both the human organism and its social environment attain optimal fulfillment of their objectives.

10

TRANSITION: TENSION AND CHALLENGE

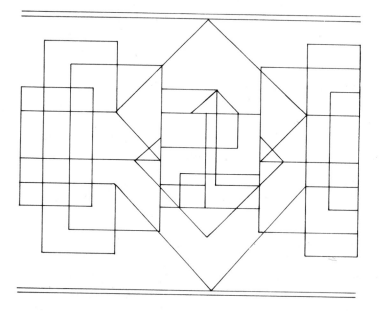

THE IMPORTANCE OF TRANSITION

The developmental imperative for change, which was discussed in Chapter 2, has its greatest influence at the entry and exit from a life stage. At these times people are particularly vulnerable. As much as change is the law of life, people seem generally to resist any modifications in the adaptation they have achieved. Some observers ascribe this resistance to a movement toward homeostasis, or dynamic equilibrium, as a characteristic of human behavior. Others view humankind as a species oriented to preserving the status quo. In either case, whether the initiatives to change originate within the person or come from outside, a certain amount of stress is likely to accompany periods of transition.

In Loevinger's studies of ego development (1976) some of the transitional periods assume the status of discrete stages "...leaving open the question of whether this is a stage in itself or a transition between stages or whether there is no real difference between these two possibilities" (p. 19).

The research of Levinson and his colleagues with adult men (1978) led to a developmental schema in which each life stage is bounded by transitional periods. Indeed, the concept of "mid-life transition" is central to his major formulations.

In their work with women's development Golden and her associates (1978) have identified the transitional periods as critical times for intervention. And, underscoring human vulnerability during developmental transitions, Lowenthal and colleagues (1977) selected couples in transition periods (such as preretirement) for their studies of the relationship between adaptation and mental health.

In terms of psychological processes it is readily understandable that periods of transition should be particularly stressful. Newly emerging intrapsychic functions intersect changing sociocultural expectations at these times. Even when this happens gradually, it requires reorganizing perception and restructuring ways of functioning. Assimilating new information and getting used to an expanded repertoire of experiences makes demands on personal energy. If, in addition, earlier developmental issues have been incompletely resolved, the strains on psychological resources can be intensified. Finally, developmentally acquired abilities that have been marginally adequate at one stage may be severely taxed when the impending life period demands their further elaboration.

How any given individual encounters the transition from one stage

to the next depends on those factors we have just examined. The specific features unique to that individual will determine how the process is experienced, and how the transition will be made. The person's ego strength, the kind of social support network that is available, existing cultural conditions, and the person's prior developmental history will all play parts in the scenario.

Turning now to the transition between adolescence and young adulthood, it is possible to anticipate those aspects that have the greatest potential for being problematic. Much less is known about established adulthood. Therefore, the exit-transition problems of young adulthood can be identified only in much less specific terms.

TRANSITION FROM ADOLESCENCE TO YOUNG ADULTHOOD

The adolescent/young adult transition is likely to be much more subtle than one might think. Entry into adult life would seem to be the occasion for major personal transformation. In most societies adulthood is defined by the taking on of prescribed role activities. Commonly, the role (for example, farmer, parent) subsumes some skills or competencies. It is typical of most cultures to prepare children for adulthood by training them gradually to acquire the skills that will be expected of them as responsible adults. The discontinuity between childhood training and adult responsibility that Benedict (1934) noted in "civilized" nations has been little improved since her observations almost 50 years ago. But training (or its absence) for stage-appropriate role behavior is only one part of developmental growth. Predictable behavioral expectations that originate from a group are designed to satisfy group needs. They may not correspond to the central concerns of the individual. In extreme cases (such as the use of children as factory workers at the turn of the century) group demands can be exploitative and harmful to the individual's health and growth.

The position tenaciously maintained throughout this book is that psychological development is grounded in psychological processes. People can successfully meet social expectations, and hence win social status, but lag in their psychological development. This is particularly true of the transition from adolescence to young adulthood.

The sociocultural evidence of attaining adulthood is, in most societies, relatively vivid. The person marries and produces children. Socioeco-

nomic independence is demonstrated by establishing separate living quarters from the family of origin or by carrying one's own share of the burden. Often the acquisition of these competencies and responsibilities promotes personal psychological growth. Sometimes it inhibits growth. But it is never the same as growth.

Intrapsychic Transition

One of the most important aspects of the psychological transition to adulthood involves what Ausubel and Kirk (1977) call *desatellization*. The child is born into a family or other social structure and grows up under the gravitational influence of significant adults. The early life of the child revolves around those adults as a planet does around the sun. Moving into adulthood, in Ausubel's terms, requires that the person disconnect from a satellite relationship and establish a psychologically autonomous path. At the level of intrapsychic organization the transition is from achieving and integral sense of one's identity to differentiating and integrating the component ingredients of who one is and what one is about. In terms we have elaborated in Chapter 7, this means moving from rudimentary identity formation of a diffuse type to self-particularization and ego integration. This evolution can be described in its cognitive/ethical and interpersonal dimensions.

Cognitive/ethical development entails a progressive disengagement from *basic dualism* (Perry, 1970). In that stage, rightness and authority are not differentiated, and the person's own reasoning and ethical alignments are identified with the authoritarian position. This simplistic developmental stage is characteristic of adolescence. In Perry's terms, it evolves into a more sophisticated level of complexity and differentiation called *relativism*. In this period the structure of thinking allows for "a plurality of points of view, interpretations, frames of reference, value systems and contingencies [and] various sorts of analysis, comparison and evaluation" [1970, Glossary]. This change, from dualism to relativism, is reflected in the development of idealism from adolescence to young adulthood.

Idealism. Little is known of the psychological origins of idealism and even less about its life-span evolution. That idealism is associated with youth has been recognized since antiquity, however. "Youth [have] exalted notions because they have not yet been humbled by life or learned

its necessary limitations. Moreover, their hopeful disposition makes them think themselves equal to great things. They would always rather do noble deeds than useful ones—*Aristotle*" (Hirth, 1972).

Lampl-de Groot (1962) is probably correct to link the formation of ideals to the development of superego and ego-ideal. But the processes by which the higher aspirations for oneself result in concern for human well-being can only be guessed at. Whether the evolution of idealism depends on prior emergence of formal operations in thinking, as described by Piaget, also remains unknown. The evidence *is* consistent that a concern about ethical/moral absolutes—truth, peace, justice, perfection—tends to merge into abstract idealism (see Chapter 5) during adolescence. Adolescent idealism seems to have little concrete personal relevance, either as an internalized value or an imperative to action. Rather, its occurrence is largely in conceptual form or as an attribute ascribed to someone else. But even in this abstract form, idealism can have strong affective pull. The attractive power of charismatic individuals or organizations who offer glib promises of peace and happiness owes much of its success to the adolescent susceptibility to idealistic purposes.

With time, narcissistic self-preoccupation recedes. And, as adolescents acclimatize to the inner changes they experience, a more allocentric awareness of the world can gradually take its place. The person's energies are more evenly distributed between self and world. This transformation in self/other orientation may be one of the causes of the metamorphosis of idealism during the transition. Other contributing factors may well be the sense of power and activist orientation that also emerge. But whatever its genesis, a more active form of idealism accompanies evolution into young adulthood. No longer content with idea or ideology, young adults are impelled to put their altruistic beliefs into practice. Idealism thus assumes human proportions during the transition.

White (1952, 1975) speaks of the "humanization of values" during this period. And Sanford's (1956) research with college students corroborates the view that what was an abstract notion begins to assume flesh-and-blood proportions. It is not enough to espouse a belief. Now the personal challenge "What can I do about it?" emerges. The psychological freedom to look beyond immediate self-interest brings young people to the gateway of perhaps the most altruistically sensitive period of the entire life span.

Unfortunately, a common consequence of that encounter between idealistic impulse and everyday reality is frustration, disappointment,

and pain. The depression found by Symonds (1961) in projective testing of young adults and by Lowenthal and colleagues (1977) in self-descriptions of young-adult women mirrors what Rappaport calls the disillusionment of adult transition: "Typical experience in this period does inevitably force young people to reevaluate and change most of their ideas about themselves and the world" (1972, p. 335).

Disillusionment and depression notwithstanding, world history is replete with examples of outrageous idealism by people in that segment of the life span approximating young adulthood. Examples that come to mind include Nathan Hale and Molly Pitcher in the American Revolution, the nameless Chinese university students who opposed invading Japanese tanks unarmed in 1932, and the Hungarian freedom fighters of 1954.

From all that is presently known, idealism as a life-stage characteristic occurs only in adolescence and young adulthood. Its natural evolution from abstract concept to a basis for action constitutes one of the more telling points in differentiating the two stages.

Underlying the distinction between the two forms of idealism are implications about prepotent modes of expression. The content of idealistic urgings does not differentiate adolescents and young adults. Rather, it is the ongoing change in personality structure that affects the role of idealism within the overall psychic economy of the individual. In particular, the shift from impulsivity to activism is critical here.

Impulsivity and activism. Impulsivity can be defined psychologically as the tendency to act unreflectively. It occurs when there are very strong affective urgings, weak ego controls, or some combination of the two. Infants are bound by impulses. And much of child development is concerned with learning how to manage emotions. The advent of adolescence is accompanied by intensified emotions and increased ego vulnerability. Consequently, the impulse control attained by late childhood is jeopardized by intrapsychic turmoil. According to psychoanalytic theory, the drives that have been "tamed" by neutralization are resexualized by the onset of puberty (Blanck & Blanck, 1974). Ego functions are less dependable and more fluid. Impulsivity is therefore a characteristic of the adolescent stage.

Through the adolescent years there is a gradual accommodation to these psychological and physiological changes. With the emergence of a

sense of coherent identity, ego functioning is enhanced. The focus of attention and energy now moves outward, into a more refined world awareness. Whereas adolescents are often occupied with containing or reacting to behaviors erupting from within themselves, young adults become more volitional. The central ingredient in this change is that behavior is increasingly being mediated by the ego. Adult ego functioning is characterized by organized, integrated coordination of activity, geared to addressing the immediate world.

Behavior thus becomes more dependable and predictable, because it is better controlled. The role of ego mediation is to enhance organismic effectiveness. Freud's early notions were that inhibition and repression are the necessary tools of ego intervention. Contemporary ego psychologists now recognize that expressive behaviors, including spontaneous and intuitive reactions, are augmented by ego mediation. Haan's listing of ego coping mechanisms (1977) includes processes from playfulness to problem solving. The evolution from adolescent impulsivity to young-adult activism, therefore, bespeaks a broadening, rather than a constriction, in the person's psychological freedom. Contrary to popular mythology, adult development liberates more than it enslaves. And in no other realm is this truer than in psychological—especially intrapsychic—development. The transition from impulsivity to activism is thus a measure of the maturation of the ego as a system of functions.

Responsibility. The transition to young adulthood also finds representation in Loevinger's mapping of ego development (1976). As I have noted previously, there is a close correspondence between Loevinger's findings and the theoretical construction evolved in this book. Much of what Loevinger ascribes to the conformist stage corresponds to qualities of adolescence: conformance to group-accepted rules, in-group/out-group stereotyping, use of moralistic clichés, and interest in appearance, social acceptance, reputation, and material things. Indeed, she states that the transition from conformist to conscientious stages, through a self-aware level, "is probably the modal level for adults in our society" (p. 19). The interdependence of ego development and identity formation is clearly implied in the self-aware transition: "Consciousness of self is a pre-requisite to the replacement of group standards by self-evaluated ones, characteristic of the next stage" (1976, p. 19).

The conscientious stage includes the long-term planning, differen-

tiated self-evaluation, social awareness of obligation and responsibility, and personal perspective that characterize intrapsychic functioning in young adulthood.

Thus, the transition to young adulthood involves a necessary process of disconnecting from primary-group allegiances and accepting responsibility for oneself. No longer can one rest secure in identifying oneself as "I'm a Kowalski" or "I'm a member of the Shantu sect." Whether or not one retains close family ties or belongs to a religious group, acknowledging and accepting the primacy of one's psychological autonomy is a critical step in the development from adolescence into young adulthood. The self-conscious adolescent may feel shunned or disliked for real or imagined shortcomings. He or she would like nothing more than group approval. The young adult, by contrast, may have to give up status as a group member to pursue personal goals and individual autonomy. Small wonder that so many people resist and delay confronting that point of transition.

Interpersonal Transition

The features of differentiation, integration, and increasing complexity describe the interpersonal transition as well as they do the intrapsychic one. The major avenues along which interpersonal growth proceeds are one's relations with parental figures and with peers.

From birth onward parents have custody, care, and control of one's life. That relationship structures the child's life experience from its earliest, most formative years. One continues to have parents, and to be their child, long after one has entered adulthood. The transitional challenge, then, is not to deny or renounce one's parents. Rather, it is to delineate one's adulthood within the context of the biological permanence of a parent/child relationship.

A major change in that relationship is from a vertical, authoritarian pattern to a horizontal, egalitarian form. Under optimum conditions, two adults—one parent to the other—meet in mutual respect for the integrity of the other. The younger adult accepts responsibility for the conduct and control of his or her life and relinquishes the relative security of being under the parental wing. Yet one's parent is forever one's parent. Thus, it is not a transferring of roles but an expansion of the earlier relationship that must be accomplished. Emerging young adults

are not confronted with choosing between parental values and peer values. Instead, they must selectively incorporate a combination of values that they can identify as their own, regardless of source.

The challenge of transition to young adulthood includes differentiating deference from dependence, respect from blind reverence, separation from rejection. Only as the absolutist constructions of adolescence give way to the relativistic forms of young adulthood can this evolution occur. Conversely, the change in the nature of parent/child relationships is likely to generalize to other relationships and also to enhance intrapsychic development. Once again it becomes apparent that development is a holistic process involving interdependent components.

In Chapter 5 I noted that adolescents retain important anchoring attachments to their parents. These ties form the secure emotional background for moving into the world of peers. The transition to young adulthood involves not only the restructuring of relationships with parents but also major refinements in peer relations. Until there is psychological autonomy from parents, peer relations will remain incomplete at best. But the critical growth issue for movement into young adulthood is the ability to develop partnership and competitor attitudes with others, particularly with one's own generation.

With parents it is necessary to undo and modify long-term patterns of relating. With peers it is necessary to create patterns of relating. Typically, the most intimate of peer relationships occur outside of the primary group. Consequently, those attitudes and expectations that evolved from contact with parents and siblings may prove to be irrelevant or counterproductive when meeting people with whom there is no long history of close association.

Part of the tension and challenge of peer relations comes from this relative newness of experience. For better or worse, one's place in the primary group is known. The freedom to choose friends, coworkers, and lovers brings with it a heavy burden of responsibility and anxiety. Out of the anxiety emerges the regressive urge to reestablish old, familiar patterns of relating—as younger sister, favored son, prima donna, or bully. To the extent that one is caught in the past, new relationships are sought that will allow old patterns to continue. But new people bring their own distinctive patterns of relating, so that, inevitably, mutual readjustment is required if the relationship is to endure.

New contacts provide new ideas, attitudes, response styles. The

transition to peer relationships therefore stimulates a broadened view of the human world as one encounters these diverse interpersonal experiences. For adolescents the transfer of locus of attention from parents to peers characterizes the developmental thrust at that stage. The preponderant effort interpersonally, as it is intrapsychically, is expended in the service of desatellization. "The burden of evidence suggests that personal friendships are of unique importance during adolescence because they provide the most effective help . . . to organize a more mature self-concept" (Rappaport, 1972, p. 299).

When that purpose nears achievement, interpersonal relations can include what Isaacs (1956) referred to as "disidentification from objects" and "appreciation of the sensibilities of others." The separation from parents lays the groundwork for the emergence of personal perspective. As one learns to stand back from self, so one learns to see oneself in relation to others. And it is in this context that a more sensitive, empathic, and differentiated view of human relations can evolve. In this evolution peers become important as individuals in their own right, beyond the adolescent needs for a refuge, sounding board, or narcissistic focus. As we saw in Chapter 8, the quality of the relationship is delineated relative to shared purposes, closeness, room for autonomy, and pursuit of individual objectives.

Both partnership and competitor relations are predicated on the prior development of some measure of autonomous identity. It is this fundamental attainment that permits a more careful exploration of how one relates to others. One of my students, Katz (1978), undertook to demonstrate intimacy operations in young-adult couples. She hypothesized that private as well as shared space was necessary for intimate bonding to be successful. Among her conclusions was the finding that intimacy evolves over three steps:

1. Couple-bonding—the discovery and building of a couple system.
2. Differentiation of partners—the validation of essential and situational differences between self and partner.
3. Dealing with impasse and breakthrough to rebonding—access to a more shared intimate space [p. 221].

Whether or not one can speak of partnership and competitor relationships as normative, they are prepotent in young adulthood. And, it is apparent, they depend on prior developmental accomplishments for their potentiation beyond mere readiness to emerge.

TRANSITION FROM YOUNG ADULTHOOD TO ESTABLISHED ADULTHOOD

Until fairly recent times scant attention has been given to established adulthood. The same theorists who divide the adult life span into early, middle, and late periods are likely to be vague or unaware of any distinctions between young-adult and established-adult stages.

Rappaport distinguishes between the disillusionment of early adulthood and the acceptance of self and one's life that marks middle age. Erikson appears to be describing an established-adult period, characterized by generativity or stagnation. People at this time contend with the stimulation and nurturance of those who are young or encounter a personal sense of "boredom and interpersonal impoverishment" or both (1968, p. 138).

The transition from young adulthood to established-adult status has been described by a number of investigators. Super (1957) was the first writer to make the connection between career development and personal development. His vocational-development theory is grounded in the evolution of personal self-concept. Super, who originated the idea of an established-adult period, does not recognize it as a discrete life stage. For him the establishment phase is a later part of early-adult vocational development. It follows on the heels of an extended "late adolescence," when people undergo a process of trial and exploration, trying to implement their evolving conception of themselves.

From this trial and exploration emerges a greater familiarity with cultural expectations and insight into oneself, a widened world awareness, and more-specialized information about one's own needs. The result is more-realistic, goal-directed behavior. For middle-class men in Western society this produces a stable career pattern. Working-class men, and women in general, often do not attain this established career status. In terms of personal development, however, this life period is characterized by modification and implementation of the self-concept.

Levinson's research team (1978) has contributed much to an understanding of transitional periods in adult development. Like Super, this group uses Buhler's model of adult life stages, which conceptualizes early adulthood as the period from 20 to 45. Distinct periods and transitions are identified within this span. *Getting into the adult world* is an exploratory period whose objective is a definition of oneself as adult such that linkages can be formed between oneself and the wider world.

Transition occurs between 28 and 32. For Levinson, the *age-30 transition* is "a remarkable gift and burden." It provides an opportunity

to revise and restructure earlier life plans. Yet it also demands that the man make a stronger commitment in the forthcoming years. Levinson's subjects describe "a sense of greater urgency. Life is becoming more serious, more restrictive, more 'for real' " (1978, p. 85). Following this transition is the period of *settling down,* which is the second part of 20–45 early-adulthood.

This period conforms most closely to what I refer to as established adulthood. "The individual now makes deeper commitments; invests more of himself in his work, family, and valued interests; and within the framework of this life structure, makes and pursues more long-range plans and goals.... The man establishes his niche in society" (1978, p. 23).

Gould's (1978) 28- to 34-year-olds correspond chronologically to the Levinson group's *age-30 transition.* He reports a feeling of disillusionment and reappraisal in his sample. Case studies done by my own students of people in this age group suggest that both men and women experience a keen awareness of having really become adults. Concomitantly there is often a wistful realization that "youth" is now behind them.

Bear in mind that these data constitute a limited historic, geographic, ethnic, and sexual sampling. For late-20th-century middle Americans, especially males, the transition from young to established adulthood is most likely to occur in the few years clustered around age 30. To the extent that the data are representative, they suggest that this transition period has consistent features in our culture:

1. There is a feeling of disappointment and disillusionment. High hopes and idealism have encountered real-world obstacles. The compromise solutions that Ginzberg and associates (1951) and Super (1957) cite as optimal resolutions are often subjectively experienced as less-than-desirable adaptions.

2. The process of getting into the world, and of learning more about oneself-in-the-world, shifts to a deepened awareness of oneself as adult. In the words of a World War I soldier, "It doesn't matter how you got here—you're in the Army now." For some the dawning awareness augments a deepening commitment to ongoing activities and purposes. For others it augurs psychic upheaval and reexamination.

For our purposes the precise chronological dating of this transition period is less important than its contents. Whatever makes age 30 so important in one place and time could occur at 25 or 35 in a different

temporal/cultural context. The psychological features of the transition are what we hypothesize to be the universal ingredients.

The Saliency of Everyday Life

What emerges from this transition is a deepened understanding of workaday reality. The life process has sometimes been described as movement from egocentrism to allocentrism (Heath, 1965). Infantile experience cannot distinguish between personal and objective reality. Only gradually, over the first decades of life, do people gain skill in differentiating perception from reality and in apprehending the interaction between oneself and the world. It may be that the advent of established adulthood is marked by a fundamental coming to terms with the fact of being an adult in a real world.

If the young adult dares to plan great things, it is the established adult who can be depended on to get everyday things done. Earlier (p. 42) we defined the intrapsychic issue of established adults as consolidation and effectuation. The established-adult stage is characterized by competent, productive performance. Established adults, more than any other age group, make their culture work. They have the acquired skills, energy, and demonstrated competence to run the everyday world they inhabit. The higher echelons of management and leadership in a society usually come from middle-age and senescent adults.

Established adulthood, then, has as its essential developmental precursor a transition from idealism to allocentrism. As defined by Heath, allocentrism is "a universal developmental trend toward accurately internalizing the external world and accommodating one's self to its demands" (1965, p. 20).

En route to this developmental achievement, the adult must become familiar with the external world in its workings. Even more important, it is necessary that the external world be assigned a value and status at least equal to knowing and experiencing one's self. Thus, while the developmental process of engaging the world as a full-time participant evolves incrementally, it comes to a watershed point in established adulthood.

To illustrate that process it may be helpful to shift to the metaphor of figure/ground relationships. A photographic lens aimed at the person-in-the-world field would in infancy be unfocused: person and world would be indistinguishable. Gradually the person would come into

focus—details of face and body clear, the rest of the world a blur. Over time, significant objects—that is, those features of the world of immediate personal importance—are included in the camera's visual field. As the camera's eye expands, more and more details of the world become clear, so much so that the person becomes briefly a vague blur but then reemerges as part of the wide-angle view. As noted in the original discussion of life stages, it is the qualitative changes in the developmental process that identify the emergence of a new stage. To complete the metaphor, when both the person and the immediate environs are in clear focus, the transition to established adulthood is accomplished.

Effectiveness

The common denominator of most adult development—which contributes to the discontinuity between childhood and adulthood—is the role of life experience. A commonly held position among developmental psychologists (for example, Kohlberg, 1978) asserts that child development is more systematic, predictable, and universal, because it involves more *structural* change. This position assumes that physiological changes occur with greater consistency during childhood and that they condition, if not create, the nature and direction of developmental maturation. Because physiological change is much slower during adulthood—and typically involves decline rather than growth—it follows that developmental changes at that time are less systematic, predictable, and universal. The argument is cogent to the extent that one accepts the reductionist view that, for change to be structural, it must be physiologically based. An alternative approach lays stress on the necessary and sufficient attributes of psychological structure, because physiological change alone provides no guarantee of a change in psychological structuring. Blasi (1976) asserts that, although structural change is essential to development, its most central features are not defined physiologically. Structure denotes stability and continuity but especially organizational integrity. "In sum, structure is defined by relations, by the basic laws of totality, that is, by laws that are independent of the elements" (1976, p. 33).

In support of this position is an impressive foundation of theory and experimental research, particularly from Heinz Werner (1940, 1957) and Gestalt psychology (for example, Kohler, 1947). These data demonstrate that perceptual and cognitive restructuring takes place with

learning and life experience, independently of physiological changes.

To the extent that psychological experiences of living are universal in the human life span, developmental restructuring can and does occur, predictably, throughout adulthood. In the transition from young adulthood to established adulthood it is life experience, not physiological change, that interacts with the total organism to produce those qualitative changes necessary to structure a different kind of developmental potential.

The effect of life experience at this transitional period is to help young adults move from a sense of capability to an awareness of their own effectiveness. One of the most consistent differences my students find when they compare young adults with established adults has to do with the impact of experience. Using both self-report and indirect-observation measures, they find that the experience of continued effectiveness in everyday living (holding a job, maintaining relationships) acts as an organizing principle in structuring self-concept, buttressing convictions, and enhancing a sense of personal solidity. These features seem to be present even when the individual's experiences have not been especially happy or successful. Compared to young adults, established adults have a better sense of what can be done that comes from feeling that they have done it. When asked what age he would most like to be, a 34-year-old research analyst answered: "I can only be where I am—it's important to realize where you are. If I were younger, I wouldn't have experienced what I have . . . . My answer probably would be different. [How?] I would want to relive it and do better."

A 25-year-old professional athlete, accomplished though he was in a skilled career, nevertheless reflected both the newness of his world experience and his anticipation that what lay ahead would be the main arena of his life's activities. He answered the same question as follows: "Twenty-five. I have enjoyed this more than any other age. I feel physically at my strongest and ready and capable to take on new things. I feel young and strong and happy. This represents a beginning. I'm optimistic about the future."

In this illustrative comparison the established adult reflects holistically on what experience has taught him about where he is in the world. The young adult seems more attuned to self-particularizing and feeling ready to encounter life's experiences. Despite his demonstrated career competence in a difficult field, his thoughts center on his readiness—not his achievements.

Circumscribed Concerns

Given free rein, the young adult would change the world. Given the same opportunities, the established adult would keep it functioning. This distinction highlights another of the qualitative differences between the two life stages. The established stage marks full-scale entry into the adult world. Of all the life stages no group bears as much the burden of responsibility of societal membership and maintenance. The work of fostering the growth of the young; taking over for aging parents; providing for the economic well-being of the social unit (family, village, clan); ensuring physical protection of members; sustaining the group's cultural integrity; presenting a model for social emulation: these are the tasks of established adults, both male and female. Is it any wonder that there is a contraction of concern?

At first blush the retraction from idealism may seem like a reversion to adolescent narcissism. The young-adult interest in larger social purposes seems to give way to deepened involvement with everyday economics and an almost exclusive concern with providing for the immediate primary group. It often appears that the adolescent's preoccupation with self has been extended one notch in established adulthood to a preoccupation with one's closest social contacts: spouse, children, parents, self. But closer inspection reveals that the energy is directed outward—a concern for affecting others. In adolescence the concern is that of being sustained psychologically by others. Established adults are the primary sustainers and providers of their social system.

The transition from young to established adulthood, therefore, entails a tradeoff between an expansion of real power in the social world and a circumscribing of scope to more immediate responsibility for one's own primary group. On another plane the transition is a movement from the periphery of adult society to its interior. Thus, the restriction in breadth of concern is accompanied by an intensification of concern within narrowed boundaries. Immediate pragmatic necessities come into priority focus, and more abstract values recede into the background. Responsibilities take the place of exploratory ventures. A sense of authority replaces the feeling of disenfranchisement.

This kind of focusing augments the sharpening of sociocultural knowledge and skill. Established adults become expert in knowing and applying the customs, rules, expectations, and social patterns of their culture. They model the cultural patterns and traditions in their own

attitudes and behavior. Because they are the primary caretakers of their society, they serve as living examples to the young. Consequently, they become both the deliberate and inadvertent transmitters of culture to the next generation.

The skills and politics of social interaction also come to the fore in established adulthood. This involves learning the more subtle ways of showing respect and exercising influence. Established adults understand and use the formal and informal channels of communication within the social network. This process is not simply a matter of learning the do's and don'ts of one's culture. Long before established adulthood, the members of a society are educated to know what various behaviors signify—for example, the differences in the way one addresses elders, children, or peers. But in established adulthood there is an assimilation and acceptance of what has previously been learned. During earlier periods of life it is common for patterns of social behavior to be accommodated automatically, in conformity with cultural expectations. But later on, questioning, criticism, or resistance to conventional authority may occur. In young adulthood acceptance or rejection of customs occurs selectively, as people test out how they can affect their world. Idealism may be suppressed, but it is not absent. The potential for outrage is never more than one defense away.

For established adults, results justify methods. Ideology has lost much of the power it exercised during adolescence and young adulthood. The burdens of responsibility—or the taste of authority—make practical outcomes, not the ethics of method, the primary consideration. But above all else, the deepening of involvement in the everyday world—the acknowledgement that one's destiny is inseparable from the fate of that world—necessitates a deepening commitment to learning its ways and managing a pathway in that world.

In virtually every society and in every era of history, the day-to-day managers have had the widest array of social contact: with elders and parents, with peers, with children; with males and females; at different degrees of intimacy and distance; under socially proscibed conditions as well as informal contact. Productive interaction—even sheer survival— has depended on the knowledge and skill the person could bring to bear on each such situation. And these situations occur dozens of times daily! Thus, the need for day-in, day-out efficiency over a multiplicity of tasks, functions, and interactions is what most characterizes the psychological demands on established adults.

The practiced skills of daily living, making the culture work, maintaining a core of stability—this is what established adulthood is about. In our own country it has been instructive to watch the evolution of social protesters who were young adults in the 1960s. Some of those who vociferously exposed the flaws of the political system have now entered politics as a way of making it function better. Many others have decentralized their dissatisfactions and have refocused their energies on local projects, such as improving neighborhoods and working for state consumer groups. Still others have entered the business world, bringing with them a sense of social responsibility and personal commitment that show signs of modifying the traditional climate of corporate enterprise.

The shift in focus of expression from the ideology of outrageous idealism in young adulthood to allocentric effectuation in established adulthood can perhaps be illustrated by people such as Mario Savio and Raymond Mungo. Savio spearheaded the Berkeley Free Speech Movement in 1964, challenging basic issues in higher education. In 1977 he was found working for a tenants' association in a California city. In 1967 Mungo jolted national leaders by publishing a front-page editorial in the *Boston University News* calling for the impeachment of President Lyndon B. Johnson over the war in Vietnam. In 1978 Mungo was a publisher and author of a book on counterculture businesses. Far from turning into apathy—as some critics have charged—the idealism of young adulthood may well have been filtered into the functionalism of established adulthood.

PERSONALITY DEVELOPMENT FROM ADOLESCENCE THROUGH ESTABLISHED ADULTHOOD

As information accumulates about the several life stages, it also sheds light on the flow of personality development across the life span. Examining the transition from one stage to the next helps to elucidate where development is continuous, where it seems discontinuous, and where there are major gaps in present thinking.

The data from these three adjacent life stages cover the critical periods surrounding entry into adult life. In the aggregate, adolescence, young adulthood, and established adulthood encompass between one-third and one-half of the human life cycle. The identification of growth dimensions over so large a span of time can thus add appreciably to our understanding of the course of human developmental history. The pres-

ent data permit a discussion of the dimensions of self-construct development, self/world interaction, interpersonal evolution, ideological change, and energy vectors. Some dimensions of personality development in later adulthood, such as disengagement (Cumming & Henry, 1961) may have little relevance for a time of life when the person is making entry into the world. Other dimensions, such as ideological evolution, may not have the salience in the rest of the life span that they exhibit during the three stages covered by this analysis.

The dimensions identified in the present examination of interstage transitions—self-construct development, self/world interaction, interpersonal evolution, ideological change, and energy vectors—cover some of the central aspects of adult development. We now proceed to a review of these central aspects, during the period of transition from adolescence through young adulthood and into established adulthood.

Self-Construct Development

Following from the intrapsychic disruptions of the adolescent identity crisis, a global reorganization seems to take place that is the first phase of identity formation. This is succeeded by a period of differentiation, called self-particularization, which allows for a new definition and identification of the content of the self. The process of organizing and articulating these parts relative to the whole is ego integration. Achievement of this level of integrity and wholeness at the core of personality constitutes a landmark of restructuring. All aspects of the personality can be better coordinated, more organized, and function more effectively. The level of effectuation achieved by the established adult must in some significant way be proportional to the degree of ego integration he or she achieves. The feedback of experiential data from the environment continues to affect and modify ongoing processes of self-particularization and ego integration. These further elaborations of the self-construct then provide new resources for continued or expanded effectuation. And thus it is that ego growth continues for as long as these reciprocal processes are operational.

These changes, from identity disruption through redefinition and reorganization and culminating in a self-construct that permits effective performance, describe a process that is probably necessary for human development in any cultural context. From the perspective of life-span psychology, these developments in self-construct are critical. They condi-

tion the transition from child to adult, from early personality formation to the structure that undergirds the rest of the adult life span.

Self/World Interaction

The self/world interaction can be conceptualized as a dialectical tension between narcissism and reality-testing, between self-centering and world centering. The narcissism of adolescence reflects the intrapsychic distress inherent to that stage's developmental turmoil. Contact with the world is tentative and is geared largely to recruiting whatever support and reassurance can be marshaled from the world, short of recreating the dependence of childhood. Yet the shift of allegiance from parents to peers is an important qualitative change in restructuring the reality component of interacting with the world. It is developmentally necessary for there to be an expansion of awareness of one's relevant environmental boundaries.

With entry into the world comes entry into young adulthood. There is increasing world awareness and a readiness to be actively involved, committed to participation. But the orientation is largely that of one on the periphery, still a relative outsider. From that vantage point the flaws and opportunities of the society are what is most visible. It is to these that the young adult gravitates, eager to grapple and make impact. But accurate reality testing and narcissistic needs for self-expression conspire to produce a world view which is typically at odds with that held by the power structure of the society. The cultural mandate has to do with serving the society's physical survival needs. These focus in founding a family and providing for it, but they may also include guarding and protecting the system. Thus, the self/world interaction of young adults is commonly characterized by an involvement fraught with frustration and disillusionment. For those people who avert disappointment by automatic compliance with social expectations, the consequences may be delayed until mid-life or middle age. Too often the compliance of young adulthood is paid for with crisis in later years.

Established adulthood is marked by full-scale entry into the world. Efficient, effective participation in maintaining the society is the hallmark of this period. But underlying this successful adaptation is a next developmental step in self/world orientation, an allocentric frame of reference. The values and goals of the society have been accurately perceived and internalized. Personal goals and values have been accommodated to correspond with—or at least not contradict—those of the

society. Participation in the power and authority structure of the culture is initiated.

Interpersonal Relationships

The evolution of human relationships is of vast significance throughout the life span. Human development is intricately enmeshed with interpersonal experience. The classic studies of Ribble (1947) and Spitz (1946) have dramatically demonstrated the impact of early parenting experience on the respiration and survival behavior of infants. Ribble found that infant breathing was improved by physical contact with the mother. Spitz observed head banging and apathetic withdrawal among infants in a foundling home. More recently, Kernberg (1972) and Kohut (1971) have attempted to relate interpersonal experience in childhood to borderline personality structure in adulthood.

But important interpersonal experiences are inherent to every stage of development, not only those of infancy and childhood. What is learned and applied in human relationships from adolescence through established adulthood has a determining influence on the most fundamental and far-reaching features of human performance. The critical process of shifting focus from the nuclear family to one's peers takes place over these three life stages. The transition in social self-concept from child to adult to partner to parent must also be negotiated during this period. But those developmental steps in sense of self can occur only when there has been a restructuring of interpersonal relationships. The way significant people are encountered and the recognition from them thus engendered are vital ingredients in this process.

In adolescence the psychological weakening of ties to parents takes shape as a developmental task. Peer standards and sexual interests exercise a powerful attractive force, pulling the adolescent from the orbit of family domination toward alternative influences. This emerging arena of peer influence brings its own set of expectations, rewards, and performance criteria.

The transition to young adulthood focuses even more attention on peer relations, as their quality becomes progressively more differentiated. Distinguishing between affiliation and affection or between assertiveness and anger ensures a more mature interaction with other people. Intergenerational relationships, especially those with parents are significantly modified. The perspective and psychological distance that have been acquired influence how one's parents are now perceived. Older,

deeply ingrained patterns of perception and response still remain, or atrophy slowly. But now they must compete with other, often dissonant, ways of perceiving and responding.

The aggregate effects of moving into the peer world and establishing a different style of relating, of evolving a more differentiated understanding of interpersonal relations, and of achieving sexual maturation and experience, all assure that relations with parents have been permanently altered.

As the developmental process continues from young adult to established adult, the interpersonal transition becomes even more clearly delineated and the cycle from succorance to nurturance is completed. The established adult's interpersonal world is one of providing for others. In some cases this entails being the "parent" of one's own aging or infirm parents. Remnants of childhood perceptions of parents (including unfulfilled needs and fantasies) may nevertheless persist and influence behavior throughout the life span (Friday, 1977). Adults, even mature adults, rarely give up all their childhood fantasies and expectations.

Ideology

One of the more fascinating products of the study of psychological development over the adult years has been the serendipitous discovery of systematic changes in ideology. The conceptualization of social needs and aspirations undergoes a sequence of changes that appears to transcend culture and history. Before adolescence and after established adulthood there may be other developmental changes in ideology, but that is beyond the scope of this book. Sources as far back as classical antiquity contrast the idealism of the young with the realism of adults. But only as modern investigators have identified the successive stages of the life cycle has the transformation been seen as an evolutionary process.

In adolescence the logical juxtaposing of ideas encounters the development of a metaphysical awareness of values and goals. According to Adelson and O'Neil (1966), adolescence "allows the birth of ideology." The character of that ideology I have described as an abstract, moralistic idealism. As such, it goes beyond the concrete, reward-and-punishment orientation of childhood. If the ideational level is simplistic in its good/ bad dualism (Perry, 1970), it nevertheless represents an advance developmentally.

However, it remains for young adulthood to provide the motive

force that transforms belief into conviction, concept into action. What makes young adults' idealism outrageous is that they seek to implement ideology, converting ideas into behavior. The advent of relativism in structuring of thought permits greater flexibility. Hence, it becomes more feasible to adapt ideology to pragmatic implementation. Thus, the ideological transition from adolescence to young adulthood entails a modulation of idealism.

Transition to established adulthood brings with it further ideological changes. The responsibilities of front-line participation in sustaining the culture—maintaining and nurturing a family, tribe, or clan—gradually educate one to the complexity of society. Being responsible for the day-to-day survival of the culture distracts one from concerns for social betterment, equal rights, or other worthy causes. Functionalism supplants idealism as the dominant ideological theme.

Energy Vectors

People typically distribute their efforts in a variety of endeavors. With ego development more and more effort comes under organized, volitional control. Major pathways of energy expenditure can be identified. These pathways, or vectors, are characterized by the amount and direction of effort that is focused and utilized. It may be possible to chart the major energy vectors in each life stage, as well as across life stages.

The locus of energy distribution, viewed across the three life stages we have been comparing, seems to follow an erratic path. In adolescence the dominant energy vector is self-directed, narcissistic. In young adulthood energy vectors are directed outward in attempts to engage and affect the world. Although energy tends to be invested in specific tasks such as finding a mate, its goal is typically of much greater scope, such as implementing a life plan. Thus the young adult's entry into the world restructures the flow of psychic energies from the self to the environment. Issues previously conceived as residing within the self are more likely to be perceived as tasks to be encountered in the world.

The advent of established adulthood is marked by a deepened and more differentiated investment of energy in the world. Finding a mate means less relative to life plan but more relative to self-support, parenting, and handling the daily problems of living. Spreading the investment of energy over a wider variety of small targets probably has the net effect of diluting personal impact on any single objective. At the same time, it

probably multiplies the likelihood of achieving tangible outcome from at least some of those efforts. Everyday projects yield results more readily than global enterprises, after all.

PROBLEMS OF TRANSITION

As we have seen, change is the law of life; nothing in human structure or function is static. Yet it is equally true that human nature over most of the life span is essentially conservative; people prefer to retain what is familiar and to resist change. The result is homeostatic tension, which allows for gradual changes and only rarely accommodates abrupt transitions. Yet the facts of biological and cultural life regularly impose an awareness that developmental evolution is proceeding at a pace not of the person's own choosing.

Developmental Crises

I have elsewhere (1977) described the escalation of these tensions of transition. It has been found useful to consider them

as *developmental crises*. Whatever other origins or issues may be identified, a significant number of adult problems can be usefully conceptualized as results of the person's (usually) adverse encounter with one or more aspects of the developmental imperative. It is possible to classify several kinds of developmental crisis:

    a. Fear of an impending life stage. The person sees forthcoming changes as threatening, frightening, damaging. Examples include fear of death as one enters senescent adulthood or fear of the demands of parenting as one concludes the young adult stage.

    b. Reluctance to leave a gratifying stage. It is not uncommon for anxiety, depression, or feelings of loss to be precipitated by an awareness that one can no longer continue as one has, that one has outgrown a period that brought satisfaction or security. Birthdays, anniversaries, and some holidays put people in touch with the passage of time. Letting go of the familiar satisfactions of college for an uncertain future (and, incidentally, having to acknowledge one's adulthood) provides a common example of this issue.

    c. Trauma of unexpected developmental demands. For some people the advent of an awaited developmental phenomenon brings with it unexpected and unpleasant side effects. The homemaker's anticipated liberation from the demands of parenting may be deadened by loneliness and the sound of an empty house. As a general feature of development, any increase in freedom and

autonomy is usually accompanied by a dystonic sense of personal isolation and responsibility.

   d. Unresolved earlier issues. To the extent that one meets cultural expectations of appropriate role behavior it is possible to obscure, even to oneself, the psychological challenge of development. Having attained sexual competence may present the appearance but lack the substance of being capable of intimacy, love, sharing. One's evolution into a committed relationship such as marriage may provide the person his/her first real confrontation with vital developmental issues heretofore skirted or avoided.

   e. Cumulative erosion of energies. Sometimes the sheer energy investment necessary to meet a developmental demand may cause a breakdown of function. Usually this occurs in people who have encountered difficulty in previous periods, or who otherwise find their psychic resources depleted at the time of a new demand. One more bill to be paid, another pregnancy, additional work responsibility—any further strain on a psychic system already extended to its limit can precipitate one of the more serious developmental crises.

   f. Positive growth experience. Some adults come to experience a satisfaction in living that calls to their attention characteristics or conditions that inhibit further self-actualization. It may be an exogenous condition (e.g., a stultifying job or marriage) or an endogenous characteristic (inhibition of emotional expression). Either way, their general level of satisfaction serves to highlight by contrast areas of relative dissatisfaction in their lives [p. 91. From "A Developmental Approach to Counseling Adults," by G. Bocknek. In N. K. Schlossberg and A. D. Entine (Eds.), *Counseling Adults.* Copyright © 1977 by Wadsworth, Inc. Reprinted by permission of the publisher, Brooks/Cole Publishing Company, Monterey, California].

Identity Foreclosure

A more subtle and pervasive problem comes from a "noncrisis," when the person successfully averts the tension and challenge of transition through the identity crisis. This method of coping with the evolution from adolescence to young adulthood is called identity foreclosure. As elucidated by Marcia (1966), foreclosure occurs when the developing person accedes to demands (or rewards!) by meeting certain role expectations rather than pressing toward continued growth of self. In return for adapting to the cultural—or subcultural—mold, one receives praise, acceptance, a secure place. Marcia (1966, 1967) describes identity foreclosers as obedient, approval-oriented individuals. They accept the role

laid out by others (commonly parents) as their identity. Foreclosure protects the person from doubt and anxiety at the cost of personal growth. One example is a young adult who reluctantly accepts a secure job in the family business rather than pursuing a long-standing interest in marine biology. Another is a married woman who adopts the stereotypic role of full-time housewife urged by her family rather than following her inclination to work in a retail business.

Such choices are everyday occurrences and can hardly be said to indicate psychopathology. But in subtly significant ways they may well lead to a blunting of personality. Davidson (1978), for instance, found evidence of less ego differentiation among identity-foreclosed college students compared with peers who had achieved some resolution of the identity crisis. The apparent ubiquity of foreclosure in a majority of post-high school North Americans (Trent & Medsker, 1969) is discouragingly supplemented by the research of Golden and his colleagues (1967), who studied 50 "normal" White males. Using unusually dependable, long-term criteria of freedom from psychopathology, they found these well-adapted people "to have little imagination and generally limited interests and social activities. They indicate limited educational and vocational aspirations for themselves, and also for their children" (p. 34).

To attempt to chronicle further the hazards of developmental transition would require an extensively detailed exposition of the focal issues at each stage. It would also necessitate a discussion of psychopathology and extend beyond the scope of this book. Wittenberg (1968) and Hanfmann (1978) deal with clinical aspects of the transition from adolescence to young adulthood. In general, there is a clinical truism that holds up well to the test of experience: the more unresolved developmental issues, the greater the likelihood that psychopathology will erupt.

Developmental changes usually equip people to function better relative to their location in the life span. People who have not successfully negotiated developmental transitions find themselves increasingly unsynchronized with their own chronological age.

DEVELOPMENTAL OPPORTUNITIES

On the other side of the coin, the developmental process provides important opportunities for reparative growth. The internal changes mandated by the developmental imperative equip people with new resources for tackling old problems.

Resolving Old Issues

One form of opportunity occurs when newly evolved psychological competencies enable people to return to earlier developmental issues that had been incompletely addressed. Jill was a shy, isolated teenager. She was tall, heavy, and plain looking. Throughout childhood she had been teased by classmates. Her adolescence was spent almost exclusively in school-work and playing the cornet. Social contact with peers was confined to impersonal "shop talk" with people who had similar interests. Gradually she achieved a positive sense of identity as an accomplished amateur musician with a satisfying career. Armored with this area of competence, she began to notice people around her and became aware that she was avoiding them—that they did not shun her. Coworkers responded to her when she offered conversations. Gradually she was able to enter into social relationships and to develop a few close friends.

In this instance, the interpersonal focus of adolescence—peer relations—had barely begun well into young adulthood. Her transition from adolescence had been based on an identity as an unattractive, unpopular person. Self-particularization allowed Jill to identify her vocational competence and musical talent. As these facets of her personality were integrated into her self-concept, her capacity for personal perspective enabled her to value herself more. She was also able to observe that peers did not reject her. Indeed, as she took steps to move into her social environment, her peers responded favorably to her. The developmental acquisitions of young adulthood in the intrapsychic and intracultural areas empowered Jill to return to some of the interpersonal issues of adolescence that she had not resolved.

Applying Life's Experiences

A second form of opportunity occurs when people apply developmental learning across generations. This occurs most frequently in parenting, although it can be manifested in many facets of people's style of living.

Most people live out the life cycle more than once: we live vicariously through our observations of others. As we go through the experiences of infancy and childhood, we learn how mothers, fathers, and grandparents (old people) act. Matings, births, working, and dying are played out by others close by while we observe as avid spectators. Witnessing these activities conditions our own expectations of what life is

about for ourselves. As we age and enter the appropriate life-span periods of our culture, we in turn mate, become parents, work, and die. But how we go about these life tasks is significantly influenced by our prior experiences with them.

At the most fundamental level, most of what we know of social-role behavior we learn from modeling. Consciously and unconsciously, intentionally and inadvertently, we learn by identification with and imitation of the significant figures around us. Throughout childhood and most of adolescence, what is right and proper may be indistinguishable from what is available and familiar. With young adulthood comes the capacity for personal perspective. That ability to observe themselves allows people to function as both director and chief performer in the enactment of their own life drama. Whether it is political belief or propensity for physical violence, the most powerful influence on adult behavior is childhood memories. But when that standard is unacceptable, conditions are ripe for change, and a revised pattern of attitudes and behavior may ensue. Either way, whether behavior conforms to or differs from childhood recollection, the opportunity exists to modify, extend, or repair one's own developmental experience. The reviewing of one's own experience from an adult perspective offers at least the possibility of affecting one's conduct.

To summarize, transitions only dramatize the essential nature of the developmental process, which is one of continuous change. Nevertheless, that experience manages to accommodate such discontinuous changes as a reversal in direction of energy vectors and the capacity to radically alter previously learned behavior patterns. The more dramatic impact of transitional phases may precipitate developmental crises. Changes can be used beneficially to modify or repair earlier inadequacies of the evolutionary experience. Or they can focus attention on current areas of difficulty in the ongoing life process.

11

SOME REFLECTIONS

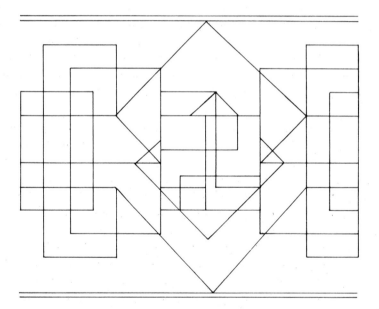

SUMMING UP

The young-adult stage is exciting and satisfying, an entry into the major life period. Yet it is also characterized by disillusionment (Rappoport, 1972) and depression (Symonds, 1961). Young adulthood is a time when one's idealism encounters painful conflict with routine self-interests. In addition, the pressures to meet social expectations inexorably wear down one's tendencies to contribute more globally. And there is a dissonance between self as perceived and self as socially recognized. We have described the young adult as the most disenfranchised of adults, experiencing self as grown yet encouraged by society to think and act as a "superteen." Thus, the person is confronted continuously with the paradox of living in a highly desirable life period yet being chronically disappointed over unfulfilled aspirations. Small wonder that this is a time when people often seek psychological help.

Happily, it is also a period when the prognosis for successful intervention is at its most favorable. Precisely because of their developmentally acquired assets, young adults are well positioned to use various types of counseling and therapy. These assets include confidence and a readiness to explore, a sense of identity, and a *sens de pouvoir.* By virtue of their capacity for personal perspective, young adults are also better able to gain insight into whatever pernicious effects social and environmental pressures may be imposing on them.

One of the most important distinctions I have tried to make is between the adolescent and young-adult life stages. They share overt behavioral similarities that lead much of society to blend them into one period of "youth." Yet they show psychological distinctions clearly indicating that the teenager is much more a child and that the young adult has passed through a vital transition into the adult domain of functioning. To the extent that adults are the decision makers and bear the burdens of a society, our own culture is shortchanging itself by failing to make this meaningful distinction.

EXPLORATION

Because the young-adult life period is still a relatively new area of study, its broad implications are not well understood. This concluding chapter will attempt to place young adulthood in a larger context.

A summarizing chapter would imply a sense of closure; however, my intention is to underscore the need for exploring young adulthood.

What follows, therefore, is a series of reflections and not a set of conclusions. Under the cover of reflecting I have ventured further afield—into social history and cultural influence—than might otherwise be justified. But these meanderings are not frivolous; the intentions behind them are quite serious. I invite you to explore them with me.

There are two sections in this chapter. The first explores the interaction between young adults and society. The social context of and the confusion between the designations *youth* and *young adult* will be examined. The largest part of this section will be devoted to the impact—historic and potential—of young adults *on* society. For me, this is one of the more important aspects of the book.

The second section raises a number of research questions. These concern the accuracy and generalizability of my findings, the relevance of longitudinal research to data on life stages, and the relationship between culture and development as they affect the study of young adulthood.

YOUTH AND YOUNG ADULTHOOD

The theoretical literature dealing with the impact of young adults on society is replete with confusion. Primarily, there is a lack of consensus on what is meant by the several labels of *youth, young people, adolescent,* and *young adult*. Those writers who use chronological age describe adolescence as anywhere from 12 to 30, depending on the particular author. Young adulthood is located anywhere from 18 to 35. Youth can be from 10 to 30. Conventional distinctions in North American society tend to locate adolescence in the teens and young adulthood in the 20s. Other investigators do not indicate how they differentiate among young people. In some instances it is unclear whether any differentiation is actually made.

Thus, Bettelheim (1965) interprets the intergenerational conflict and dissent of "youth" as a manifestation of the Oedipal complex displaced onto the world scene. "Youth" protests are viewed as ways of living out the unresolved Oedipal components of adolescent development. Feuer (1969) ascribes dissent to a more primitive archetype of adolescent rebellion. In one large sweep he incorporates both the local and international protest of the 1960s as a reversion to primal-horde behavior. His thesis is that the antiwar demonstrations and college takeovers of that period were analogous to the sons' attempt to wrest power from the patriarchal leader.

These writers share a belief that dissent in young people lacks substantive content, that it is to be understood psychodynamically as the turmoil of adolescence. Yet neither author indicates how he determined that the dissenters in several countries were all adolescents or, in fact, were dealing with unresolved adolescent problems. In actuality, a number of on-site studies (for example, see Trimberger, 1968) reported that student protest leaders tended to be postadolescent teaching fellows who were "moderate and legitimate student leaders." Dissent and dispute over campus procedures and the Vietnam War were critical and substantive issues for many dissenters of that period.

An alternative approach is reflected in the writings of Keniston (1965) and Erikson (1970). For Keniston, the term *youth* refers to a special group of postadolescents. They are located typically in Eastern, private, liberal-arts universities. They come from predominantly White, upper-middle-class backgrounds. He conceptualizes youth as a discrete life stage, but one that is severely constrained by geography and socioeconomic status. Erikson imposes no such limitations. He also speaks of "youth" but seems to refer to aspects of late adolescence that extend into an undefined later period. The qualities of youth Keniston and Erikson identify are idealism, ethics, activist energy, and a capacity for moral leadership.

What most writers who describe youth identify is a short-term action orientation, an ahistoric approach to experience, and the rhetoric of idealism. However, few investigators take cognizance of the data indicating that there are important developmental differences within the population called youth. The justification for invoking a youth life stage depends heavily on phenotypic role behavior. In this sense *youth* could be considered a sociocultural life stage—along with parenthood, the "empty nest," and retirement. But this is quite different from an approach to psychological development that addresses the evolution of genotypic, intrapsychic processes.

Social Impact of Young Adults

Bits and pieces of evidence are available throughout history and across cultures of the characteristic contributions young adults make to their society. From the first marathon runner at Thermopylae to the Warsaw ghetto uprising, this impact has been felt. However, the post–World War II opening up and restructuring of society around the world has set the stage for young adults to affect culture in historic ways and

proportions. Thus, a recapitulation of the recent era can perhaps better exemplify the distinctive contributions made by young adults.

A companion phenomenon of the period since 1945 has been the incredible explosion of technological knowledge. The awesome and dehumanizing implications of that revolution have been highlighted in books such as Orwell's *1984*. The threat of technocracy becomes ever more real as machines and systems challenge their creators to devise ways in which to optimize control over them. Industrialized societies find themselves increasingly bureaucratized, classified, regimented, isolated, and restricted.

Young adults have been in the forefront of the reaction against these encroachments. Their initiatives have taken the form of expanding sensory experience and enhancing human worth. To these efforts they have brought the qualities distinctive of their life stage—innovativeness, activism, outrageous idealism, sense of capability, world consciousness, and a reservoir of confidence.

Expansion of Sensory Experience

The objective, impersonal, and coldly logical approach of the machine and the bureaucratic organization have stimulated a counter-emphasis on personal and private experience. This reaction includes a deepening awareness of one's own emotions, an examination of the nonrational and mystical, and a movement toward experiencing pleasure, personal achievement, and affective expression. This has manifested itself in many forms, most of which have had immediate aversive impact on the larger society.

Drug use. One form this reaction has taken is the use of drugs. There is an ironic twist here. Although community reaction has been punitive, people have always relied on stimulants and inhibitants to mitigate the pain and stress of daily existence. Beer, wine, peyote, and betel are as old as civilization. Yet the same people who abominate marijuana typically consume daily quotas of tobacco, coffee, alcoholic beverages, and a dazzling array of other "soothing medications." Meanwhile, evidence mounts for the social and medical utility of the ingredients contained in cannabis and lysergic acid. Marijuana is demonstrably less toxic than alcohol, tobacco, or morphine, whether it is used as a social facilitant or to relieve the suffering of terminally ill patients. LSD is a traditional psycho-therapeutic aid in European psychiatry.

In the post–Korean War period, the use of marijuana, hashish, LSD, and mescaline had as their purpose not avoidance but expansion of awareness into new dimensions of conscious experience. Governments that profit from covertly permitting drug traffic in heroin piously retain harsh laws against marijuana. It is unfortunate that so little has been done to clarify and publicize the distinction between the consciousness-expanding use of mild forms of hallucinogens, compared with the pathological and escapist use of heroin, barbiturates, and amphetamines. Nevertheless, despite international efforts to repress its production, distribution, and use, marijuana gains increasing acceptance across the broad spectrum of society.

Music. In another area of social impact, the preferences of young people have produced a musical renaissance. The advent of musicians developing new rhythmic varieties—who are both performers of high caliber and composers of note and distinction—is a phenomenon not witnessed on this scope in a century or more. Even more remarkable is the seeming preponderance of young adults in the creation of these musical forms.

Sex. Sexuality has undergone what must legitimately be termed a revolution. Wars traditionally weaken sexual restraints, especially among young adults, who are the cannon fodder. The period since World War II has witnessed the devaluation of virginity and the popularization of casual sex. Sex for pleasure has acquired much of the public acceptance once reserved to sex for procreation. Personal interest in abortion and birth control has resonated with global concerns for population control. The reverberations from this revolution will undoubtedly continue across the planet into the 21st century.

At the level of human interaction, sexual freedom has had ramifications well beyond the bed. Throughout the Western world, but especially in the United States, all relationships between the sexes have become more open. The demystification of virginity symbolizes the changes in the customs and perceptions that have governed relations between men and women. What some social critics call moral degeneration others view as evidence of a new age of sociosexual enlightenment. Relaxation of the double standard of sexual behavior has reopened questions about what is appropriate sexual behavior. The research of Masters and Johnson (1966, 1970) shattered established beliefs about the nature of orgasm. And a

number of authors (such as Comfort, 1972) have published manuals that teach the pursuit of sexual pleasure for both men and women.

Bringing sex out of the closet has opened the door to reconsideration of more fundamental issues, such as choice of sexual partner and gender identity. The study of homosexuality and transsexualism indicates how much remains unknown about gender development and object choice (Money & Ehrhardt, 1972). Thus, the sexual revolution precipitated by young adults has led to a searching inquiry into sexuality and the nature of sexual identity development.

Color. Another form of sensory expansion has been the explosion in the use of color. Color stimulates emotionality, and it is no accident that the most dazzling of greens, yellow, blues, reds, and oranges have enjoyed the greatest popularity. Brilliant colors have found their way into architecture, furniture, cars, and clothing. Vivid color combinations that were previously considered unacceptable, pigments and hues previously unavailable—all have been mobilized into a visual assault comparable only to the auditory impact of popular music groups with their improbable names. The deliberate use of contrast and incongruity is clearly intended to intensify the sheer power of the sensory experience.

Nonrational experience. It is in this context that one can legitimately combine ventures into witchcraft and magic with renewed interest in psychic research. They find common ground as part of a general quest into a different kind and dimension of experience. It is precisely the nonrational, illogical, experiential character of these areas that makes them so attractive. One benefit is an increasing awareness of well-established scientific data that heretofore have lain on back shelves, more because of public scepticism than lack of verification. Ample data already exist to indicate the legitimacy of such phenomena as extrasensory perception, psychokinesis, telepathic transmissions, and a variety of other so-called psychic events. In a similar vein, astrology and extra-terrestial events have attracted wider attention.

In the broad field of psychological services, a comparable trend has been in evidence. Eschewing traditional psychotherapists, young adults have increasingly supported nonintellectual, experience-centered approaches as varied as Gestalt therapy, primal scream, encounter groups, and meditation. Health and growth now command as much interest among young and established adults as does treatment.

Chapter 11

Focus on Human Worth

A cliché phrase of the 1960s was "Do your own thing." In its sociohistoric context this can be understood as a reaction of young adults to the progressive intrusion of computers, automation, and external regulation into private life. "Do your own thing" speaks to the value of the individual's own interest. It is a nonconformist, antiprogrammatic sentiment aimed at supporting the efforts of individuals and groups to differentiate themselves from the conglomerate whole, to affirm their unique worth in an impersonal world.

A second, and more historic, aspect of this movement was its challenging of the melting-pot philosophy of assimilation into the mainstream. The tradition that heterogeneous immigrants should blend together encountered a radically different proposal: that disparate and dissonant components are worthwhile. An offshoot of this emphasis on human worth has been a more visible identification of minority groups and of the oppressive impact of mainstream society on their members.

Minority pride. One early form this movement took was a resurgence of Black nationalism, led typically by young adults such as Stokely Carmichael and Huey Newton. Their focus was on instilling a sense of pride in being Black—a sense of distinctiveness about negritude to counter the notion that the dominant White society possessed the ultimate standards and values. Although the history of Black nationalism goes back to the writings of Marcus Garvey, W. E. B. Du Bois, Langston Hughes, and others, its implementation into a pragmatic mass movement did not occur until the emergence of militant young Blacks. These young adults did not merely accept the virtues of a distinctive style of music, foods, customs, dress, and attitudes. Within the Black community those cultural features were already well known. The contribution of Black nationalism was to publicize and assert the value of Black culture for the nation at large.

American assimilationist philosophy dictated that groups abandon their distinctive qualities and adopt the values of the mainstream society. The Black-nationalist movement insisted on respect and retention of differences, on vindicating the constitutional and social rights of minorities. Black people thus reversed the melting-pot tradition. This has been a historic contribution. It has allowed a slave population of the 19th century to gain fuller social status. It has set a precedent for other social

minorities—ethnic, sexual, and political—to gain access to the mainstream. These people thus experience greater personal worth and also become more effective contributors to the whole society.

One major beneficiary of the Black-nationalist movement has been the women's movement. Feminism, a movement in the United States since the turn of the century, has enjoyed a flourishing reactivation, again under the sponsorship of groups of young adults. These modern feminists argue that women have for too long functioned as an oppressed minority group. In fact, they contend, women have documented their ability to function with intelligence, responsibility, and maturity in a variety of activities and tasks having little to do with the culturally prescribed roles of housekeeper and nursemaid.

One's identification as woman, rather than being a limitation in terms of social function, has been refocused to identify unique and distinctive qualities that are resources of particular talent. For example, Gilligan (1977) notes that women differ from men in valuing human relations over autonomy. The cultural implications are different from those suggested by describing men as independent and women as dependent or by asserting that development proceeds from dependence to independence. Insights gained about the distinctive contributions of women enrich the entire society. If sex differences are inborn, then clearly the distinctive contributions of women and men should be more widely distributed across the society, in industry as well as in parenting.

Eastern thought. Under considerations of human worth should also be included a preoccupation with Eastern meditative philosophies and religions. Distinctive here is the emphasis on individual awareness and private experience as opposed to public performance and ritualistic practice. It is not surprising in light of the other events I have described that there should be an awakened concern with self-exploration. Although some critics view this trend as narcissistic, it does not have as its intention withdrawal from the world. Rather, it is concerned with the exploration of the inner space of the individual. Consequently, an interest in yoga, Zen Buddhism, and other Eastern traditions is consistent with a centering of awareness on the importance of personal experience.

Social revisionism. Another reaction to technology's dehumanizing aspects is *social revisionism,* so called because it is intended to restructure the style and quality of everyday life. Numerous students and workers,

including some of the most talented, have left school or quit attractive jobs. Some chose the voluntary poverty of rural life, behavior that was virtually unintelligible to the mainstream of middle-class thinking. Others brought human values to executive positions in large corporations or helped to staff citizen groups lobbying in the public interest. Those with much to gain from the status quo—intelligent, middle-class Whites— were in the forefront of the movement. The hippies of the '60s found spiritual community with the revisionists of the '70s.

Another feature of this revisionism has been the movement toward *communalism*. Its direction has been away from society's hierarchy and toward the development of small cooperative communities. Those communities function within a self-regulating system of principles, and individual members may enter or leave at their own discretion. Thus, in effect, an alternative social organization was achieved. Depending on the particular commune, it could substitute for a social group, a family, a work organization, or a religious institution.

For one particular social organization—a central structure in the life of many young adults—social revisionism has enforced changes that were resisted for over 1000 years. I am referring to the university. Up to the middle of the 20th century, colleges reserved to themselves the rights and privileges of surrogate parents. This, in effect, established a domicile away from home for young adults in which their lives, both on and off campus, were regulated and determined by an older group of adults. The latter presumably had access to the wisdom of age to guide them in setting up what was best for the enrichment of their charges.

The changes that have occurred in the U. S. college system since the 1950s are revolutionary. Most of them reflect modifications generated by the students themselves, which administrators and boards of trustees only reluctantly acceded to after much difficulty and occasional active insurrection. The hallmark of these changes has been to grant students greater autonomy in their campus lives, to treat them more as adults.

Consumerism. These changes also reflect another new movement, *consumerism*. It maintains that those who are the users of a product or service should have a voice in structuring its content. In the case of higher education, the student consumers were able to make their wishes known with sufficient visibility and strength to enforce changes that many educators had long believed were overdue. These faculty members had argued that in higher education, at least, androgogy—the teaching of

adults—should replace pedagogy (Knowles, 1974). In the public sector of consumerism, young people have once again pioneered in a major area of social reform. Beginning with the leadership of Ralph Nader, numbers of young adults spent large amounts of time investigating and exposing a wide variety of practices designed to deceive or otherwise bilk consumers.

One of the more remarkable facets of this consumer movement has to do with the concern shown in two of the most traditional professions, medicine and law. These fields have increasingly been accused of self-centeredness, of having a primary concern for individual profit rather than social welfare. In recent years young medical students and law clerks have spearheaded notable reform movements within their professions. The former have challenged existing inadequacies in hospital practices. The latter have joined in legal-aid projects to help provide counsel for individuals and groups lacking the resources to take to the courts the injustices they feel they are facing.

On the individual level, young adults have pressed industry to create working hours and conditions more conducive to variable life-style needs. Where it had been typical for only unions to negotiate contracts with management, now both individuals and groups bargain for more flexible working arrangements. Under young-adult pressure the previously immutable 9-to-5 work week has become more flexible.

Naturalism. Perhaps the most prominent general movement has been towards *naturalism* as a reaction to the artificial environment humans have been progressively creating for themselves. A major aspect of this movement has been agrarianism. Rural communities have been established, endeavoring to become economically self-sufficient. Another aspect of this naturalistic direction has been the resurrection of an interest in crafts and skilled trades. Young men and women in various parts of the country are pursuing such arts as weaving, pottery, or leatherwork. Others have opened their own small businesses, featuring such things as motorcycle repair, computer technology, or natural foods.

What characterizes many of these ventures is an abjuring of tradi-. tional work hours, profit levels, worker/boss relationships, and the like. Whether these systems are viable, only time will tell. Suffice it to say that the interest and direction have been toward finding alternative styles to those of the dominant society.

Another area in which naturalism has made itself felt is in the rise of interest in organic farming and foods. Vegetarianism, macrobiotics, and

the concern for growing foods without benefit of chemical fertilizers and insecticides have enjoyed an impressive popularity. This has reflected both a reaction against modern technology and a desire to get back to self-reliant experiences, more wholesome foods, and the holistic styles of living of an earlier period. The energy crisis that surfaced in the 1970s further justified the return to a simpler life-style, oriented to conservation rather than consumption.

Idealistic Expression

Another major social impact has been from idealistic ventures of young adults, the outrageous idealism referred to earlier in the text. In the realm of civil rights the original impetus came from those Black college students who, forcefully but nonviolently, desegregated restaurants and bus stations. They were followed by other young people who also volunteered, literally risking death, to help in voter registration drives. More recently the American Indian Movement has been spearheaded by young adults concerned to protect the rights of their own oppressed minority.

Perhaps no movement was so idealistic and far-flung as the Peace Corps, proposed by the late Senator Hubert H. Humphrey. Once again it was young adults—teachers, carpenters, and students—who offered themselves as a basic resource to alleviate some of the misery to be found throughout the world.

In the areas of pollution and ecology it has also been the young who responded to Rachel Carson's plea (1951) that the world be saved from destroying itself. In local areas this movement has taken the form of recycling campaigns and picketing of industries that seemed unconcerned about environmental consequences. Arousing the community through the formation of consumer boards, action committees, and demonstrations has brought about greater awareness and modification of destructive practices.

Probably the most dramatic of the idealistic movements to gain practical expression in recent years has been political. Here the young people of the United States were virtually responsible for the resignation of President Lyndon B. Johnson by dint of their diligent sponsorship of Senator Eugene McCarthy in the 1968 presidential campaign. The bitter experiences of the Democratic National Convention of 1968 in Chicago—where young people, as usual, were excluded from real participation in nominating a president—were sharply reversed only four years

later in the 1972 convention. Specific quotas were established for the inclusion of minority groups, women, and young people among the voting delegates—a historic event in U. S. politics.

But Governor George Wallace of Alabama, a different sort of figure who symbolized dissatisfaction with the direction of the nation at that time, also attracted a large percentage of young-adult advocates to his cause. Outrageous idealism seemingly can be focused on both political extremes, not just liberal causes. Another illustration of how underlying attitudes influence overt behavior is the refusal by a disproportionate number of young adults to vote at all, even for presumably progressive candidates. For this latter group it would appear that the act of voting itself is seen as a nonfunctional type of behavior. This group insists that the electoral process is ineffectual in reflecting the needs and wishes of the electorate. To vote would mean support of the system. Thus, both voting and nonvoting apparently served as expressions of the same psychological attitude of idealism for two dissimilar groups of young adults.

Probably the most frustrating and demoralizing experience of recent times, particularly as it relates to young people, was the Vietnam War. Almost from the very beginning, young adults opposed by word and by action U. S. involvement in Southeast Asia. Their opposition resulted in all manner of activism, including mass demonstrations, draft dodging, fleeing the country, deserting, and attempting to disrupt the draft system. Young people experienced frustration after frustration over the course of two different presidencies in an effort to end the war. It is by no means coincidental that the legal basis for this war remains problematic and that its very legitimacy (in terms of actual provocation) has since come under critical scrutiny.

I recognize that the examples cited refer to only one culture during one particular time period. Thus, they are vulnerable to the criticism of not being representative of either a particular age group or developmental period. The counter to this argument states that the events in the United States are cited because they are more accessible. There is ample evidence that the same kinds of phenomena have occurred at other times and in other countries. The Hungarian freedom fighters were a coalition of workers and students who attempted to overthrow the Soviet-controlled regime of Janos Kadar in 1953. Much of the other recent active insurrection and terrorism—in Europe, Africa, and Asia—provide evidence of efforts by young adults to alter their society. Moreover, many of

the changes we have referred to in the realm of human worth are not only typical of Western civilization but are also evident across the globe.

To more fully understand the impact of young adults on their own society, one would need to examine the particular cultural context at the time. Imperial Japan was a society in which reverence for ritual and antiquity was paramount. There was no sign before 1945 of dissidence on the part of young people. But it awaited only the opportune circumstances—crushing military defeat, in this instance—to become activated. A not dissimilar set of conditions in post–World War I Germany—economic and political crisis—led to the rise to power of Adolph Hitler. His followers, unemployed "brown shirts," were largely young adults seeking to rekindle personal and national pride, idealistic sentiments that his rhetoric successfully exploited (Shirer, 1960).

Potential for Young-Adult Impact

To consider the implications of young-adult impact, one must extrapolate beyond present data. What might the future hold if young adults and their culture gain the awareness to optimize each other's potential? Young adults can be a unique force for human betterment by utilizing their potential for idealism, vitality, innovation, and social prophesy.

Young adults' qualities. As a repository for idealism, they have no peer among adults. They would be the first to accept as good and sufficient motivation the opportunity to improve the welfare of others or of society in general. They can be an effective counterbalance to the conservatism and narrowed focus that seem to overtake many adults as they get older. To the traditional council of elders young adults bring an enthusiasm for noble causes and the willingness to work for them. In ironic contrast to the common stereotypes of irresponsibility and hedonism is the fact that no greater moral leadership has emerged in recent times than that of young adults. The fields of civil rights, sexual equality, voluntarism, consumerism, participatory democracy, and church reform exemplify, but do not exhaust, areas where young adults have been in the forefront of social progress. Their sense of capability and activistic orientation ensure that, unlike their adolescent siblings, they conceptualize ideals in action terms.

Positioned as they are at the gates of adulthood, young adults are

relatively unencumbered by past frustrations in dealing with society's problems. In addition, they bring the fresh perspective of the newly arrived. Consequently, they have significant potential for contribution in social prophesy. They have little commitment to the past and an eagerness to be part of the present; they come recently equipped with a world consciousness and concern to make a place in their culture. This combination of life circumstances seems to provide young adults with a special ability to sense emergent trends in a society. Their reactions to these observations are dependable harbingers of the impending future. What seasoned adults adapt to by habit, young adults react to as a stimulus. Because they lack the social and political power to dictate policy, their reactions do not determine the future but only anticipate it. But where young adults go, the horizon will soon extend.

Unlike both adolescents and older adults, young adults are amenable to change. The innovative prepotency of young adulthood has important cultural implications.

As Toffler (1970) indicated in *Future Shock,* it has become increasingly necessary for people to live with uncertainty and to face the world with a readiness to change. To be irrevocably committed to any point of view or doctrine is to be in danger of obsolescence or worse. The continuing explosion of knowledge and technique makes radical change a predictable part of the everyday future. No group is better adapted by nature to deal with just such a state of affairs than young adults. As more people experience the obsolescence of traditional sources of moral authority—such as religion and the family—there is an increasing need for new moral leadership. Complex moral and ethical issues arise. Genetic control of future offspring, euthanasia, abortion, the continuing automation of industry, the viability of marriage as an institution—these are some of the impending issues that industrialized nations will need to resolve in the decades ahead. In addition, there are the global problems of population control, food and energy distribution, and prevention of nuclear war.

In earlier periods of history, knowledge accumulated slowly, over generations of experience. Older adults had time-tested wisdom on which to base their judgments. But in a world where knowledge multiplies every decade, it is vital that decision-making be influenced by people who are not committed to past beliefs, some of which are now obsolete. The inclusion of young adults in policymaking levels of the social structure is mandated by more than considerations of ethical justice. It is apparent

that the wisdom of age in and of itself cannot provide the richness and depth necessary to meet the problem-solving tasks that lie ahead. Equally obvious, it seems, is that some combination of historical perspective and positive response to change is vital.

How young adults can lead. Erikson (1970) has forecast a "revolt of the dependent," an upheaval involving those members of society who have been kept—or who exist—in a state of dependence on the mainstream of power and privilege. He refers here to the economically dependent, the poor; the culturally dependent, the minorities; and the developmentally dependent, the young. He points to the fact that of these groups it is primarily the young—the young adults—who have the ethical concern to deal with the issues that lie ahead. In addition, he points out that young adults serve as natural leaders for youth and children. Consequently, with the population of the world increasingly becoming younger, this group has the potential to mobilize the dependent across the globe in the quest for a more equitable share of power and goods. One of the great problems for the future will be to find a way that older adults and young adults can not only come to the same conference table but also learn to profit from what each has to offer the other. The young adults will come as idealists and agitators for change. The older adults will come as more historically wise and attuned to compromise, with a preference for quiescent adaptation rather than progress at the most rapid rate.

All too often the basic conflict between young adults and their elders has not been over goals but over whether they can be implemented and, if so, how soon. For many older adults the burning issue consuming a younger colleague is an old familiar one that they have earlier contended with. To be confronted with the need for once more engaging in the battle may be more than they care to do. More poignantly, perhaps, for some older people it may be a battle in which they all too keenly recall having made important compromises that in turn affected their own moral views. In at least some instances, therefore, the critical question may be the extent to which older adults can tolerate the guilt engendered by their younger colleagues' reawakening issues they have themselves with difficulty suppressed. As Erikson puts it, "To share true authority with the young, however, would mean to acknowledge something that adults distrust in themselves: a truly ethical potential" (1970, p. 21).

This is a time when moral leadership and ethical imperatives are desperately needed, as nations confront the juncture of technology with ethics in a way perhaps never before experienced on this planet. History

records the hesitancy with which existing power structures acknowledge and incorporate newly emerging groups. Entrenched power is conservative, and it is most resistive when pressed to share its authority. Yet history also reveals that traditional approaches are most vulnerable to failure during periods of rapid change. The response of established power to the challenge to incorporate new groups within the policymaking body may well dictate the future course of world events.

In the case of young adults, what is at issue is the willingness of older generations to enfranchise as peers a generation rarely acknowledged to be adult. People need recognition, and they are susceptible to social definition as a means of self-definition. Young adults treated as less-than-responsible "youth" tend to live out the social role prescribed for them. Both young adults and their older peers need to recognize and nurture this reservoir of innovative potential if it is to be exploited successfully. Developmental proclivity in no way guarantees potentiation. It is thus vital that both young adults and their elders become sensitized to the opportunities that do exist for broadening the councils of policymaking if we are to witness maximum progress for humankind in the years ahead.

BROAD RESEARCH ISSUES

I should perhaps apologize to you for having indulged in what must seem a theoretical tirade in a book designed to be a dispassionate coverage of a significant period of life. The events and the stakes involved are my justification for such a digression. To return to a more scientific stance of inquiry, a number of issues deserve much further explanation and clarification.

How Valid Are the Findings?

Primary among these is the need to test the theoretical constructs offered here for their accuracy, universality, viability, and irreversibility. The data presented—as noted earlier—possess some empirical justification, a good deal of clinical validity, and experiential grounding. Nevertheless, legitimate questions can be raised about the precision with which these processes have been defined and explicated. When one speaks of idealism or innovativeness, are these the actual characteristics and features that are being distinguished. Or are there more basic or more subtle processes that as yet have eluded recognition? To what extent are the observations truly universal?

A developmental theory purports to be measuring human nature and human function independently of time and culture. That is, these events, these processes, are asserted to be true over wide cultural variations. To what extent are they indigenous to the unfolding of the natural history of human beings? Multidisciplinary, longitudinal, and cross-cultural investigation—taking care to study intrapsychic processes—will be the only true test of this proposition. To what extent are the traits and qualities observed modifiable? Are they as dependent on a beneficent environment as would often appear to be indicated? Conversely, is the sequence so tied to preconditions that later events simply do not emerge into prepotency without them? Finally, is development truly an irreversible sequence? Or can the individual leap ahead and drop back, even omitting particular stages in the developmental process? To what extent is human development sex-specific? Again, one must continuously test the validity of the theory as it relates to these points.

Complicating the issue yet further is the basic question of what is acceptable as evidence. When we discuss developmental processes, it is clear that we are distinguishing between cultural and historical opportunities—between overt, phenotypic, behaviors and latent, genotypic, potentialities for expression that are based on the maturation of psychological processes. Because the processes themselves are not directly observable, they must be inferred from available behavior. Inevitably inference leads to the possibility of misinterpretation or distortion. Further problems arise as one endeavors to separate out the impact of culture and environment on these developmental processes. But inference and interpretation are necessary in all research, in physics as well as in psychology. Those problems should not deter inquiry.

If young adulthood is determined by psychological processes that are inferred and interpreted rather than directly observed, how can groups of people be called "young adult"? In terms of scientific verifiability, a young adult can be identified only by assessing behavior for signs of the underlying processes associated with that life stage. But young adulthood does occur at that period of the life span when physical development is complete. Thus, a careful observer may watch a group of young people, note their physical appearance, examine their behavior, and draw inferences about underlying psychological characteristics. As with other types of naturalistic research, experience and training sharpen perception and improve accuracy of interpretation.

The added advantage of a theoretical schema is that it serves as a

directional lens, sensitizing the investigator to observations that may clarify the underlying intent of the behavior in view. What is the relationship between observed behavior and the situational context? How is the group's behavior affected by situational changes? To what kind(s) of group leadership are the individuals most responsive? Which genotypic constructs best account for what is observed? Ultimately, the utility of this approach will depend on "models that elevate genotypic (competence) and phenotypic (performance) relationships from the level of theoretical conjecture and interpretation to one of empirically testable assertions." (Baltes & Schaie, 1973, p. 385).

Historical precedent for the empirical value of this approach is exemplified by the action research of Lewin (1947) and the naturalistic research of Jane Goodall (1968).

Still another question deals with the extent to which the listed number of life stages is in fact the actual number. We have seen that the earlier theorists (Jung, Buhler) typically identified but three adult stages: early, middle, late. More recent work (Vaillant, Levinson) asserts that there are five or more adult periods. In the history of ideas, as in other developmental phenomena, it is common to move from simpler to more complex formulations. This is yet another example of the room for legitimate differences of opinion and differences in point of approach in exploratory research.

Adult Personality Development: Longitudinal

But, as fundamental as stage theory is to an understanding of human development, we have seen that it is also important to account for longitudinal continuity. The emerging data from the Berkeley Institute of Human Development, now beginning to report on some 50 years of longitudinal research, indicate the continuity of personality development. Symonds (1961) and Vaillant (1977) have similarly been able to provide empirical support for the thesis that basic features of personality evolve well into the adult years.

Arthur Chickering (1967) has suggested the conceptualization of personality "vectors." These are major motivating forces that vary over the course of the life span. They provide dimensions around which the continuity of personality can be studied from stage to stage. In a similar vein Jones (1943) reports from the Berkeley research on the natural history of particular drive areas, such as aggressiveness, and other per-

sonality traits. He finds that a particular feature may undergo a number of changes over the course of personality development in the individual. Aggressiveness seen in childhood may be latent in adolescence and then resurface in adulthood.

Changing traits. The larger question becomes how we can identify the ways in which features and characteristics of personality undergo *systematic change* as a function of personality development. Underlying this approach is the need to identify those dimensions of personality that are most susceptible to longitudinal study. It is not yet known whether there are few or many dimensions of personality functioning that remain with the subject as determining features over the life span. Various authors have been able to identify a number of significant areas that seem to be germane to such longitudinal study. The research of Piaget and Perry describes the evolution of thinking from childhood into adulthood. Morality (Kohlberg, 1973, 1964), intelligence (Schaie, 1973), time sense (Neugarten & Datan, 1973), and ego development (Loevinger, 1976; Mahler, 1963) have similarly acquired life-span scope.

Other dimensions of development continue to emerge. Heath (1965) Piaget (1963), and Guttmann (1975) suggest a dimension that can be called *reality orientation.* It ranges from an egocentric approach at a less mature level of development to the allocentric orientation of mature adults. Related to this is a dimension that might be referred to as the self/world relationship. It is characterized by movement from narcissism through idealism and into ultimate pragmatism.

A vital area that has received almost no systematic attention is the natural history of interpersonal relationships. What changes occur in the nature of these relationships over the course of the life span? The early promise of Sullivan (1947), Isaacs (1956), and Guntrip (1964) has generated little subsequent documentation. Lowenthal and associates (1977) have produced interesting data on adult interpersonal functioning, but without providing a developmental rationale for their findings. As the life-span-development approach gains wider acceptance, one can anticipate more-systematic investigations of basic dimensions of human functioning along a natural-history sequence of evolution. Ultimately, such an approach will require the coordinated efforts of a number of disciplines, including various branches of psychology, anthropology, and biology.

Structural changes. For the present, having identified several con-

tent areas of personality development, what of structural changes in personality over the life span? The increasing awareness of ego development as a central factor provides some basis for optimism that this area will receive continuing attention. Erikson's identification of the adolescent identity crisis and subsequent identity formation culminated the earlier thinking of investigators who attempted to follow the development of personality structure into adulthood. From a structural perspective, however, Erikson's theory ends with adolescence. *Identity formation* seems too final a term to apply to ego development when the entire adult life cycle lies ahead.

I have proposed that young adults go through a process of differentiation called self-particularization. Ego integration then organizes the component ingredients into a coordinated, integral whole. Kurt Lewin (1935) is among those who describe personality structure in later adult years as one of "dedifferentiation," the "primitivization" of "innerpersonal regions." That is, the differentiated parts of the personality reduce in number and their interaction becomes less fluid and more rigid. This is a reversal of the process described in young adulthood. Clearly these theoretical formulations require extensive study. But even if they were verified, what of structural evolution in the periods intervening between young adulthood and senescent adulthood? Is Werner's theory (see Chapter 7) of development (diffuse-differentiated-integrated) an adequate paradigm for ego development in adulthood? These are but some of the basic issues that will compel attention as we endeavor to learn more about the natural evolution of personality structure.

How Does Culture Affect Development?

A second broad area for investigation is the relationship between development and cultural pressure. That is, to what extent and in what ways do cultural, environmental, and familial conditions affect individual characteristics? At the outer limit, to what extent can such conditions act to foster or inhibit developmental prepotencies? Conventional wisdom cannot dependably answer such questions. Unfortunately, the issue is muddled further by a common clinical observation. The same basic cultural custom or social institution can either aid or detract from optimum growth. Does marriage help or hinder growth? Does the demand for a career choice and a career commitment enhance or stunt development? The best answers available indicate that either, or both, can occur.

For any given individual, marriage or career may act as an important stimulus to growth or, conversely, restrict and narrow the breadth of development.

The underlying principle seems to be the extent to which a cultural pattern presses the individual toward social conformity or provides a nurturant environment for potentiation. Here we encounter the differences between personal and cultural objectives in a particular social situation. When the concern is for individual growth, the results may be quite different from when the intention is to produce a particular kind of socially desired outcome. Thus, a society that urges people to marry so that they will propagate may, incidentally, enhance personal development through that expectation. But its primary purpose, and a necessary and sufficient objective of urging marriage, may have little to do with promoting individual growth and development.

It is a fundamental assertion that maturation ultimately depends on the activation of potentialities within the individual. At the same time, environment and culture have an important role to play in the potentiation of these features. Learning originates within the individual, as well as in response to environmental stimulation. Cultures are created by people; yet they are more than the product of their creators. Young adults contribute to their society and are also shaped by it. By furthering our understanding of the interactive processes between culture and development, we may be able to bring out what is best in both.

REFERENCES

Abraham, K. *Selected papers of Karl Abraham*. London: Hogarth Press, 1927.

Adelson, J. The mystique of adolescence. *Psychiatry,* Summer 1964, (1), pp. 1–5.

Adelson, J., & O'Neil, R. Growth of political ideas in adolescence. *Journal of Personality and Social Psychology,* 1966, (4), 295–306.

Adler, A. *Understanding human nature* (W. Wolfe, trans.). New York: Greenberg, 1927.

Allport, G. *Personality: A psychological interpretation.* New York: Holt, Rinehart & Winston, 1937.

Allport, G. *Pattern and growth in personality.* New York: Holt, Rinehart & Winston, 1961.

Ames, L., Métraux, R., & Walker, R. *Adolescent Rorschach responses.* New York: Hoeber, 1959.

Atkinson, J., & Raphelson, A. Individual differences in motivation and behavior in particular situations. *Journal of Personality,* 1953, *24,* 349–363.

Ausubel, D., & Kirk, D. *Ego psychology and mental disorder: A developmental approach to psychopathology.* New York: Grune & Stratton, 1977.

Baldwin, J. *Another country.* New York: Dial Press, 1962.

Baltes, P., & Schaie, W. On life-span developmental research paradigms: Retrospects and prospects. In P. Baltes & W. Schaie (Eds.), *Life-span developmental psychology.* New York: Academic Press, 1973.

Bayley, N. The life span as a frame of reference in psychological research. In F. Rebelsky (Ed.), *Life: The continuous process.* New York: Knopf, 1975.

Beck, S. *The Rorschach experiment.* New York: Grune & Stratton, 1960.

Benedict, R. *Patterns of culture.* Boston: Houghton Mifflin, 1934.

Bettelheim, B. The problem of generations. In E. Erikson (Ed.), *The challenge of youth.* New York: Anchor, 1965.

Birket-Smith, K. *Primitive man and his ways.* New York: Mentor, 1963.

Blanck, G., & Blanck, R. *Ego psychology: Theory and practice.* New York: Columbia University Press, 1974.

215

Blank, G., & Blank, R. *Ego psychology: Theory and practice* (vol II). New York: Columbia University Press, 1979.

Blasi, A. Concept of development in personality theory. In J. Loevinger (Ed.), *Ego development*. San Francisco: Jossey-Bass, 1976.

Blos, P. *On adolescence*. Glencoe, Ill.: Free Press, 1962.

Bocknek, G. *The relationship between motivation and performance in achieving and non-achieving college students*. Unpublished dissertation, Boston University, 1959.

Bocknek, G., A developmental approach to counseling adults. In N. Schlossberg & A. Entine (Eds.), *Counseling adults*. Monterey, Calif.: Brooks/Cole, 1977.

Bortner, R., & Hultsch, D. Personal time perspective in adults. *Developmental Psychology*, 1972, 7, 98–103.

Brammer, L., & Shostrum, E. *Therapeutic psychology* (2nd ed.). Englewood Cliffs, N.J.: Prentice-Hall, 1968.

Brenner, M. Casualty rate of unemployment. *APA Monitor*, July 1978 (1).

Buhler, C. The curve of life as studied in biographies. *Journal of Applied Psychology*, 1935, 19, 405–409.

Buhler, C., & Massarik, B. *The course of human life*. New York: Springer, 1968.

Carson, R. *The sea around us*. New York: Oxford University Press, 1951.

Chickering, A. The young adult: A new and needed new course. *Journal of the National Association of Women Deans and Counselors*, 1967, pp. 98–111.

Cole, L. *Psychology of adolescence* (7th ed.). New York: Holt, Rinehart & Winston, 1970.

Comfort, A. *The joy of sex*. New York: Crown, 1972.

Cumming, E., & Henry, W. *Growing old*. New York: Basic Books, 1961.

Datan, N., & Ginsberg, L. (Eds.), *Life-span developmental psychology*. New York: Academic Press, 1975.

Davidson, S. *Relationship between differentiation and identity status in college students*. Unpublished dissertation, Boston University, 1978.

Detroit turns to young designers. *Parade Magazine*, Feb. 1966.

Deutsch, H. *Psychology of women: A psychoanalytic interpretation*. New York: Grune & Stratton, 1944.

Douvan, E. & Adelson, J. *The adolescent experience*. New York: Wiley, 1966.

Durkheim, E. *Suicide* (Spaulding & Simpson, trans.). New York: Free Press of Glencoe, 1951.

Duvall, E. *Family development* (3rd ed.). New York: Lippincott, 1967.

Eisdorfer, C., & Lawton, P. (Eds.). *The psychology of adult development and aging*. Washington: American Psychological Association, 1973.

Elkind, D. *Children and adolescents* (2nd ed). New York: Oxford University Press, 1974.

Ellis, A. *Reason and emotion in psychotherapy*. New York: Lyle Stuart, 1962.

Erikson, E. *Childhood and society*. New York: Norton, 1950.

Erikson, E. The problem of ego identity. *Journal of American Psychoanalytic Association*, 1956, 4, 56–121.

Erikson, E. Identity and the life cycle. *Psychological Issues,* 1959, *1,* 1–171.

Erikson E. *Youth: Change and challenge.* New York: Basic Books, 1963.

Erikson, E. *Identity: Youth and crisis.* New York: Norton, 1968.

Erikson, E. Reflections on the dissent of contemporary youth. *International Journal of Psychoanalysis,* 1970, *51,* 11–22.

Etkind, S. *Two patterns of ego identity formation in underachieving "special needs" adolescents.* Unpublished dissertation, Boston University, 1979.

Evan, E. (Ed.). *Adolescents: Readings in behavior and development.* New York: Dryden Press, 1970.

Ewey, R., & Humber, W. *The development of human behavior.* New York: Macmillan, 1951.

Feuer, L. *The conflict of generations: The character and significance of student movements.* New York: Basic Books, 1969.

Freedman, M. *The college experience.* San Francisco: Jossey-Bass, 1967.

Fenichel, O. *Psychoanalytic theory of neurosis.* New York: Norton, 1945.

Freud, A. *The ego and the mechanisms of defense.* London: Hogarth Press, 1937.

Freud, S. *The basic writings of Sigmund Freud.* New York: Random House, 1938.

Friday, N. *My mother/my self.* New York: Delacorte Press, 1977.

Fromm, E. *Escape from freedom.* New York: Farrar & Rinehart, 1941.

Fromm, E. *Man for himself: An inquiry into the psychology of ethics.* New York: Rinehart, 1947.

Fromm, E. *The art of loving.* New York: Harper, 1956.

Fromm-Reichmann, F. Psychiatric aspects of anxiety. In L. Rabkin & J. Carr (Eds.), *Sourcebook in abnormal psychology.* Boston: Houghton Mifflin, 1967.

Gagnon, J. Scripts and the coordination of sexual conduct. In J. Cole & R. Diensibier (Eds.), *Nebraska Symposium on Motivation.* Lincoln: University of Nebraska Press, 1973.

Garmezy, N. Vulnerable and invulnerable children. *Catalog of Selected Documents in Psychology,* 1976, 6, 96.

Gesell, A. *The child from five to ten.* New York: Harper & Row, 1946.

Gilligan, C. In a different voice: Women's conception of self and morality. *Harvard Educational Review,* 1977, 47(1), pp. 481–517.

Ginzberg, E., Ginzberg, S. W., Axelrad, S., & Herma, J. L. *Occupational choice.* New York: Columbia University Press, 1951.

Gitelson, M. The emotional problems of the elderly. In W. Sze (Ed.), *Human life cycle.* New York: Jason Aronson, 1977.

Goethals, G., & Klos, D. *Experiencing youth.* Boston: Little, Brown, 1970.

Golden, J., Mandel, N., Glueck, B., & Feder, Z. A summary description of fifty "normal" white males. In L. Rabkin & J. Carr (Eds.), *Sourcebook in abnormal psychology.* Boston: Houghton Mifflin, 1967.

Golden, S., et al. *Facilitating psychosocial transitions in normal adult development.* Ann Arbor: University of Michigan Center for Continuing Education of Women, 1978.

Goldin, R. *Therapy as education.* Unpublished dissertation, Boston University, 1977.

Goodall, J. The behavior of free-living chimpanzees in the Gombe Strea Reserve. *Animal Behavior Monographs,* 1968, *1,* 161–311.

Goodenough, F., & Tyler, L. *Developmental psychology: An approach to the study of human behavior.* New York: Appleton-Century-Crofts, 1959.

Gould, R. The phases of adult life: A study in developmental psychology. *American Journal of Psychiatry,* 1972, *129,* 521–531.

Gould, R. *Transformations.* New York: Simon & Schuster, 1978.

Guntrip, H. *Personality structure and human interaction.* New York: International Universities Press, 1964.

Gutmann, D. Parenthood: A key to the comparative study of the life cycle. In N. Datan & L. Ginsberg (Eds.), *Life-span developmental psychology.* New York: Academic Press, 1975.

Haan, N. *Coping and defending.* New York: Academic Press, 1977.

Haan, N., Smith, M., & Block, J. Moral reasoning of young adults. *Journal of Personality and Social Psychology,* 1968, *10,* 183–201.

Hanfmann, E. *Effective therapy for college students.* San Francisco: Jossey-Bass, 1978.

Harlow, H. The nature of love. *American Psychologist,* 1958, *13,* 673–685.

Hartmann, H. *Ego psychology and the problem of adaptation.* New York: International Universities Press, 1958.

Havighurst, R. *Developmental tasks and education.* London: Longmans, Green, 1952.

Heath, D. *Explorations of maturity.* New York: Appleton-Century-Crofts, 1965.

Hemmendinger, L. *Perceptual organization and development as reflected in the structure of Rorschach test responses.* Paper read at the convention of the American Psychological Association, Chicago, 1951.

Herbert, W. Mental health parley focuses on economy. *APA Monitor,* July 1978, pp. 1, 14.

Hirth, P. Youth unrest. *Israel Magazine,* 1972, *4*(5), p. 75.

Huntington, D. Personal communication, 1968.

Hurwitz, I. *A developmental study of the relationship between motor ability and perceptual processes as measured by the Rorschach test.* Unpublished dissertation, Clark University, 1954.

Isaacs, K. *Relatability, a proposed construct and an approach to its validation.* Unpublished dissertation, University of Chicago, 1956.

Jones, H. *Development in adolescence.* New York: Appleton-Century-Crofts, 1943.

Jung, C. [The stages of life.] In R. Hull (trans.), *The structure and dynamics of the psyche* (2nd ed.). Princeton, N. J.: Princeton University Press, 1969.

Katz, A. *Intimacy: The role of awareness in young adult couples.* Unpublished dissertation, Boston University, 1978.

Keniston, K. *The uncommitted.* New York: Dell, 1965.

Keniston, K. Youth as a stage of life. In W. Sze (Ed.), *Human life cycle.* New York: Jason Aronson, 1975.

Kernberg, O. Early ego integration and object relations. *Annals of the New York Academy of Sciences,* 1972, *193,* 233–247.

Kimmel, D. *Adulthood and aging.* New York: Wiley, 1974.

Kinsey, A., Pomeroy, W., & Martin, C. *Sexual Behavior in the human male.* Philadelphia: Saunders, 1953.

Knowles, M. *The adult learner: A neglected species.* Houston: Gulf, 1974.

Knox, A. *Adult development and learning.* San Francisco: Jossey-Bass, 1977.

Kohlberg, L. Development of moral character and moral ideology. In M. Hoffman & W. Hoffman (Eds.), *Review of child development research* (Vol. I). New York: Russell Sage Foundation, 1964.

Kohlberg, L. Stage and sequence: The cognitive-developmental approach to socialization. In D. Goslin (Ed.), *Handbook of socialization theory and research.* Chicago: Rand McNally, 1969.

Kohlberg, L. Personal communication, 1978.

Kohler, W. *Gestalt psychology,* New York: Liveright, 1947.

Kohut, H. *The analysis of self.* New York: International Universities Press, 1971.

Kruger, A. *Direct and substitutive modes of tension-reduction in terms of developmental level.* Unpublished dissertation, Clark University, 1954.

Kuhlen, R., & Murphy, G. The psychological needs of adults. *Notes and essays.* Chicago: CSLEA, 1955, (12).

Labouvie-Vief, G. Adult cognitive development: In search of alternative explanations. *Merrill-Palmer Quarterly,* 1977, *23,* 228–263.

Lampl-de Groot, J. Ego ideal and superego. *Psychoanalytic Study of the Child,* 1962, *27,* 94–106.

Lane, J. Social effectiveness and developmental level. *Journal of Personality,* 1955, *23,* 274–284.

Lee, J. *Commitment: Its nature and development in later adolescence.* Unpublished manuscript, Cambridge, Mass.: Harvard University School of Education, 1965.

Levine, L. *Personal and social development.* New York: Holt, 1963.

Levinson, D., Darrow, C., Klein, E., Levinson, M., & McKee, B. The psychosocial development of men. In D. Ricks, A. Thomas, and M. Roff (Eds.), *Life history research in psychopathology.* Minneapolis: University of Minnesota Press, 1974.

Levinson, D., Darrow, C., Klein, E., Levinson, M., & McKee, B. *The seasons of a man's life.* New York: Knopf, 1978.

Lévi-Strauss, C. [*Structural anthropology*] (C. Jacobson & B. Schoepf, trans.). New York: Basic Books, 1963.

Lewin, K. *A dynamic theory of personality.* New York: McGraw-Hill, 1935.

Lewin, K. Group discussion and social change. In T. Newcomb & E. Hartley (Eds.), *Readings in social psychology.* New York: Holt, 1947.

Lidz, T. *The person* (Rev. ed.). New York: Basic Books, 1976.

Loevinger, J. The meaning and measurement of ego development. *American Psychologist,* 1966, *21,* 195–206.

Loevinger, J. *Ego development.* San Francisco: Jossey-Bass, 1976.

Loevinger, J. & Wessler, R. *Measuring ego development I: Construction and use of a sentence completion test.* San Francisco: Jossey-Bass, 1970.

Lofchie, S. The performance of adults under stress: A developmental approach. *Journal of Psychology,* 1955, *39,* 109–116.

Lowenthal, M., Thurnher, M., & Chiriboga, D. *Four stages of life.* San Francisco: Jossey-Bass, 1977.

Macfarlane, J. The guidance study. *Sociometry,* 1939, *2,* 1–23.

Mahler, M. Thoughts about development and individuation. *The Psychoanalytic Study of the Child,* 1963, *18,* 307–324.

Mahler, M. *On human symbiosis and the vicissitudes of individuation.* New York: International Universities Press, 1968.

Marcia, J. Development and validation of ego-identity status. *Journal of Personality and Social Psychology,* 1966, *3,* 551–559.

Marcia, J. Ego-identity status: Relationship to change in self-esteem, "general maladjustment," and authoritarianism. *Journal of Personality,* 1967, *35,* 118–133.

Marcuse, H. *Eros and civilization.* Boston: Beacon Press, 1955.

Maslow, A. *Motivation and personality.* New York: Harper, 1954.

Maslow. A. *Toward a psychology of being.* Princeton, N. J.: Van Nostrand, 1962.

Masters, W., & Johnson, V. *Human sexual response.* Boston: Little Brown, 1966.

Masters, W., & Johnson, V. *Human sexual inadequacy.* Boston: Little Brown, 1970.

May, R. *Psychology and the human dilemma.* Princeton, N. J.: Van Nostrand, 1967.

McClelland, D. *The achieving society.* New York: Van Nostrand, 1961.

McDougall, W. *An introduction to social psychology* (14th ed.). Boston: John W. Luce, 1921.

McLeish, J. *The ulyssean adult.* Toronto: McGraw-Hill Ryerson, 1976.

McMillan, J. Peer review and professional standards for psychologists rendering personal health services. *Professional Psychology,* 1974, *5,* 51–58.

Mead, M. Adolescence in primitive and in modern society. In T. Newcomb & E. Hartley (Eds.), *Readings in social psychology.* New York: Holt, 1947.

Mead, M. Marriage in two steps. *Redbook,* July 1966.

Menaker, S., & Menaker, I. *Ego in evolution.* New York: Grove Press, 1965.

Mohr, G., & Despres, M. *The stormy decade: Adolescence.* New York: Random House, 1958.

Money, J., & Ehrhardt, A. *Man and woman, boy and girl.* Baltimore: Johns Hopkins Press, 1972.

Moore, A. *The young adult generation.* Nashville, Tenn.: Abingdon Press, 1969.

Mosher, R., & Sprinthall, N. Deliberate psychological education. *The Counseling Psychologist,* 1972, *2,* 3–82.

Murphy, G. *Personality: A biosocial approach to origins and structure.* New York: Harper, 1947.

Murphy, G. *Human potentialities.* New York: Basic Books, 1965.

Murphy, G. Personal communication, 1972.

Murray, H. *Explorations in personality.* New York: Oxford University Press, 1938.

Mussen, P., Conger, J., & Kagan, J. *Child development and personality* (2nd ed.).

Neugarten, B. (Ed.). *Middle age and aging.* Chicago: University of Chicago Press, 1968.

Neugarten, B. Continuities and discontinuities of psychological issues into adult life. In F. Rebelsky (Ed.), *Life: The continuous process.* New York: Knopf, 1975.(a)

Neugarten, B. Personality and the aging process. In F. Rebelsky (Ed.), *Life: The continuous process.* New York: Knopf, 1975.(b)

Neugarten, B., Wood, V., Kraines, R., & Loomis, B. Women's attitudes toward menopause. *Human Development,* 1963, *6,* 140–151.

Neugarten, B., & Datan, N. Sociological perspectives on the life cycle. In P. Baltes & W. Schaie (Eds.), *Life-span developmental psychology.* New York: Academic Press, 1973.

Offer, D. *Psychological world of the teen-ager.* New York: Basic Books, 1969.

Offer, D., & Offer, J. *From teenage to young manhood.* New York: Basic Books, 1970.

O'Neill, N., & O'Neill, G. *Open marriage.* New York: Avon Books, 1972.

Peck, R. Personality factors in aging. In B. L. Neugarten (Ed.), *Middle age and aging.* Chicago: University of Chicago Press, 1968.

Peck, R. Psychological developments in the second half of life. In W. Sze (Ed.), *Human life cycle.* New York: Jason Aronson, 1975.

Perry, W. *Forms of intellectual and ethical development in the college years.* New York: Holt, Rinehart & Winston, 1970.

Piaget, J. *The moral judgment of the child.* New York: Collier, 1962.

Piaget, J. [*The origins of intelligence in children*] (M. Cook, trans.). New York: Norton, 1963.

Pressey, S., & Kuhlen, R. *Psychological development through the life span.* New York: Harper & Row, 1957.

Rapoport, R. *Pilot project on family research and mental health.* Cambridge, Mass.: Harvard University School of Public Health, 1961.

Rappaport, L. *Personality development.* Glenview, Ill.: Scott, Foresman, 1972.

Ribble, M. The significance of infantile sucking for the psychic development of the individual. In S. Tomkins (Ed.), *Contemporary psychopathology.* Cambridge, Mass.: Harvard University Press, 1947.

Riegel, K. Adult life crises: A dialectical interpretation of development. In N. Datan & L. Ginsberg (Eds.), *Life-span developmental psychology.* New York: Academic Press, 1975.

Rubin. L. *Worlds of pain.* New York: Basic Books, 1978.

Rudolph, S., & Rudolph, L. Rajput adulthood. *Daedalus,* 1976 (105), 149–164.

Sanford, N. Personality development during the college years. *Journal of Social Issues,* 1956, *12,* 61.

Sanford, N. *The American college.* New York: Wiley, 1962.

Sanford, N. *Self and society.* New York: Atherton Press, 1966.

Schaie, W. A field theory approach to age changes in cognitive behavior. In D. Charles & W. Loofts (Eds.), *Readings in psychological development through life.* New York: Holt, Rinehart & Winston, 1973.

Schaie, W., Labouvie, G., & Buech, B. Generational versus cohort-specific differences in adult cognitive functioning. *Developmental Psychology,* 1973, *9,* 151–166.

Self, P. The future evolution of the parental imperative. In N. Datan & L. Ginsberg (Eds.), *Life-span developmental psychology.* New York: Academic Press, 1975.

Shirer, W. *The rise and fall of the Third Reich.* New York: Simon and Schuster, 1960.

Skolnick, K., & Skolnick, V. *Families in transition.* Boston: Little, Brown, 1971.

Spitz, R. Anaclytic depression: An inquiry into the genesis of psychiatric conditions in early childhood. *The Psychoanalytic Study of the Child,* 1946, *11,* 313–342.

Sullivan, H. *Conceptions of modern psychiatry.* Washington: William Alanson White Foundation, 1947.

Super, D. *The psychology of careers.* New York: Harper, 1957.

Super, D., Starishevsky, R., Matlin, W., & Jordaan, J. Career development: self-concept theory. *CEEB Research Monographs,* 1963.

Symonds, P. *From adolescent to adult.* New York: Columbia University Press, 1961.

Tanner, J. M., & Inhelder, B. (Eds.). *Discussions on child development* (Vols. I & II). New York: International University Press, 1957.

Tanner, J. M., & Inhelder, B. (Eds.). *Discussions on child development* (Vol. III). New York: International University Press, 1958.

Toffler, A. *Future shock.* New York: Random House, 1970.

Trent, J., & Medsker, L. *Beyond high school.* San Francisco: Jossey-Bass, 1969.

Trimberger, E. Why a rebellion at Columbia was inevitable. *Transaction*, 1968, *5*, 28–38.

Vaillant, G. *Adaptation to life*. Boston: Little, Brown, 1977.

van den Daele, L. Ego development and preferential judgment in life-span perspective. In N. Datan & L. Ginsberg (Eds.), *Life-span developmental psychology*. New York: Academic Press, 1975.

Van Gennep, A. *The rites of passage*. Chicago: University of Chicago Press, 1960.

Webster, H. Some quantitative results of studying college women. *Journal of Social Issues*, 1956, *12*, 29–43.

Wechsler, D. *The measurement and appraisal of adult intelligence* (4th ed.). Baltimore: Williams and Wilkins, 1958.

Werner, H. *The comparative psychology of mental development*. Chicago: Follet, 1940.

Werner, H. *The concept of development*. Minneapolis: University of Minnesota Press, 1957.

Whipple, J. Especially for adults. *Notes and essays*. Chicago: CSLEA, No. 19, October 1947 (19).

Whitbourne, S., & Weinstock, G. *Adult development*. New York: Holt, Rinehart & Winston, 1979.

White, R. Ego and reality in psychoanalytic theory. *Psychological Issues*, 1963, *3*(3), 210 pp.

White, R. *Lives in progress* (3rd ed.). New York: Holt, Rinehart & Winston, 1975. (First edition 1952.)

Wittenberg, R. *Postadolescence*. New York: Grune & Stratton, 1968.

Wittenborn, J., Brill, H., Smith, J., & Whittenborn, S. (Eds.). *Drugs and youth*. Springfield, Ill.: Charles C Thomas, 1969.

Wohlwill, J. Methodology and research strategy in the study of development and change. In L. Goulet & P. Baltes (Eds.), *Life-span developmental psychology*. New York: Academic Press, 1970.

NAME INDEX

SUBJECT INDEX

Acceptance in marriage, 157
Accommodation, 30
Activism in young adulthood, 76,
   109–110
Adolescence:
  biosexual maturity in, 72–73
  discontinuity in, 67–68
  ego fluidity in, 74–76
  ego integrity, 39
  ego synthesis in, 68
  emancipation in, 69
  fantasy in, 89
  foreclosure in, 39
  idealism in, 76–78, 113
  identity in, 151
  identity crisis in, 38, 72, 81
  identity formation in, 39, 68
  impulsivity in 75–76, 89, 170–171
  love in, 138
  narcissism in, 73–74, 169
  peers in, 38–39, 69–72
  pressure in, 66–67
  rejection in, 70
  Rorschach studies, 38, 68
  self-consolidation in, 68
  self-esteem in, 90
  self-exploration in, 68
  separation, 39, 69
  sexual references in, 89
  sociological maturity in, 69
  stage, period, 4
  status consciousness in, 71
  stereotypic thinking in, 90

Adulthood:
  allocentrism in, 49
  attributes of, 51–53
  autonomy in, 49
  defense mechanisms in, 56, 61–62
  dominance/submission in, 56
  expansion and defense in, 56
  fantasy productions in, 56
  growth/decline interaction in, 60–61
  integration in, 49
  option in, 53
  polarities in, 60
  potential in, 62–63
  roles in, 167
  sense of history in, 58
  sense of loss, 56
  sexual competitors in, 59
  sexual partners in, 59
  stability in, 49
  stages of, 4, 7
  symbolization in, 49
  time sense in, 56, 57
Affection:
  and love, 150
  in marriage, 151
Alienation, 21
Allocentrism, 177
  in adulthood, 49
Anomie, 21
Assimilation, 30
Autonomy, 159
  in adulthood, 49
  functional, 158

227

— *A Sentimental Journey through France and Italy by Mr. Yorick,* edited by Gardner D. Stout Jr. (London, 1967).

SUTHERLAND, JAMES: 'Some Aspects of Eighteenth-Century Prose', in *Essays on the Eighteenth Century. Presented to David Nichol Smith* (Oxford, 1945), pp. 94-110.

TENGARRINHA, JOSÉ: 'A oratória e o jornalismo no Romantismo', in *Estética do Romantismo em Portugal. Primeiro Colóquio, 1970* (Lisboa, 1979), pp. 185-90.

THORPE, CLARENCE DEWITT: 'Addison and Hutchinson on the Imagination', in *English Literary History,* Vol. 2 (1935), pp. 215-34.

TIEGHEM, PHILIPPE VAN: *Les Influences étrangères sur la littérature française (1550-1880)* (Paris, 1961).

TRAUGOTT, JOHN (ed.): *Laurence Sterne. A Collection of Critical Essays,* Twentieth Century Views, A Spectrum Book (Englewood Cliffs, New Jersey, 1968).

— 'The Shandean Comic Vision of Locke', in *ibid.,* pp. 126-47.

VICENTE, GIL: *Côrtes de Júpiter,* prefácio, notas e glossário de Marques Braga, Col. Textos Literários (Lisboa, 1937).

WALLER, R. D.: Introduction to John Hookham Frere's *The Monks and the Giants* (New York, 1926).

*WALTER, FÉLIX: *La Littérature portugaise en Angleterre à l'époque romantique* (Paris, 1927).

WATKINS, W. B. C.: 'From Yorick Revisited', in *Laurence Sterne. A Collection of Critical Essays,* pp. 168-79.

WEDGWOOD, JULIA: 'Sir Walter Scott and the Romantic Reaction', in *Scott — The Critical Heritage,* pp. 499-521.

WELFORD, R.: *Men of Mark 'twixt Tyne and Tweed,* 3 Vols (London, 1895), Vol. I.

WELSH, ALEXANDER: 'Scott's Heroes', in *Walter Scott,* ed. by D. D. Devlin, pp. 63-70.

WILLIAMS, IOAN (ed.): *Sir Walter Scott on Novelists and Fiction* (London, 1968).

portuguesa e de teoria literária, ed. João José Cochofel (Lisboa, 1977), Vol. I, pp. 426-52.

RIDENOUR, GEORGE M.: *The Style of «Don Juan»*, Reprint of Yale Studies in English, Vol. 144 (Archon Books: Hamden, Connecticut, 1969).

RIVAS, DUQUE DE, ÁNGEL DE SAAVEDRA: *El moro expósito* (Madrid, 1967).

ROCHA, ANDRÉE CRABBÉ: *A epistolografia em Portugal* (Coimbra, 1965).

RODRIGUES, ANTÓNIO GONÇALVES: *A novelística estrangeira em versão portuguesa no período pré-romântico* (Coimbra, 1951).

RODRIGUES, URBANO TAVARES: *O mito de D. Juan e o donjuanismo em Portugal* (Lisboa, 1960).

QUILLINAN, EDWARD: *The Lusiad of Luis de Camoens*, trans. by E. Quillinan, with notes by John Adamson (London, 1853).

SÁ, VICTOR DE: *A crise do liberalismo e as primeiras manifestações das ideias socialistas em Portugal (1820-1852)* (Lisboa, 1969).

SARAIVA, ANTÓNIO JOSÉ: *Herculano e o liberalismo em Portugal — Os problemas morais e culturais da instauração do regime (1834-1850)* (Lisboa, 1949).

SCHLEGEL, A. W.: *Cours de litterature dramatique*, 3 Vols translated from the German (Paris, 1814), t. III.

SCOTT, SIR WALTER: *Sir Walter Scott's Minstrelsy of the Scottish Border*, edited by T. H. Henderson, 4 Vols (Edinburgh, 1902).

— *The Miscellaneous Works of Sir Walter Scott*, 30 Vols (Edinburgh, 1869-71).

— *The Poetical Works of Sir Walter Scott*, with the Author's Introduction and Notes, edited by J. Logie Robertson, M. A. (London, 1926).

— *The Waverley Novels*, Dryburgh Edition, 25 Vols (London, 1892): Vol. II: *Guy Mannering;* Vol. IV: *Rob Roy;* Vol. VIII: *The Bride of Lammermoor;* Vol. IX: *Ivanhoe;* Vol. XI: *The Abbot;* Vol. XV: *Peveril of the Peak.*

— *Waverley*, Everyman's Library, with a preface by James C. Corson (London, 1969).

* SÉRGIO, ANTÓNIO: 'Notas sobre a imaginação, a fantasia e o problema psicológico-moral na obra novelística de Queiroz', in *Livro do centenário de Eça de Queiroz*, ed. L. M. Pereira and C. Reys (Lisboa, 1945), pp. 449-59.

SERRÃO, JOAQUIM VERÍSSIMO: *Herculano e a consciência do liberalismo português* (Lisboa, 1977).

SERRÃO, JOEL: *Temas de cultura portuguesa — II* (Lisboa, 1965).

— *Temas oitocentistas*, 2 Vols (Lisboa, 1959-62).

— (ed.) *Antologia do pensamento político português. I — Liberalismo, socialismo, republicanismo* (Porto, 1970).

SHAKESPEARE, WILLIAM: *The Works of Shakespeare*, with Life, Glossary, etc., by the Editor of the «Chandos», The «Albion» Edition (London, n. d.).

SHELLEY, MARY W.: *Letters of Mary W. Shelley (Mostly Unpublished)*, edited by Henry H. Harper (Minneapolis, 1918).

— *The Letters of Mary W. Shelley*, collected and edited by Frederick L. Jones, 3 Vols (Norman, Oklahoma, 1944).

SHELLEY, PERCY BYSSHE: *The Complete Works of Percy Bysshe Shelley*, 10 Vols (London, 1927), Vol. II: *Prometheus Unbound.*

SHKLOVSKY, VICTOR: 'A Parodying Novel: Sterne's *Tristram Shandy*', in *Laurence Sterne. A Collection of Critical Essays*, pp. 66-89.

SMITHERS, PETER: *The Life of Joseph Addison* (Oxford, 1968).

* SOUSA, R. W.: *The Rediscoverers: Major Writers in the Portuguese Literature of National Regeneration* (Univ. Park, Pa., 1981).

SOUTHEY, REV. CHARLES CUTHBERT: *The Life and Correspondence of the Late Robert Southey*, 6 Vols (London, 1850).

SOUTHEY, ROBERT: *Journals of a Residence in Portugal 1800-1801, and a Visit to France*, edited by A. Cabral (Oxford, 1960).

STEDMONT, J. M.: *The Comic Art of Laurence Sterne* (Toronto, 1967).

STENDHAL: *Racine et Shakespeare*, préface et notes de Pierre Martino (Paris, 1928).

STERNE, LAURENCE: *The Life and Opinions of Tristram Shandy, Gentleman*, edited by Graham Petrie, introduced by Christopher Ricks, The Penguin English Library (Harmondsworth, 1967).

KNOWLES, RICHARD BRINSLEY: *The Life of James Sheridan Knowles* (London, 1872).

KROEBER, KARL: *Romantic Narrative Art* (London, 1966).

LAMB, NORMAN J.: 'Notes on some Portuguese «Emigrado» Journals Published in England', in *Bulletin of Hispanic Studies*, 30 (1953), pp. 151-60.

LANG, ANDREW: *Sir Walter Scott and the Border Minstrelsy* (London, 1910).

LARDNER, REV. DIONYSIUS (ed.): *The Cabinet Cyclopaedia, Biography: Eminent Literary and Successful Men of Italy, Spain and Portugal*, Vols 63, 71, 96 (London, 1837).

LEAVIS, F. R.: 'Byron's Satire', in *Revaluation*, Penguin Books (Harmondsworth, 1967).

LEHMAN, BENJAMIN H.: 'Of Time, Personality and the Author', in *Laurence Sterne. A Collection of Critical Essays*, pp. 21-33.

LEY, CHARLES DAVID: *A Inglaterra e os escritores portugueses* (Lisboa, 1939).

LLORENS CASTILLO, VICENTE: *Liberales y Románticos. Una emigración española en Inglaterra (1823-1834)* (México, 1954).

* LOPES, ÓSCAR: 'Alguns trabalhos sobre românticos portugueses', in *Modo de ler — Crítica e interpretação literária*, Vol. II (Porto, 1969), pp. 201-9.

LUKÁCS, GEORG: *The Historical Novel*, translated from the German by Hannah and Stanley Mitchell, Penguin Books (Harmondsworth, 1976).

MACAULAY, ROSE: *They went to Portugal* (London, 1946).

McKILLOP, ALAN DUGALD: *The Early Masters of English Fiction* (London, 1956).

— 'Laurence Sterne', in *Laurence Sterne. A Collection of Critical Essays*, pp. 34-65.

MAIGRON, LOUIS: *Le Roman historique à l'époque romantique. Essai sur l'influence de Walter Scott* (Paris, 1898).

MAISTRE, XAVIER DE: *Voyage autour de ma chambre par «Chevalier X» O. A. D. M. S. (Xavier au service de Sa Majesté Sarde)* (Turin, 1795).

MANDEL, OSCAR: 'The Function of the Norm in *Don Quixote*', in *Modern Philology*, 55 (1957-8), pp. 154-63.

MARTINS, J. P. OLIVEIRA: *Portugal contemporâneo*, 3 Vols, 7ª ed. (Lisboa, 1953).

MENDILOV, A. A.: 'The Revolt of Sterne', in *Laurence Sterne. A Collection of Critical Essays*, pp. 90-107.

MILIC, LOUIS T.: 'Observations on Conversational Style', in *English Writers of the Eighteenth Century*, edited by John Middendorf (London, 1971).

MOORE, HELEN: *Mary Wollstonecraft Shelley* (Philadelphia, 1886).

MOORE, THOMAS: *The Poetical Works of Thomas Moore*, with commentaries and notes by C. Kent, Centenary Edition (London, 1879).

MORNET, DANIEL: *La Pensée française au XVIIIᵉ siècle*, 9th ed. (Paris, 1956).

* MOSER, GERD: *Les Romantiques portugais et l'Allemagne* (Paris, 1939).

NELSON, ROBERT J.: *Play within a Play* (New Haven, 1958).

NEMÉSIO, VITORINO: *Exilados 1828-1832. História sentimental e política do liberalismo na emigração* (Lisboa, n. d.).

— *A mocidade de Herculano até à volta do exílio (1810-1832)*, 2 Vols (Lisboa, 1934).

* — *Relações francesas do Romantismo português* (Coimbra, 1936).

NERVAL, GÉRARD DE: 'Lettres d'Allemagne', in *Oeuvres*, Vol. II, Bibliothèque de la Pléiade (Paris, 1956), pp. 883-98.

NICOLL, ALLARDYCE (ed.): *A History of English Drama 1660-1900*, 6 Vols (Cambridge, 1952-59), Vol. II, 3rd ed. (1955).

OATES, J. C. T.: *Shandyism and Sentiment, 1760-1800* (Cambridge, 1968).

PIRES, MARIA LAURA BETTENCOURT: *Walter Scott e o Romantismo português* (Lisboa, 1979).

Plutarch's Lives. The Translation called Dryden's, corrected from the Greek and revised by A. H. Clough, 3 Vols (Liverpool, 1883), Vol. II: *The Life of Caesar*, Vol. III: *Life of Cato the Younger*.

PRAZ, MARIO: *The Romantic Agony* (London, 1970).

* REBELO, LUÍS FRANCISCO: *O teatro romântico (1838-1869)*, Biblioteca Breve, Vol. 51, Lisboa, 1980).

* REBELO, LUÍS DE SOUSA: 'Armas e letras', in *Grande dicionário da literatura*

ERÄMETSÄ, ERIK: *A Study of the Word «Sentimental» and of Other Linguistic Characteristics of Eighteenth-Century Sentimentalism in England* (Helsinki, 1951).

ESCARPIT, ROBERT: *Lord Byron. Un tempérament littéraire*, 2 Vols (Paris, 1955).

ESTÈVE, EDMOND: *Byron et le romantisme français. Essai sur la fortune et l'influence de l'oeuvre de Byron en France de 1812 à 1850* (Paris, 1907).

* *Estética do Romantismo em Portugal*, Centro de Estudos do Século XIX do Grémio Literário, Primeiro Colóquio 1970 (Lisboa, 1974).

FANSHAWE, SIR RICHARD: *Original Letters of His Excellency Sir Richard Fanshawe* (London, 1702).

FARRELL, WILLIAM J.: 'Nature versus Art as a Comic Pattern in *Tristram Shandy*', in *English Literary History*, Vol. XXX (1963), pp. 16-35.

* FERREIRA, ALBERTO: *Perspectiva do Romantismo português (1834-1865)*, Textos de Cultura Portuguesa (Lisboa, 1971).

FESTING, GABRIELLE: *John Hookham Frere and his Friends* (London, 1899).

FIELDING, HENRY: *Journal of a Voyage to Lisbon* (Cambridge, 1913).

* FIGUEIREDO, FIDELINO DE: *História da literatura romântica (1825-1870)*, 2ª ed. revista (Lisboa, 1923).

— *Pyrene* (Lisboa, 1935).

FITZPATRICK, WILLIAM JOHN: *Lady Morgan, her career, literary and personal, with a glimpse of her friends, and a word to her calumniators* (London, 1860).

FLUCHÈRE, HENRI: *Laurence Sterne. De l'homme à l'oeuvre* (Paris, 1961).

— *From Tristram to Yorick. An Interpretation of «Tristram Shandy»*, translated and abridged by Barbara Bray (Oxford, 1965).

* FRANÇA, JOSÉ AUGUSTO: *O Romantismo em Portugal*, 6 Vols (Lisboa, 1974).

FUSSELL, JR., PAUL: *Theory of Prosody in Eighteenth-Century England*, Archon Books (Hamden, Connecticut, 1966).

GRIERSON, H. J. C. (ed.): *Sir Walter Scott To-day, Some Retrospective Essays and Studies* (London, 1932).

— *Sir Walter Scott, Bart. A New Life Supplementary to, and corrective of, Lockhart's Biography* (London, 1938).

HASBERG, LUDWIG: *James Sheridan Knowles' Leben und dramatische Werke, Ein Beitrag zur Geschichte des englischen Dramas* (Lingen, 1883).

HAYDEN, JOHN O.: *Scott. The Critical Heritage*, The Critical Heritage Series (London, 1970).

HOLLAND, LORD, HENRY RICHARD FOX: *Foreign Reminiscences*, edited by Henry Edward Lord Holland, 2nd ed. (London, 1851).

The Holland House Diaries 1831-1840, The Diary of Henry Richard Vassal Fox, third Lord Holland, with extracts from the Diary of Dr. John Allen, edited with introductory essay and notes by Abraham D. Kriegel (London, 1977).

HOUGH, GRAHAM: *The Romantic Poets*, 3rd ed. (London, 1967).

HOWES, ALAN B.: *Yorick and the Critics. Sterne's Reputation in England, 1760-1868* (New Haven, 1958).

HUSTVEDT, SIGURD BERNHARD: *Ballad Books and Ballad Men* (Cambridge, Mass., 1930).

JEFFERSON, D. W.: '*Tristram Shandy* and the Tradition of Learned Wit', in *Laurence Sterne. A Collection of Critical Essays*, edited by John Traugott, Twentieth Century Views (New Jersey, 1968), pp. 148-67.

JENNY, LAURENT: 'Intertextualités — La stratégie de la forme', in *Poétique*, n° 27 (1976), 257-81.

JOSEPH, M. K.: *Byron the Poet* (London, 1966).

KINSEY, WILLIAM MORGAN: *Portugal Illustrated; in a series of letters. Embellished with a Map, Plates of Coins, Vignettes, Modinhas and various Engravings of Costumes, Landscape Scenery*, etc., 2nd ed. (London, 1829).

KNIGHT, G. WILSON: *The Golden Labyrinth, a Study of British Drama* (London, 1962).

KNOWLES, JAMES SHERIDAN: *Lectures on Dramatic Literature by James Sheridan Knowles*, revised and edited by F. Harvey (London, 1873).

— *Lectures on Dramatic Literature by James Sheridan Knowles (Never before published) — Macbeth*, edited by Francis Harvey (London, 1875).

BLACK, FRANK GEES: *The Epistolary Novel in the Late Eighteenth Century* (Eugene, 1940).
BLOOM, HAROLD: *The Anxiety of Influence, A Theory of Poetry* (Oxford, 1973).
BOCAGE: *Poesias várias,* introdução, selecção e notas de Vitorino Nemésio, 2ª ed., Col. Clássicos Portugueses (Lisboa, 1961).
BOUSSAGOL, G.: *Ángel de Saavedra, duc de Rivas; sa vie, son oeuvre poétique* (Toulouse, 1926).
BOWLES, WILLIAM LISLE: *The Poetical Works of William Lisle Bowles with Memoir, Critical Dissertation and Explanatory Notes,* by the Rev. George Gifillan, 2 Vols (Edinburgh, 1855).
— *The Spirit of Discovery; or the Conquest of Ocean. A Poem in five books with notes, historical and illustrative* (Bath, 1804).
BOYD, ELIZABETH FRENCH: *Byron's «Don Juan». A Critical Study* (New York, 1958).
BRAEKMEN, W.: *Letters by Robert Southey to Sir John Taylor Coleridge,* Studia Germanica, Gandensi VI-1964.
BUCHAN, JOHN: *Sir Walter Scott* (London, 1932).
BYRON, LORD: *Poetry and Prose. With Essays by Scott, Hazlitt, Macaulay, etc.,* with an Introduction by Sir Arthur Quiller-Couch and Notes by David Nichol Smith (Oxford, 1940).
— *Poetical Works,* edited by Frederick Page, new ed. corrected by John Jump (London, 1970).
— *Don Juan,* edited by T. G. Steffan, E. Steffan and W. W. Pratt, Penguin Books (Harmondsworth, 1977).
CALIXTO, MARIA LEONOR: *A literatura «negra» ou de «terror» em Portugal nos séculos XVIII e XIX* (Lisboa, 1956).
* *Catalogue of the Valuable Library of the Late Robert Southey, Esq. LL.D. Poet Laureate,* in Auction Catalogues (1844).
* CHAVES, CASTELO BRANCO: *O romance histórico no Romantismo português,* Biblioteca Breve, nº 45 (Lisboa, 1980).
CIDADE, HERNANI: *A Marquesa de Alorna. Sua vida e obras. Reprodução de algumas cartas inéditas* (Porto, n. d.).
— *A obra poética do Dr. José Anastácio da Cunha,* precedido de *O anglo-germanismo nos proto-românticos portugueses* (Coimbra, 1930).
COCKSHUT, A. O. J.: *The Achievement of Walter Scott* (London, 1969).
COELHO, JACINTO DO PRADO: 'Presença da França nas letras portuguesas dos séculos XVIII e XIX', in *Boletim da Academia das Ciências de Lisboa,* Nova Série, 34 (1962), pp. 123-49.
— *Introdução ao estudo da novela camiliana* (Coimbra, 1964).
* — 'Pré-Romantismo', in *Dicionário das literaturas portuguesa, galega e brasileira,* Vol. II, pp. 866-8.
CONRAD, PETER: *Shandyism. The Character of Romantic Irony* (Oxford, 1978).
CRAIK, T. W. (ed.): *The Revels History of the Drama in English,* Vol. V (1660-1750) (London, 1976).
CROLL, MORRIS W.: *Style, Rhetoric and Rhythm* (Princeton, 1966).
CRUTWELL, PATRICK: 'Walter Scott', in *The Pelican Guide to English Literature,* Vol. 5 (Harmondsworth, 1969).
CURRY, KENNETH: *New Letters of Robert Southey* (London, 1965).
— 'The Published Letters of Robert Southey. A Checklist', in *Bulletin of the New York Public Library,* 71 (March, 1967).
DEVLIN, D. D. (ed.): *Walter Scott,* Modern Judgements (London, 1968).
DUNCAN, JOSEPH E.: 'The Anti-Romantic in *Ivanhoe*', in *Walter Scott,* edited by D. D. Devlin, pp. 142-7.
DYSON, E.: 'Sterne: The Novelist as Jester', in *Critical Quarterly,* 4 (1926), pp. 309-20.
EICHLER, ALBERT: *John Hookham Frere, sein Leben und seine Werke, sein Einfluss auf Lord Byron* (Leipzig, 1905).
ELIOT, T. S.: 'Tradition and the Individual Talent', in *Selected Essays,* 3rd ed. (London, 1969), pp. 13-22.

Foreign Quarterly Review (1827-33); * Vol. I (1827), * Vol. II (1828), * Vol. X (1832).
Foreign Review and Continental Miscellany, 5 Vols (1828-1830).
Gentleman's Magazine (1844-5).
Literary Gazette (1819-33).
Literary Guardian, 2 Vols (1831-1832).
Monthly Magazine (1796-9).
Morning Chronicle (1826-7); * 31.1.1826; 5.2.1827; 2.3.1827; 29.3.1827; 10.5.1827; 6.8.1827; 25.8.1827; 30.8.1827.
Penny Magazine (1832-9).
People's Journal (1809) (1847).
Quarterly Review (1809-51); * Vol. 79 (1846).
Spectator, ed. with introductory notes by D. F. Bond, 5 Vols (Oxford, 1965).
Tait's Edinburgh Magazine (1846-7).

e) *General Bibliography*

Works which contain material bearing directly on Garrett or his writings are marked with an asterisk (*).

ADAMSON, JOHN: *Dona Ignez de Castro* (Newcastle, 1808).
— *Sonnets from the Portuguese of Luis de Camoens* (Newcastle, 1810).
— *Memoirs of the Life and Writings of Luis de Camoens*, 2 Vols (Newcastle, 1820).
* — *Bibliotheca Lusitana* (Newcastle, 1836).
* — *Lusitania Illustrata: Notices on the History, Antiquities, Literature, etc. of Portugal, Part I: Sonnets* (Newcastle, 1842), *Part II: Minstrelsy* (Newcastle, 1846).
* — *Ballads from the Portuguese*, translated and versified by J. A. and R. C. C. (Newcastle, 1846).
ADDISON, JOSEPH: *Cato*, in *Eighteenth Century Plays—Gay—Lillo—Rowe—Colman—Garrick—Addison—Fielding and Cumberland*, Everyman's Library, 818 (London, 1964).
— (ed.) *The Spectator* [see d) English Periodicals].
ALONSO, DÁMASO: 'Tradition or polygenesis', in *Annual Bulletin of the Modern Humanities Research Association*, n° 32 (1960), pp. 17-34.
ALORNA, MARQUESA DE: *Inéditos, cartas e outros escritos*, selecção, prefácio e notas do Professor Hernani Cidade (Lisboa, 1941).
— *Poesias*, selecção, prefácio e notas do Professor Hernani Cidade (Lisboa, 1941).
ANON.: *Iu-Kiao-Li ou les deux cousines. Roman chinois*, prefaced and translated by Jean-Pierre Abel Rémusat (Paris, 1826).
ANON.: *(José Anastácio da Cunha). Notícias literárias de Portugal, 1780*, conforme o manuscrito do Arquivo Nacional do Rio de Janeiro (Colecção de Memórias), Vol. III, Códice 807. Texto francês do original. Tradução portuguesa, prefácio e notas de Joel Serrão. Col. Paralelos, n° 1, 2ª ed. revista (Lisboa, 1971).
ATKINSON, WILLIAM C.: *British Contributions to Portuguese and Brazilian Studies* (London, 1974).
BARTON, FRANCIS BROWN: *Étude sur l'influence de Laurence Sterne en France au dix-huitième siècle* (Paris, 1911).
BATHO, EDITH: 'Scott as a Mediaevalist', in *Sir Walter Scott. Some Retrospective Essays and Studies*, ed. by H. J. C. Grierson (London, 1932).
BECKFORD, WILLIAM: *Italy, with Sketches of Spain and Portugal*, 2 Vols (London, 1834).
— *Recollections of an Excursion to the Monasteries of Alcobaça and Batalha* (London, 1835).
— *The Journal of William Beckford in Portugal and Spain* (1787-8), ed. by Boyd Alexander (London, 1954).
BERTHIER, ALFRED: *Xavier de Maistre, Étude biographique et littéraire* (Paris, 1821).

PINA, LUIS DE: 'Garrett e o *Romanceiro*', in *Studium Generale*, Centro de Estudos Humanísticos, Vol. IV (Porto, 1975), pp. 5-37.
— 'Panorama psicológico das *Viagens na minha terra*', Centro de Estudos Humanísticos (Porto, 1961).
PRESTAGE, EDGAR: *Brother Luiz de Sousa: a study; with translated extracts* (Altrincham, 1900).
QUILLINAN, E.: '*Um auto de Gil Vicente*, por J. B. de Almeida Garrett', in *Quarterly Review*, 79, n° clvii (1846-7), pp. 197-202.
RAMALHO, AMÉRICO DA COSTA: 'Garrett tradutor de Catulo', in *Colóquio*, n° 27 (Lisboa, 1964), pp. 38-41.
— 'Versões garrettianas de Safo', in *Humanitas*, Vols. XVII-XVIII (Coimbra, 1965-6).
RAMOS, FELICIANO: «*Frei Luís de Sousa*» *de Almeida Garrett* (Braga, 1956).
— *A presença histórica do Norte na obra de Garrett* (Braga, 1956).
ROCHA, ANDRÉE CRABBÉ: 'Présence et absence du théâtre portugais', in *Bulletin d'Histoire du Théâtre Portugais*, 4, fasc. I (1953).
— *O teatro de Garrett*, 2ª ed. (Coimbra, 1954).
— 'Garrett homme de théâtre', in *Bulletin d'Histoire du Théâtre Portugais*, 4, fasc. I (1954).
— 'Garrett e o Brasil', in *Estrada larga*, Vol. I, pp. 331-6.
— 'Garrett epistológrafo', in *Colóquio*, n° 22 (Fev. 1963), pp. 47-9.
SARAIVA, ANTÓNIO JOSÉ: 'O conflito dramático na obra de Garrett', in *Para a história da cultura em Portugal*, Vol. I (Lisboa, 1961), pp. 61-79.
— 'A evolução do teatro de Garrett. Os temas e as formas', in *ibid.*, Vol. II, pp. 15-45.
— 'A expressão lírica do amor nas *Folhas caídas*', in *ibid.*, Vol. II, pp. 46-52.
— 'Garrett e o Romantismo', in *ibid.*, Vol. II, pp. 53-9.
— 'Garrett lido hoje', in *Estrada larga*, Vol. I, pp. 373-6.
SEIXO, MARIA ALZIRA: '*O arco de Sant' Ana* de Garrett — Marcas românticas numa atitude narrativa e num esquema romanesco', in *Estética do Romantismo em Portugal*, pp. 113-20.
SIMÕES, JOÃO GASPAR: *Garrett. Biografia, exame crítico e antologia* (Porto, 1954).
— *Garrett. Quatro aspectos da sua personalidade: o homem público, o poeta, o dramaturgo, o romancista* (Porto, 1954).
— *Almeida Garrett* (Lisboa, 1964).
SOVERAL, CARLOS EDUARDO DE: 'Actualidade clássica e romântica de Garrett', in *Ao ritmo da Europa* (Lisboa, 1962).
TERRA, JOSÉ F. DA SILVA: 'Les Exils de Garrett en France', in *Bulletin des Etudes Portugaises*, Nouvelle série, 28-29 (1967-8), pp. 163-211.
VIANA, MÁRIO GONÇALVES: *Almeida Garrett*, série Figuras Nacionais, 3 (Porto, 1937).

Collective Works

— *Almeida Garrett. No I centenário da sua morte* (Porto, 1954).
— *Gazeta Literária*, Vol. 2, n°ˢ 26-7 (Porto, 1954).
— *Vértice*, Vol. 14, n° 135 (Coimbra, 1954).
— *Comemoração do primeiro centenário do Visconde de Almeida Garrett (1854-1954)* (Lisboa, 1959).

d) *English Periodicals consulted:*

Periodicals which contain material bearing directly on Garrett or his works are marked with an asterisk (*).

Annual Review, II (1804).
Blackwood's Edinburgh Magazine (1825-32).
Dublin University Magazine (1847-54).
Edinburgh Monthly Review, 5 Vols (1819-1821).
Edinburgh Review (1813-41).

da literatura, tradução portuguesa de Paulo Quintela, 5ª ed., 2 Vols (Coimbra, 1970); see in Vol. II the chapter 'Interpretação de *Frei Luís de Sousa'*, pp. 285-300.

LAMB, NORMAN, J.: 'The Romanticism of Almeida Garrett's *Viagens na minha terra',* in *Bulletin of Hispanic Studies,* 26 (1949), pp. 227-40.

LAWTON, R. A.: *Almeida Garrett, l'intime contrainte* (Paris, 1966).

— 'O conceito garrettiano do Romantismo', in *Estética do Romantismo em Portugal,* Centro de Estudos do Século XIX do Grémio Literário, Primeiro Colóquio (Lisboa, 1974), pp. 95-104.

LIMA, AUGUSTO DE CASTRO PIRES DE: 'Garrett e o *Romanceiro',* in *Estrada larga,* Vol. I, pp. 353-9.

LIMA, HENRIQUE DE CAMPOS FERREIRA: 'A livraria de Garrett', in *Livros,* nº 6 (Lisboa, 1925), pp. 161-4.

— *Estudos garretteanos* (Porto, 1926).

— *Garrett e a Academia* (Coimbra, 1926).

— 'Garrett na Bélgica', in *Boletim da Academia das Ciências de Lisboa,* Nova Série, 1 (Coimbra, 1929).

— *Garrett diplomata* (Vila Nova de Gaia, 1932).

— 'Garrett em Espanha', in *Memórias da Academia das Ciências de Lisboa,* Classe de Letras, t. III (1939).

— *Inventário do espólio literário de Garrett* (Coimbra, 1948).

— 'Garrett no estrangeiro', in *Memórias da Academia das Ciências de Lisboa,* Classe de Letras, t. V (1949).

— *Garrettiana. Catálogo de exposição bibliográfica, iconográfica e de recordações de Almeida Garrett em Angra do Heroísmo* (Angra do Heroísmo, 1954).

LOURENÇO, EDUARDO: 'Romantismo e tempo e o tempo do nosso Romantismo a propósito do *Frei Luís de Sousa',* in *Estética do Romantismo em Portugal,* pp. 105-11.

MACEDO, HELDER: 'As *Viagens na minha terra* e a menina dos rouxinóis', in *Colóquio-Letras,* nº 51 (Sept. 1979), pp. 15-24.

MALPIQUE, CRUZ: *História de um elegante do Romantismo* (Porto, 1954).

METZELTIN, M.: *'O alfageme de Santarém',* in *Aufsätze zur Portugiesischenkulturgeschichte,* 15 (1978), pp. 90-106.

MONTEIRO, OFÉLIA MILHEIRO CALDAS PAIVA: 'Viajando com Garrett pelo Vale de Santarém. Alguns elementos para a história inédita de Carlos a Joaninha', in Vol. IV de *Actas* do V Colóquio Internacional de Estudos Luso-Brasileiros (Coimbra, 1966).

— *A formação de Almeida Garrett. Experiência e criação,* 2 Vols (Coimbra, 1971).

— 'Algumas reflexões sobre a novelística de Garrett', in *Colóquio-Letras,* nº 30 (Março 1976), pp. 13-29.

MOURÃO-FERREIRA, DAVID: 'Para um retrato de Garrett', in *Hospital das letras* (Lisboa, 1966), pp. 65-79.

— 'Garrett e a poesia confidencial das *Folhas caídas',* in *ibid.,* pp. 81-96.

NEMÉSIO, VITORINO: 'Almeida Garrett', in *Perspectiva da literatura portuguesa do século XIX,* dirigida por João Gaspar Simões, Vol. I (Lisboa, 1949), pp. 33-44.

— 'Situação de Garrett', in *Conhecimento de poesia* (Lisboa, 1958), pp. 89-100.

— 'Os primeiros amores de Garrett', in *Ondas médias. Biografia e literatura* (Lisboa, n. d.), pp. 225-32.

— 'Garrett e Herculano', in *ibid.,* pp. 233-42.

OLIVEIRA, JOSÉ OSÓRIO DE: *O romance de Garrett,* 2ª ed. revista e ampliada (Lisboa, 1952).

PAVÃO, JR., JOSÉ DE ALMEIDA: *Garrett clássico e romântico* (Ponta Delgada, 1955).

— *'Frei Luís de Sousa:* o trágico e uma intromissão do cómico', in *Arquipélago,* nº 2 (1980), pp. 189-99.

PIMPÃO, ÁLVARO DA COSTA: 'O Romantismo das *Viagens* de Almeida Garrett', in *Ocidente,* 31, nº 108 (Lisboa, 1947), pp. 189-204; also in *Gente grada* (Coimbra, 1952), pp. 1-26.

139

CIDADE, HERNANI: 'Almeida Garrett — o poeta', in *Revista da Faculdade de Letras de Lisboa*, 2ª série, 21, nº 1 (1955), pp. 5-17.

— 'Almeida Garrett. Como as viagens no estrangeiro prepararam as *Viagens na minha terra*', in *Século XIX. A revolução cultural em Portugal e alguns dos seus mestres* (Lisboa, 1961), pp. 7-40.

CINTRA, LUÍS F. LINDLEY: 'Notas à margem do *Romanceiro* de Almeida Garrett', in *Boletim Internacional de Bibliografia Luso-Brasileira*, 8, nº 1 (Jan.-Março 1967), pp. 105-35.

COELHO, JACINTO DO PRADO: 'Garrett prosador', in *Revista da Faculdade de Letras de Lisboa*, 2ª série, 21, nº 1 (1955), pp. 18-39; also in *A letra e o leitor* (Lisboa, 1968), pp. 72-100.

— 'O amor e o tempo das *Folhas caídas* de Garrett', in *Problemática da história literária* (Lisboa, 1961), pp. 163-70.

— 'A novela da «Menina dos rouxinóis»', in *ibid.*, pp. 171-7; also in *Estrada larga*, Vol. I (Porto, s. d.), pp. 326-30.

— 'Garrett e os seus mitos', in *Problemática da história literária*, pp. 179-87.

— 'A dialéctica da História em Garrett', in *A letra e o leitor*, pp. 101-5.

— 'Garrett, Rousseau e o Carlos das *Viagens*', in *ibid.*, pp. 106-11.

— 'Garrett perante o Romantismo', in *Estrada larga*, pp. 299-308.

— 'Garrett perante o Iluminismo', in *ibid.*, pp. 360-4.

— 'João Baptista da Silva Leitão de Almeida Garrett', in *Dicionário das literaturas portuguesa, galega e brasileira*, ed. J. Prado Coelho, 2 Vols (Porto, 1968), pp. 363-6.

CORNIL, SUZANNE: 'Garrett en Belgique (1834-1836)', in *The Analysis of Literary Texts: Current Trends in Methodology*, ed. by Pope and Randolph D., 3rd and 4th York Coll. Coloquia. Ypsilanti: Bilingual Prose (1980), pp. 603-11.

DACOSTA, LUISA: 'Garrett e a geração neo-garrettiana de 1890', in *Seara Nova*, nº 1411 (1963), pp. 122-3 and 138.

DIAS, AUGUSTO DA COSTA: 'Estilística e dialéctica', in *Viagens na minha terra* (Lisboa, 1963), pp. XII-LXVI.

— 'O jovem Garrett, esboço de ensaio sobre um grande vulto ignorado da filosofia portuguesa das Luzes', introdução a *O roubo das sabinas* (Lisboa, 1968), pp. VII-C.

— 'Garrett republicano', in *Seara Nova*, nºˢ 1505 and 1507 (Lisboa, 1971).

— 'O jovem Garrett e o *Portugal na balança da Europa*', in *Seara Nova*, nº 1504 (1971).

DÍAZ, DAVID S.: 'Psychological Motivation in Almeida Garrett's Drama *Frei Luís de Sousa*', in *Spenser at Kalamazoo*, proceedings of the 13th Conference on Medieval Studies in Kalamazoo, Michigan (5-6 May 1978).

ESTORNINHO, CARLOS: 'Garrett and England: English Reminiscences in the Life and Work of Almeida Garrett', in *Annual Report & Review of the Historical Association, Portugal Branch*, Twelfth Annual Report & Review (Lisbon, 1954), pp. 729-32.

— 'Letters from British Correspondents to Almeida Garrett', in *ibid.*, pp. 711-29.

— 'Garrett e a Inglaterra. Reminiscências inglesas na vida e obra de Almeida Garrett', in *Revista da Faculdade de Letras de Lisboa*, 2ª série, 21, nº 1 (1955), pp. 40-75.

FERREIRA, ALBERTO: 'Garrett e o poder burguês', in *Seara Nova*, nº 1518 (Abril 1972).

FERREIRA, JOAQUIM: *Mensagem de Garrett* (Porto, n. d.).

FERRO, TÚLIO RAMIRES: 'Perfil de Garrett poeta', in *Estrada larga*, Vol. I (Porto, n. d.), pp. 337-41.

FIGUEIREDO, FIDELINO DE: 'Le Donjuanisme de Garrett', in *Donjuanisme et antidonjuanisme en Portugal* (Coimbra, 1933), pp. 13-20.

— *Shakespeare e Garrett* (São Paulo, 1970).

FRAZÃO, J. VASCONCELOS: *O temperamento de Almeida Garrett* (Lisboa, 1951).

FREIRE, ANTÓNIO BARATA: 'Nacionalismo, tradicionalismo e mais ideias de Garrett', in *Lusíadas*, 3, nº 9 (Porto, 1956).

KAYSER, WOLFGANG: *Análise e interpretação da obra literária. Introdução à ciência*

de Santarém (Lisboa, 1973), ed. de J. Prado Coelho, precedida de 'Introdução geral ao teatro de Garrett' por Andrée Crabbé Rocha.

b) *Periodicals of which Garrett was founder or editor, or to which he contributed:*

O Biografo (1839).
Borboleta Constitucional (1821).
O Chaveco Liberal (London, 1829).
Chronica Constitucional de Lisboa (1833-1834).
O Chronista (1827).
O Constitucional (1838).
O Correio das Damas (1836).
Correio de Lisboa (1839).
A Época (1848).
Gazeta de Lisboa (1819).
O Génio Constitucional (1820).
Mnemósine Constitucional (1820).
O Nacional (1837).
O Patriota (1820-1821).
O Patriota Funchalense (1821).
O Pelourinho (1831-1832).
O Popular (Londres, 1824-1825).
O Portuguez (1826-1827).
O Portuguez Constitucional em Londres (1832).
O Portuguez Constitucional (1836).
O Toucador (1822).

c) *Works on Garrett:*

Books and articles

ALGE, CARLOS D': *As relações brasileiras de Almeida Garrett,* Tempo Brasileiro (Brasília, 1980).
— 'Garrett e o Brasil', in *Revista de Cultura Vozes,* 73 (1979), pp. 769-72.
ALMEIDA, VIEIRA DE: 'Barão e frade', in *Estrada larga,* Vol. I (Porto, n. d.), pp. 294-8.
AMORIM, GOMES DE: *Garrett. Memorias biographicas,* 3 Vols (Lisboa, 1881-4).
ANON.: Review of *Parnaso Lusitano* (Paris, 1826) and *Adozinda* (London, 1828), in *Foreign Quarterly Review,* 10 (1832), pp. 437-74.
ANTSCHERL, OTTO: *J. B. de Almeida Garrett und seine Beziehungen zur Romantik* (Heidelberg, 1927).
AZEVEDO, NARCISO DE: *A Nau Catrineta e Miragaia (Estudos da sua génese)* (Porto, 1956).
BERARDINELLI, CLEONICE: 'Garrett e Camilo: Românticos heterodoxos?', in *Bulletin des Études Portugaises et de l'Institut Français au Portugal,* 37-8 (1977-8), pp. 61-81.
BOM, LAURINDA: *Almeida Garrett, uma proposta de trabalho* (Lisboa, 1980).
BOTREL, J.-F., MASSA, J.-M., et POUGET, A.: *Quelques documents sur les premières representations de «Frei Luís de Sousa» (1843-1850)* (Paris, 1966).
BRAGA, THEOPHILO: *História do theatro portuguez. IV — Garrett e os dramas românticos* (Porto, 1871).
— *História do Romantismo em Portugal* (Lisboa, 1880); see the chapter 'Almeida Garrett', pp. 119-218.
— *Garrett e o Romantismo* (Porto, 1903).
CABRAL, A.: *O nacionalismo na obra de Garrett* (Lisboa, 1954).
CARDOSO, P.: *Frei Luís: uma leitura esotérica* (Lisboa, 1978).
CARVALHO, ADALBERTO D. DE: 'Almeida Garrett: o tribuno e o educador', in *Seara Nova,* nº 1580 (1977), pp. 24-6.

de 1834 até 183... entre os dois irmãos A. J. L. A. Garrett e João Baptista Leitão de Almeida Garrett — Membro da «Comissão Eclesiástica» e deputado da nação, introdução e notas de Segismundo Spina (São Paulo, 1961).

D. Branca, ou a conquista do Algarve, Obra posthuma de F. E. (Paris, 1826).

Doutrinas de estética literária, prefácio e notas de Agostinho da Silva, Col. Textos Literários, 2ª ed. (Lisboa, 1961).

Flores sem fruto; Folhas caídas, texte établi, avec variantes, notes et introduction par R. A. Lawton (Paris, 1975).

Folhas caídas, introdução de José Gomes Ferreira, 2ª ed. (Lisboa, 1969).

Folhas caídas, prefácio, notas e glossário por Augusto C. Pires de Lima, Col. Portugal, 23 (Porto, n. d.).

Frei Luís de Sousa, texto revisto, notas e prefácio de Rodrigues Lapa, Col. Textos Literários, 7ª ed. (Lisboa, 1964).

Magriço ou os doze de Inglaterra, ed. organizada e comentada por Alberto Pimenta, Col. Textos Breves, Edições 70 (Lisboa, 1978).

Miragaia, romance popular pelo autor de Adozinda, Bernal Francez, etc. (Lisboa, 1844).

Narrativas e lendas, ed. crítica, prefácio e notas de Augusto da Costa Dias (Lisboa, 1979).

Portugal na balança da Europa (Londres, 1830).

Portugal na balança da Europa, prefácio de Joel Serrão, Col. Horizonte, 5, Livros Horizonte (Lisboa, n. d.).

Romanceiro, ed. revista e prefaciada por Fernando de Castro Pires de Lima, 3 Vols, Col. Cultura e Recreio (Lisboa, 1963).

Roubo das Sabinas, O, ed. crítica, fixação de texto, introdução e notas de Augusto da Costa Dias (Lisboa, 1968).

Textes inédits d'Almeida Garrett. Fragments d'oeuvres dramatiques, ed. by Damien Saunal in *Bulletin d'Histoire du Théâtre Portugais,* Vol. III, fasc. I (Lisboa, 1952).

Viagens na minha terra, introdução e notas de Augusto da Costa Dias (Lisboa, 1963).

Viagens na minha terra, ed. organizada e anotada pelo Prof. José Pereira Tavares, Col. Clássicos Sá da Costa (Lisboa, 1966).

Selections

Almeida Garrett: doutrina restauradora nacional, selecção, prefácio e notas de J. de Castro Osório (Lisboa, 1960).

'Camões' e 'D. Branca', introdução, selecção e notas de António José Saraiva, Col. Clássicos Portugueses (Lisboa, 1943).

Folhas caídas e outros poemas, introdução, selecção e notas de António José Saraiva, Col. Clássicos Portugueses (Lisboa, 1943).

O «Romanceiro» de Garrett, introdução, selecção e notas por A. do Prado Coelho, Col. Clássicos Portugueses (Lisboa, 1943).

Sentido e unidade das «Viagens na minha terra» de Almeida Garrett, aparelho crítico, selecção, notas e sugestões para análise literária de Alberto Carvalho, Col. Textos Literários (Lisboa, 1979).

Viagens na minha terra, introdução, selecção e notas de Ofélia Milheiro Caldas, 2 Vols, Col. Literária 'Atlântida' (Coimbra, 1960-1).

Complete Works

Obras completas de Almeida Garrett, grande edição popular ilustrada, prefaciada, revista, coordenada e dirigida por Theophilo Braga, 2 Vols (Lisboa, 1904).

Obras posthumas, Vols. xxix e xxx da ed. *Obras completas de Almeida Garrett* (Lisboa, 1914).

Obras de Almeida Garrett, 2 Vols (Porto, 1966).

Obras completas de Almeida Garrett: Teatro I: Catão, 7ª ed. (Lisboa, 1972), *Teatro II: Mérope,* 6ª ed. (Lisboa, 1973), *Teatro III: Um auto de Gil Vicente; O alfageme*

BIBLIOGRAPHY

It would be impossible to give here a complete bibliography of works concerned with Anglo-Portuguese relations or with Garrett; the reader is referred for the latter to Ofélia Milheiro Caldas Paiva Monteiro's *A formação de Garrett. Experiência e criação* for the period up to 1971. The bibliography given here is confined to the works consulted or quoted in the preparation of the present study.

I. MANUSCRIPTS

a) *Garrett:*

— *Fragmentos. O Magriço* (B. Nac., Col. Cartonense, 51).
— *A Madame Shelley* (MS 57 Esp. f. 21 r-v).
— *A livraria de Garrett* in *Inventário judicial a que se procedeu em seguida à morte de Garrett* (Sala F. L., Mov. 5-7-1).

b) *Others:*

— Letter from John Adamson of 4 January 1819 to the Literary and Philosophical Society of Newcastle.
— Shelley Collection belonging to the Bodleian Library, Oxford, and the section of Lord Abinger's papers that is deposited in the same library.

c) *P. R. O. Ashridge:*

— Home Office, Entry Books:
Vol. 25 (1826-1828).
Vol. 27 (1832-1834).

II. PUBLISHED WORKS

a) *Works by Garrett:*

Individual Works

Adozinda, romance (London, 1828).
Camões, edição conforme a revista pelo autor, com um estudo de Camillo Castello Branco, Col. Lusitânia (Porto, n. d.).
Camões, prefácio de José Augusto França, Col. Horizontes Clássicos, Livros Horizonte (Lisboa, 1973).
Cartas de amor à viscondessa da Luz, coordenadas e anotadas por José Bruno Carreiro (Lisboa, n. d.).
Cartas apologéticas e históricas sobre os sucessos religiosos em Portugal nos anos

— 'Thomas Moore Musgrave's translation of A. Ferreira's *Ignez de Castro*' (review).

1826 — '*Sketches of Portuguese Life, Manners, Costume and Character.* Illust. by twenty coloured plates (London, 1826)' (review).

— '*The Lusiad: an Epic Poem.* By Luis de Camoens. Translated from the Portuguese by Thomas Moore Musgrave (London, 1826)' (review-article).

— Letter from J. Adamson, on the above article.

1827 — 'Southey's *History of the Peninsular War*' (review-article).

— '*Personal Narrative of Adventures in the Peninsula during the War of 1812-13.* By an Officer, Late in the Staff Corps, etc. (London, 1827)' (review-article).

— '*An Historical View of the Revolution of Portugal since the Close of the Peninsular War; exhibiting a full Account of the Events which have led to the Present State of that Country.* By an Eye-Witness (London, 1827)' (review).

— '*Rambles in Madeira and in Portugal in the Early Part of 1826.* By C. and J. Revington (London, 1827)' (review-article).

1828 — '*Portugal in 1828,* by William Young (London, 1828)' (review).

New Monthly Magazine

Vol. CXL (1867) — 'Legendary lore of Portugal' by an Old Traveller (article).

The People's Journal

Vol. III-IV (1847) — Excerpt from Southey's *History of Brazil.*

Quarterly Review

Vol. XXIX-XXX (April 1823-Jan. 1824) — Review of Southey's *History of the Peninsular War;* review-article of Major Moyle Shorer's *Recollections of the Peninsula* (it gives no indication of the author).

Vol. LIII-LIV (Feb. 1835-Sept. 1835) — '*Rough Leaves from a Journal kept in Spain and Portugal* by Lieut.-Col. Badcock (London, 1835)' (review); '*Recollections of a Visit to the Monasteries of Alcobaça and Batalha* by W. Beckford (London, 1835)' (review).

Tait's Edinburgh Magazine

Vol. XIV (1847) — ' "Iberia won" by Thomas Hughes' (review).

APPENDIX II

In the course of my researches I have found the following items which appear to have escaped the notice of biographers to date, and which are of some relevance to Anglo-Portuguese relations in this period:

Blackwood's Edinburgh Magazine

Vol. XXIII (Jan.-June 1828) — *A Narrative of the War in Spain and Portugal*, by Lieut.-General the Marquess of Londonderry (London, 1828), pp. 716-35 (review).

Dublin University Magazine

Vol. XXXVIII (1851) — Anonymous translation of a poem by Camoens in 'Our Garland for June'.

Vol. XL (1852) — Article on Portuguese literature by MEM including the translation of Bocage's 'Voaste, Alma innocente, Alma querida.'

Vol. XLIV (1854) — Translation of a sonnet by José B. Andrada, 'Adeus, fica-te em paz, Alcina amada', by MEM.

Edinburgh Monthly Review

Vol. V (1821) — 'Letters from Portugal, Spain and France during the Memorable Campaigns of 1811, 1812 and 1813; and from Belgium and France in the year 1815. By a British officer (London, 1819)' (review).

Literary Gazette

1819 — 'Dr. Robert Southey's *History of Brazil*' (review-article).

1823 — 'Recollections of the Peninsula. By the Author of *Sketches in India* (London, 1823)' (review-article).

1824 — Notice of a new edition of the translation of Camoens's Works by Lord Strangford.

1825 — 'Lisbon in the Years 1821, 1822 and 1823. By Marianne Baillie' (review).

— 'Excursions in Madeira, Porto Santo &Ca. By the late T. Edwards Bowdich, Esq. (London, 1825)' (review).

Eh bien! ce fut alors, vous l'avez entendue,
Et j'en frissone encor — cette voix inconnue
«Partez» dit elle. — Helas! J'allais rever bonheur
Et avant de dormir on eveille mon coeur.

Oui, le sort a parlé, et j'accepte l'augure:
Il faut s' resigner, je le fais sans murmure.
Et peutetre ce dieu dont on a tant d'effroi
Sent par fois la pitié et en a eu de moi.
Son Eden, s'il existe, oui ce lieu de délice
A peutetre ce fruit qu'on appelle *caprice*,
Dont le gout plus trompeur que la pomme jadis
Promettant le bonheur, chasse du paradis.

Et ou va-t'-on alors, missionaire charmante
Quand l'ange nous poursuit
Ou va-t-on poursuivi de l'épée flamboyante?
Il le faut bien, helas! vous avez beau prêcher,
Il faut bien mon amie que ce soit a l'enfer.
3   4   5   1   2

APPENDIX I

The following poem, which is MS 57 of *Esp.*, f. 21 r-v, of which nine lines only have been published by O. Paiva Monteiro in *A formação de Almeida Garrett*, Coimbra, 1971, Vol. II, p. 139, is given here for the first time in full. In terms of spelling, grammar and correctness of rhyme the French of this poem is very far from perfect; however, in order not to overburden the text, I have not thought it necessary to put [*sic*] every time it would have been justified.

A Madame Shelley

Qui me conseillait de croire et d'esperer

Londres Juillett 1831

Non, charmante prêcheuse, il faut y renoncer;
Sans foi, sans espérance on ne peut se sauver.
Ta sublime doctrine je l'aime et la respecte
Mais mon athée de coeur l'admire et la rejette.
—Oh qu'il doit être beau ce charmant paradis
Ce printems eternal, ces bosquets, ces hourys!
Si ce n'était un rêve... et si votre croyance
Etait vraye après tout! —Si, fatale ignorance!
Cet horrible néant, ce goufre ou j'ai tombé,
Ouvrage de mes mains, n'était que mon péché;
Si, trompé jusqu'ici, ma coupable paupière
S'était fermée rebelle à la sainte lumière! ...
Il sera bien affreux le funeste réveil
Qui viendra dissiper mon coupable sommeil!

Mais non, je n'y crois pas, je ne veux point y croire;
Les peines sont toujours à cotê de la gloire.
Et peutetre j'irais, en cherchant le bonheur,
Trouver la mort, le crime — et me perdre l'honneur...
Vous en rappelez vous? — C'était hier encore:
S'il y a un paradis, si ce dieu qu'on adore,
Ce dieu qu'on craint si fort et auquel je ne croi
N'est pas un songe vain — il était près de moi:
Tout athée que je suis, je sentis dans mon ame
Penetrer peu à peu un raion de sa flamme;
Et mon lache de coeur a demi moitié ebranlé
Se reprochait déja son incredulité.

131

he is not one, but both. Every man's mind is, in this respect, modified by all the objects of nature and art, by every word and every suggestion which he ever admitted to act upon his consciousness; it is the mirror upon which all forms are reflected, and in which they compose one form. Poets, not otherwise than philosophers, painters, sculptors, and musicians, are, in one sense, the creators, and, in another, the creations, of their age. From this subjection the loftiest do not escape.'

It is then beyond question that Garrett's debt to English writers is both varied and significant, indeed vital to his development, probably surpassing that which he contracted to any other group of authors. But it should not be thought that this in any way casts doubts on his own originality or suggests that he spent his time looking for themes or devices which he could borrow. Garrett was a profoundly sincere and committed writer, whose greatest ambition was to bring Portuguese literature up to the standard which he saw being achieved elsewhere in Europe; he was also a man with an extremely lively sensibility, intensely aware of all that was going on in the art of countries other than his own. That he may have been receptive and impressionable is undeniable. But he was not only an acute and discerning judge, who was well able to detect that which in foreign literature was both valuable in itself and relevant to Portuguese circumstances; he was also a man of strong individuality who only accepted and assimilated such elements from the outside as awakened genuine echoes in his own nature. He was no slave to fashion or plagiarism: those authors who were popular in their time but whose temperament was alien to his own leave no traces on his work. Where, with his keen and subtle sense for what was new and at the same time authentic, he detected something that evoked a real and lasting resonance in him, he opened his mind and his art to all that he could derive from it; where contemporary celebrities had no intimate appeal to him, he left them alone.

The result is that, with the exception of Addison's *Cato,* read when he was very young and inexperienced, Garrett only appropriated to himself those aspects of English authors which revealed to him things already existing and obscurely felt in his own personality. His love for English literature does not make Garrett a derivative or unoriginal writer. On the contrary, they enabled him to be himself, a strongly marked and distinctively Portuguese creator, who only took from them what he could absorb into his own being and recreate in a highly personal manner. His place in the first ranks of Portuguese literature is undisputed and requires no further encomium. The totality of Garrett's work, with such prominent seminal features as his aesthetic nationalism, his innovatory contribution to the art of narrative, and the creation of modern Portuguese prose, had a lasting and irreversible effect on later generations, and it is not possible to study a Ramalho, an Antero, an Eça or a Nobre without referring back to him. Together with Herculano, Garrett impelled Portuguese literature to join the Romantic rebellion, and his was the major force that steered it towards English romanticism. In Garrett literary excellence was achieved through the very things that Addison had prescribed, and which he explicitly admired in Scott: the enrichment and the strengthening of the native tradition through the knowledge of other literatures — and it was above all his knowledge of English literature that enabled him to reach the status of one of the greatest and most original of Portuguese writers. The aspect of his work which has been under scrutiny in this study is best appreciated in the light of Shelley's words in the Preface to his *Prometheus Unbound:* 'A poet is the combined product of such internal powers as modify the nature of others; and of such external influences as excite and sustain these powers;

from Bacon's *Essays* to Gibbon's *Decline and Fall,* and various volumes of English, Portuguese, African and ecclesiastical history, Blackstone's *Commentaries on the Laws and Constitution of England,* the *Lawyer's Cabinet, English and Jewish Tithe Systems Compared,* treatises on education and on economy, a cookery book, a classical dictionary, a Greek lexicon... It is thus evident that Garrett's English culture was extremely wide and varied. But, as we saw at the beginning of this study, he also had a thorough knowledge of and love for the literature of his country, which was one of the great and absorbing passions of his life. This is amply demonstrated not only in the Portuguese section of his library, but also in his early collecting of José Anastácio da Cunha's poems in Oporto, and in his reverence for Filinto, in works like his *Brief Review of the Literary History of Portugal* and *Bosquejo da história da poesia e língua portuguesa,* in his prefaces and indeed in the writings themselves, as well as in his multiple efforts to create a national theatre. He was familiar with the literature of Greek and Roman antiquity, he had some acquaintance with Italian authors —Alfieri and Dante, amongst others, left traces in his work—, and with Spanish literature; he even read some modern Germans in the original, like Herder,[3] Schiller[4] and Goethe, whom he admired exceedingly and from whose *Faust* he translates a passage in *Viagens.* Above all, he knew French literature, both classical and modern, very thoroughly, and, over and above that part of it which would naturally have been included in the standard equipment of an educated Portuguese at the beginning of the nineteenth century, he had come to familiarise himself with much more of it during his two periods of exile in France, from 1824 to 1826, and the two or three months in 1831-2. There is no doubt that his creative activities were very much affected by all these things, and if we are to assess accurately the importance of his debt to English literature, it is essential that we should also take account of the profit he may have derived from other external sources, which in this case means mainly French literature.

The French authors whom he seems to have known and liked best before his first exile were Racine, Voltaire, Ducis, Rousseau, Chateaubriand and Mme de Staël; Schlegel, though German, may be included in this group for the affinities of his thought with that of Mme de Staël. Racine gave him a model of a neo-classical theatre; the tragedies of Voltaire and Ducis showed him a more flexible yet still classical mode of dramatic writing which had considerable appeal for him. Rousseau with his individualism, his cult of nature and his mellifluous style, Chateaubriand with his extolling of the beauties of religion, his emphasis on the artistic inspiration to be found in Christianity and his glorification of melancholy, Mme de Staël with her defence of national differences in art and her discernment of the importance of historical and climatic circumstances in moulding culture, all helped to open new horizons to him. By the time he left Portugal, his

---

[3] Antscherl, p. 100.

[4] O. P. Monteiro, Vol. I, p. 512 ff., sees Schiller's influence in *Namorados extravagantes.*

reading of French writers, probably more than his reading of English authors, had helped to draw him closer to what was definable throughout Europe as the pre-romantic cast of mind, and there are distinct traces of his admiration for Chateaubriand and for Mme de Staël not only in *Retrato de Vénus* and *Ensaio de pintura,* but also in later works, like *Camões* and *D. Branca, Adosinda, Viagens, O arco* and the fragment *Helena.*[5]

However, when one comes to examine his relations with the French Romantics properly speaking, the picture changes somewhat. It is noteworthy that there is no evidence that he had read any of them until the late 1820s or even after — nor is that surprising, considering that, although Lamartine's *Méditations poétiques* appeared in 1820, the major works of Hugo, Vigny and Musset were not published until 1827 and the following decade. Since Garrett kept himself scrupulously abreast of what was happening in the French literary scene, we can be sure that he was not ignorant of the revolutionary developments around 1830, and there is textual proof that Hugo and Lamartine were authors whom he appreciated; [6] on the other hand, one would search in vain for signs of any familiarity with Vigny,[7] Musset, Balzac, Stendhal, Nerval and Gautier. But by this time, Garrett had already spent those seminal years in England which had done so much, especially through the affection for Byron and Scott which they bred in him, to change his outlook on literature and make him into a mature and individual writer.

In any case, although it is possible and perfectly legitimate to draw parallels between Garrett and various authors as Antscherl has so skilfully done, that does not of itself mean that Garrett's development was in any significant way affected by them, and on examination, textual evidence for any lasting effect on him from authors of the generation of 1830 is surprisingly thin. He does, it is true, compare Lamartine to Byron, but only to say that in his view Byron is the greater poet. He also acknowledges, in his letter of 12 June 1833 to Gomes Monteiro, that *O arco* is in the same style as Hugo's *Notre-Dame de Paris,* but, as we have seen, his intentions for that novel changed over the years, and there is reason to believe that, by the time he completed it, Scott was more important to him as an inspiration than Hugo — to say nothing of the fact that *Notre-Dame* itself is very heavily indebted to Scott. If we look at Garrett's epigraphs, usually a good indicator of the authors whose works sprang most readily to his mind, a similar picture emerges: only six epigraphs are from French

[5] Antscherl refers to the presence of Mme de Staël in *Retrato de Vénus* and *Ensaio* in pp. 17-18, to Chateaubriand's in *Retrato de Vénus* in pp. 14-17, in *Camões,* in pp. 43-4, in *D. Branca* in pp. 47, 53-4, in *Adosinda* in pp. 76, 78, in *Viagens* in p. 152, in *O arco* in pp. 173-4, and in *Helena* in p. 179; he thinks there are other traces of their influence, but only those that seem convincing are indicated here.

[6] His admiration for Hugo is expressed in a letter to Gomes Monteiro, of 12 June 1833, and for Lamartine in MS 122 of *Esp.,* quoted by O. Paiva Monteiro, Vol. II, p. 143.

[7] Note that in *O Chronista* he refers scornfully to *O Cinco de Março.* This is evidently a reference to Vigny's *Cinq-Mars,* but the fact that he translates it as though it were a date, obviously not realizing it was the name of a man, shows he had not read it.

authors, and of those only two, by Lamartine, are from a contemporary writer...

One is therefore entitled to conclude that, although French literature was always important to Garrett, and although French authors like Chateaubriand and Mme de Staël may have played an important part in widening his youthful sensibility, the really critical moment in his literary evolution comes in his first English exile. It would no doubt be exaggerated to talk of a 'conversion'; Garrett never held to a rigidly classical or neo-classical view, and the process by which he established himself as a leading Romantic figure was a gradual one; even then, especially in theatrical matters, he still retained a relatively conservative attitude. But that the English writers whom he learned to know or love during his years in England had a decisive influence in revealing new and unsuspected paths to him cannot be doubted.

At the beginning of Garrett's career Addison's *Cato* was very important to him, providing him with a model in which political ideas akin to his own were expressed in dramatic poetry that he admired to the point of imitating it freely, taking the view that one could be original despite dependence on another's text. But it cannot be said that the semi-classical form of the play incited him to any dramatic experimentation that he could not have learned from eighteenth-century French dramaturgy. His admiration for Addison the editor of *The Spectator* was long-lasting. It met his concerns as a scholar, as a journalist, as a man of unflagging interest in the improvement and instruction of the middle classes; it may well have had a bearing on his own periodicals, and it was certainly reflected in the essay-type pages of *Viagens na minha terra*.

As for Shakespeare, it is certain that Garrett had read at least the best known plays in the original, that he was familiar with their text and that he admired them greatly. Though there are traces and reminiscences of Shakespeare in his work, some of which show that he was moved by the humanity of his dramas, he felt on the whole that Shakespeare was a writer to be admired rather than to be imitated: he was not tempted to model his own theatre on Shakespearean lines, except in so far as, at an early stage, Ducis's semi-classical adaptations of *Othello* and other works seemed to represent for him a high point of dramatic excellence. He had a continuous appreciation of and enthusiasm for Shakespeare and he played the part of a precursor in fostering the knowledge of his dramas in Portugal.

Unlike Addison and Shakespeare, Sterne does not appear to have made any impression on Garrett until the years of full maturity, when he wrote *Viagens*. But if, as seems likely, Garrett discovered Sterne only late in life, that does not give him a lesser place among his English influences. Garrett studied him minutely and absorbed with enthusiasm Sterne's lesson in spontaneity, irony and humour: the cult of sensibility tinged with mild derision, the authorial pose of exhibitionism and self-mockery, the personal relationship with the reader, the registering of the pulsations of thought and emotion. Sterne was to Garrett a master in the search for expressiveness, and in the expert handling of language as a tool of infinite precision. Sterne's explorations in language were intelligently transposed

into the prose of *Viagens na minha terra,* and he is undoubtedly a main source of inspiration for Garrett's decisive contribution to the transformation of literary Portuguese from a stiff and formal idiom to a flexible and natural language. No less important was Sterne's contribution to Garrett's search for freedom in form: in Sterne's ironical flouting of set values and of narrative conventions, and in his innovatory technique is to be found a major key to the modernity of *Viagens.*

Byron emerges as the most important and sustained English influence, a figure whom Garrett follows in his search for form, and with whom he has a parallel spiritual evolution, from the world of subjectivism and romance of *Childe Harold* and *Camões* to the final acceptance of the duality symbolized by Quixote and Sancho in *Don Juan* and in *Viagens,* by way of satires like *The Age of Bronze* and *Magriço.* In Byron's poetry Garrett found an echo of his own feelings of nostalgia and rejection in exile, of growing bitterness and disenchantment, and of awareness of life as at once tragedy and comedy. They were both taught by experience to see such primary motivations in their lives as love, politics, and literature, in terms of a mobility that was incompatible with one fixed system, and yet they both strove to reach an ideal harmony, Quixotes looking up despite the jostles of reality.

All this was transmuted in their work, in their rejection of schools, in the psychology of a Byronic hero which was part of themselves and which they learned to regard with humour, in the ambiguity created by the shift of voice and time, in these and other components of the irony that is their distinctive hallmark; it also showed itself in their struggle to make form, of which they both were loving craftsmen, a vigorous expression of their conflicting tensions. Because he recognized a kindred spirit in Byron, Garrett saw in his art a model of his own personality and experiences, and reflected its development, in form and content, in his own writings.

Byron and Scott complement each other as the fundamental formative figures of Garrett's romanticism. If in aspects of Byron's compositions Garrett had a poetical model for his own individual passions and preoccupations, in Scott he found the most important foreign inspiration for such main features of his work as nationalism and medievalism. Just as, in his own evolution, Garrett follows a course similar to that taken by Byron from *Childe Harold* to *Don Juan,* so does his *Romanceiro* occupy in relation to later writings, such as the theatre, *O arco de Sant' Ana,* and *Viagens na minha terra,* a position that can be compared to that of *The Minstrelsy* and of the early poetical works in relation to the Scottish Novels. Unlike so many other Romantics, Garrett appreciated Scott's medievalism not as a mere source of the picturesque but in its deep historical sense, and balladry and other forms of antiquarian interest were to him, as they had been to Scott, as valid a contribution to the reconstitution of the past as historical documents. Scott's original creation, based on a native tradition, could not fail to appeal to Garrett, who had himself, since his youth, aspired to create a national drama and who wanted to free Portuguese literature from indiscriminate dependence on others. Scott was an inspiring guide in leading Garrett along paths that he was anxious to explore.